Owning the Olympics

Joseph Turow

SERIES EDITOR

Broadcasting, Voice, and Accountability: A Public Interest
Approach to Policy, Law, and Regulation
*Steve Buckley, Kreszentia Duer, Toby Mendel, and Seán Ó Siochrú,
with Monroe E. Price and Marc Raboy*

Owning the Olympics: Narratives of the New China
Monroe E. Price and Daniel Dayan, editors

DIGITALCULTUreBOOKS
is a collaborative imprint of the University of Michigan Press and
the University of Michigan Library dedicated to publishing innovative
work about the social, cultural, and political impact of new media.

Owning the Olympics

Narratives of the
New China

Monroe E. Price and Daniel Dayan, Editors

THE UNIVERSITY OF MICHIGAN PRESS and
THE UNIVERSITY OF MICHIGAN LIBRARY
Ann Arbor

Copyright © by Monroe E. Price and Daniel Dayan 2008
All rights reserved
Published in the United States of America by
The University of Michigan Press
Manufactured in the United States of America
⊛ Printed on acid-free paper

2011   2010   2009   2008   4   3   2   1

A CIP catalog record for this book is available from the British Library.

ISBN-13: 978-0-472-07032-9 (cloth : alk. paper)
ISBN-10: 0-472-07032-0 (cloth : alk. paper)
ISBN-13: 978-0-472-05032-1 (paper : alk. paper) .
ISBN-10: 0-472-05032-X (paper : alk. paper)

Contents

III. Theaters of Representation

IV. Conclusion

Introduction

Monroe E. Price

It was precisely one year before the 2008 Olympic Games would begin, and a deep smog covered Beijing. The day, August 8, 2007, was filled with the symbolism of anticipation. An official ceremony, triggered by the magic moment marked on a special clock, began the grand unveiling, with 10,000 carefully selected people celebrating in Tiananmen Square. This would be the best and the biggest Countdown Ceremony in Olympic history precisely because it could be no other way. Everything about Beijing 2008 had to be spectacular, superlative, outsized. At least such was the hope of China and the Beijing Organizing Committee for the Games of the XXIX Olympiad (BOCOG). Even the smog, reframed as just another barrier for the powers that be to overcome, would be turned into a sign of what Beijing could and would accomplish.

That day and the week surrounding it were a dress rehearsal not only for the Olympics' officials but also for those seeking to seize the occasion to make their own global point. The very day of the countdown ceremony a group of young Canadians and others sought to subvert the official line and gain global press notoriety by rappelling down a portion of the Great Wall to reveal a banner emblazoned with the words "One World, One Dream, Free Tibet." That week, as well, Reporters Without Borders staged a demonstration with participants wearing T-shirts that depicted the Olympic Rings transmogrified into handcuffs. And Amnesty International (2007), Human Rights Watch, and the Committee to Protect Journalists (2007) all used the countdown moment to issue sober and critical reports on China's shortcomings in the field of human rights.

The staged happenings that week, official and unofficial, serve as a metaphorical preface to this book on narratives and counternarratives. They offered a foretaste of this extraordinary chapter in the history of sport, media events, the evolution of China, and the shaping of global civil society. What occurred then encapsulated the contradictions in the Games, the many and diverse efforts to control how they are understood, and the global interest in their outcome. Rather than one strong unified message, the Beijing Olympics had already become polyphonic, multivoiced, many themed.

In view of this multiplicity of competing voices and themes, it may be worth starting with what, from an Olympics point of view, could be deemed the official story. The chair of the International Olympic Committee (IOC), Jacques Rogge, was present at the Tiananmen celebration to give the blessing of the IOC, and he praised the already completed achievements. The physical markers of the Olympics—the great stadia—were almost all standing, built not only on time but ahead of schedule and, thus, strong symbols of China's ability to conceive grandly and execute with efficiency. Another high official, Liu Qi, BOCOG's president, attributed to the people of Beijing a phrase that captured the sense of solidarity that China wished to communicate. Beijingers, he said, had expressed their relationship to the Games with this minor chant: "I participate, I contribute, I enjoy" (Yardley 2007). Xinhua, the official Chinese news agency, also conveyed the impression that a nationwide consensus marked this hallmark moment:

> Across the country, Chinese people are celebrating the occasion in various ways. In the city square of Urumqi, capital of northwest China's Xinjiang Uygur Autonomous Region, residents performed roller-skating, martial arts and Taiji under red banners reading "Fitness campaign to welcome the 2008 Olympics." More than two thousand Tibetan natives and tourists gathered on Wednesday morning in Lhasa to mark the countdown. The celebration starts with a domino display by 2,008 middle school students from Lhasa as they dropped to the ground one after another on the plaza before the Potala Palace, forming the pattern of the Olympic rings and the number "2008." "I am honored to be part of the celebration and I hope I can visit Beijing to watch the games next year," said Ouzhu, an 18-year-old Tibetan student. Residents in

Beijing found various ways to express their joy. A resident named Zhao Yue'e in Huanghuamen community around Jingshan in downtown Beijing gathered with friends at the countdown clock in her community. "We are not just waiting for the Games, we are welcoming and expecting it to come," she said. (2007)

With a remarkable lack of irony, the authorities were responding to various kinds of global criticism. While the Olympics had undoubtedly united the residents of Beijing present, these images of Beijing solidarity were in stark contrast to the claims of many, including the Geneva Centre on Housing Rights and Evictions, which had in June published an extensive critical study on the impact of the Olympics on the destruction of housing (COHRE 2007). And Xinhua, by invoking joy in Tibet, was taking on the highly controversial issue of China and human rights.

One could feel the tensions generated by the various efforts to fix the meaning of and define these Games through news accounts across the world, a large number of which featured unofficial narratives not sponsored or devised by the IOC or China. The big story in the *New York Times* on Countdown Day dealt with the counternarrative that was the subject of the Geneva study: the human and aesthetic cost involved in the massive patterns of destruction in Beijing (Yardley 2007). Under the headline, "In Beijing, a Little Building Is Defying Olympic Ambitions," Jim Yardley wrote, "The two-story building where Ms. Sun's ancestors opened a bakery in the 1840s—their clientele included the Qing emperor and his court—has been on Beijing's demolition list since Monday. Local officials have notified the Sun family that the building is along the route of the Olympic marathon. Land is needed for a beautification project. A bulldozer is parked outside. Demolition is not new in the surrounding Qianmen area, a historic neighborhood being razed and rebuilt as a shopping district for the Olympics. What is unique is that Ms. Sun is refusing to leave. She is the last holdout on a street once lined with shops. Landscapers have already covered the rest of the block with saplings and a sheet of green grass. Her building is an unsightly stump marring the view."

The *Los Angeles Times* marked the occasion by raising other themes relating to human rights. In an editorial, it concluded that "it is consumers, the international media and cultural colossi such as Steven Spielberg—not preachy foreign governments—who can best further reform in China by speaking out before the Olympic torch arrives. We wish China peace, prosperity and successful Games—but not a system that jails journalists, silences dissidents and ignores the brutalization of the people who make the products the world enjoys" (2007).

The *Guardian* celebrated with a long essay, of more than 7,000 words, that included the following summary: "As the first Olympics in a communist state since Moscow in 1980, a battle looms over the message of the 2008 games. For the ruling party, it is the ultimate propaganda opportunity to show the government's success in lifting hundreds of millions of people out of poverty. For Tibetan independence activists, human rights campaigners, supporters of the banned Falun Gong spiritual movement, persecuted peasants and environmentalists, it is a chance to expose the dark side of the planet's biggest one-party state. But perhaps more than anything, it will show how China's market reforms, begun 30 years ago, have transformed the country into one of the great centres of globalisation; how movement—from the countryside to the city, and between the homeland and the rest of the world—has changed millions of lives" (Watts 2007).

Other media focused on themes relating to the environment, labor abuses, Tibet, and Darfur. Canadian papers reveled in the story about their young citizens who had been arrested for the Great Wall Tibet event. The group was interrogated for 36 hours and bundled off by plane to Hong Kong and then back to Canada. According to the *Globe and Mail,* at least one participant was unapologetic about "her role in the audacious stunt. 'As a Canadian who enjoys the rights we have, I feel we have a responsibility to step up and take action on behalf of others who don't have those rights,' she said. 'When I see something wrong, I was taught to do something about it. Well, Tibet has been brutally occupied by China for 50 years, and that's wrong'" (Mickleburgh 2007).

The German press (Wolf 2007) gave significant coverage to German politicians who struck the human rights theme with respect to China. Martin Zeil, an official with the Free Democratic Party, threatened the possibility of a German boycott of the Olympic Games (two U.S. members of Congress had introduced boycott resolutions that week as well). "We must not stand idly by, but need to build up public pressure instead," Zeil said. He had been "shaken by the deplorable incidents in China brought to light" in human rights reports. "We cannot say: sport is one thing and politics another." An article in the Russian press nevertheless suggested that the world is not of one opinion on China and the Olympics (Kashin 2007). The piece suggested that with a year to go before the Beijing Games, the West was "launching a China-criticism campaign," apparently concerted, and that not only would pressure on China increase but "the anti-China campaign" should be seen as a warning for Sochi (site for the 2014 Winter Olympics), where propaganda pressure on Moscow "was likely to be even more intense."

All of this—the world spinning narratives and counternarratives from the phenomenon that was already becoming the Olympics of Beijing—was grist for our editing mill. By summer of 2007, many of the main themes, official and nonofficial, surrounding the Olympics were beginning to fall into place. One of our authors, Briar Smith, who taught at Peking University that summer, describes her experience of domestic press coverage, where the Beijing Olympics were frequently tied to an important national historical narrative.[1] In this context, the Olympics were seen literally as a Chinese renaissance, a term used over and over again by Smith's Chinese students. According to Smith's observations, limited to be sure, of the reactions of one group of students, the Olympics were intended to suture the painful wounds of colonization and humiliation at the hands of foreign powers. They would heal the wounds of the past partly by forcing the rest of the world to take notice of the strength and power of the PRC. Again and again Smith heard that the Games were a historical mandate, part of the country's birthright and part of what it was owed for its decades of decay and loss of face in the world. In the national consciousness, a triumphant Olympics will mark the return of the Middle Kingdom's reputation for acting as a proud host to the rest of the world, as epitomized during the Tang dynasty—a time of great cultural sophistication, complex infrastructure, and technological advancement.

Smith's students also used the Olympics to develop a new and highly compressed history of modern China. According to this narrative, when China was colonized by Japan, there was no Olympic team. During the civil war and transitory period when the Communists took over, troubled China had a paltry medal count. Taking a nearly 30-year break from the Olympics, a period that included the turbulent era of the Cultural Revolution, allowed Taiwan to get its Olympic team off the ground (inflicting a wound on PRC national pride that has endured ever since). When China reemerged in the 1980s, stronger economically and ideologically, the country immediately stunned the world with its medal count in Los Angeles and has remained in the ascendancy ever since. But the dramatic climax would come now, in 2008, with China (or Beijing) acting as host astride a great economy and increasing world influence.

One of the central themes of this book is that there is an inherent instability about great events that makes them subject to capture in surprising and unanticipated ways. China intended the "One World, One Dream" theme to project a benign, harmony-seeking China emerging as a powerful yet positive global force. Reinforcing the idea of a renaissance or restoration of political place, the Olympics were presented time after time as China's "coming out party," its reinvention for world recognition as an economic, political, and social power. China wished to show itself as having a massive population that was united in wanting China to succeed. Internally, the desire was to surmount what China might characterize as the sideshows of quarreling over the means by which the state was making one of the great transitions in world history. If this were to be the century of China, then the Olympics would be a useful point of departure.

But this did not mean that there would not be jockeying to be on the global public agenda or involved in the defining of China. On Countdown Day in August 2007, a representative of the thousand-strong Uighur community who lived in the United States appeared on WNYC in New York in an effort to bring global attention, through the Olympics, to that Muslim ethnic minority who are living on the identity margin of China and seeking greater autonomy. Those concerned with the future of Darfur and China's related role at the UN and in Sudan were closely calibrating what Olympics-related steps to take, and at what stage to leverage them, in order to affect China's policy in Sudan. The Falun Gong had somehow fallen out of the mainstream news coverage of China and human rights, but there were undoubtedly strategies in place to reintroduce that narrative as well.

The various actors or authors involved—China, global civil society, corporations, religious organizations, and others—have displayed a variety of techniques for affecting public understanding. Each recognizes the potential of surprise: unanticipated global crises, guerrilla approaches to alter agendas, the locus and efficacy of demonstrations, tactics that will attract press attention. Before the Games, there will be gestures, even grand gestures, dramatically designed to affect global perceptions. It is clear that the Chinese government and its spokespersons have been taking intense lessons in crisis management though the consequences have thus far been mixed. Some Chinese Olympic officials and IOC officials sought to defuse controversy by arguing that advocacy organizations should not "exploit the Games" to further their own agendas. Others took a cooler approach, growing accustomed to a steady stream of criticism from a wide range of groups in China and around the world. Jiang Xiaoyu, an executive vice president for the Beijing Olympic Committee, said, on Countdown Day, "We are mentally prepared that such voices will become louder in the future." After the Games, there will be a studied effort to measure the reaction of authorities: how prepared they were; how China and its massive security machinery exercised force; and how the Federations, the IOC, and others exercised control through kindness and offers of assistance.

Of course, there have already been "surprises." The efforts to link the issue of Darfur to China and the Olympics are one. In the summer of 2007, it was the rise of stories about product defects, from pet foods to toothpaste to lead-tainted toys. These stories would have been significant without the Olympics in the background. But the proximity of the Games, the significance of establishing a positive redefining narrative for China, made each negative story linked and cumulative, creating its own swarm effect. No one knows what other large issues loom, ready to seize the attention of a public that might otherwise remain attuned to the well-rehearsed and established Olympic narrative.

As can be seen from the chapters in this book, one task for those who are seeking to leverage the public power of the Games on behalf of issues they deem important has been to seek a connection between their cause and the Olympics story. In some cases, the linking has not been difficult. As we have seen, the question of urban development and the displacement of populations could be easily tied to the planning of an Olympics-ready Beijing. And, as other chapters in this collection demonstrate in greater detail, global civil society groups were able to link the exploitation of child labor to the manufacture of Olympics-related mementos, mascots, and clothes. Among the questions worth posing here is which groups are most effective (and why) at gaining a public window or platform for their themes.

This project has its intellectual origins in the insights of my coeditor, Daniel Dayan, insights that grew partly from his collaboration with my colleague Elihu Katz. In 1992, Dayan and Katz published *Media Events: The Live Broadcasting of History,* which has become one of the canonical texts in the field of communications and society. The present volume takes its cue from *Media Events* in a number of ways. In addition to being inspired by that earlier book, it also attempts to build on and refine it by using the 2008 Olympics to understand how such events function in a differently mediated world. *Media Events* captured a significant structure of communications in modern society—great political transformations (the coming of Anwar Sadat to Jerusalem), extraordinary global celebrations (the marriage of Charles and Diana), and occasions like the Olympics—to tell the story of a new relationship between audience and subject. Dayan and Katz demonstrated how these events marked a dramatic reformulation of the idea of the public and the function of the media. But 15 years is an eternity in modern broadcasting, and the idea of revisiting this subject through the lens of the 2008 Olympics seemed a useful one. The forces of globalization, the establishment of a stronger global civil society, the technological changes shaping public opinion, and China's increasingly central role in the new geopolitical environment—these and other developments suggested that the 2008 Olympics would be a rich field for study.

Part 1, "Defining Beijing 2008: Whose World, What Dream?" comprises three chapters, each of which was designed to help understand Beijing 2008 as a media event. Jacques deLisle's chapter builds an agenda for the rest of the book by describing how narratives and counternarratives become a challenge both to the organizers and to those who set out to seize the public's attention. His chapter outlines specific ways in which China has attempted to use the Olympics to win greater global acceptance by establishing a general perception of itself as a prosperous, stable, normalized country. DeLisle also weighs the possible modes of countering this agenda.

Alan Tomlinson explores the relationship between Olympic ideals and contemporary capitalism. Examining the bidding rhetoric for Beijing and London against the involvement of sponsors in The Olympic Partner program, he finds a central contradiction in the political economy of the Games. The chapter by Monroe E. Price specifically explores Dayan's theories of the "hijacking" of the Olympics platform as a modification of a general approach to media events and demonstrates how this Dayanesque turn is the source of thinking about narrative and counternarrative. Price then tries to show how global civil society organizations use Dayan's approach in their efforts to seize the Olympics and define them to their advantage.

Part 2 of the book, "Precedents and Perspectives," captures the 2008 Olympics through a somewhat wider lens. Our purpose here was to invite scholars to place these Games in a series of distinct contexts. For example, in his chapter, Nicholas J. Cull looks at the Olympics as an exercise in public diplomacy. He locates Beijing and China's administration of the Games in the government's efforts to engage in public diplomacy (with respect to the Olympics and in other areas) over half a century. Heidi Østbø Haugen allows us to look at the philosophical underpinnings of the Beijing Olympics not through the implementation but rather through the bidding process. She examines the themes of the winning bid as a window on China and the Games award processes as well. Jeffrey N. Wasserstrom discusses the long history of dual or binary perspectives on China. Wasserstrom traces this global schizophrenia, defined by those who demonize China on the one hand and those who praise it on the other, to the nineteenth century, if not earlier. And he notes that the current narratives and counternarratives surrounding the 2008 Olympics continue patterns of demonization and romanticization that emerged long before. Complementing this discussion, Sandra Collins's chapter contrasts Beijing 2008 with the shadow history of the voided Tokyo Olympics of 1940 and the legacy of Seoul, portraying them as part of a dual approach that highlights both tradition and modernity. Collins explores a hybrid identity that trades in a celebrated past and a vaunted technological future. The chapter by Briar Smith dissects Beijing's recent decision to relax restrictions on foreign journalists for a set period, noting how this decision relates to Beijing's assurances on human rights to the International Olympic Committee while enabling it to retain a grip on information circulated by its domestic press.

Part 3 is entitled "Theaters of Representation." Here we have asked our contributors to identify and discuss the sites where the authors of the official and unofficial narratives of China are playing out their dramas and seeking to influence opinion. Carolyn Marvin, for example, writes about architecture and public space, or megaspace, as she puts it. She draws on the social theorist Henri Lefebvre's idea that every society produces its characteristic space and uses it to describe the contending forces that have helped to shape the physical environment of the current Olympic drama. Building on their own research on the Olympics in Barcelona, Christopher Kennett and Miquel de Moragas report on the closing ceremony in Athens, describing it as one of the first opportunities in which China was able to develop its themes before a global audience. Lee Humphreys and Christopher J. Finlay show how the promise of a "High Tech Games" establishes an important feature of the "modernity arc," as described in Collins's earlier chapter. Humphreys and Finlay look at how Lenovo, now one of the leading personal computer companies in the world, is using sports sponsorship (of the Olympics especially) to define itself as both an international and a distinctively Chinese company that exemplifies, in particular for those at home, some of the most notable achievements of the state itself. Their chapter also examines how the effort to implement 3G technology to push and expand the uses of mobile telephony (in diffusing information about the Games) has become part of the official High Tech narrative and its opposition.

Hai Ren examines the IOC's choice of sports to be included or excluded as an index of the failure of the Games to globalize. He uses Wushu (Chinese martial arts) as a case study of the role China could play in altering the Games. Andy Miah, Beatriz García, and Tian Zhihui expand on a theme that has become especially significant as a result of our expanding definitions of the term *journalist* and the large number of reporters and writers who will cover the Olympics. They look at a growing approach of creating legitimated opportunities for "nonaccredited journalists." Their contention is that "narratives about the Olympics arise largely from the stories filed by the mass of journalists—press and broadcasters—who attend the Games and spew forth accounts of what occurs on and off the competition ground. Who those journalists are, what they do, how they are channeled through the Olympics world—each has implications for what is represented, what the billions around the globe see and read." The final chapter in this section, by Sonja K. Foss and Barbara J. Walkosz, reviews how the "elite press" in the United States has framed China in the American imagination in the run-up to Beijing 2008. Looking at some of the same indicators as deLisle, Foss and Walkosz identify four "ideological spaces": definition, equivocation, accumulation, and anticipation.

In our concluding section Christopher J. Finlay looks forward to the London Olympics (2012) and other future settings for the Games. He asks what we are learning, or think we have learned, from Beijing that can be used to understand the major players as they move on to other forums, other audiences, other narratives and counternarratives. Is Beijing the progenitor of a new kind of Olympic internationalism? And Daniel Dayan reflects on the ways in which geopolitical events have radically transformed the context of media events.

There are many areas we would like to have covered more extensively. Our understanding of narrative and counternarrative still comes primarily from the printed press and from broadcasting, and our account is consequently somewhat tilted toward representations in newspapers and published reports. We have been more concerned with efforts outside China's borders to alter the Olympic narrative, paying insufficient attention to the civil society activities within the country. The power of the Internet to mobilize, to seize, to quickly alter agendas, is worthy of separate and substantial focus. We were not able, to the extent we desired, to capture the narratives that will be projected by NBC, the global broadcast licensees, and advertisers. What they say interstitially about China and about the themes highlighted in this book—or, more likely, do *not* say—will probably also be a significant factor in the integrated final impact of the Games. Some of the terms that we use in our analysis—such as, for example, *ambushing*—come from the internecine fighting among advertisers for control of the platform, but it is clear that more attention must be given to understanding ambushes organized by civil society players. And the control of symbols (explored by many of our authors) and intellectual property clearly has become vital to our ability to do so. Surveillance, control, exercise of authority: all these appear in the book, but here, too, these themes will develop far beyond the scope of this particular collection, in the public accounts that will struggle to define the Beijing Olympics for years to come.

Virtually no part of this book focuses on the sports and athletics of the Olympic Games themselves. But, of course, athletics and athletic prowess spin their own narratives of power. It is not for nothing that China seeks to top the medal table and use the symbol of gold as an index of its place in the world. Sports are implicated in narratives of gender, race, and class; the manifestations of sports tell much about a society, and all of that will be on view at the Olympics. But these questions—including the narrative of doping—represent a substantial and different field of scholarship from what is at play in these pages. As BOCOG, China, and others continue to prepare, this book is an experiment in taking a longer view of the "event," thinking of it as something that stretches over a prolonged period and includes the run-up as well as the occasion itself.

There are many people to thank and acknowledge. The book was one of the first efforts of a new Project (now Center) for Global Communication Studies (CGCS) at the Annenberg School for Communication, established by the dean, Michael X. Delli Carpini. It became clear that one area for focus by CGCS should be China, and Professor Joseph Turow suggested that one possibility would be to encourage a network of communication and communication-related academics who were interested in the 2008 Olympics. This led, in due course, to a joint effort with the Communication University of China (CUC). The distinguished Dr. Hu Zhengrong, now vice president of CUC, was an energetic coconvener of a one-day conference in China in 2006 that brought together many scholars, some of whom are participating in this book. Several of Dr. Hu's graduate students were instrumental in planning that effort.

At Annenberg, two graduate students, Chris Finlay and Briar Smith, were indispensable. They were creative in terms of the themes of the book; resourceful in considering potential authors; and vigorous, generous, and immensely valuable in terms of actual editing functions. They functioned virtually as coeditors of the book. Libby Morgan became research and editorial coordinator during the midstage of the book's development and has played a strong hands-on role in refining the project and identifying the precise work necessary in the drive toward editorial completion. She maintained contact with authors and was the liaison with the publisher. Our authors were immensely game. They welcomed a time line that would allow the publication of the book in advance of the 2008 Olympics, and cooperation and performance were generally superb.

The Annenberg Foundation, responsible for the endowment for the Center for Global Communication Studies, is also to be recognized for making this research project, and its potential links to communication studies in China, possible. At the University of Michigan we were fortunate to be in the excellent hands of Alison Mackeen, our editor, and to be included in the New Media World series, edited by Professor Turow.

NOTE

1. Correspondence with author. Smith's chapter in the book covers other significant themes but not this one.

REFERENCES

Amnesty International. 2007. One Year Left to Fulfil Human Rights Promises. August.

Centre on Housing Rights and Evictions. (COHRE). 2007. Fair Play for Housing Rights: Mega Events and Olympic Games and Housing Rights. June 5. Available at http://www.cohre.org/store/attachments/COHRE%27s%20 Olympics%20Report.pdf.

Committee to Protect Journalists. 2007. Falling Short: As the 2008 Olympics Approach, China Falters on Press Freedom. August 7. Available at http://cpj.org/Briefings/2007/Falling_Short/China.

Kashin, Vasili. 2007. Beijing Olympics under Threat; China Faces Criticism for Human Rights Abuses. Trans. Elena Leonova. *Vedomosti,* August 8. Accessed through Agency WPS.

Los Angeles Times. 2007. Beijing Couldn't Care Less about Human Rights, but It Does Care about Its Image. The World Should Speak Up. August 9, pt. A, 20.

Mickleburgh, Rod. 2007. Cut Off from Canada for 36 Hours; Chinese Authorities Isolate and Interrogate Pro-Tibet Activists before Expelling Them. *Globe and Mail,* August 9, 1.

Watts, Jonathan. 2007. One Year to Go. *Guardian,* August 9, features sec., 6.

Wolf, Christian. 2007. China Criticized—Demands to Observe Human Rights Intensify One Year Prior to Opening of Olympic Games. German News Agency ddp through BBC Monitoring, August 8.

Xinhua. 2007. China Celebrates One Year Countdown to Olympics. General News Service, August 9.

Yardley, Jim. 2007. In Beijing: A Little Building Is Defying Olympic Ambitions. *New York Times,* August 8, sec. A, 8.

I

Defining Beijing 2008:
Whose World, What Dream?

"One World, Different Dreams"

The Contest to Define the Beijing Olympics

Jacques deLisle

"One World, One Dream"—SLOGAN OF THE BEIJING 2008 GAMES

"Same Bed, Different Dreams"—CHINESE COLLOQUIALISM

The Olympics are as much about stories—many of them political—as they are about sports. The ancient Games famously included an imperative to warring city-states to cease hostilities, an affirmation of a Greek identity coextensive with civilization, and other matters beyond athletics. Political narrative also has been central to the modern Games. Particularly in the television age, the host nation, journalists, and others have sought to define the plotline of each Olympiad. Many recent Games have been entangled with weighty political themes: Nazi Germany's rise (Berlin 1936), Middle East conflicts (Munich 1972 and Melbourne 1956), the Cold War (Helsinki 1952, Moscow 1980, and Los Angeles 1984), and host states' political rehabilitation (Tokyo 1964, Rome 1960, and arguably Munich) or arrival on the world stage (Seoul 1988 and arguably Tokyo).

Politics and narrative are again prominent in the Beijing Games. The host regime is determined to assure a positive story, especially on politically charged issues. The 2008 Olympics have produced propaganda and mobilization efforts on a scale unseen in China since the beginning of the post-Mao Zedong Reform Era. Regime efforts, along with genuine popular enthusiasm, brought huge crowds to the streets the night Beijing won the right to host the Games (MacLeod 2001c; Pan and Pomfret 2001; *People's Daily* 2001). Starting years earlier and accelerating as 2008 approached, Beijing authorities covered the city with billboards and banners urging citizens to welcome the Olympics and make Beijing an impressive host city. Major, mostly state-linked Chinese companies touted—loudly, even by Olympic sponsorship standards—their support for the Games (*China Daily* 2005a; Xinhua 2004b).[1] Olympics-related content grew pervasive in state media and on ubiquitous television screens in public spaces. A giant countdown clock was erected at Tiananmen Square, the political heart of China, with satellite versions elsewhere. Much fanfare attended milestones such as the 500- and 365-day marks. The one-year point brought more than a million to central Beijing and a countdown by a chorus of thousands led by film star Jackie Chan and accompanied by fireworks.[2] China even sought out Steven Spielberg and China's most internationally famous film director Zhang Yimou for the Games' opening and closing ceremonies (Coonan 2006; *Deutsche Presse-Agentur* 2007b).

This agenda has been especially urgent and these regime efforts have been especially ardent because the 2008 Games offer potential redemption from the failure of Beijing's bid for the 2000 Olympics. When the International Olympic Committee (IOC) denied the PRC's quest to host the Games of the XXXVII Olympiad, it brought outrage, anger, and embarrassment among China's leaders and ordinary citizens (Tyler 1993b; E. Rosenthal 2000).

The 2008 Games also provide a compelling opportunity to press very different—but equally political—counternarratives. For many of the concerns that motivate international civil society organizations, foreign governments, and others, and that generate friction in international political and economic relations, China is uniquely important. On human rights issues, China combines massive scale with a notoriously poor record in matters ranging from political dissent and democratic participation; to religious, media, and reproductive freedoms; to self-determination for ethnic minorities; to social justice. On environmental questions, China's sheer size, rapid industrialization and weak regulation have made the PRC a rival to the United States in greenhouse gas emissions, home to many of the world's most polluted cities and waterways, and a source of environmental harms throughout East Asia and beyond.

For those concerned with these global issues, and for those—both foreign and Chinese—who focus on China's practices and policies, the 2008 Olympics offer exceptional conditions for bringing international attention to these matters and pressure on the PRC. The Games demand extraordinary openness in China's restrictive political and media environment and shine a rare spotlight on Chinese circumstances that still receive disproportionately little global coverage and consideration.

For outsiders seeking to change China and Chinese reformers as well, the Games offer extraordinary opportunities to advance their broader agendas through linkage to the Olympics—whether deeply resonant or shallowly ad hoc. The Games present mirror-image opportunities—as well as risks—for a regime seeking to enhance its stature at home and abroad. On both sides, multiple actors pursuing diverse agendas and seeking to define the story of the 2008 Games can draw upon Olympic ideals in ways that range from invoking to resonating to hijacking. While struggle for control of the 2008 Olympic narrative is dramatic, confrontational, and centered on the fortnight when the world comes to Beijing, more significant effects likely will be more subtle, diffuse, and long-term.

The Regime's Main Narrative: Prosperous, Orderly, Normal, and Globalized China

The Chinese regime's preferred narrative began to emerge years before the Games. It includes several strands that are broadly, if not fully, consistent with one another and Olympic ideals. First, the Olympics offer an opportunity to present China as a developed, prosperous and therefore powerful country. China's economic prowess and modernity pervade Chinese discussions of the Olympics. President and Party General Secretary Hu Jintao and other current top leaders have explicitly linked Beijing's ability to host the Olympics to the regime's central policy of promoting economic development. A year before the Games, a Politburo Standing Committee member declared that the "rapid economic and social development" China had attained under policies of "reform and opening up to the outside world" had given China the "capability and conditions to host" the Games and display China's "splendid accomplishments." When Beijing's bid for the 2008 Games was still pending, Hu's predecessor Jiang Zemin similarly cited China's and Beijing's "healthy growth" and "steady [economic] development" as a "powerful material guarantee for hosting the Games." In his 2002 New Years message, Jiang ranked winning the right to host the Olympics alongside China's WTO entry as the preceding year's key milestones in China's pursuit of prosperity through international openness and engagement (Xinhua 2006b; *Renmin Ribao* 2000; Chen J. 2007).

One of the official concepts of the Beijing Organizing Committee of the Olympic Games (BOCOG) underscores the desire to showcase China's economic advancement, promising a "High Tech" Olympics. So too does the original—and still ubiquitous—slogan of the bid committee, "New Beijing, Great Olympics." The same idea animates unofficial discussions in Beijing that express hope the Games can dispel foreign misperceptions that the capital's residents wear Mao suits, rely more on bicycles than cars, or otherwise trail the modern world (author's interviews, 2007).[3]

Material foundations for the "developed and prosperous China" image are in place. They are the product of three decades of post-Mao economic reforms and near-double-digit annual growth, the skewing of development to major eastern cities, and the regime's formidable ability to mobilize resources for favored projects.

China's new wealth has transformed Beijing. Almost all of the city's gleaming office and residential towers, international hotels, and luxury shopping malls are less than twenty years old. The most impressive ones are of more recent vintage. The notorious traffic jams of foreign-branded, joint-venture-produced vehicles are a phenomenon mostly of the last decade. Like many arriviste metropolises, China's capital has sprouted would-be iconic architecture. New facilities for the Games are massive and designed to impress, with a price tag of over $3 billion and a scale that recalls the sensibilities of the emperors who created the Forbidden City. Many of Beijing's older architectural treasures—including the Imperial Palace and the Temple of Heaven—have undergone extensive restoration timed for the 2008 Games. Major infrastructure projects, including subway lines, roads, a rail link to the airport and its new world's-largest terminal, and environmental improvement projects are part of the pre-Games construction agenda as well—at a cost of $40 billion (*Financial Times* 2007a; Abrahamson 2005; *Japan Economic News-wire* 2005).

When reality inconveniently has fallen short of image, Chinese authorities have turned to Potemkin village tactics to hide, or distract attention from, the incompleteness or the deleterious side effects of China's breakneck modernization. For an IOC visit during Beijing's unsuccessful bid for the 2000 Games, buildings along the guests' route received fresh coats of paint and slogans welcoming the Olympics. Decrepit athletic facilities were patched up. Peddlers, homeless people, and beggars were kept out of sight. Traffic restrictions were imposed, and coal-fired furnaces were shut off (despite the impact on production and the comfort of city residents) (Associated Press 1993; Cater 1993; United Press International 1993). Although reforms responding to vote-buying scandals limited IOC visits eight years later, Beijing deployed similar tactics in its successful quest to land the 2008 Games. Authorities "greened" the city through planting trees and painting brown winter grass. They cleared the air by ordering factories to close and reprising earlier restrictions on residential coal heating. They again signaled enthusiasm with numerous banners and enthusiastic citizens (including a bicycle rally of 10,000 in central Beijing) (Byers 2001; *Japan Economic Newswire* 2001; Kuhn 2001).

To the extent that intervening years of economic growth, real estate development, and Olympics-related construction have not solved such problems (and have worsened some of them), means redolent of the 1993 and 2001 efforts to land the Games are in the repertoire for the 2008 Games. Some have been clearly and explicitly adopted—for example, limiting pollution and traffic congestion. Others are not officially acknowledged but certainly will be in the mix—for example, removing or hiding those whose presence or advocacy reveals persisting poverty and rising inequality, including Beijing-based dissidents, provincial petitioners who come to the capital seeking redress for their grievances, and migrant laborers who work in countless construction projects and other more marginal jobs in the city. Less certain is whether such measures, some of which worked reasonably well for brief site visits, can succeed when 30,000 journalists, and half a million participants and spectators, stay for two weeks.

The hosts' use of the Games to display China's modernity and prosperity fits a pattern of the Olympics as grand spectacle and, more importantly, reprises prior Olympics' roles as national "coming out parties." The Beijing Games here resemble the Seoul Games of 1988 or perhaps the Tokyo Games of 1964. The Seoul Olympics came shortly after Korea's ascension to the ranks of lower-middle-income countries—a group the PRC has now joined (World Bank n.d.). Although Japan decades earlier had become a developed, industrialized country, the 1964 Games underscored its recovery from postwar economic devastation. The parallel to the Seoul Games has become a cliché in foreign commentary and informal discussions in China. (The analogy unsurprisingly occupies a much lower profile in orthodox Chinese commentary. PRC authorities are unsurprisingly averse to outsiders' speculative suggestions that the Games also might portend political change similar to Korea's democratization. And, like Chinese leaders before them, they are hardly inclined to celebrate the former vassal state as an appropriate model or worthy predecessor for China in any significant international endeavor—with the limited exception of Korea's rise as one of several "tiger" economies from which post-Mao economic reforms drew lessons.)[4]

For China, the link between prosperity and development is reinforced by promises of more concrete economic effects. Official sources tout the Games' contribution to "the nationwide struggle" to achieve the Reform-Era goal of a "well-off society." Olympics spending may add as much as 1 percent annually to Beijing's economic growth. The impact of Olympics-driven infrastructure improvements will extend far beyond 2008 (Xinhua 2001c; Xu 2007). The rapid growth of Beijing's economy, population, and need for infrastructure means the host city faces less danger of common Olympic hangovers of white-elephant projects and popular resentment of vast expenditures on Olympics-related projects to the neglect of other needs. A mid-course retrenchment—directed by Premier Wen Jiabao and prompted by concerns about excessive and inefficient spending and doubts about the future utility of the Games' venues—promised to reduce such risks further (Xxz.gov.cn 2007; Ling and Lee 2007).

The Games are also expected to spur upgrading of Beijing's service industries. Unlike resident expatriates and experienced visitors who have become accustomed to many frustrations, the foreigners who will come for the Games are expected to demand—and thus Chinese authorities, determined to win favorable press, are pushing to provide—services that meet international standards. Sectors targeted for improvement range widely, including hospitality, transportation, media, and health care (*China Daily* 2006b; Xinhua 2005b; *China Daily* 2007e).

A second central theme in the official narrative is to portray China as politically stable and orderly. All host governments, and the international Olympic authorities, want to avoid Games marred by poor organization or political disruption. This is a core (if not explicit) Olympic value, reflected in the factors considered in the site-selection process, the insistence that the Olympics are about sport (not politics), and the related mantra that the Games should not be politicized. Commitment to political order and control looms especially large for Beijing in 2008, as top Chinese officials have noted (Xinhua 2001a). The harsh measures to relocate migrant workers, provincial petitioners, and development-besieged poor urbanites are as much about securing order as showcasing prosperity.

PRC leaders also have been sensitive to the influence of Chinese dissidents, who have embarrassed the regime abroad and who, properly handled, might aid the regime's Olympic pursuits. In the most notable example, Wei Jingsheng, China's internationally best-known dissident, was released from prison during the quest for the 2000 Games, in part to burnish the regime's image and respond to foreign human rights critiques. Wei was soon jailed again, having irked authorities by criticizing to foreign media the regime's attempts to trade political prisoners for the Games, and meeting with the U.S. State Department's chief human rights official to urge continued pressure on the PRC (Tyler 1993a; Tempest 1994).

The period preceding the 2001 vote on the 2008 Games brought similar tactics. By this time, China had sent Wei into exile as part of its effort to lessen the foreign condemnation of China's human rights record that had helped scuttle Beijing's bid for the 2000 Olympics. With the 2008 site choice nearing, Chinese authorities detained known dissidents, keeping them from IOC visitors and the press, and imprisoned at least one democracy activist who signed a letter urging the IOC to press China on human rights. Authorities also reined in media, both traditional organs and newly emerging channels for heterodox opinion, including the Internet and *wangba* (Web cafes) that provided many users with access points, as well as anonymity (Faison 1997; MacLeod 2001a; E. Rosenthal 2001; Pan and Pomfret 2001). The more-immediate run-up to the Olympics—and the politically sensitive Chinese Communist Party Congress the preceding fall—brought tighter restrictions and increased harassment of political dissidents, regime-criticizing NGOs, and old and new media.[5]

The regime's commitment to staging a trouble-free Olympics is sometimes overstated (for example in the occasional suggestion—firmly and credibly rejected by PRC authorities—that the pre-Olympics period might permit Taiwan to move toward formal independence because fear of a Moscow or Los Angeles Games-style boycott would deter Beijing from using force to check secession).[6] Still, the storyline of a smooth and successful Olympics is a high priority for a regime with considerable commitment and capacity. Maintaining order and control is a particularly deeply entrenched imperative in China, where "fear of chaos" (*paluan*) is a centuries-old political trope and where the ruling regime initially drew much of its legitimacy from having ended decades of civil war, foreign invasion, anarchy, and semicolonial encroachment. Of more immediate relevance, the forcible suppression of the Democracy Movement, the smothering of dissent during the nearly two decades since, and the ongoing repression of Falun Gong under-score the regime's ability to maintain political order and quash challenges when leaders perceive sufficiently strong reasons to do so. For the Beijing Games, the prospects for disruption are dim, at least on anything approaching the scale of the Tiananmen Democracy Movement of 1989 or the Falun Gong activities of a decade later (including the surprise assembly of 10,000 followers outside the top Chinese leadership's residence). Enforced silence predictably awaits dissidents, and expulsion, confinement, or other restrictions face vagrants, petty criminals, mental patients, rural-to-urban migrants, and other unsightly types, for the 2008 Games.[7] To further assure order, PRC authorities have devoted massive resources to security work for the Games. It may also help that major venues are clustered in areas removed from both central Beijing and the chronically politically troublesome university district.

In more quotidian but economically significant ways, PRC authorities have used their power to control citizens' and enterprises' behavior to create an impression of orderliness and cleanliness during key Olympics-related moments. They shut down factories and limited driving for IOC visitors in 2001, creating unusually clear skies and quiet streets (*Japan Economic Newswire* 2001; Kuhn 2001). Two years before the Beijing Olympiad, capital-area factories, taxi drivers, and others were on notice that their "fog"-producing and traffic-snarling activities would be severely curtailed during the Games. Factories were to close for months preceding and during the Olympics, and much of the city's workforce was to be told, or encouraged, to take vacations.[8] The China-Africa summit in October 2006 and a test ban on driving for 1.3 million vehicles in August 2007 provided small-scale dress rehearsals for Olympic traffic restrictions. A year before the Games, authorities announced that hundreds of domestic flights would be canceled in the weeks surrounding the Games to reduce airport delays (McGregor 2006a; *China Daily* 2007a; Harvey and McGregor 2007; Xinhua 2007l). And, most expensively of all, much of the Olympics-driven infrastructure building blitz served this same goal of avoiding chaos from an inadequate transportation system.

Other official efforts also show commitment to orderly, trouble-free Games. For example, city authorities launched a campaign to improve Beijingers' manners in advance of the Olympics. Targeted behavior included booing athletes who perform badly, spitting or swearing in public, failing to queue for buses, and using embarrassingly bad English (Xinhua 2006a; Yardley 2007b; Xinhua 2007m). Methods were developed and tested to seed clouds to reduce the chance of rain during the image-defining opening and closing days and to wash pollution from the skies (*China Daily* 2007c; Xinhua 2007i). With controversy erupting over Chinese exports of dangerous food, medicine, and toys in the summer of 2007, PRC authorities rushed to address another perceived threat to a smooth and orderly Olympics, pledging high-tech tracking and inspection systems to assure the safety of consumables at the Games (Yardley 2007c).

A third element in the preferred official narrative uses the Beijing Olympics to assert China's achievement of, or return to, international respectability and normal membership in the global community. The Olympics' utility in promoting such political rehabilitation and acceptance is not a formally recognized Olympic principle. It is understandably not stressed in official Chinese discussions. But it is an obvious power of the Olympics and figured prominently in debates over whether China should be awarded the Games and motivated the Chinese regime's desire to host.

The still-fresh memory of the 1989 Tiananmen Incident (and human rights issues generally) helped defeat Beijing's bid for 2000. The awarding of the 2008 Olympics marked zealously pursued and hard-won progress from this dismal baseline. The Games will offer further opportunities. The visual richness of the Olympics and the worldwide attention they draw provide a singularly promising chance to supplant images from 1989, such as a lone man standing in the path of tanks or an army vehicle toppling the Goddess of Democracy.[9]

Here, the 2008 Games can give China what the 1960 Rome Games; the 1964 Tokyo Games; and, arguably, the 1972 Munich Games (especially read against the backdrop of the 1936 Berlin Games) gave their hosts: a symbolic affirmation of the country's recovery from political pariah status that had followed odious actions. To be sure, the Tiananmen Incident and other recent PRC human rights violations pale in comparison to Axis governments' atrocities in World War II. On the other hand, China's quest for reacceptance is complicated by the continuing in power of the regime responsible for the behavior that led to ostracism.

Ongoing, post-Tiananmen human rights abuses have remained a challenge for China's rehabilitation and normality agenda. China's former recalcitrance toward the international human rights regime has softened, grudgingly, in the face of regular critical reports from NGOs, the U.S. State Department, and others; threats by the U.S. to remove trading privileges; the remarkable (if modest and constrained) growth of human rights discourse and advocacy in China; and the partly human rights–based and temporarily successful international opposition to China's entering the WTO and hosting the Olympics.

As the role of human rights concerns in China's Olympics bids underscores, China's efforts to use the Games to enhance its normal, accepted state status partly depend on more effectively engaging the international human rights norms that have become a feature of the Olympic movement. This connection between human rights and the Games may have its roots in venerable Olympic ideals of sport free from politics and open to individual merit. It expanded through the resonance of human rights issues with Olympic tragedy and controversy at Munich in 1972, retrospectively for Berlin in 1936 and arguably in the Afghanistan invasion–linked boycott of Moscow in 1980. The tie has strengthened further through Olympics-focused efforts of human rights NGOs in recent years. The Olympic Charter and Code of Ethics now include such human rights–related provisions as preservation of human dignity, harmonious development of man, and prohibition of discrimination on the basis of race, religion, gender, or politics (IOC 2004).

Recognizing the seriousness of international discontent and concern, Chinese Olympics authorities assured wary Olympics decision makers and decision influencers that awarding Beijing the Games would promote human rights in the PRC and bring Games-specific changes in such key areas as press freedom, especially for foreign media. These arguments and promises helped China land the Games but have limited prospects for wider effect. Poor implementation, continued abuses, and tighter controls (some Olympics driven) have produced a torrent of criticism as the 2008 Games draw near (Xinhua 2006f; Tian 2007; Dickie 2007a).[10]

For China, the rehabilitation-and-arrival theme extends beyond recovery from Tiananmen and later human rights problems. Beijing's successful bid to host the Games, and the Olympics' placing the host city at the center of world attention, are seen as bringing closure to China's "century (and a half) of humiliation" that began with the Opium Wars, the shattering of a Sinocentric world order, and China's relegation to the margins of the international system. While this issue has not been central to official views, it is a significant theme, especially common in unofficial and foreign discussions of the Beijing Olympics and China's rise more generally. It likely also helps explain the seemingly outsized importance that the Games appear to have for China's leaders (C. Smith 2001; Frank 1993; Chen J. 2007; Xu 2007; author's interviews 2007).

Addressing environmental problems is also part of the "normal" or "conforming" nation strand in the officially preferred narrative. China increasingly draws international opprobrium for failing to engage this set of international norms. It faces criticism and alarm for having rejected the Kyoto accords, allowing its waterways and urban air to become among the world's most polluted, threatening the environment and public health of its neighbors and, on some views, using lax pollution controls as an export subsidy.

The Olympics bring special pressures, incentives, and opportunities for China to address its environmental rogue status. Environmental issues have distinctive ties to the Olympics. The environment formally joined culture and sport as international Olympic themes in the 1990s. Environmental concerns and the Games are broadly and informally linked by the connection between sport and public health and the impact of pollution on the Olympics' many outdoor events. And Olympics officials early and often raised the environment as a serious concern for a Beijing Games (Cha 2007; United Nations n.d.; *China Daily* 2007b; IOC 2004; World Health Organization 2005; Japan and China 2007).

Against this problematic backdrop, PRC authorities made a "Green" Olympics one of the Beijing Games' official concepts. They have adopted and publicized regulations incorporating international "green" standards and pursued cooperation on Games-specific environmental measures with the United Nations Environmental Program and environmental protection authorities abroad. They have made and emphasized pledges to minimize energy use and adopt solar energy, water recycling, and other green technology for Games-related building projects, transportation, and other activities during the Games. They have touted campaigns to plant trees, directives to curtail or close (permanently or temporarily) polluting factories in the Beijing area, convert capital-area power plants from coal to cleaner fuels, and restrict driving during the Games. Some of these undertakings have been costly and somewhat effective. They command greater official attention and extra public resources (totaling several billion dollars) partly because they seem vital to the regime's Olympic story that China is a responsible and respectable participant in an increasingly important aspect of the international system (Xinhua 2006c; *China Daily* 2005b; *China Daily* 2004c; Xinhua 2007n; Landsberg 2007b; MacLeod and Wiseman 2007).

Prospects for success remain questionable, however. The measures are small relative to China's problems, both of substance and image. Some of the commitments surely will be honored in the breach or will prove inadequate (Harvey and McGregor 2007; *Deutsche Presse-Agentur* 2007c). The latter problem was underscored when, with a year to go, the IOC warned it might postpone endurance events if pollution remained severe (Blitz and Dickie 2007). Other pledges risk diminished impact because they may be recognized as only symbolic (seeming green without being green), temporary and local (reducing haze and traffic jams only in Beijing and only during the Games), or cost-shifting (moving factories elsewhere in China).

Intellectual property plays a similar role in the official Olympic narrative of China's international normalcy and conformity. The PRC has faced mounting criticism for being ineffective or unwilling to implement international norms—and China's WTO-related commitments—for the protection of intellectual property rights (IPR). China's behavior has brought growing calls for action, including chronic complaints from foreign companies and industry groups and the United States' initiating long-contemplated WTO proceedings before the one-year mark in the countdown to the Games (Puzzanghera and Iritani 2007; USTR 2007).

Like human rights and the environment, IPR is a special concern of the Olympics that poses serious risks and possible opportunities for the Beijing Games' hosts. Olympics-related IPR protection has become a major IOC focus. Selling sponsorship rights and licensing Olympic logos are highly lucrative and vital to paying for costly Olympics operations. China's broader record of rampant piracy has compounded such concerns for the 2008 Games.

PRC authorities have sought to assuage those worries and, in turn, avoid reinforcing an important count in the international indictment charging China with shirking global rules. Across Beijing, specialized stores and booths have sprung up, prominently and apparently accurately proclaiming that they sell "officially licensed" Olympics products and offering them at premium prices. PRC authorities have pledged increased IPR enforcement, adopted Olympics-specific IPR regulations, declared that those rules "meet usual international practices"

(*China Daily* 2004a; PRC State Council 2002), launched contests to increase popular knowledge of Olympics-related IPR laws (Xinhua 2007j), devoted a disproportionate share of antipiracy enforcement efforts to Olympics knockoffs, and publicized enforcement successes.[11] Authorities clearly are sensitive to reports of Olympics IPR piracy, apparently believe that they may face significant costs if they fail to follow through on high-profile commitments to improve IPR protection, and surely are solicitous of the interests of state-owned or state-affiliated enterprises that produce licensed Olympics merchandise.

Here too, the impact of promises and efforts is doubtful. Unlicensed Olympics paraphernalia has been on offer from street hawkers many months before the peak demand that will accompany the Games. Officially touted crackdowns on Olympics counterfeiters are still few relative to the likely scale of 2008 Games-related piracy. And the authorities' moves face a skeptical international audience that may well regard publicized efforts as being more about image than efficacy.

A fourth theme in the officially favored narrative is a "globalized" China (to be inferred from an apparently globalized Beijing). This element is facially consistent with international Olympic norms of internationalism and universality. It is also imbedded in the Beijing Games' principal slogan, "One World, One Dream," which tellingly enjoys a special place as a giant billboard at the most heavily touristed—and photographed—part of the Great Wall. One of the Games' official themes—a "Humanistic" or "People's" Olympics—emphasizes benevolent cultural and social implications of the Olympics and similarly signals cosmopolitanism, harmony, and universality.[12]

Much that supports the "normal" and "accepted" nation strand also serves this element of the regime's preferred interpretation of the 2008 Games. The claim that China is "globalized" is a key aim of the PRC's self-congratulatory embrace of international norms—generally and in specifically Olympics-related moves—on issues ranging from intellectual property to environmental protection to labor standards.

Similarly, developments that support the officially preferred Olympics story line of China's economic prowess also help the regime's claim to cosmopolitanism. Because foreign trade and investment have loomed so large in China's rapid development and because coastal urban China's burgeoning consumer class has a strong taste for foreign brands, the advertisements (many of them invoking the Olympics) that festoon the capital's main roads and shopping areas are mostly for internationally famous companies. In the Olympics context, the regime has not left this visible commercial face of internationalism at risk of shabbiness. As the Olympics-driven urban facelift that followed the awarding of the Games began in 2002, city officials ordered the removal of down-market signs (including some of longtime Olympics sponsor McDonald's) (Xinhua 2002).

Many of the most recent additions to the architectural backdrop for such signage also embody the regime's globalization narrative. Prominent examples include controversial French architect Paul Andreu's National Theater with its flattened, reflective dome and Rem Koolhaas's "twisted arch" headquarters for China Central Television. Major Olympic venues are similarly internationalized. The main stadium for the Games, designed by the Swiss firm Herzog and de Meuron, has an open-weave facade that has prompted the moniker "bird's nest." While this popular nickname evokes Chinese cuisine, the design is not discernibly Chinese. A leading architect at the local firm that collaborated on the project tellingly described the stadium as "such a good, modern design that it would be accepted and liked by Chinese culture" because of those virtues, not because of its Chineseness. Another Chinese architect with a major role in the project similarly described the stadium as "a very bold design for a nation that wants to prove itself part of the international family, to show we share the same values." Australia's PTW Architects' fanciful natatorium evokes blue bubbles—and the sobriquet "water cube"—and has no discernibly Chinese features (Pomfret 2000; *South China Morning Post* 2007; *China Daily* 2006c; Watts 2007). This internationalization of building styles has displaced former mayor Chen Xitong's more nativist directives that prompted often-tacky Chinese motifs on many buildings from the 1980s and early 1990s.

These changes to Beijing's cityscape have been so striking that that they have generated a backlash. Local companies and officials have attacked foreign brands' outdoor advertisements for overwhelming Chinese competitors (Xinhua 2005c). Chinese architects, officials, and commentators have lamented displacement of Chinese aesthetic traditions and criticized foreign-designed projects for not fitting their environment. Such charges (along with concerns about cost and safety) were sufficiently powerful to bring retrenchment of key projects and reconsideration of the rush to foreign styles (Xinhua 1993b; Hawthorne 2004; *China Daily* 2004b). Chinese celebrities' contributions to packaging the Beijing Games also have supported the cosmopolitan theme but without drawing nationalist critiques. Some of the most prominent roles, tellingly, have gone to movie actor Jackie Chan, basketball star Yao Ming, and film director Zhang Yimou—whose appeal goes far beyond the Chinese world and much of whose fame comes from accomplishments in non-Chinese settings.

This official narrative of universality and globalization that echoes and appropriates established Olympic ideals also serves a broader Chinese foreign policy agenda. The Olympics story line of a cosmopolitan, internationalized China dovetails with the PRC's drive to assure skittish neighbors and a wary world that China's inexorable "rise" will be a "peaceful" one in which China will continue to emphasize its own economic development; deepen engagement with the outside world; and eschew "hegemonism," "imperialism," and other modes of dominating other states or abusing its new power. Chinese Olympic rhetoric has picked up these themes, stressing that the Games will help make Beijing and China more internationally open, and adopting as one of the organizing committee's three official themes a "People's" or "Humanistic" Olympics that will have transformative and internationalizing effects on China's citizenry (Zheng 2005; Xinhua 1993a; Moon 2006).

Efforts to weave the strands of development, stability, normality, and globalization into an effective narrative for the Beijing 2008 Games have faced significant challenges. Among the difficulties are the weakness of empirical foundations for some key claims, and the themes' uneasy coexistence with another, very different dimension of official China's preferred vision of the Games.

The Regime's Other Narrative: Chinese Nationalism

Nationalism is a familiar element in the Olympic experience and— though less so—Olympic ideals. It has particular force and volatility for the Beijing Games. While the most audible parts of the official narrative have stressed international cooperation and assimilation and domestic prosperity and order, nationalism has always been central to China's Olympic quest. It predictably comes more to the fore as the Games approach.

Partisan patriotism may not be among the Olympics' most lofty values, but it is an important facet of the Games, especially for the host nation. For the 2008 Beijing Olympiad, the Chinese regime has cast winning the right to host the Games and staging a smooth and successful Olympics as major points of national pride and signal moments in China's rise as a great power. A chest-thumping tone pervades discussions of the Olympics as a reflection of China's recent accomplishments and return to international prominence and acceptance.

Against this background, Chinese successes at the Games are sure to bring much official triumphalism, both reflecting and feeding popular sentiment and perhaps pushing beyond the point that serves the regime's longer term interests and reflective preferences. China's status as a major and rising sports power and the Games' typical home court advantage promise many occasions for celebration of Chinese on-the-field accomplishments and China's pursuit of first place in the medal count. Long before the Games, public displays in Beijing celebrated Yao Ming, 2004 hurdles gold medalist Liu Xiang, and other Chinese athletes alongside Jesse Owens and other stars of past Olympiads.

Other Chinese characteristics of the 2008 Games may amplify the ordinary Olympic temptations of nationalism. Head-to-head competition between PRC and U.S. teams invites jingoistic responses, especially given two backstories. The approach and arrival of the Games of the XXIX Olympiad recall the United States' role in denying Beijing the 2000 Games and political efforts in the United States that opposed awarding China the 2008 Games. Some of that opposition continued long after the IOC's site selection and included pointed (if futile) calls in Congress, among NGOs, and elsewhere for a boycott of the Beijing Games (Lengell 2007; *Los Angeles Times* 2007; *China Daily* 2007d; Smith 2007; Perlez 2001; Xinhua 2001b; Schweisberg 1993; Xinhua 1993c).

The Games will unfold against the backdrop of China's rapid and self-conscious rise as a great power and official and popular chafing at perceived American efforts to deny China its rightful place in the world or to subject China to unfair standards and unwarranted criticisms. Key irritants are unlikely to abate before the Games: a cavernous bilateral trade imbalance; charges that China has not allowed its currency to appreciate adequately; concerns about shoddy and dangerous Chinese exports; Washington's characterization of China as less than a "responsible stakeholder" in the international system on matters ranging from economics to human rights to international security to public health; and sharp disagreements over the propriety, necessity, and motivation of China's quest for a blue-water navy, satellite-killing weapons, information warfare capacity, and other military capabilities. The nationalist strand in the Chinese official narrative and the developed and powerful China theme that PRC authorities also press (and that, in any event, will be inescapably on display at the Games) are a heady combination that may provide ample fodder for the "China threat" school of PRC critics in the United States.

The likelihood of Sino-American conflict-fueled nationalism becoming a major element in the Olympics story line will rise if these or other aspects of U.S.-China relations become foci of the American presidential campaign and party conventions that will be held nearly opposite the Olympics, or if PRC leaders—or unforeseen events—increase such issues' political salience (Luce and Ward 2007). Once accepted, China's invitation to President Bush to attend the 2008 Games promised some assurance on this front, but at the risk of greater U.S. attention to the Games and, in turn, greater impact on U.S. opinion and policy of any developments that depart from the Chinese regime's preferred Olympic narrative (Stolberg 2007).

Japanese Olympic successes and direct competition with Chinese athletes could become another flashpoint for Chinese Olympic nationalism. Bilateral relations remain chronically troubled, and clashes have erupted after matches between Chinese and Japanese teams in recent years and brought international expressions of concern about what they portended for 2008 (Makinoda 2007; McNeill 2004; McGregor and Pilling 2004).

Taiwan's Olympic role—always nettlesome for China—is more problematic at a PRC-hosted Games. For decades, China has grudgingly endured Taiwan's participation under the name "Chinese Taipei." At a Beijing Games, however, the prospect of Taiwanese athletes competing as representatives of an entity distinct from the PRC, or standing atop medal platforms on mainland Chinese soil, puts Chinese authorities to harder choices. In this setting, China's customary acquiescence risks implying greater PRC acceptance of Taiwan's status in an event at which competitors typically represent sovereign states, not lesser entities. Given the broader nationalist tenor of the Olympics for China, temptation and pressure to push back may be formidable, despite the cost to China's efforts—at the Games and more broadly—to appear accommodating and nonbellicose. This prospect will loom larger still if Taiwanese athletes, media, or politicians cast Taiwan's Olympic participation or successes strongly in Taiwanese nationalist terms.

Here too, broader politics, including election politics, likely will play a role. A new president will have taken office in Taiwan three months before the Games. If past patterns hold, the campaign will have included conflict over Taiwan's relations with the mainland and whatever initiatives concerning the island republic's "status" the retiring "pro-independence" incumbent Chen Shui-bian will have undertaken during his final months in office. Among these is a ruling-party-backed proposed referendum for the early 2008 balloting that calls for Taiwan's entry into the United Nations. This long has been anathema to Beijing (which insists that Taiwan is ineligible for what the PRC characterizes as a states-member-only organization), and the referendum is among the reasons offered for pressing a tough line on Taiwan policy at the Chinese Communist Party Congress held ten months before the Games.

Well before the Games, the Taiwan issue and the nationalist strand in China's Olympics agenda already had produced friction. In early 2007, controversy erupted over whether the Olympic torch would pass through Taiwan on its way to the opening ceremonies. Beijing offered, and Taipei rejected (and negotiations for a mutually acceptable alternative arrangement failed to resurrect), the flame's journey through the island as part of a final, intra-Chinese segment that also would include the Hong Kong and Macao Special Administrative Regions.[13]

Tibet too has become part of an Olympics-related and politically charged nationalist narrative concerning a region of disputed Chinese sovereignty. Beijing Olympics organizers pointedly included Tibet as a domestic leg of the torch relay and as the source of one of the Games' mascots. Chinese authorities reacted sharply to efforts to use the Olympics to display Tibetan opposition to China's rule, quashing Olympics-and-Tibet-related protests and restricting foreign media access to the region (Macartney 2007; Yardley 2007e).

Chinese nationalism—or at least Chinese culturalism—pervades official symbols and slogans of the 2008 Games, sometimes in ways not obvious to outsiders. This is particularly significant as an attempt to define the meaning of the 2008 Olympics because culturalism and nationalism long have been closely linked in China and because Chinese political discourse remains highly attuned to metaphor and symbol.[14]

The logo for Beijing 2008 is a human figure evoking an Olympic athlete and incorporating a stylized variant of the ancient seal-style version of the character *jing*, as in Beijing. (To some observers, it resembled not *jing* but *wen*, referring to culture [*wenhua*]—implicitly Chinese culture.) The logo provoked nationalism-related criticism on two fronts: some complained that the design attempted to make a universal event excessively Chinese; others attacked it for being insufficiently nationalist in snubbing the rest of China in favor of Beijing (BOCOG n.d.a; Fang 2004b; Fang 2004a).

Olympic medals will feature the logo and incorporate rings of jade—the quintessential Chinese stone and symbol of honor, virtue, and fortune—in descending levels of quality on the gold, silver, and bronze medallions (Gao 2007). The *fuwa*—the omnipresent and insufferably cuddly mascots for the Games—are an oppressive mélange of Chinese symbols, leavened with Olympic icons. The five creatures represent the carp, panda, Olympic Flame, Tibetan antelope, and swallow. Each is color coded to one of the Olympic rings and one of five basic elements that mostly track traditional Chinese cosmology.[15] Each is also associated with a traditional Chinese blessing. The mascots' names take kitschy national-culturalism further still: Beibei, Jingjing, Huanhuan, Yingying, and Nini use mandarin Chinese's dense homophony to echo the venerable tourism slogan, *Beijing huanying ni* (Beijing welcomes you!) (BOCOG n.d.b; Gao 2005).

This pervasive cultural symbolism extends, with more subtlety and less media hype, to the Games' physical setting. As references to the influence of the "five elements theory" on the design of the Olympic village underscore, traditional motifs are hardly absent. The Olympic Green follows principles of Chinese geomancy (*fengshui*). The Games complex is laid out to extend and remain harmonious with the capital's ancient north-south axis—an orientation that the founders of the People's Republic once sought to pivot with the postrevolutionary construction of the broad east-west boulevard that passes before Tiananmen. Construction for the Games also has unearthed archaeological finds, which are always occasions for officially sanctioned expressions of national-cultural pride (Xinhua 2004a; Xiao 2002; Yardley 2007a). Cultural nationalism is also reflected in the vast Olympics-driven restoration program for the city's imperial-era architectural treasures, and in plans for elaborate—even by Olympics standards—events showcasing Chinese performing arts.

Even small and seemingly trivial matters convey attempted sinicization. The moment chosen for the Games' opening—8:08 p.m. on August 8, 2008—is a string of Chinese superstition's lucky number. The Chinese version of the Games' widely used English slogan replaces the bland "New Beijing, Great Olympics" with the more proprietary and transforming "New Beijing, New Olympics."

Some host country cultural nationalism in the Olympics is commonplace and consistent with the inclusion of "culture" alongside "sport" in the pantheon of Olympic values. Still, the Chinese hosts' efforts have been unusually pervasive and often overwrought. Less clear are the prospects for success of this strand in the officially preferred narrative. Much of the content is, by any measure, clunky and contrived. Anecdotal evidence suggests that educated and cosmopolitan segments of the Beijing population (and perhaps others) wince at dated-sounding, simplistic, and excessively nationalistic tones in the official fervor for and pride in China's Olympic moment and expected successes. The nationalist drumbeating over the Olympics also seems to have little carry beyond Beijing. Shanghai is far more focused on its own World Exposition for 2010. The Olympics figure far less prominently in conversations and local media coverage beyond Beijing, and many comments are critical of the perceived waste and the expenditure of national resources on the already rich and subsidized capital (author's interviews, 2006–2007; *Economic Reference News* 2004; Wei 2007).

Moreover, the purveyors of the officially preferred narrative surely appreciate that moves that evoke or fan popular nationalism in China can be dangerous and must be relatively carefully calibrated. Although manipulable and often mobilized to regime ends (ranging from supporting the Olympic bid to criticizing Japanese prime ministerial visits to the Yasukuni Shrine to U.S. bombing of the Chinese embassy in Belgrade), Chinese nationalism is a genuinely popular phenomenon that is sometimes virulent and difficult for the regime to control.

The nationalist strand in the officially preferred story line also must contend with more accommodating and cosmopolitan themes in the regime's principal narrative and the weight those derive from Chinese authorities' having emphasized them in their bid to secure the Games and advance broader PRC foreign policy goals. Moreover, purveyors of officially preferred narratives must contend with other contestants in a struggle to define the meaning of the 2008 Olympics. These rivals' aims conflict with the official agenda's nationalist elements—and others as well.

Counternarratives: Appropriating Olympic Ideals, Playing Chinese Politics, and the Games as Foreign Policy and Guerrilla Theater

The Olympics often spawns transnational, multisided contests to shape a Games story line. Those battles are especially complex and high-stakes for the XXIX Summer Games. Challenges to official China's preferred narrative come from diverse sources, including groups that fall within the loose rubric of "global civil society"; foreign governments with China policies and issue-specific foreign policies; and other organizations, industry associations and firms, and individuals in China and elsewhere. Well before the Games, these actors began to press Olympics-related agendas on a wide range of issues. These efforts to expose, publicize, or affect repressive, illiberal, or otherwise international norm–violating PRC policies and practices predate and extend beyond China's pursuit of the Games. Several features of the Olympics, however, create especially promising contexts for long-standing participants and newcomers to try to change China.

First, the Olympics has facilitated linkages between agendas that critics and promoters of reforms press and goals that the Chinese leadership values, including hosting the Olympics as a sign of China's status and prowess and, more broadly, securing China's standing as an internationally accepted, normal state. Foreign actors' influence on the IOC's choice of hosts and their ability to threaten credibly to diminish the Beijing Games' success (through high-profile protests, boycotts, reports, and the like) gave outsiders special leverage with the Chinese leadership. Echoing the saga of China's quest for WTO membership, Beijing's quest for the Games prompted pledges that otherwise would not have been forthcoming from the PRC on issues that mattered to foreign governments, international NGOs, and influential interest groups.[16]

In seeking the Olympics, as in pursuing WTO accession, China's promises gave new tools to critics and reform-promoters at home and abroad. They could monitor China's compliance and depict PRC shortfalls as not meeting requirements that Chinese authorities could not dismiss as externally imposed, nonbinding benchmarks. A year before the Games, this tactic became more prominent. Notable examples included foreign media and international human rights NGOs and dissident and critical Chinese issuing high-profile condemnations of Chinese authorities' failures to live up to Olympics commitments on press freedom, labor rights, and human rights more generally.

Second, as these examples of linkage suggest, agendas of activists, critics, and other proponents of change in China can invoke or appropriate Olympics values. Where they do, their preferred story lines have a better chance of being woven into the Games' principal narrative and leveraging the Olympics' capacity to affect PRC regime behavior and Chinese circumstances.

Human rights issues are the most notable example. The Beijing Games' background includes much that reinforces the already robust linkage between the Olympics and human rights. NGOs and foreign political leaders cast their opposition to Beijing's unsuccessful bid for the 2000 Games largely in human rights terms (Bondy 1993; Sun 1993). As the IOC considered awarding Beijing the 2008 Olympics, critics and opponents reprised earlier tactics and argued that China's human rights record disqualified the PRC from hosting the Games.[17] In one widely noted example, Amnesty International timed the release of a major report on torture in China to coincide with IOC representatives' predecision visit to Beijing (MacLeod 2001b).

Chinese authorities have made it easier for NGOs and other critics to connect human rights agendas, including maltreatment of political prisoners and China's suppression of political dissent, to the Beijing Games. The release of selected dissidents to parry foreign criticism made the former prisoners potent spokesmen and foci for linking criticisms of China's political repression to assertions of Beijing's unsuitability as a host for the Games. Perhaps the most striking case is twice-imprisoned and exiled Wei Jingsheng's call to deny China the 2008 Olympics, which was more potent because his first release had been widely seen as a move to boost Beijing's bid for the 2000 Games.

The seemingly ordinary practice of the host city's mayor being a prominent presence on the bidding and organizing committees strengthened the human rights connection because of two incumbents' problematic records. In the 2000 Games process, Chen Xitong brought the burden of a significant role in the bloody crushing of the 1989 Democracy Movement. For the 2008 round, Liu Qi's presence spotlighted the suppression of Falun Gong, most dramatically when his visit to the Salt Lake City Winter Games made possible service of process against him in a suit over his leadership of a government body tasked with eradicating the "evil cult" (Pomfret 2002; *Doe v. Liu Qi* 2004). Such damaging linkages were reinforced further by the aspiring hosts' tone-deaf short-lived contemplation of using Tiananmen Square—site of the 1989 military action against peaceful demonstrators—as the venue for the 2008 beach volleyball competition (Mackay 2001; Sohu.com 2005). More calculatingly and ultimately more powerfully, Chinese authorities made the connections stronger still with their bid-supporting reassurances that the Games would foster human rights improvements and their pledges of specific Olympics-related legal reforms with human rights content.

Since the decision on the 2008 site, those seeking to press the regime have continued Olympics-linked critiques and calls for improvement of China's human rights laws and practices. NGOs have played the Olympic card and won related media attention in several ways. Some have proclaimed "minimum human rights standards" that China should be required to meet as host for the Games and published periodic reports highlighting China's failures to fulfill Olympics-related human rights promises (Olympic Watch 2004; Magnier 2004; Pierson 2007; Lague 2006). The pace and profile of this approach surged at the one-year-to-go point with a series of headline-grabbing publications. Amnesty International issued a report denouncing an ongoing crackdown on Chinese media, an Olympics-related "cleanup" ousting Beijing vagrants and migrants, a general failure to implement Olympics-related pledges on press freedom and other matters, and continuing abuses in criminal justice and media censorship. Invoking the link to the Games, the NGO's secretary general warned that "[u]nless Chinese authorities take urgent measures to stop human rights violations over the coming year, they risk tarnishing . . . the legacy of the Beijing Olympics." Human Rights Watch simultaneously issued a similar report, criticizing the regime's overall record on human rights, a growing crackdown on dissent and the media, and Olympics-related increases in abuses of labor rights and forced evictions (Amnesty International 2007; Human Rights Watch 2007b; Yardley 2007d; Cody 2007b).

Chinese activists and critics have undertaken kindred efforts. Perhaps most famously, a group of more than forty prominent intellectuals and activists issued an open letter to Hu Jintao, Wen Jiabao, and National People's Congress head Wu Bangguo at the one-year mark, calling for a recasting of the Beijing Games' principal slogan as "One World, One Dream, *and Universal Human Rights*." The letter cataloged familiar human rights problems, including media controls, persecution of lawyers and activists who expose human rights abuses and environmental problems, and aggrieved citizens petitioning for redress, forced evictions, residency restrictions, violations of labor rights, and so on. It added calls for amnesty for political prisoners, expanded and equal freedoms for foreign and Chinese journalists, and establishment of a system of citizen oversight over Olympics spending.[18] Less elite Chinese, including thousands of peasants, have expressed similar sentiments in their own letters and petitions.[19] Such moves by PRC and international actors foreshadow further efforts to promote scrutiny of

PRC human rights conditions through the Games themselves—a prospect that the regime clearly finds disconcerting.

As the abuses cataloged in such omnibus human rights reports suggest, the Olympics-linkage strategy extends to more specific human rights agendas. Connecting their issues to the Beijing Games has been a promising project for opponents of China's harsh treatment of rural-to-urban migrant workers and urban dwellers whose homes stand in the path of property development. Massive and rapid Olympics-related construction brought dramatic residential displacement, by one NGO's account ousting nearly 10 percent of the city's population. This helped the Geneva-based Centre on Housing Rights and Evictions (COHRE) and other NGOs, activists, and media draw greater attention to the broader issue of property seizures. Chinese activists similarly linked their long-standing complaints about housing rights and forced evictions to Olympics-driven projects, commencing their bold and risky efforts several years before the Games and prompting the imprisonment of one activist who had sought permission for a protest march (COHRE 2007; Watts 2003; Goff 2005; *Daily Yomiuri* 2007; Xinhua 2007d; Xinhua 2007k; Callick 2007).

Similarly, the army of construction workers who came to Beijing to build the Games' venues helped foreign NGOs and domestic critics highlight, and gave an Olympic face to, the problems of poverty, insecurity, and discrimination facing internal migrants (Eimer 2007; *Guardian Unlimited* 2007). So too did the authorities' moves to eliminate migrant villages and rumored plans to remove unauthorized residents prior to the Games, lest the capital's unregistered underclass damage the image of an orderly Olympics hosted by a prosperous China (Xinhua 2005a; Shi 2006a).[20] More than their foreign counterparts, Chinese activists and critics added other social and economic rights concerns to their Olympics-invoking agenda, for example, linking inadequate investment in health care and other public goods to profligate spending on the Games.

Olympics-related developments also provided regime critics with means to bring greater exposure to labor rights violations. A British NGO reported that PRC firms were using child workers to produce Olympics logo-bearing products. The revelations, media coverage, and PRC promises of remedial action helped bring international attention to broader child labor abuses that labor rights NGOs argue are widespread and growing in rural China. An Olympics-focused union-based campaign, PlayFair 2008, reported "gross violations" of labor standards at four factories making Olympics-branded merchandise (McLaughlin 2007; Xinhua 2007h; PlayFair 2008 2007). Such reports increased pressure on Chinese authorities to investigate and sanction problems of underage labor and forced overtime among other producers of Olympics licensed goods. The host regime thus helped NGOs bring further attention to such issues while seemingly gaining little credibility with skeptical foreign audiences that became increasingly concerned over Chinese factory conditions in the wake of scandals over the low cost and poor safety of Chinese exports (*Financial Times* 2007b; Barboza 2007).

Attempts to pressure the Chinese regime on "rights of peoples" issues also invoke the Olympics. PRC authorities' efforts to use the Olympics to assert their claim to sovereignty over Tibet—by including Tibet on the torch route and a Tibetan animal among the Games' mascots—have facilitated their nemeses use of Olympic linkages to advance their own Tibet agendas. Thus, exiled Tibetans have proposed a separate "Tibetan Olympics" and asked the IOC to allow a Tibetan team at the 2008 Games. Free Tibet groups have staged widely reported protests, unveiling banners near the proposed torch route and at the Great Wall, where the one-year countdown saw soon-to-be-deported activists unfurl a call for "One World, One Dream, Free Tibet" (*Hindustan Times* 2007; *New Zealand Herald* 2007; *Statesman* 2007; *Kyodo News Agency* 2007). PRC officials have fairly openly expressed concern that long-repressed domestic dissident groups favoring separatist agendas in Tibet and Xinjiang will attempt to seize the Olympic spotlight to advance their causes (Cody 2007a).

The banned Falun Gong sect poses similar threats and raises similar concerns. Its supporters and advocates abroad have linked calls to cease persecuting the group to the PRC's broader Olympics-related human rights commitments and Olympics-heightened international concern over China's human rights performance. Their tactics have included a "Global Human Rights Torch Relay" (HRTR) alternative to the official Olympic torch relay. The authorities reportedly worry that Falun Gong adherents remaining in China will try to use the Olympic stage to highlight their plight. And such worries seem plausible, given the extraordinary determination evident in domestic Falun Gong followers' and activists' persistence in challenging the regime despite extraordinary suppression efforts and through sometimes desperate measures (including self-immolation).[21]

Activists, including foreign celebrities, also have used Beijing's hosting of the Games to focus attention on human rights violations in Darfur and China's support for the Sudanese regime. China's recalcitrance on international sanctions and Hu Jintao's uncritical tone during his Africa trip a year and a half before the Games created a useful platform for NGOs and activists. They dubbed the 2008 Games the "Genocide Olympics," arguing that China's Darfur policy (as well as China's domestic human rights record) made Beijing an unfit host, and planned their own alternative torch routes through sites of twentieth and twenty-first century genocides and through more than twenty U.S. states. Despite official PRC denials, some analysts credit such efforts— and the attention those efforts received from foreign governments— with making the PRC more cooperative in multinational efforts on Darfur, including acquiescence in a Security Council Resolution endorsing peacekeeping forces (Farrow and Farrow 2007; Dinmore 2007; Xinhua 2007e; Cooper 2007; Yardley 2007e).

Media freedom and related issues of openness and free exchange are another area in which critics and activists (as well as journalists, who depend upon such freedoms) exploit resonance with Olympic ideals. The now-entrenched Olympic expectation of unrestrained international media access provides important leverage against any host government's restrictions on coverage. The principles are particularly salient for the 2008 Games, where the host regime is accustomed to imposing severe constraints on media coverage, information flows, and free expression. PRC authorities have given proponents of media freedom additional leverage by bowing to strong international pressure and promising a free (or at least freer than is normal in the PRC) media environment for the Games (*China Daily* 2006d; McGregor 2006b).

This has provided a sturdy platform for NGOs' and news organizations' criticisms of moves by PRC authorities that portended Olympics-related media restrictions, refused to extend promised Olympics-related freedoms to Chinese journalists or non-Olympics stories, and harassed or restricted media in China during the run-up to the Games (Yan 2005b; Reporters Sans Frontières 2006; Allen 2007). Here too, the countdown's reaching the one-year mark brought high-profile critiques by NGOs of tightening censorship of local media, harassment of foreign media, and unfulfilled promises of Olympics-related liberalization. At the same time, Reporters Without Borders sponsored a demonstration in Beijing criticizing the failure to implement the press freedom reforms China had pledged when seeking the Games. The demonstration gained extra publicity and impact when authorities detained Chinese journalists who covered it (*BBC Monitoring International* 2007; Amnesty International 2007; Human Rights Watch 2007b; Landsberg 2007a).

Those with more commercial interests also press their regime-criticizing and regime-pressuring agendas by invoking another established—if less exalted—feature of the Olympics: the Games as business venture. Those concerned with China's IPR record especially can build upon the IOC's and official corporate sponsors' concern with Olympic branding and licensing, and exploit Chinese authorities' interest in avoiding high-profile criticism of Olympics-related shortcomings in an area that has been a source of conflict and embarrassment in China's external relations. A prominent example of this tactic is the Motion Picture Association of America's airing familiar criticisms of Chinese IPR protection from an Olympics-invoking platform. Another perhaps is the U.S. government's taking formal steps before the WTO to address Chinese IPR infringement and negotiating enhanced bilateral cooperation against piracy (Glickman 2006; Puzzanghera and Iritani 2007; Associated Press 2007). While factors unrelated to the Olympics surely drove such decisions, the Olympics connection was often cited in discussions of Washington's moves and may well have made China more pliable.

Environmentalists also are employing linkages to the Olympics in pressing their China-related agendas. International groups' efforts resonate with the Olympic movement's official concern with environmental issues. They leverage the IOC's highly public worries about environmental conditions for the 2008 Games (including the mid-2007 threat to postpone endurance events). They exploit the PRC regime's proclaimed commitment to a "Green" Olympics and its desire to avoid images of athletes struggling with choking haze, Olympics-related feature coverage of Beijing's pollution problems, or the embarrassment of pollution-postponed events. Even PRC successes have provided fodder for such critiques, inviting NGO questions about why Games-related clean-ups did not extend beyond the Olympics period or outside the capital region (Magnier 2007). Efforts from Chinese NGOs and activists generally have been broadly similar but more tempered. Thus, PRC environmental advocates report, and observers confirm, unprecedented success in getting the authorities to take their concerns seriously, and they attribute such developments largely to Beijing's "Green" Olympics pledge and Olympics-driven international scrutiny. At the same time, prominent Chinese environmentalists have faced criticism for being too timid and cooperative—charges that are not often made against their besieged counterparts who press various human rights agendas often at the cost of harassment or imprisonment (Yan 2005a; Larmer 2001; Fan 2007).

As these patterns of internal and external criticism and pressure imply, Chinese actors have been less visible in pressing counternarratives months or years in advance of the Games. They, of course, have much less freedom, far fewer resources, and more constrained media access. As the Chinese authorities' reaction to some of the more bold domestic critics (such as housing activists) makes clear, Chinese challengers to the regime's preferred Olympics story line can pay a high price for their temerity. As PRC officials' reported worries over foreign-media-targeting surprises from domestic dissident groups suggest, PRC proponents of counternarratives likely understand that their best hope may be to wait for the Games themselves to make their most dramatic and visible moves.

Third, Olympics norms and practices have combined with features of Chinese politics to help proponents of critical counternarratives and advocates for Chinese reform by limiting PRC authorities' use of means they ordinarily could employ against activities and actors that they find threatening or deem unacceptable. The Beijing Games will bring an international media and visitor presence of vast proportions and diverse worldwide provenance that the PRC's security apparatus will be hard pressed to monitor and evaluate, much less control, despite allocating formidable resources to the task. For the 2008 Games, the familiar effects of international media and other Olympic visitors are likely to be magnified, given the extraordinary interest that the Beijing Games have generated among traditional print and broadcast journalists and the presence of an unprecedentedly large, diffuse, and particularly hard-to-control cohort from new media. In this context, aspects of PRC behavior that support critical counternarratives and mediagenic actions that regime critics undertake in connection with the Beijing Olympics are likely to receive extensive coverage that Chinese authorities will be unable to stop at all or, at least, not without unacceptable financial and political cost.

The Olympics' status as a singularly supranational event makes the venue for the Games a global space in which ordinary sovereign prerogatives of the host are limited. In the context of the Games, familiar and otherwise internationally tolerated restrictions that PRC authorities use to disable protesters, silence critics, or stifle public debate may well appear illegitimate and face unusual international opprobrium when exposed, as they are sure to be, in the glare of the Olympics spotlight.

As this suggests, the "Olympic effect" of greater scrutiny and openness may be especially significant for Games held in China. For Beijing in 2008, the "gap" between the Olympic media frenzy and ordinary coverage is unusually large. Although foreign audiences increasingly appreciate China's global importance, developments in China still receive disproportionately little international attention under ordinary circumstances. This is partly a matter of the inherent difficulties of covering a large; poor; rapidly changing; and physically, culturally, and linguistically remote country. It is also a function of political regime type. While China has undergone a breathtaking opening during the last generation, the PRC is still among a small handful of authoritarian states, and (with the exception of the Soviet Union in 1980) the most strongly authoritarian state since before World War II, to host an Olympics. Such regimes severely restrict information and journalists and do so in crude and obvious ways that are hard to sustain amid the global interest and expectations of openness that come with hosting the Games.

As Chinese authorities are acutely aware, an extraordinarily dense foreign press presence and relaxed media controls previously have had powerful political effects in China. Outside journalists who arrived to cover Soviet President Gorbachev's visit to Beijing helped catalyze, and bring international attention to, the Tiananmen Democracy Movement in 1989. In an exceptionally liberal period in Chinese politics and regime policy toward students, intellectuals, and the press, the Democracy Movement attracted an unusually large and unfettered media contingent—both foreign and indigenous—that reported extensively and dramatically on the movement and its violent suppression, with correspondingly greater harm to the Chinese leadership's international—and domestic—reputation.

Many of the organizations and actors that seek to shape the story of the Beijing Games and, in turn, the PRC's behavior (and the media that cover them) also enjoy insulation from some of the more subtle pressures Chinese authorities ordinarily use to restrain those who are more durably on the ground in China. The NGOs, corporations, government officials, interest groups, celebrities, and others that are primarily focused on China for the Olympics differ from the foreign businesses, foreign-linked foundations and civil society organizations, and resi-

45

dent foreign diplomats and journalists in China in a key respect: the former are more nearly nonrepeat players. They have less need to worry about angering Chinese authorities or putting Chinese counterparts in difficult positions. They need not be so concerned about future license denials, regulatory hassles, adverse decisions on matters within government discretion, and alienating Chinese partners who are wary of dealing with foreigners who have fallen into official disfavor or shown questionable political judgment. The contrast with the concerns and constraints facing domestic Chinese NGOs, dissidents, and critics is, of course, greater still.

At the same time, those who seek to use the Olympics as a platform for rival narratives and critical agendas benefit from the host regime's Olympics-based reasons for self-restraint. The Chinese leadership shows every sign of feeling strongly the "pull" of securing a story line that echoes the international "seal of approval" provided at Seoul in 1988 or Tokyo in 1964, and the "push" of avoiding the politicization and loss of international goodwill that befell the 1980 Moscow and 1984 Los Angeles Games, or, much worse, the 1936 Berlin Games. While this is to be expected from a political system that emphasizes symbolic politics and national pride, PRC authorities have magnified the effect by binding themselves to the mast in so publicly staking their reputation on staging a "successful" Olympics.

Another structural feature of Chinese politics promises greater space for international civil society NGOs and other regime critics, including domestic ones, to advance their goals in connection with the 2008 Olympics. The commitments to hosting a successful Games and to advancing the regime's preferred overarching narrative do not mean that the Chinese Party-state will function as a disciplined machine pursuing a coherent agenda. Although the PRC's political system is authoritarian, it is also famously "fragmented": different components of the Party and state pursue diverse and sometimes conflicting aims.[22] This is reflected in the great but uneven importance that the Olympics has assumed for Party and government organs, and the extensive but varied responsibilities and commitments that various state and state-linked entities have undertaken in conjunction with the Games.

Although the specific alignments are too opaque and uncertain to map in detail, different "pieces" of the Beijing and broader PRC Party-state (as well as elite leaders and social constituencies) well may react very differently to steps that NGOs, activists, and others take on the

46

Olympic stage. For example, those portions of the Party and state apparatus (and their patrons and constituents) that are especially deeply invested in staging an Olympics that wins international praise are likely to be more willing to tolerate actions critical of the regime, or at odds with regime preferences, as a cost of achieving their goals. They therefore are more likely to push, in the complex and informal world of Chinese politics, against peer or rival organs (and their patrons and constituents) that favor less accommodating lines.

Signs of this pattern emerged well before the Games. BOCOG and the Beijing municipal authorities seem genuinely to accept an imperative of greater tolerance for media freedom while other state entities that traditionally regulate the media, international journalists, and the Internet (including the State Administration of Radio Film and Television, the Foreign Ministry, the Ministry of the Information Industry, and the public security authorities) appear to have taken harder lines and adopted contrary measures, leading to difficulties for those who made and must defend China's Games-related pledges of increased openness (Reporters Sans Frontières 2006). The apparent understanding among authorities most involved in hosting the Games that it is important to liberalize the political climate (albeit temporarily) diverges sharply from—and foretells friction with—public security authorities, who have held forth loudly about the extraordinary resources devoted to keeping order and the need for security forces to be "combat ready" (Wang 2007).[23]

BOCOG, environmental protection authorities, city leaders, and others have taken significant and unpopular measures (including cutting off coal-fired heaters for a wintertime IOC delegation visit, ordering restrictions on cooling and other electricity usage during the Games, and banning more than a million cars from the streets) to improve the environmental image and reality for the Olympics. Chinese environmental activists and advocates have had kind words for state environmental protection authorities and their Olympics-enhanced interest in enforcing rules and cooperation addressing environmental issues. Yet, with the Games barely three years off, speculation continued that one of the capital region's most polluting enterprises—a steel company with powerful state patrons and many employees—might succeed in resisting directives to curtail or suspend operations for the Games. A year before the Games, a company spokesman sniffed that, while sharp reductions in operations would be phased in through the

Games and beyond, the final relocation in 2010 would have occurred eventually anyway and had only been hastened somewhat by the Olympics (Cha 2007; *China Daily* 2004c; Larmer 2001; Fan 2007; United Press International 2005; Dickie 2007a; MacLeod and Wiseman 2007).

Beijing Olympics officials and IPR enforcement organs sought to strengthen (at least somewhat) measures to limit pirated Olympic goods. But they seemed certain to find little cooperation from officials in China's major fakes-producing regions where entanglements and alignment of interests between local government and IPR-violating enterprises can be very close (Clark and Cheng 2007).

To the extent that more accommodating fragments of the Party-state win out in such conflicts or have autonomy to implement their preferred approaches, there will be a more favorable environment for outsiders and local reformers to push agendas that diverge from the principal narratives favored by the Chinese regime as a whole. At the same time, some moves that more recalcitrant components of the Party-state, or the regime as a coordinated whole, might undertake against foreign critics' or domestic dissidents' agendas can redound to the targets' benefit. For those pressing counternarratives and challenging regime behavior, sometimes nothing succeeds like official repression, at least where it is high profile and ham fisted or tin eared. Instances of this phenomenon already have occurred in the run-up to the Beijing Olympics. Examples from around the one year countdown mark include PRC security forces' detention of local journalists who covered a foreign journalist organization's protest in Beijing of China's failure to implement Olympics pledges of media freedom, and detention and deportation of "Free Tibet" supporters who unfurled a banner at the Great Wall.

Still, such regime missteps—and other factors that limit Chinese authorities' capacity or will to suppress—provide little reason for complacency among critics of the PRC regime and proponents of counternarratives.

The Empire Can Strike Back

Although facing significant constraints and capable opponents in the contest to define the narrative of the Beijing Games, the host regime also has considerable advantages. These derive in part from key features of the Olympics, Chinese politics, and the critics and opponents of official China's preferred story line.

First, despite the partly self-inflicted erosion of its means of control and intimidation over the last three decades, the Chinese Party-state remains formidable, especially when it faces relatively short-term challenges. For the fortnight of the Games, Chinese authorities can maintain a level of vigilance and, if needed, repression that might not be sustainable over a long period. In doing so, they will have human and material resources beyond the considerable ones ordinarily on hand in Beijing (Xinhua 2006e; Xinhua 2005d; Daley 2003; Xinhua 2007a; Kwok 2007). They can use methods recently practiced in suppressing remarkably determined Falun Gong adherents, honed in concerted pre-Olympics drills, and enhanced by foreign-assisted Olympics-related security forces training programs. The latter have proceeded despite international criticism of liberal states for helping a repressive regime build capacity and concern that heavy-handed security measures might mar the Games (Xinhua 2007f; Xinhua 2007g).

Second, despite the decline of ideology's importance in post-Mao China, symbolic politics and political theater remain important in Chinese politics and stiffen official resolve to control the rich image-making power of the Olympics. PRC authorities likely see it as vital to prevent definitive moments that serve a heterodox political agenda— anything analogous to the raised fists of African American athletes at the Mexico City Games, much less the hostage crisis at the Munich Olympics, or the Olympic equivalent of the lone man standing before a tank near Tiananmen in 1989.

In trying to forestall such adverse imagery and broader counternarratives, official Chinese sources and sympathetic commentators have been adept (if not unchallenged or entirely successful) at invoking the Olympic principle that the Olympics should not be "politicized" by those who wanted to deny Beijing the Games or who want to use the Olympics to change China's human rights practices or political system (Cody 2007a; Magnier 2004; Mackay 2001). Here, PRC authorities have had help from the IOC and others who have a stake in the 2008 Games' success and have made more muted versions of anti-"politicization" arguments (B. Smith 2007; Rogge 2007).

Third, the PRC regime may well be able to blunt or deflect criticisms of its failure to satisfy external demands or expectations that China adopt international norms. And it may be able to do so without major changes in its own behavior. On many fronts, China has been adept at pledging conformity to foreign standards or global rules, avoiding robust implementation, and escaping the degree of condemnation from abroad that would have accompanied flat rejection of the norm or commitment. That is, at least, a plausible characterization of how the PRC has engaged international human rights law and international intellectual property rights—both areas that have been especially at issue in connection with the Beijing Olympics. Quasi-official Chinese sources and defenders of the Beijing Games also have worked to undercut or preempt criticism of human rights, press freedom, and other shortcomings by pointing to China's recent progress and asserting that hosting the Games will help foster improvement well beyond 2008.[24]

Pursuit of official China's preferred narrative may benefit also from low expectations that many Olympics participants and observers likely hold because of their lack of familiarity with contemporary China. First-time visitors and relative neophytes can be favorably surprised by the cosmopolitanism, openness, sophistication, wealth, and lack of obvious political repression in Beijing. Experiences of Beijing tend to color impressions of the unvisited "rest of China," notwithstanding an intellectual appreciation that much of the country does not resemble the glittering capital. This effect likely will be more pronounced given the care taken to present Beijing's best face for the Games.

Finally, the hosts' prospects for controlling the Beijing Games' story line are enhanced by structural disadvantages among proponents of rival narratives. Those seeking to invoke or hijack Olympic ideals and use the Games as a platform to pursue alternative, regime-criticizing agendas are ideologically cacophonous and institutionally fragmented. Their aims are strikingly varied: democratic reform; civil liberties and civil and political rights; social and economic justice for migrants and displaced urban residents; media freedom; environmental protection; intellectual property rights protection; labor rights; "separatist" or "independence" goals for Tibet, Taiwan, and the Muslim regions of Xinjiang; religious freedom, primarily for Christians; ending repression of Falun Gong; relaxation of population control policies; and so on. Elements in international civil society and foreign political circles that endorse such ends range across a broad political spectrum. They have little demonstrated or likely capacity for close cooperation with one another.

Perhaps more importantly, they have only modest accomplishments and dim prospects for cooperation with their Chinese counterparts who have begun to pursue parallel tactics. Chinese dissidents, intellectuals, activists, and NGOs have emerged to address—with varying degrees of success and risk—many of the same issues, including the environment, forced evictions, migrant workers, human rights more generally, and media freedom. While these local proponents of change also have adopted tactics of linking their causes to the Beijing Olympics, their actions have shown little coordination with or even apparent impact upon the undertakings of the many foreign actors seeking to define the meaning of the Beijing Games.[25] The most internationally visible example of a domestic Chinese undertaking is the August 2007 "open letter" from dozens of prominent intellectuals and dissidents calling for adding "Human Rights" to the slogan "One World, One Dream," and asserting that the regime's violation of Olympics-related human rights promises and human rights abuses more generally "violate the Olympic spirit" and worsen a "crisis of rule" in China (Qianming.net 2007; Wu 2007; Cody 2007b). Even that letter, however, prompted mostly citation and not collaboration abroad (and much of the attention it received reflected the preexisting fame of its principal signatories abroad).

The Chinese regime benefits from the many impediments to such parallel undertakings' blossoming into full alliances. Domestic and foreign critics' aims are far from fully parallel. The Chinese intelligentsia that provides ideas and leadership for such groups (and many "ordinary" Chinese as well) has limited interest in agendas associated with "separatism" or "cults," attacking China's Africa policy, and so on. They also tend to be more susceptible to at least the more benign elements in the regime's nationalist narrative and more modest in their expectations of immediate reform in China. Compared to foreign governments and international civil society groups, Chinese activists have placed greater emphasis on linking the Olympics to education and public health spending and release of political dissidents. More significantly, Chinese and foreigners face radically different threats of retaliation from Chinese authorities. Cooperation and the trust it requires when grappling with an authoritarian regime are far more difficult when domestic actors face threats of ruined careers and imprisonment but foreigners rarely need worry about more than interrogation and expulsion. Such factors surely reduce the authorities' need to worry about a coordinated foreign or transnational effort to capture the narrative of the Beijing Games.

A Journey of a Thousand *Li* or the
Death of a Thousand Cuts?

The victor (if any) in the contest to define the meaning of the XXIX Olympiad will be determined only in retrospect. Rivals in the struggle to shape the Beijing Games' narrative have sufficient strengths and weaknesses, and the dominant story of any Olympics can be so strongly affected by exogenous factors and unpredictably resonant moments, that pre-Games predictions are little more than speculation. Similarly uncertain, but more important, is the impact on bigger questions of "changing China" that have made the story line of the Games, and China's hosting, worth fighting over.

A bleak assessment conjures the specter of a Beijing Olympics that deepens China's repression in domestic politics and intransigence in foreign policy. Some who opposed awarding Beijing the Olympics, or fear that the regime will win the battle over the Games' narrative, see the 2008 Olympics providing a propaganda coup and reinforcement of self-image reminiscent of what the Berlin Games gave Hitler's Germany (A. M. Rosenthal 1993; Kynge 2001; Larmer 2001; Sun 1993; Frank 1993). Accounts of Chinese authorities' actions sometimes have fed these concerns, perhaps most astonishingly when foreign media reported that they consulted with Hitler's favorite architect's son and namesake on the design of the main axis for the Games site (Becker 2003).

This analogy has gained relatively little traction, and rightly so. It overreaches. It overstates the impact of the Berlin Games (Terrill 2007). It also oversimplifies the range of possible consequences of the Beijing Games. If official China succeeds in holding the Games—and selling the plotline—it wants, the regime might not become more set in its ways or emboldened. It might become more tolerant of the types of international links and liberalizing influences that the Olympics will have promoted. A "successful" Games may increase confidence among Chinese political elites that the regime can endure and benefit from increased openness. Or it may strengthen the image of China as a powerful—and therefore potentially threatening—state and, in turn, the Chinese leadership's appreciation that China needs to appear, and therefore perhaps to be, more open to international scrutiny and influence and willing to conform to international norms.

More rosy assessments foresee the 2008 Games spurring rapid transformation in China. One line of analysis imagines the 2008 Games as a possible reprise of the 1988 Seoul Olympics, which are often credited with speeding South Korea's transition from military dictatorship to democracy, or the 1980 Moscow Games, which are sometimes depicted as having helped open the door to Gorbachev's reforms and, in turn, the demise of communism in the former Soviet Union. IOC sources, veteran U.S. diplomats, and foreign observers and proponents of Beijing's bid embraced moderate versions of this argument or folded the Olympics into a broader pattern of using negotiated commitments, foreign advice and assistance, and other tools of engagement to move China toward greater liberalism at home and cooperation abroad (Wilson 2001; Liu 2006; Longman 2001; Lilley 2001; Rogge 2007). Official Chinese sources concertedly—if perhaps sometimes disingenuously—encouraged this view, promising that a Beijing-hosted Olympics would lead to a more open China and promote further improvement in China's human rights conditions (Wilson 2001; Lev 2001; Longman 2001).

A less harmonious variation on this theme sees much potential for foreign governments, international NGOs, Chinese dissidents and re-formers, and media coverage to push China along this same path of transformation by Olympics-focused or Olympics-enhanced pressure on the PRC leadership, global exposure of problematic Chinese practices and policies, coordinated responses to PRC failures to implement international promises and obligations, and success in the struggle for a critical counternarrative of the 2008 Games. If this occurs, then post-Olympics China may face greater and more sustained pressure on human rights, the environment, and other issues that have drawn criticisms and calls for reform during Beijing's two campaigns to host the Olympics, the run-up to the 2008 Olympiad, and the Games themselves.

Prognostications of major near-term change are likely overly optimistic and simplistic. The more strident critics and pessimists do have a point: for the Chinese regime, Olympics success may reinforce the status quo and its excesses. So too, the Chinese leadership has demonstrated—most extremely in the aftermath of Tiananmen—the ability and will to use political repression and endure international isolation when openness, liberalization, and their sequelae embarrass or seem to threaten the regime. Or the Games may simply fail to have any dramatic impact on China. Once the flurry of attention and scrutiny has passed, there may be a relatively rapid return to much that looks like the ordinary regime practices that predated the Games and the broader quest for the Olympics.

More importantly, any lasting impact of the Beijing Olympics and any significant transnational influences it will yield likely lie beyond immediate or dramatic success or failure at the Beijing Olympics or in shaping the "meaning" of the 2008 Games. Any such more subtle and lasting influences are likely to favor liberalization and openness in the long run. During the nearly three decades of China's Reform Era, the trend has been strongly toward greater engagement with and influence from the outside world. Qualitative shifts toward openness and conformity in Reform Era China generally have proved to be "one-way ratchets," not vulnerable to permanent reversal. The Games may well not have that level of impact. If they do, and perhaps even if they do not, they may mark another chapter in this long-unfolding story. Such developments can create space not only for previously repressed or ignored critics of the regime but, perhaps more importantly and more durably, for Chinese proponents of more moderately critical or reformist perspectives as well.

Here, the Olympics-related emergence and Olympics-focused efforts of Chinese activists for human rights, the environment, and media freedom are modestly encouraging signs despite their lack of success, their political and legal vulnerability, and the weakness of their connections to foreign counterparts. From a relatively long-run perspective, the organizational and ideological fragmentation on all sides— among Chinese leaders, institutions, and interest groups and among foreign and Chinese actors seeking to expose and change Chinese behavior—may be a positive factor. It multiplies the number of actors and points of contact, and, in turn, prospects for meaningful transnational ties and resilient channels of influence and cooperation (including the diffusion of techniques for successful NGO and civil society activities). The resulting numerosity, small scale, and seeming lack of connection among such actors and networks also are likely to make them less vulnerable and seem less threatening to the regime and thus less likely to provoke effective repression.

If the 2008 Olympics has these effects (and it is far from a foregone conclusion that it will), it will have contributed to a much larger and longer term process that has been transforming China in ways that are generally consistent with many of the international norms that global civil society groups; foreign governments and other external actors; and Chinese NGOs, activists, and dissidents have been pressing in the more immediate and perhaps less promising context of the contest over the Beijing Games and its story line. The Games then will have been a step in a journey of a thousand *li* toward a more liberal and open environment in China, or one slice among the thousand cuts that will bring the end of a closed and repressive order.[26]

NOTES

1. The first "partners" and "sponsors" included: Sinopec and CNPC (the giant oil companies), Bank of China, Air China, Haier (the white goods maker), People's Insurance Company of China, Tsingtao and Yanjing beer companies, China Netcomm, China Mobile, Sohu.com (a major internet portal), Volkswagen (China), Adidas and Johnson & Johnson. Almost without exception, the sponsoring companies are variously state-owned, majority-state-owned, in especially highly regulated sectors, or joint-ventures (or partners to joint ventures) in which the Chinese partner is state-owned or state-controlled. Lenovo (the Chinese computer company that bought IBM's PC division) announced that it would spend up to two percent of its yearly turnover for Olympics-related marketing efforts (Xinhua 2007b).

2. See, for example, Chua 2007a, *Deutsche Presse-Agentur* 2007a, Chua 2007b, and Xu 2007.

3. See also Dickie 2007b.

4. See, e.g., Lilley 2001, Chen K. 2007, deLisle 2001, and *China Daily* 2006a.

5. These developments have been the foci of NGO and media reports and are discussed more fully later in the chapter.

6. See, for example, Xinhua 2003 and Xinhuanet.com 2004.

7. See, for example, Shi 2006b.

8. See, for example, Spencer 2006 and Shi 2006b.

9. See, for example, Pan and Pomfret 2001, MacLeod 2001c, and Cater 1993.

10. The regulations, among other things, permit travel and interviewing without prior permission, but are in effect only from January 2007 to October 2008. Critiques of shortcomings are discussed more fully later in the chapter.

11. On many of these issues, see Clark and Cheng 2007, Xinhua 2007c, China Online 2002, and Tsang 2007.

12. The Chinese term is *renwen aoyun,* fairly translated as "humanistic Olympics." The more common English translation of the phrase for the Games is "people's Olympics," which would be the ordinary English rendering of the Chinese phrase *"renmin aoyun"*—a term that would refer inescapably to the Chinese people and that strongly evokes Chinese nationalism. See also Humanistic Olympic Studies Center, Renmin University.

13. See, for example, *Central News Agency* 2007, Ni 2007, Shi and Chung 2007, and Lague 2007.

14. For a strong and classic statement of this position, see Pye 1978.

15. The associated elements are water, wood, fire, earth, and air. The final traditional Chinese element is metal, not air (which is among other cultures' traditional lists of basic elements), and some Chinese sources have mistakenly substituted metal for air. The "internationalist" departure parallels—albeit perhaps unintentionally—the inclusion of the Olympic Flame as the central mascot alongside the four Chinese animals. The traditional blessings are prosperity, happiness, passion, health, and good luck.

16. On the WTO experience, see, generally, deLisle 2006 and Panitchpakdi and Clifford 2002.

17. See, for example, Larmer 2001, Kynge 2001, and Powers 2001.

18. For the text of the letter, see SperoNews 2007 and Cody 2007b.

19. Such petitions are described in He 2007.

20. Treatment of these groups figured prominently in the Chinese intellectuals' and dissidents' August 2007 "open letter" (SperoNews 2007).

21. See CIPFG (n.d.) and HRTR (n.d.). See also deLisle 1999, Li 2003, and Cody 2007a.

22. See, for example, Lieberthal and Lampton 1992.

23. Security preparation issues are discussed in more detail later in the chapter.

24. See Pierson 2007, Wilson 2001, and Rogge 2007.

25. See, for example, RTHK Radio Web site 2000, Quan 2005, Shi 2006b, Eimer 2007, and C. Smith 2001.

26. Lao-tzu so spoke of a journey of 1000 *li* (see Lao Tsu, Feng, and English 1997, 125); the thousand cuts refers to late imperial Chinese modes of execution and dismemberment and often appears—sometimes in exaggerated forms—in Western accounts of the cruelty of Chinese imperial justice. See Isaacs 1948, 63–64, and Costanzo 1997, 4.

REFERENCES

Abrahamson, Alan. 2005. Built-in Commitment: Beijing Has Become a Huge Construction Site. *Los Angeles Times,* July 14.

Allen, Kate. 2007. The Terrible Growth of Internet Repression. *Independent,* June 6.

Amnesty International. 2007. People's Republic of China: The Olympics Countdown—One Year Left to Fulfil Human Rights Promises. Available at http://web.amnesty.org/library/print/ENGASA170242007.

Associated Press. 1993. With an Eye toward 2000, Beijing Puts on a Good Face for Olympic Panel. March 4.

Associated Press. 2007. China, U.S. to Step up Joint Anti-Piracy Effort. June 15.

Barboza, David. 2007. U.S. Group Calls Conditions at China Toy Plants "Brutal." *International Herald Tribune,* August 22, 6.

BBC Monitoring International. 2007. China Watchdog Report Disputes Government Media Freedom "Promise," August 7.

Becker, Jasper. 2003. Empire Building. *Independent,* March 24.

Beijing Municipality. 2004. Provisions for the Protection of Olympics-Related Intellectual Property Rights.

Blitz, Roger, and Mure Dickie. 2007. IOC Warns Beijing on Air Quality Threat to Olympics. *Financial Times,* August 9, 7.

BOCOG. n.d.a. The Olympic Emblem. Official Web site of the Beijing 2008 Olympic Games. Available at http://en.beijing2008.cn/spirit/beijing 2008/graphic/n214070081.shtml.

BOCOG. n.d.b. The Official Mascots of the Beijing 2008 Olympic Games. Official Web site of the Beijing 2008 Olympic Games. Available at http://en.beijing2008.cn/spirit/beijing2008/graphic/n214070081.shtml.

Bondy, Filip. 1993. I.O.C. Pressured to Make Beijing a Forbidden City. *New York Times,* April 21, B18.

Byers, Jim. 2001. In Beijing, They're Painting the Grass Green. *Toronto Star,* February 14.

Callick, Rowan. 2007. China Puts a Sunny Spin on Clouds of Criticism. *Australian,* August 17, 10.

Cater, Nick. 1993. Enter the Dragon. *Advertiser* (Sydney), September 21.

Central News Agency (Taiwan). 2007. Olympic Torch Relay Issue Poses Test for Taiwan, China—Analysts, April 27.

Cha, Ariana Eunjung. 2007. Olympic Trials for Polluted Beijing. *Washington Post,* March 30, A1.

Chen Jiaxing. 2007. Jia Qinglin Meets with Representatives to Youth Exchange Activity. Xinhua News Agency, August 20.

Chen, Kuide. 2007. Two Historical Turning Points: The Seoul and Beijing Olympics. *China Rights Forum* 3:36–40.

China Daily. 2004a. Forum Stresses IPR Protection for Games. April 3.

China Daily. 2004b. Is Synthetic Fusion in Harmony with Traditional Chinese Culture? October 1.

China Daily. 2004c. Environment Pledge of 2008 Olympic Committee on Track. October 4.

China Daily. 2005a. Sohu.com Celebrates Olympics Contract. November 9.

China Daily. 2005b. China, UN Agree on Environmental Protection at 2008 Olympics. November 18.

China Daily. 2006a. Olympics to Add Oomph to Beijing Economy. January 17.

China Daily. 2006b. Beijing Ready for Rehearsals. August 4.

China Daily. 2006c. Architect's Story of Grand "Bird's Nest." September 22.

China Daily. 2006d. Olympics to Introduce New Media Relationship. December 22.

China Daily. 2007a. Traffic to be Cut by 30% ahead of Games. April 19.

China Daily. 2007b. Beijing Olympic Committee Wins High Praise from IOC. April 20.

China Daily. 2007c. Don't Rain on Our Parade. April 26.

China Daily. 2007d. Don't Politicize Olympics, Official Says. May 30.

China Daily. 2007e. Hotel Chain Offers to Help Olympics. May 30.

China Online. 2002. Beijing Tackles Intellectual Property Rights Violations. January 23.

Chua Chin Hon. 2007a. Beijing on Track for Olympics: 500 Days to Event and Some Chinese Are Suffering from Publicity Overload. *Straits Times*, April 2.

Chua Chin Hon. 2007b. China Begins Countdown to Beijing Olympics. *Straits Times*, August 9.

CIPFG (Coalition to Investigate the Persecution of Falun Gong in China). http://cipfg.org/en.

Clark, Grant, and Wing-Gar Cheng. 2007. China Aims at Olympic Knockoffs. *International Herald Tribune*, April 27, 10.

Cody, Edward. 2007a. One Year out from Olympics, a Test of Openness in Beijing. *Washington Post*, August 7, A1.

Cody, Edward. 2007b. Before Olympics, a Call for Change: Chinese Dissidents Join Foreign Appeals for Beijing to Honor Rights Commitments. *Washington Post*, August 8, A9.

COHRE. 2007. Fair Play for Housing Rights: Mega-Events, Olympic Games and Housing Rights.

Cooper, Helene. 2007. China Acts on Sudan after Hollywood Push. *New York Times*, April 14, 2.

Coonan, Clifford. 2006. Chinese Olympics Get the Spielberg Treatment. *Independent*, April 18.

Costanzo, Mark. 1997. Just Revenge: Costs and Consequences of the Death Penalty. New York: St. Martin's.

Daley, Kieran. 2003. Olympic Games: Beijing to Boost Security Budget by up to £ 280 Million. *Independent*, July 19.

Daily Yomiuri. 2007. China's Countdown to the Olympics; Beijing Olympics Coming at a Price. August 9, 1.

deLisle, Jacques. 1999. Who's Afraid of Falun Gong? Foreign Policy Research Institute, August 5. Available at http://www.fpri.org/enotes/19990805.asia.delisle.delisle.afraidfalungong.html.

deLisle, Jacques. 2001. Politics, Law and Resentment along the China Coast. Foreign Policy Research Institute, July 17. Available at http://www.fpri.org/enotes/asia.20010717.delisle.chinacoast.html.

deLisle, Jacques. 2006. China and the WTO. In *China under Hu Jintao*, ed. Tun-jen Cheng, Jacques deLisle, and Deborah Brown. Singapore: World Scientific Press.

Deutsche Presse-Agentur. 2007a. Beijing Celebrates 500 Days to 2008 Olympics. March 26.

Deutsche Presse-Agentur. 2007b. China Urges Spielberg to Continue as Olympic Adviser. August 6.

Deutsche Presse-Agentur. 2007c. Beijing Sees Little Improvement in Air Quality during Driving Ban. August 20.

Dickie, Mure. 2007a. China Tries to Clear Air for Olympics. *Financial Times,* March 12, 4.

Dickie, Mure. 2007b. Landmarks Rise as Civil Rights Prospects Fall. *Financial Times,* August 6, 6.

Dinmore, Guy. 2007. Darfur Adds to US Doubts over Beijing's Foreign Policy. *Financial Times,* June 14, 6.

Doe v. Liu Qi. 2004. 349 F.Supp.2d 1258 (N.D. Cal. 2004).

Economic Reference News. 2004. Is an Olympic Gold Medal Worth 700 Million Yuan? Coldly Pondering the National Sports System. September 6. Available at http://rich.online.sh.cn/rich/gb/content/2004–09/06/content_954510.htm.

Eimer, David. 2007. China Races to Olympic Glory while 20 Million of Its Children are Denied School. *Sunday Telegraph,* March 4.

Faison, Seth. 1997. Out of China. *New York Times,* November 17, A1.

Fan Baihua. 2007. Looking beyond the 2008 Olympics. *China Rights Forum* 3:93–97.

Fang, David. 2004a. Olympics Logo Loved and Loathed. *South China Morning Post,* August 5.

Fang, David. 2004b. The Olympic Logo: What? Why? Who? *South China Morning Post,* September 1.

Farrow, Ronan, and Mia Farrow. 2007. The Genocide Olympics. *Wall Street Journal,* March 28.

Financial Times. 2007a. Beijing Invests Heavily for Spectacular Olympic Games. April 10.

Financial Times. 2007b. Chinese Olympic Souvenir Firms Fined for Forced Overtime. August 7.

Frank, Jeffrey A. 1993. China's Dead Serious Games. *Washington Post,* May 30, C3.

Gao Peng. 2005. Beijing Unveils 2008 Olympic Mascots. Xinhua General News Service, November 11.

Gao Peng. 2007. Medal Design Unveiled to Mark 500-Day Countdown. Xinhua General News Service, March 27.

Glickman, Dan. 2006. No More Pirate Games. *Los Angeles Times,* December 18.

Goff, Peter. 2005. IOC Urged to Take a Stand on Evictions. *South China Morning Post,* December 4, 10.

Guardian Unlimited. 2007. China's Rapid Growth Creating Migrant Underclass, Says Amnesty. March 1.

Harvey, Fiona, and Richard McGregor. 2007. Beijing Hails Success of Anti-Smog Trial. *Financial Times,* August 22, 8.

Hawthorne, Christopher. 2004. China Scales back Ambitious Design Plans. *New York Times,* September 21, 10.

He Qinglian. 2007. Human Rights: The True Gold Standard. *China Rights Forum* 3:26–30.

Hindustan Times. 2007. Tibetans Plan Their Own 2008 Olympics ahead of Beijing. May 16.

HRTR. http://www.humanrightstorch.org.

Humanistic Olympic Studies Center. Renmin University. http://www.c2008 .org/index.asp.

Human Rights Watch. 2004. China: Release Housing Rights Activist. Available at http://hrw.org/english/docs/2004/09/28/china9400.htm.

Human Rights Watch. 2007a. China Backtracking on Media Freedoms. Press release, May 31.

Human Rights Watch. 2007b. China: No Progress on Rights One Year before Olympics. August 2. Available at http://china.hrw.org/press/china_no_ progress_on_rights_one_year_before_olympics.

IOC. 2004. *Olympic Charter* and *IOC Code of Ethics.*

Issacs, Harold R. 1948. *Scratches on Our Minds.* New York: John Day.

Japan and China. 2007. Joint Statement on the Further Strengthening of Bilateral Cooperation on Environmental Conservation. April 11.

Japan Economic Newswire. 2001. Olympics Inspectors Leave Beijing after Getting "Royal Tour." February 24.

Japan Economic Newswire. 2005. Beijing to Spend Millions to Fix Cultural Relics before Olympics. April 1.

Kuhn, Anthony. 2001. Beijing Puts on Its Best Game Face. *Los Angeles Times,* February 25, 2.

Kwok, Kristine. 2007. Secretive Arm of the Law. *South China Morning Post,* August 4, 6.

Kynge, James. 2001. Mind Games: China Is Heavily Fancied to Win Its Bid for the 2008 Olympic Games. *Financial Times,* July 7, 11.

Kyodo News Agency. 2007. China Deports Eight Tibet Activists Who Protested on Great Wall. August 9.

Lague, David. 2006. Rights Group Accuses China of Failing to Honor Olympic Pledges. *International Herald Tribune,* September 22, 3.

Lague, David. 2007. Taiwan and China Squabble over Olympic Torch. *International Herald Tribune,* September 17.

Landsberg, Mitchell. 2007a. Beijing Is Accused of Unfair Play. *Los Angeles Times,* August 7, A1.

Landsberg, Mitchell. 2007b. Clearing the Air for the Olympics. *Los Angeles Times,* August 11, A6.

Lao Tsu, Gia-Gu Feng, and Jane English. 1997. *Tao Te Ching.* New York: Vintage.

Larmer, Brook. 2001. Olympic Dreams. *Newsweek,* February 26, 22.

Lengell, Sean. 2007. Bush Urged to Boycott Olympics: Rohrabacher Cites Beijing on Human Rights. *Washington Times,* August 23, A4.

Lev, Michael A. 2001. Beijing Beautifies for '08 Olympic Bid. *Chicago Tribune,* February 18, 3.

Li, John. 2003. After Four Years of Repression, It's Time to Let Go: China vs. Falun Gong. *International Herald Tribune,* July 22, 8.

Lieberthal, Kenneth, and David M. Lampton, eds. 1992. *Bureaucracy, Politics, and Decision Making in Post-Mao China.* Berkeley: University of California Press.

Lilley, James R. 2001. The Golden Handcuffs. *Newsweek,* July 16, 30.

Ling, Bonny, and Trevor Lee. 2007. Where Is the Frugal Olympics? *China Rights Forum* 3:54–61.

Liu, Melinda. 2006. Beijing Starts to Feel the "Olympic Effect." *Newsweek,* December 25, 54.

Longman, Jere. 2001. Beijing Wins Bid for 2008 Olympic Games. *New York Times,* July 14, 1.

Los Angeles Times. 2007. Leveraging the Olympics: Celebrity Pressure against China. May 30, A20.

Luce, Edward, and Andrew Ward. 2007. Democratic Rivals United in Tough Line on Beijing. *Financial Times,* August 16, 5.

Macartney, Jane. 2007. Beijing Tightens Tibet Travel Rules. *Australian,* May 16, 8.

Mackay, Duncan. 2001. Olympic Games: Big Boost for Beijing 2008—but Do Keep Beach Volleyball out of Tiananmen Square. *Guardian,* May 16.

MacLeod, Calum. 2001a. Free Political Prisoners to Host Olympics, China Told. *Independent,* January 18, 15.

MacLeod, Calum. 2001b. China's Use of Torture Exposed by Amnesty. *Independent,* February 13, 15.

MacLeod, Calum. 2001c. Olympic Games: China Celebrates with Rare Burst of Genuine Celebration. *Independent,* July 14, 5.

MacLeod, Calum, and Paul Wiseman. 2007. Whatever It Takes, China Aims for Dazzling Games. *USA Today,* August 6, 1A.

Magnier, Mark. 2004. Trying to Get Beijing to Go for Gold on Rights. *Los Angeles Times,* October 11, 3.

Magnier, Mark. 2007. Games Run-up Exposes the Dark Side of China. *Los Angeles Times,* August 8, A1.

Makinoda, Toru. 2007. Japanese Soccer Fans Taunted in China. *Daily Yomiuri,* August 5.

McGregor, Richard. 2006a. African Summit Set to Be Diplomatic Triumph for China. *Financial Times,* November 3, 8.

McGregor, Richard. 2006b. China Eases Rules on Media for Olympics. *Financial Times,* December 2, 7.

McGregor, Richard, and David Pilling. 2004. Beijing Crowd Behaviour Augurs Ill for 2008. *Financial Times,* August 9, 2.

McLaughlin, Kathleen E. 2007. Ahead of Olympics, China Faces Charges of Child Labor. *Christian Science Monitor,* June 13, 1.

McNeill, David. 2004. Rioting Chinese Football Fans Vent Anti-Japanese Feelings. *Independent,* August 9, 24.

Moon Gwang-lip. 2006. China Shows Olympic Confidence. *Korea Times,* April 4.

New Zealand Herald. 2007. Tibet Asks to Send Its Own Team to Beijing. August 8.

Ni, Ching-Ching. 2007. China's Olympic Torch Route Ignites an Uproar. *Los Angeles Times,* April 27, A3.

Office of the United States Trade Representative (USTR). 2007. United States Files WTO Cases against China over Deficiencies in China's Intellectual Property Laws and Market Access Barriers to Copyright-Based Industries. April 9. Available at http://www.ustr.gov/Document_Library/Press_Re leases/2007/April/United_States_Files_WTO_Cases_Against_China_Over _Deficiencies_in_Chinas_Intellectual_Property_Rights_Laws_Market_Ac cess_Barr.html.

Olympic Dream for Darfur. http://savedarfur.org/content/torchrun.

Olympic Watch. 2004. Human Rights Organizations Unveil "Minimum Standards for Beijing 2008." Joint statement by Olympic Watch ISHR/IGRM and Laogai Research Foundation, August 29. Available at http://www.olympicwatch.org/news.php?id=7.

Pan, Philip P., and John Pomfret. 2001. Elated Chinese Fill Tiananmen Square. *Washington Post,* July 14, A1.

Panitchpakdi, Supachai, and Mark L. Clifford. 2002. *China and the WTO.* Singapore: John Wiley.

People's Daily. 2001. A Sleepless Night! A Sleepless Night for 1.3 Billion! July 14.

Perlez, Jane. 2001. U.S. Won't Block China's Bid for Olympics. *New York Times,* July 11, A6.

Pierson, David. 2007. China Gets Low Grade in Human Rights. *Los Angeles Times,* May 1, A3.

PlayFair 2008. 2007. *No Medal for Olympics on Labor Rights.* Available at http://www.playfair2008.org/docs/playfair_2008-report.pdf.

Pomfret, John. 2000. On the Bubble: Opera Divides Beijing. *Washington Post,* July 8, A11.

Pomfret, John. 2002. Fight over Banned Sect Moves to U.S. *Washington Post,* March 12, A15.

Powers, John. 2001. Beijing Looks to Win Games. *Boston Globe,* July 13, E7.

PRC State Council. 2002. Regulations on the Protection of Olympic Symbols.

Puzzanghera, Jim, and Evelyn Iritani. 2007. U.S. to Step up Piracy Battle. *Los Angeles Times,* April 10, C1.

Pye, Lucien. 1978. Aesopian Language in Chinese Politics. *Proceedings of the American Philosophical Society* 122(5):336–39.

Qianming.net. 2007. "One World, One Dream": The Same Human Rights— Our Opinions and Appeal Concerning the Beijing Olympics. August 8. Available at http://www.qian-ming.net/gb/default.aspx?dir=scp&cid= 125.

Quan Xiaoshu. 2005. New NGO Founded to Rally All Chinese People against Worsening Pollution. Xinhua News Agency, April 23.

Renmin Ribao. 2000. Beijing Fully Capable of Hosting High-Level Olympic Games. October 5.

Reporters Sans Frontières. 2006. China's Media Crackdown Gathers Pace in Run-up to Olympics. Press release, August 7.

RTHK Radio 3 Web site. 2000. Chinese Activists Urge Olympic Ruling Body to Put Pressure on Beijing. December 31 (Hong Kong).

Rogge, Jacques. 2007. A Catalyst, Not a Cure: Beijing Olympics. *International Herald Tribune,* August 8.

Rosenthal, A. M. 1993. Here We Go Again. *New York Times,* April 9, A27.

Rosenthal, Elisabeth. 2000. For a Prize That's Olympian, China Jumps the Gun. *New York Times,* September 6, A4.

Rosenthal, Elisabeth. 2001. Beijing Tries to Woo Olympics and Keep Dissidents in Check. *New York Times,* February 23, A8.

Schweisberg, David R. 1993. Olympic Loss Leaves China Seething. United Press International, September 23.

Shi Jingtao. 2006a. Beijing Denies It Will Have Games Purge. *South China Morning Post,* September 16, 1.

Shi Jingtao. 2006b. Olympic Expulsions Break Law, Says Expert. *South China Morning Post,* September 16, 5.

Shi Jingtao, and Lawrence Chung. 2007. Accept Torch Route, Taipei Told. *South China Morning Post,* August 7, 4.

Smith, Bill. 2007. China, IOC Stand Firm against Boycott. *Deutsche Presse-Agentur,* August 2.

Smith, Craig S. 2001. Critics at Home Surfacing in Wake of China's Successful Bid for the Games. *New York Times,* July 15, 6.

Sohu.com. 2005. Beach Volleyball Will Not Be Held in Tiananmen Square. Available at http://news.sohu.com/20050603/n225805057.shtml.

South China Morning Post. 2007. Xenophobia Has No Place in Building the New China, January 17, 14.

Spencer, Richard. 2006. China to Shut Heavy Industry and Give Olympians Fresh Air. *Daily Telegraph,* December 29, 17.

SperoNews. 2007. Open Letter Denounces China Human Rights Abuse. *Asia News,* August 9. Available at http://www.speroforum.com/site/article .asp?id=10675&t=Open+letter+denounces+China+human+rights+abuse.

Statesman (India). 2007. Tibet's Banner of Revolt at Everest. April 29, 2007.

Stolberg, Sheryl Gay. 2007. Bush Tells Hu He'll Go to 2008 Olympics. *International Herald Tribune,* September 7, 1.

Sun, Lena H. 1993. China Has Biggest Stake in Olympic Games. *Washington Post,* September 21, A1.

Tempest, Rone. 1994. Chinese Dissident Is Back in Custody after "New" Crimes. *Los Angeles Times,* April 6, A7.

Terrill, Ross. 2007. In Beijing, Orwell Goes to the Olympics. *New York Times,* August 22.

Tian Qi. 2007. Liu Jianchao: Degree of China's Opening to World Media Will Be Greater and Greater. *Zhongguo Xinwen She,* August 21.

Tsang, Denise. 2007. US Takes Beijing to WTO again over Piracy Row. *South China Morning Post,* August 15.

Tyler, Patrick E. 1993a. Chinese Dissident Emerges, Still Unbowed. *New York Times,* September 21.

Tyler, Patrick E. 1993b. There Is No Joy in Beijing as Sydney Gets Olympics. *New York Times,* September 24, B9.

United Nations. n.d. UNEP and the International Olympic Committee. Available at http://www.unep.org/sport_env/Olympic_Games/index.asp.

United Press International. 1993. Beijing Leaves Residents Cold for Olympic Inspection. March 4.

United Press International. 2005. Steel Company Drags Heels Leaving Beijing. March 1.

USTR. *See* Office of the United States Trade Representative.

Wang Yong. 2007. Four Police Helicopters to Conduct Air Patrols during Beijing Olympic Games. Xinhua News Agency, May 30.

Watts, Jonathan. 2003. China's New Cultural Revolutionaries: They Wave Not Mao's Book but Eviction Orders. *Guardian,* September 6, 19.

Watts, Jonathan. 2007. One Year to Go. *Guardian,* August 9, 6.

Wei Lu. 2007. A Worm's-Eye View of the Beijing Olympics. *China Rights Forum* 3:62–65.

Wilson, Bruce. 2001. Chinese Games. *Sunday Telegraph* (Australia), July 15.

World Bank. http://go.worldbank.org/K2CKM78CCo.

World Health Organization. 2005. Environmental Health Country Profile—China. June 9, 5.

Wu, Vivian. 2007. No Olympic Glory without Human Rights, Beijing Told. *South China Morning Post,* August 8, 4.

Xiao Liu. 2002. Winning Design Caught in Public Dispute. *China Daily,* July 23.

Xinhua. 1993a. Olympics Will Mean a More Open China—Chen Xitong. General Overseas News Service, August 14.

Xinhua. 1993b. Chen Xitong: Beijing Should Be Like Beijing. General News Service, August 25.

Xinhua. 1993c. Chinese Diplomat Rejects Olympic-Related Human Rights Allegation by U.S. Senator. September 13.

Xinhua. 2001a. Premier Calls for Modern, Socially Stable Beijing. January 22.

Xinhua. 2001b. Official Dismisses U.S. Lawmakers' Opposition to Beijing's Olympic Bid. May 20.

Xinhua. 2001c. Chinese Economy to Benefit from Olympiad: Economist. Economic News Service, July 17.

Xinhua. 2001d. Jiang Zemin: Make Joint Efforts to Promote World Peace and Development—Congratulatory Message Delivered at the Beginning of the Year 2002. December 31.

Xinhua. 2002. Beijing Brings down McDonalds Signs to Make City More Beautiful for Olympics. March 1.

Xinhua. 2003. Chen Shui-bian Accused of Taking 2008 Olympics to Seek Independence. November 22.

Xinhua. 2004a. Five-Element Theory Inspires Olympic Village Design. Business Daily Update, April 7.

Xinhua. 2004b. Sinopec Designated 2008 Beijing Olympic Sponsor. Economic News Service, October 11.

Xinhua. 2005a. "Slums" Sting Chinese Cities, Hamper Building of Harmonious Society. September 8.

Xinhua. 2005b. Beijing Vows to Improve Quality Media Services in 2008 Olympics. Economic News Service, September 22.

Xinhua. 2005c. Outdoor Advertising Expanding but Still Vulnerable. General News Service, December 3.

Xinhua. 2005d. China Sets up Special Police Unit to Tighten Olympics Security. December 20.

Xinhua. 2006a. Beijingers Taught to Behave Themselves for Olympic Games. February 21.

Xinhua. 2006b. President Calls for Scientific Development. March 6.

Xinhua. 2006c. Chinese Capital Builds Energy-Saving Projects for Olympics Games. July 4.

Xinhua. 2006d. Green Olympics Underway. Business Daily Update, July 11.

Xinhua. 2006e. Chinese Politburo Member Zhou Yongkang on Security of Beijing Olympic Games. August 19.

Xinhua. 2006f. Regulations on Reporting Activities in China by Foreign Journalists during the Beijing Olympic Games and the Preparatory Period. Article 6, December 1.

Xinhua. 2007a. Beijing Forms Helicopter Police Team for 2008 Olympics. March 11.

Xinhua. 2007b. Lenovo Initiates Beijing Olympics Marketing Program. Economic News Service, March 28.

Xinhua. 2007c. China to Issue New Plan to Protect Olympic Logo. General News Service, April 17.

Xinhua. 2007d. No Forced Eviction for Olympic Games—Foreign Ministry Spokesman. June 5.

Xinhua. 2007e. China Opposes U.S. House Resolution on Darfur Issue. June 7.

Xinhua. 2007f. FBI Willing to Help China with Olympic Security. June 13.

Xinhua. 2007g. China Ready to Work with Other Countries on Olympic Security. June 14.

Xinhua. 2007h. Guangdong Stationery Producer Did Use Child Labor. June 14.

Xinhua. 2007i. China Practices Artificial Rain Reduction for Sunny Olympics. August 9.

Xinhua. 2007j. China to Hold Online Contest on Olympics-Related Laws. Economic News Service, August 13.

Xinhua. 2007k. China Denies Displacing 1.5 Million Beijing Residents. Financial News Network, August 16.

Xinhua. 2007l. China to Slash Domestic Flights to Regulate Air Transport. General News Service, August 15, 2007.

Xinhua. 2007m. China Calls for Standardized Use of Languages for 2008 Olympics. August 20.

Xinhua. 2007n. IOC Supports Beijing's Clean-Air Measures: Jacques Rogge. General News Service, August 24.

Xinhuanet.com. 2004. State Council Taiwan Affairs Office: Mainland Will Not Tolerate "Taiwan Independence" to Hold Successful Olympics. Available at http://news.xinhuanet.com/taiwan/2004-07/28/content_1662889 .htm.

Xu Jingyue. 2007. Ceremony Celebrating the One-Year Countdown to the Beijing Olympics Held in Grand Fashion. *Xinhua News Agency,* August 8.

Xxz.gov.cn. Beijing Development and Reform Commission Official: Post-Games Utilization Is a Real Question. May 15, 2007.

Yan, Alice. 2005a. Environmental Watchdogs Hungry for Action. *South China Morning Post,* March 28.

Yan, Alice. 2005b. US Foundation Quits Olympic Media Project. *South China Morning Post,* May 14, 6.

Yardley, Jim. 2007a. Olympic Construction Unearths Ancient Treasure Trove. *New York Times,* February 7, 4.

Yardley, Jim. 2007b. As Games Near, Beijing Tackles "Auspicious Clods." *New York Times,* April 18, 1.

Yardley, Jim. 2007c. China Praises Its Progress toward Olympics. *New York Times,* August 7, 8.

Yardley, Jim. 2007d. Abuses Belie China Pledge on Rights, Critics Say. *New York Times,* August 8, 10.

Yardley, Jim. 2007e. An Unwelcome Team at the Beijing Olympics. *International Herald Tribune,* August 14, 2.

Zheng Bijian. 2005. China's "Peaceful Rise" to Great Power Status. *Foreign Affairs* September–October.

Olympic Values,
Beijing's Olympic Games, and the
Universal Market

Alan Tomlinson

Whether it is a comparative cultural, critical investigative, anthropologically rooted, or media-oriented approach to understanding the Olympic phenomenon, it is notable that the place of the sponsor in the cultural and social construction of the Games is less subject to scrutiny than are other aspects of the event, such as the media coverage, the nationalist elements, and selected ceremonial dimensions. The relationships within the purported Olympic Family—in particular, the increasing profile and influence of corporate partners of the International Olympic Committee (IOC)—have received less extensive or sustained critical analysis.

In a trilogy of studies, Andrew Jennings has pursued a relentless course of investigative journalism (Symson and Jennings 1992; Jennings and Sambrook 2000; Jennings 1996). His works have revealed the underlying political and economic interests that have driven the Games in the period since the former Francoist Juan Antonio Samaranch's succession to the IOC presidency in 1980, and the success of the 1984 Los Angeles Games that rewrote the rules for the staging of the international sporting event. If the modern Olympics was in its early years (1896–1928) based upon fragile alliances of political, cultural, and economic interests, developing as a more explicitly political phenomenon from 1932 to 1980, Los Angeles 1984 introduced a new economic order that underpinned the initial survival of the Games—on the withdrawal of Teheran, Los Angeles was the only candidate to stage the event—and its consequent expansion and escalation (Tomlinson 2005a, 50–56; Tomlinson 2005b). Writing on the eve of the 1984 event, Richard Gruneau argued that for some time sporting practice had been incorporated into an expanding international capitalist marketplace, but that Los Angeles' capacity to rewrite the rules of the host city's game produced a "unique" and "one of the most publicly visible business deals in the history of corporate capitalism" (Gruneau 1984, 11). Anything was now up for sponsorship, from the AT&T-sponsored torch relay to the only two newly constructed sites, the McDonald's Olympic pool and the Southland Corporation velodrome (Tomlinson 2006a, 167); after the event, the organizing committee reported a surplus of more than US$222 million. The claimed and perceived success of the Los Angeles Olympics in 1984 established the framework for the political economy of future Games, based upon escalating media rights and forms of corporate sponsorship secured by both the IOC and the local organizing committees of the host city: "From that point on, the Games were guaranteed a future as one of the most high-profile global commodities" (Tomlinson 2005a, 56).

A study focusing upon the Beijing event has foregrounded this political economy, arguing that "there is an *extraordinary convergence,* or *elective affinity,* between modern Olympism and the *ideals and tendencies* of modern market capitalism" (Close et al. 2007, 1–2, 117). The Beijing Olympiad and Olympics are seen, in this light, as a catalyst "in the re-alignment process of the global political economy" (Close et al. 2007, 2, 117), as well as a focus for some potential internal reform, in relation to human rights. The term *elective affinity* derives from the work of the German sociologist Max Weber, whose studies were, to some degree, framed as a methodological and epistemological debate with what he saw as a form of economic determinism in the work of Karl Marx. An elective affinity could be identified, Weber proposed, between, say, a set of religious beliefs and a particular social group or system (Weber 1948, 62–63), and he referred—in contemporaneous exchanges concerning his study *The Protestant Ethic and the Spirit of Capitalism* (Weber 1965)—to "the unique and long-established elective affinity of Calvinism to capitalism" (Weber 2001, 107). The notion of elective affinity refers, therefore, to a correspondence between sources of meaning that may not initially seem to be connected: "the contents of one system of meaning engender a tendency for adherents to build and pursue the other system of meaning" (Scott and Marshall 2005,

182). Adapted to the Olympic context the argument goes that the Olympic Ideals or Movement converge with the spirit of contemporary market capitalism. The implication here is that neither one determines the other, but that the values of the two meaning-systems are conducive to a kind of reciprocal development. Weber concluded *The Protestant Ethic and the Spirit of Capitalism* on a cautionary note, claiming that it was not his aim to "substitute for a one-sided materialistic an equally one-sided spiritualistic causal interpretation of culture and history" (Weber 1965, 183). "Historical truth," he implied, does not lie in the application of such theoretical extremes.

Close et al. offer the synonyms for elective affinity of *mutual attraction* and *irresistible mutual desire* (2007, 118). When referring to Beijing as a catalyst they refer to how the city/event and the period (the Olympiad) leading up to the event will contribute to re-alignments of both the overall global political economy (2) and the "political economy arena of Chinese society" (117). They highlight five developments: deepening institutionalization, on a global scale, of Olympism; a global spread of the doctrine of individualism, in Western terms; global scales of advance in liberal democracy and market capitalism; a consolidation of global society within the continuing progress of globalization; and China's emergence as a superpower and player in the political economy, in both regional and global terms. These developments are said to share "a formidable array of elective affinities" (2). All five developments are presented with the adjectival label "global," which seems to be the core feature of the meaning-systems that are claimed as converging in the period of the Beijing Olympiad and Games. This is a bold claim: that one sporting mega-event crystallizes political, economic, cultural, and social changes at all conceivable levels of social organization. The boldness of the conception may blur the specifics of the analysis, and this question will be returned to in the concluding section of this chapter.

Close et al., though, rightly recognize the corporate partners as at the heart of what the authors call the "Olympic social compact." The Beijing Organizing Committee of the Olympic Games (BOCOG) is cited as embracing, in its own sponsorship program, the "IOC's commitment to a market-oriented, private-sector partnership approach to financing the Olympics . . ." (99):

> . . . the response of the local (China's), regional (East Asia's), and global *business communities,* and above all *business elites,* will have been at one

with the way in which the IOC seems to have been convinced by the Chinese delegation's presentation and promises at the IOC's session in Moscow on 13 July 2001. (Close et al. 2007, 99)

Short (2004) has also focused upon the corporatization of the Olympics, in terms of both the connected interests of key actors in the Olympic network and the expansion of international product markets more generally. In the light of these interpretive debates, this chapter now presents a critical reading of the discourses characterizing the last two winning bids for Summer Olympic Games, Beijing's in 2001 and London's in 2005; followed by a commentary on the profile of the twelve select Olympic partner sponsors as presented on the International Olympic Committee's Web site; and a concluding discussion of how the contribution of corporate sponsors to the Olympic phenomenon might best be understood.

Beijing's Bid: Historical Pedigree and Modernity

In a lull during the program of the Sydney Olympics in September 2000, the press hall in the Main Press Centre at the Olympic Park in Homebush Bay turned away from the events of the competitive program or the cultural politics of the Australian event. A solemn, unsmiling delegation of Chinese sport diplomats—four men and two women—lined up on the platform of the hall, and a far from capacity audience (of around 150) was invited into the thinking of the city aspiring to stage the Games eight years hence. The Beijing bidding committee was hiding nothing: Beijing's success in landing the 2008 Olympics was, with little doubt, the expectation in the minds of state and city authorities, after years of campaigning and lobbying; failure would mean that several individuals' dedication to a lifetime's professional goal would count for nothing, deleted in a blur of shame and failure. No wonder, then, that the delegation looked so serious and joyless. The mood was lifted by the presentational video, *New Beijing Great Olympics* (Beijing ShengYang 2000), a little more than four minutes of beaming faces, colorful landscapes and carefully orchestrated individual and collective physical performance. The opening shot of nonelite male athletes bursting from the starting line on a running track was succeeded by shots of urban and historical skyscapes and landscapes;

traditional culture and artistic performance; and gymnasts, cyclists, and tennis players. The more serious performers were young, establishing the aspirational motif for a coming generation. As the video short progressed, this mix of urban modernity and classical allusion was sustained, with shots of fun runs, urban calisthenics, mass fitness sessions, happy-looking consumption in theme-park rides and smart-looking urban transport systems, and soaring flocks of birds speeding into a gloriously clear sky. Images of youth predominated, but elder people too could be seen exercising in the public spaces of the city. The soundtrack of the video transitioned from heavy orchestra to opera, as images of ballet, dance and the concert hall were interspersed with acrobats and children skipping in the streets. The focus switched to Olympic sports, more intensely competitive forms of ice skating, skating, swimming, football, gymnastics, martial arts, hurdling/running, basketball, and memorable moments and footage of China's Olympic triumphs, with a finishing focus back on youth and children, representing a welcoming and proud new China in the flag-waving groups of grinning children, and superimposing the "New Beijing, Great Olympics" slogan on the running track.

The press release accompanying the video reiterated this slogan, and expanded the message:

> Beijing in the new century will host the great Olympic Games and welcome athletes and friends worldwide with a new look and in a new spirit: the modern Olympic Games will open a new chapter in its unusual history of over one hundred years with its first ever hosting by China, the home to 1/5 of the population. And the time-honored charm of the Olympic sports will also appeal to the world in a wholly new way. (Beijing 2008 Olympic Games Bid Committee [BOBICO] 2000b)

Seen as "a noble sport undertaking" which aims at "promoting mutual understanding, friendship and safeguarding world peace by way of sport," the Olympic Games and the Olympic spirit were presented as "the common desire and shared dream of the whole nation." All this talk of new looks and spirits matching Chinese values to those of the historically and culturally established Olympics was given little elaboration. But the elision of Chinese values and Olympism was smoothly achieved. The attraction of the Games to Beijing and China as a vehicle for bringing the world in to the city and the nation was expressed more convincingly:

Either applying for the hosting of the Olympic Games or the actual hosting of such games will help promote the city's open-up commitments, economic development and social progress, offering the world a unique opportunity to better understand China and its capital Beijing and facilitating integration between China and its capital and the rest of the world. (BOBICO 2000b)

This is where the committee was getting to the core of the matter, after the rhetoric of the new and the shared. "Open-up commitments" linked to economic development and social progress—what is this if not new international markets, and expanded consumption in both internal and external forms, in the expanding global marketplace?[1] The Olympics in Beijing:

> . . . will provide a fit platform for the common celebration of humanity, civility, Olympic spirit, human achievements as well as an occasion for self-improvements and progress. We 12 million citizens of Beijing have the right infrastructure, the right expertise and the right people to host the 2008 Olympic Games. We are in a position to make the 2008 Olympic Games a green, cultural and high-tech sporting event to highlight environmental protection, cultural exchanges between the east and west, and the use of new and high technologies . . . The economy of Beijing, and that of China in general, are now growing faster than ever before. Its urban infrastructure, from telecommunication, traffic, to hospitality industry, and to sporting facilities, has been markedly improved. (BOBICO 2000b)

Lest those of us in the audience doubted some of these infrastructural claims, further points and accompanying glossy literature and handouts bombarded us with facts and figures. The four concluding points to the press release indicated that the "current bidding work" focused on five areas: the control of air pollution and the improvement of the ecological environment, based on an investment of US$6.8 billion; second, the problem of traffic bottlenecks, with a priority being a 65-kilometer Olympic Boulevard, road-widening schemes, a subway line connecting the city with the Olympic stadiums and the Olympic Village, and a light-track railway around the village; third, building from scratch thirteen new stadiums to complement the fifteen existing ones; fourth, the development of the telecommunications infrastructure; and finally, foreign-language training in all levels of Beijing's education system.

Further facts and figures presented as evidence of Beijing's preparedness defied logic, from the number of engineering research centers in
the city, to the number of medals, titles, and awards won by Beijing
sportsmen and women since the founding of the People's Republic of
China in 1949 (Beijing Foreign Cultural Exchanges Service Center
2000a). The most interesting and—if at all reliable—categories in the
"facts and figures" pamphlet concerned foreign trade, commerce, industry, construction and housing, and telecommunications, all of
which were presented as evidence of the opening-up and (economic)
reform theme. These were listed after sections on history and culture,
marking the typical mix of history and modernity that bidding cities
tend to emphasize. In this presentational barrage of facts, images, and
statistics, the nature of the Olympic Games as a commercial phenomenon was never mentioned or raised. It is an extraordinary rhetoric of
international commonality that underlies the vision of would-be
Olympic hosts such as Beijing. Images and soundtracks supersede language and analysis; a smiling child symbolizes the innate sweetness
and charm of humanity; a classical architecture invokes cultural charm
and historical significance, whatever might have gone on inside the
walls of the building; a determined youth represents the worldwide
generations and their future possibilities. Drawn into these bidding
rhetorics you would not know that McDonald's or Coca-Cola existed,
let alone were at the heart of an Olympic political economy in which
up to 40 percent of Olympic finances have been reported as coming
from partner sponsors.

A Famous Day in London Town:
Perpetuating the Bidding Rhetoric

When London unexpectedly won the race to host the 2012 Summer
Olympics, managers cheered in their highly-pressured offices in the
city of London. It is claimed that London 2012's successful bid was
clinched by two factors: the audience granted by UK prime minister
Tony Blair to various IOC members in his hotel room in Singapore; and
the presentational video fronting London 2012 on the day of the decision itself (Lee 2006). No evidence exists concerning the former, and
the nature of the diplomatic discourse employed by Blair and his aides;
the latter is a matter of public record, available on the London 2012 organizing committee's Web site, and deserves some scrutiny. The com-

monalities in the presentational rhetoric of the Beijing and London bids are striking.

The video (Full Moon 2005) was divided into three parts, the first and the third entitled "Inspiration," and the middle section comprising Blair's address to the IOC. The video built up with symphonic precision, the first part a fraction under 2 minutes, the Blair address 2 minutes 49 seconds, the culminating inspiration slightly over 4 minutes. The first part introduced children of the world in 2005 dreaming of success seven years on: a black boy runner from Nigeria; an Asian girl gymnast; a white Western female swimmer; and a male cyclist. Four individual sports, three of them accessible worldwide, the other widely recognizable as accessible. The voiceover stressed the nobility and potentially heroic aspiration of the athlete, in the familiar tones of Lord of the Rings mega-star Sir Ian McKellan. His voice was framed against an original score that blended the elegiac feel of English classical music with a Vangelis-style sound resonant of the *Chariots of Fire* anthem that has come to embody the theme of heroic human striving.

Blair's address promised the IOC its "very best partner," assuring the voters that the bid had "excited people throughout the country." Nelson Mandela was recruited to the cause, and spoke of how a London Games could fulfill a dream for future generations "beyond our own time and borders." The inspiration of the London 2012 vision would draw in millions more young people, not just from Britain but across the world. In the closing section the viewer was invited back into a seductive world of youthful aspirations from across the world, skillfully interwoven images and shots of young people growing toward the London 2012 moment. The sweat of hard work was blended with the tears of frustration and elation, as the video led in to its final textual message and appeal: "CHOOSE LONDON AND INSPIRE YOUNG PEOPLE EVERYWHERE TO CHOOSE OLYMPIC SPORT."

There is a marked consistency of the messages transmitted in the Beijing and the London visual shorts/presentations: youth, aspiration, and the future are at the center of the frame. Prominently absent from both is the actual fact of Olympic finances, whether broadcasting, the main source of Olympic revenues, or the partner sponsors who contribute the second highest proportion of Olympic revenue. If, as Close et al. (2007) argue, there is a convergence between the aims and values of Olympism and those of contemporary capitalism, then these are at most a subtext in the representational devices and strategies of aspiring Olympic hosts.

TOP VI: The Hidden Presence

IOC president Jacques Rogge is unambiguous on the contribution of corporate sponsorship to the Olympics:

> Without the support of the business community, without its technology, expertise, people, services, products, telecommunications, its financing—the Olympic Games could not and cannot happen. Without this support, the athletes cannot compete and achieve their very best in the world's best sporting event. (IOC 2007a)

The TOP ("The Olympic Programme" is the source of the acronym) scheme is a huge success story in the history of sport sponsorship and marketing, and transformational in terms of the political economy of international and media-based sport (Tomlinson 2005b, 51; Barney et al. 2002, 153–80). Since 1986, the IOC has granted exclusive worldwide partner status to a limited number of sponsors; in the sixth phase of this scheme, running from 2005–2008, there were twelve such sponsors. It is interesting to consider the profile of these "members" of the Olympic Family on the IOC Web site (IOC 2007b). The twelve 2005–2008 partners were (in alphabetical order):

1. Atos Origin—information technology
2. Coca-Cola—nonalcoholic beverages
3. GE—technical services and select products
4. Johnson & Johnson—healthcare
5. Kodak—film, photography, imaging
6. Lenovo—computing equipment
7. Manulife—insurance/annuities
8. McDonald's—retail food services
9. Omega—timing, scoring, and venue results services
10. Panasonic—audio/TV/video equipment
11. Samsung—wireless communication equipment
12. Visa—consumer payment systems (credit cards, etc.)

The following profiles are summaries of the Web profiles, and include no interpretive commentary. A thematic interpretation follows this listing.

Atos Origin, the worldwide technology partner, became a TOP partner in 2001 under the label Schlumberger Sema, and confirmed the position as Atos Origin for 2004–2012. It manages and integrates all of the IOC's technology partners, specializing in the management of (large-scale) operations. The company has annual revenues of more than 5 billion Euros, employing 45,000 people in 50 countries.

Coca-Cola boasts the longest continual relationship with the Olympic movement, from the 1928 Olympics in Amsterdam onward. "The company has developed a strong tradition of creating programs and events to bring the spirit of the Games to consumers in Olympic host cities and around the world," working closely with the IOC to support athletes and teams in more than 19 countries. It was a charter member of the first TOP scheme in 1986. In 2005, the IOC and Coca- Cola "extended their partnership agreement for an unprecedented 12 years until 2020." Coca-Cola has 230 brands of products and local operations in more than 200 countries around the world.

GE is the specialist provider of power, lighting, security, and "modular space solutions," and supplies ultrasound and MRI equipment to help doctors treat athletes. "NBC Universal, a division of GE, is the exclusive media partner of the Games" through 2012.

Johnson & Johnson is, the profile boasts, the first "broad health-care products company" to be a TOP partner. "Johnson & Johnson and the Olympic Movement share the common mission of developing the healthy mind, body and spirit. Our common values of striving for excellence, achievement, high performance, teamwork, service and commitment to the community provide a strong foundation for achieving that mission." Johnson & Johnson companies "support Olympic-related programmes that promote the health of people around the world." With more than 200 operating companies, Johnson & Johnson employs around 115,600 men and women in 57 countries.

Kodak claims a major role in capturing the "most memorable images in Olympic history," having provided film for 27 Olympiads from 1896 onward. Kodak was a charter TOP member in 1986, and is presented as "the leader in helping people take, share, print and view images for memories, for information, for entertainment."

Lenovo Group, previously the Legend Group Limited, reports an established commitment to supporting sport, including women's soccer, in China. It joined the TOP program in January 2005. As the largest manufacturer of personal computers (PCs) in China, it has led sales of the product in the country (and across the Asian Pacific region apart from Japan) since 1994. In December 2004 Lenovo announced a "major acquisition" of IBM, discussed in more detail below, that would make it the third largest maker of PCs in the world.

Manulife Financial Services merged with the established TOP partner John Hancock (which joined the scheme in 1993) in spring 2004. It "shares the Olympic spirit with its sales intermediaries, consumers and employees through an array of innovative grassroots initiatives. The company has also developed a range of community outreach programmes that promote the Olympic ideals, particularly to young people." It gives support to athletes across the world, for training and competition, so supporting "their ultimate dreams" of representing their country at the Olympic Games. The fifth largest life insurance company in the world, Manulife has 20,000 employees in 19 countries and territories.

McDonald's has a longstanding commitment to the Olympics. The company became an official sponsor in 1976, but its profile recalls an earlier relationship still: "At the 1968 Olympic Winter Games, McDonald's airlifted hamburgers to U.S. athletes competing in Grenoble, France, who reported they were homesick for McDonald's food." Since then the company has served "its menu of choice and variety" to millions of athletes, family, and fans. McDonald's is committed to TOP through 2012. It has 30,000 local restaurants, conducting almost 50 million transactions each day, in more than 100 countries. Around 70 percent of McDonald's worldwide are independently owned and operated.

Omega is one of the Swatch group's 16 brands, and is "the largest manufacturer and distributor of finished watches in the world." A long-time Olympic provider and licensee, it has provided the Olympic Games with timing services in all but three Olympic Games since the Los Angeles Games of 1932. It joined TOP as a worldwide Olympic partner in 2003.

Panasonic, as a branch of the Matsushita Electric Industrial Company, provides state-of-the-art digital audio, TV, and digital equipment. Its technology plays "a vital role in delivering the sights, sounds and unique excitement of the Olympic Games, from the field of play to the spectators through its large on-site video screens and professional audio-systems, and to people around the world with its digital broadcasting equipment."

Samsung is the provider of wireless telecommunications equipment "to the Olympic Family to support the operations of staging the

Olympic Games. Samsung . . . helps Olympic athletes share their experiences with family and friends around the world."

Visa International, the exclusive payment card and official payment system of the Games, is said to have "developed a tradition of programs that support Olympic athletes in many countries, as well as programs that teach the youth of the world about the history, values and ideals of the Olympic Movement." Visa joined TOP as a charter member in 1986. Its annual card sales volume is more than US$3 trillion, in more than 150 countries and involving 21,000 member institutions. It is a leader in Internet-based payments and a pioneer of what it calls u-commerce: "the ability to conduct commerce anywhere, anytime, and any way."

Several themes warrant comment in response to the summaries of the sponsor profiles. First, these are giant companies that, on the whole, want to become bigger; several have achieved this via mergers. Second, they are primarily Western companies with worldwide profiles, seven of them U.S.-based, two from Western Europe (Germany and Switzerland), and three from Asia (Japan, South Korea, and China). Third, they are in the TOP program for longer-term benefits, as testified by the three continuous partners since 1986 (though the price is now so high for such rights that this may be introducing some volatility in the program, and this is considered further at the end of the chapter, with reference to the Kodak case). Fourth, most of them employ a rhetoric of support for excellence in performance and for the wider population(s) that are necessary to the Olympics as a large-scale media phenomenon, though few if any of these are instanced or exemplified in any specific way. Fifth, all generate products and services that have potential for penetration into expanded and lucrative markets, and all but one, Lenovo, will be excited by the presence of the Games in the massive and still-expanding new market of Chinese consumers (for Lenovo, the benefit is exposure outside of China). Sixth, their presence (though still not adorning the Olympic stadium) will dominate the official sites of the Games, their employees enjoying the best hotels, hospitality events and "Olympic Family" tickets at the blue-ribbon and most high-profile events.

Lenovo, as the sole sponsor based in China, is a revealing case-study of the emergent Chinese economy, in which enterprises and companies aspire to a global level of business competition (Ling 2006), and not just to compete in local markets. Its IOC Web site highlights the company's repositioning of itself as a global company. This was achieved when US$1.5 billion was paid for the PC business of IBM, a move designed to place Lenovo closer to the two world leaders, Dell and Hewlett-Packard. This strategy was aimed at establishing the company as "one of China's first home-grown brand names," not just clinching its TOP status but also "enlisting celebrities to promote its products, hiring foreign executives and refashioning a company" (Barboza 2006) that had grown from modest and small-scale roots. Lenovo, with executive offices in Beijing, Singapore, and Purchase, New York,[2] was establishing its international profile and worldwide infrastructure, and appointed William Amelio as its president and chief executive. Amelio was a former chief executive at Dell, and went on to bring several more top Dell personnel into the Lenovo operation.

This close-up on Lenovo illustrates a central contradiction of the political economy of the Olympics. Though it invokes values of universal appeal and the "celebration of humanity," (Carrington 2004) the IOC's financial well-being is dependent upon the patronage of aggressive multinational companies more interested in monopolizing global markets than in so-called Olympic values. If Beijing's Olympics is to be a catalyst for anything, it is for the expansion of capitalist and consumer markets in the post-communist world.

Conclusion: Reaching Beyond the Rhetoric

Some of the gaps between idealist rhetoric and the realities of the Games' finances, economics, and political economy are further highlighted by giving space to the voices and postulations of the organizers and the IOC itself. As an event like the Olympic Games comes closer in operational terms, idealism can give way to pragmatism, and the organizers must always face practical problems of policy and implementation. BOCOG's priorities change, its preoccupations less to do with idealism and more concerned with market protectionism, or even profits and surplus (Bloomberg 2006). Typical of the organizers' concern are the comments made at a June 2007 press conference, in which marketing official Chen Feng addressed assembled journalists in the Beijing Olympic Media Center:

> If we don't prevent and fight ambush marketing, more and more interest-driven enterprises will join the ranks of ambush marketing com-

panies, which will reduce the value of the Olympic brands and dampen the sponsors' enthusiasm. The Olympic Movement will lose its financial support and this may imperil the 2008 Olympic Games . . . If ordinary citizens refrain from buying fake Olympic products and report infringement cases, they will be making a sterling contribution to the Olympics and to the protection of Olympic intellectual property rights. (BOCOG 2007)

So your Olympic duty becomes to be an over-directed consumer and an everyday snoop.

The IOC (2007b) in fact sees marketing as "the driving force of the Olympic movement":

The Olympic marketing programme has become the driving force behind the promotion, the financial security and stability of the Olympic Movement.

The challenge of financing the Olympic Games has been a recurring theme throughout Olympic history. Since its founding in 1894, the Olympic Movement has depended on partnership with the business community to stage the Olympic Games and to support the Olympic athletes. Today, marketing partners are an intrinsic part of the Olympic Family.

This is an historical distortion: though commercialization was sought early on in the history of the Olympics (Barney et al. 2002), systematic and consistent business support was piecemeal and fragmented in those early years. The IOC did not permit advertisements in brochures and programs for the London 1948 Olympics, endeavoring "to ensure that they are promoted not so much as a commercial venture but in the best interests of sport" (Burghley 1951, 26). Ninety-two years into the organization's history the TOP scheme was transformative of the political economy of a financially moribund institution. It is therefore disingenuous to locate the TOP sponsors within an established historical tradition. A more accurate interpretation is available in former IOC marketing chief Michael Payne's account of this transformation (Payne 2005), and in his description (Tomlinson 2006b) of the contemporary Olympics as a business sponsor's dream, "commercially controlled and ambush-free."

The IOC recognizes the central place of its "support from sponsors." Corporate sponsors provided US$1.5 billion over a four year period, 34 percent of the US$4 billion of IOC revenue in the Olympic "quadrennium" from 2001–2004, and 11 sponsors (before the arrival of Lenovo as the twelfth) committed US$866 million for the 2005–2008 period:

> The Olympic Movement provides unparalleled returns on the investment for sponsors. The Games provide a marketing platform that is based on ideals and values. The Games provide unparalleled opportunities for a company's sales, showcasing, internal rewards, and community outreach programmes.
>
> Support from the business community and other benefactors helps the athletes and the teams promote the Games. In addition, many sponsors' products, services and expertise are essential to the staging of an Olympic Games. Olympic marketing has developed significantly over the past two decades to ensure the viability of the Olympic Games for many decades to come. (IOC 2007a)

Here, the IOC confirms its commitment to the sponsoring model, playing up the convergence of corporate and Olympic ideals. All Olympic Games, though, confirm the malleability and flexibility of these ideals in what I have called a "necessary arrogation" (Tomlinson 1999). Beijing is an interesting case of such an arrogation—behind its claimed and expressed values Beijing is doing the modern IOC and the new China's work, opening up vast potential consumer markets to ambitious and aggressive multinational companies in a consolidation of the commodification of the Games (Tomlinson 2005c). Braverman (1974), in his critique of monopoly capitalism, talked of how the universal market penetrates into the crevices of our life, in the creation of new products related to personal and cultural aspirations. Some of sport's highest achievements and lofty ideals are now inextricably woven into the universal market, dictating what you can wear as a competitor, how you can pay as a customer, what film you use for your souvenir shot, what quick bite or soft drink you can refresh yourself with.

The interests of the Olympics and of the corporations placing their products through the Olympic brand are certainly a case of "mutual attraction," to cite Close et al. again. But there is more to say: global corporatism existed and would continue to exist without the Olympics; the Olympics, without the TOP programme, would be enfeebled and relatively insignificant. As Short (2004, 96) has argued, the Olympic Games have provided both a vehicle for economic globalization, and "a platform for the penetration of selected corporations into global markets and global consciousness." There will be changes to the lineup,

and in October 2007 Kodak announced its decision to end its partnership with the IOC, citing its digital-led directions and changing market
conditions (Dobbin 2007; Christie 2007). Some top executives also
consider that the IOC and its host partners are setting too high a price,
as one has revealed (interview with author, September 2007). The
Olympics keeps its stadia free of perimeter advertising, and some companies consider this too restricting a model for the high cost of the exclusivity: imagine, then, an alternative scenario for a multinational. If
Paris had gained the 2012 Games, sponsoring the Eiffel Tower, for instance, might look like better value than sponsoring events in a brand-
free area of the Stade de France. New forms of ambush marketing such
as this hypothetical French case might change the marketing landscape
of the Olympic event. But the basic formula of corporate and media un-
derpinning of the event remains in force, and the corporate partner
continues to be a primary player. Short also comments on the influence
of corporate sponsorship on the site of the Games: "The major corporations have been very eager to get the Games into China as a strategy
of promoting their products and name recognition to one of the largest
faster-growing markets in the world" (2004, 97). There is as yet little direct evidence of this eagerness, as corporate sponsors balance the
rhetoric of their partner with the representation of their own global
profiles: the eagerness is without doubt there, but the nature of the
influence is not at all clear in empirical terms, and remains to be re-
searched. Key questions include: What is the proportional commitment to TOP of each sponsor's marketing budget? What evidence is
there of value-for-money in terms of marketing profile and market
share? How many hotels and tickets are taken up by sponsors at the
Games? How do the sponsors participate more widely in the affairs of
the "Olympic Family" and the decisions of the IOC?

A closer look and deeper understanding of the role of the corporate
sponsors in the Olympic story is likely to reaffirm the major influence
of multinational capital upon that narrative. John MacAloon (2006,
32) has observed that Olympic officials are perfectly capable of signing
sponsorship contracts while at the same time proceeding "to battle
those sponsors in defense of the values of the Olympic movement. In
the flame relay, the values of ritual and festival continue to prevail over
those of spectacle, due in great part to the effective political action of
such leaders and their volunteer staff." But in pre-event discourse and
representational forms at least, the Beijing case reaffirms the process
whereby an Olympic rhetoric masks some primary motives of the cho-

sen host, and its main partners. And this makes of the Olympics-Sponsor partnership less of an elective affinity, and more of an ideological contradiction. As the Games are further commodified in the interests of corporate sponsors and global consumption, the Olympics survives as a lucrative brand in the international marketplace, not merely converging with a system and ideology of consumer capitalism, but reshaped by it.

NOTES

1. The term *open up commitments* draws upon the concept of "open" or "openness" which, I am informed by an anonymous reviewer, is a translation of the Chinese term *kaifang*. The words that I have cited from the bidding team's documentation have a specific meaning: again I am indebted to this reviewer—"For the Chinese listener, the words 'the city's commitments on opening up' is code for great political liberalization, and greater integration with the world order, whatever it is." Nevertheless, the words were not being addressed to "the Chinese listener," but presented in the press release to an assembly of the international press. I may misunderstand the specifics of Chinese semantics here, including a particular take on the politics of progress and transformation, but the connection of such forms of openness with the internationalization of markets is at the heart of the committee's statement.

2. Lenovo no longer has offices in Purchase, New York. The U.S. offices are in Raleigh, North Carolina. The company had not made this change at the time it appointed Amelio as president and chief executive.

REFERENCES

Barboza, David. 2006. Exodus from Dell to Lenovo. *International Herald Tribune*, August 25. Available at http://www.iht.com/articles/2006/08/25/business/lenovo.php (accessed June 22, 2007).

Barney, Robert K., Stephen R. Wenn, and Scott G. Martyn. 2002. *Selling the Five Rings: The International Olympic Committee and the Rise of Olympic Commercialism*. Salt Lake City: University of Utah Press.

Beijing Foreign Cultural Exchanges Service Center. 2000a. *Beijing: Facts and Figures*. China: Information Office of Beijing Municipal Government.

Beijing Foreign Cultural Exchanges Service Center. 2000b. *History-City-People: Beijing in Focus*. China: Information Office of Beijing Municipal Government.

Beijing ShengYang Century Advertising Co. 2000. *New Beijing Great Olympics*. Copyright Beijing 2008 Olympic Games Bidding Committee.

Bloomberg. 2006. Beijing 2008 Games May Be Most Profitable Olympics,

IOC Says. (Reporter in Beijing, Grant Clark). Available at http://www
.bloomberg.com/apps/news?pid=10000060&sid=a8XHFh9VKJfg   (accessed June 18, 2007).

BOBICO. 2000a. Action Plan for Green Olympics. Produced by Beijing Foreign Cultural Exchanges Service Center, China.

BOBICO. 2000b. Untitled press release, September 20.

BOCOG. 2007. BOCOG to Strengthen Anti-ambush Marketing Efforts. The Official Web site of the Beijing Olympic Games—Beijing 2008, One World One Dream, updated June 13, 2007. Available at http://en.beijing2008.cn/news/official/preparation/n214097245.shtml (accessed June 18, 2007).

Braverman, Harry. 1974. *Labor and Monopoly Capital: The Degradation of Work in the Twentieth Century.* New York: Monthly Review Press.

Burghley, Lord, general ed. 1951. The Official Report of the Organizing Committee for the XIV Olympiad. London: Organizing Committee for the XIV Olympiad, London, 1948. Consulted in the library of the Olympic Museum, Lausanne, Switzerland.

Carrington, Ben. 2004. Cosmopolitan Olympism, Humanism and the Spectacle of "Race." In *Post-Olympism? Questioning Sport in the Twenty-First Century,* ed. John Bale and Mette Krogh Christensen, 81–97. Oxford: Berg.

Christie, James. 2007. Kodak Hits Delete Button. *Globe and Mail,* October 13. Available at http://www.theglobeandmail.com/servlet/story/LAC.2007 1013.OLYKODAK13/TPStory/Sports (accessed October 15, 2007).

Close, Paul, David Askew, and Xin Xu. 2007. *The Beijing Olympiad: The Political Economy of a Sporting Mega-event.* London: Routledge.

Dobbin, Ben. 2007. Kodak to cut Olympic Sponsorship after 2008 Games. *Daily Southtown,* October 12. Available at http://www.dailysouthtown .com/business/600828,dst_kodak_12.article (accessed October 15, 2007).

Full Moon. 2005. Inspiration: London 2012 Bid Video Presentation. London.

Gruneau, Richard. 1984. Commercialism and the Modern Olympics. In *Five-Ring Circus? Money, Power, and Politics at the Olympic Games,* ed. Alan Tomlinson and Garry Whannel, 1–15. London: Pluto Press.

IOC. 2007a. Introduction to Olympic Marketing. Available at http://www .olympic.org/uk/organisation/facts/introduction/index_uk.asp (accessed June 22, 2007).

IOC. 2007b. Listing and Profiles of TOP Partners. Available at http://www .olympic.org/uk/organisation/facts/programme/profiles_uk.asp (accessed June 15, 2007).

Jennings, Andrew. 1996. *The New Lords of the Rings: Olympic Corruption and How to Buy Gold Medals.* London: Simon and Schuster.

Jennings, Andrew, and Clare Sambrook. 2000. *The Great Olympic Swindle: When the World Wanted Its Games Back.* London: Simon and Schuster.

Lee, Mike. 2006. *The Race for the 2012 Olympics: The Inside Story of How London Won the Bid.* London: Virgin Books.

Ling Zhijun. 2006. *The Lenovo Affair: The Growth of China's Computer Giant and Its Takeover of IBM-PC.* Trans. M. Avery. New York: John Wiley.

MacAloon, John. 2006. Reviewing Olympic Ethnography. In *National Identity and Global Sports Events: Culture, Politics, and Spectacle in the Football World Cup and the Olympic Games,* ed. Alan Tomlinson and Christopher Young, 13–29. Albany: State University of New York Press.

Payne, Michael. 2005. *Olympic Turnaround.* London: Business Press.

Scott, John, and Gordon Marshall. 2005. *Oxford Dictionary of Sociology.* 3rd ed. Oxford: Oxford University Press.

Short, John R. 2004. Going for Gold: Globalizing the Olympics, Localizing the Games. In *Global Metropolitan: Globalizing Cities in a Capitalist World,* 86–108. London: Routledge.

Simson, Vyv, and Andrew Jennings. 1992. *The Lords of the Rings: Power, Money, and Drugs at the Olympic Games.* London: Simon and Schuster.

Tomlinson, Alan. 1999. *The Game's Up: Essays in the Cultural Analysis of Sport, Leisure, and Popular Culture.* Aldershot, UK: Ashgate.

Tomlinson, Alan. 2005a. Olympic Survivals: The Olympic Games as a Global Phenomenon. In *The Global Politics of Sport: The Role of Global Institutions in Sport,* ed. L. Allison, 46–62. London: Routledge.

Tomlinson, Alan. 2005b. The Making of the Global Sports Economy: ISL, Adidas and the Rise of the Corporate Player in World Sport. In *Sport and Corporate Nationalisms,* ed. M. L. Silk, D. L. Andrews, and C. L. Cole, 35–65. Oxford: Berg.

Tomlinson, Alan. 2005c. The Commercialization of the Olympics: Cities, Corporations and the Olympic Commodity. In *Global Olympics: Historical and Sociological Studies of the Modern Games,* ed. K. Young and K. B. Wamsley, 179–200. Oxford: Elsevier.

Tomlinson, Alan. 2006a. Los Angeles 1984 and 1932: Commercializing the American Dream. In *National Identity and Global Sports Events: Culture, Politics, and Spectacle in the Olympics and the Football World Cup,* ed. Alan Tomlinson and Christopher Young, 163–76. London: Routledge.

Tomlinson, Alan. 2006b. The Commercialization of the Olympics: Cities, Corporations, and the Olympic Commodity. Available at http://alantom linson.typepad.com/alan_tomlinson/observations_on_the_olympics/in dex.html.

Weber, Max. 1948. *From Max Weber.* Ed. H. Gerth and C. Wright Mills. London: Routledge and Kegan Paul.

Weber, Max. 1965. *The Protestant Ethic and the Spirit of Capitalism.* Trans. Talcott Parsons. London: Unwin University Books.

Weber, Max. 2001. Weber's Second Reply to Rachfahl, 1910. In *The Protestant Ethic Debate: Max Weber's Replies to his Critics, 1907–1910,* ed. David J. Chalcraft and Austin Harrington, 93–132. Liverpool: Liverpool University Press.

On Seizing the Olympic Platform

Monroe E. Price

When Daniel Dayan and Elihu Katz wrote *Media Events*, their masterful analysis of mass ceremonies of the twentieth century (coronations, the moon landing, the Kennedy funeral), the emphasis was on the celebratory or cohesion-building qualities of such global incidents. Now, reflecting on geopolitical changes that have intensified since the publication of the book, they have come to think more of the brutal competition that occurs to appropriate these phenomenona by a variety of groups and powers in society. Katz has argued that "terrorism" has created a new category of media event. Dayan, with whose modification this chapter is more concerned, has used the word *hijack* to imply the sometimes forceful, but certainly involuntary or antagonistic, seizure of world attention by altering the expected and legitimated narrative of these singular moments (2005). Dayan reflects the hunger by a multitude of groups to gain the extraordinary benefit of huge investments in platforms established by others, and, in so doing, take advantage of elaborately created fora to advance political and commercial messages. Media events become marked by efforts by free riders or interlopers to seize the opportunity to perform in a global theater of representation.

The most dramatic kind of hijacking is asymmetric, where small, seemingly powerless groups gain momentary attention and sometimes enduring strength by storming (literally or figuratively) a platform media event so as instantly to control the narrative (the Palestinian gunmen in the Munich Olympics). But the concept of hijacking raises more complex questions of power and how narratives are generated and diffused in society. Societies or public spaces are hijacked, ways of living are altered, and the predominant notion of propriety and normal behavior displaced. Hijacking can be supplemented by softer versions, such as piggybacking, which I describe subsequently, and that too may involve both marginal and established players (as in "ambush marketing," described later).

Within these ideas there is a torque-like twist that transforms the emphasis, place, and analysis of *Media Events*. This chapter, and this book, co-edited with Dayan, locates this idea of hijacking or seizure, looking at the 2008 Olympics as a case study. Through this study, I look at the more abstract questions surrounding "platforms," as the thing that is hijacked, looking at the category as a relatively underexplored vehicle for systematic communication. I turn next to the historic use of the Olympics as a platform and, finally, to a few examples of seeking to seize the Olympic platform by external civil society advocacy groups and others to exploit the 2008 Olympics to their advantage. I dwell specifically on a campaign to increase China's pressure on Sudan over the Darfur crisis. Because of the centrality of China and narratives of China in the global and domestic imagination, the stakes in producing and controlling the stories produced through the Beijing Olympics have been great. Through this, the event has become something of a watershed for altering perceptions and engendering change.

Platforms and Their Uses

What do we mean by platforms? For the purposes of this analysis, I consider as a "platform" any mechanism that allows for the presentation of information and its transmission from a sender to a receiver. The term grants a sense of solidity and implies a locus for action, for platforms that exist physically, in the electronic universe or simply as the relationships or links between various entities. Platforms have enormous value if they are successful in attracting large, indeed massive, audiences and serving the need of their sponsors, whether they are selling goods or ideas or have the potential to do so. Of course, one can consider newspapers and broadcasting as not only "media" but as historic platforms, and the process by which various groups gain access and influence with them has, of course, been much studied (Montgomery

1990). But in this chapter, I want to use the term *platform* in a special way. What I wish to emphasize is the appropriation of already created platforms by those who seek new opportunities to deliver messages and pathways to persuade. By restricting this approach to "already created" platforms, I want to distinguish between the fostering of a new event as a platform and the effort to take a platform created by others.

This phenomenon of platforms exists in a world in which much clamoring for attention—to sell goods or alter political attitudes—encounters few effective channels to reach the desired audience. Furthermore, the existing channels are often tightly controlled and present significant barriers to entry. Globalization plays a large role in the shifting efforts to perform and persuade. In the twentieth century, media systems were designed so that issues would be articulated, framed and discussed largely within national boundaries, and the residue of that system persists. Increasingly, however, issues such as human rights, environmentalism, and even the impact of domestic political choices are seen with respect to their vast transnational implications. The interests and actions of civil society and other groups shift from a national to a global level. These passions are made all the more frustrating by the fact that they are often blocked from entry (purposely or merely because of patterns of scarcity) into domestic media systems. As a result, these groups seek new ways of reaching widely distributed elites (and masses).

There is, of course, a very long history of alternate modes of gathering audiences together through various mechanisms that allow persuasive messages to be articulated and widely diffused. Demonstrations, marches, strikes or manifestations are exemplary. In the last several decades, global civil society groups have organized huge concerts, terrorists have caused immense catastrophes, and political figures have staged gatherings of dignitaries: all widely differing efforts to create an opportunity for significant audiences to experience arguments or assertions that would not otherwise come to their attention—or not with such emphasis. Media coverage of such events plays a major role in bringing them to the attention of the public. Much of the work in Dayan and Katz's well-known book, *Media Events,* is about the communications-related aspects of creating such platforms.

But in this chapter the emphasis is on the effort (and this is a rough distinction) not to create a platform, but rather to appropriate one that was already established or constructed for another purpose, turning the message from that of its sponsors to those of others, commercial entities or global civil society groups. It is that specific irony—the notion of hijacking or piggybacking—that becomes of interest with respect to the Olympics. The central idea is to find a platform that has proven highly successful in establishing a major constituency for one purpose and then convert that constituency to a different, unintended objective. The cost of creating the platform (very likely considerable) is borne by one player, but the benefits are then obtained by another. The Olympic Games, which offer advocacy groups opportunities for alliances among disparate groups that make up global civil society, provides an important example of this phenomenon. Embedded in this idea are a variety of subnotions: (a) that the Olympic Games are such a platform; (b) that one can identify a dominant narrative that is the intended and approved narrative for which the platform was designed; and (c) in contrast, one can categorize other uses of the platform as counternarrative in ways that are worthy of distinction. In other words, there is some (possibly illusionary) accepted use for the Olympics that is crowded out or violated and that it is possible to tell, sometimes in advance of the event, who the contenders are for the secondary use.

Because of the ever-present danger of appropriation, one defining characteristic of significant platforms is the effort to protect them from unwanted or unremunerated uses. In the Internet world, platform software is created to protect a site from hacking. But what about complex platforms like the Olympic Games? These are protected through physical modes of security (limiting who may actually enter the Olympic facilities or who receives press accreditation for coverage). They are protected through assertion of intellectual property and contractual rights, using highly developed legal mechanisms to enjoin or impose high costs on those who seek to be free riders. The International Olympic Committee (IOC) sets terms for the uses of the platform (and limitations on those uses) by the organizers, the sponsors, and the athletic federations. And platforms are protected, most subtly, through intense management of narrative and response to efforts to subvert or countermand what is chosen to be dominant.

In the case of the Olympics, some fundamental problems present themselves. First, there is a built-in ambiguity as to the "ownership" of the Olympics platform. In some Games, the platform has belonged more to the International Olympic Committee, and in some more to the Organizing Committee; in recent Olympics, ownership is increasingly a combination of these two. Further ambiguity is added as the host city or country seeks to control part of the narrative. In China, while 2008 is the Beijing Olympics, there is no doubt that the Games are an opportunity for China to tell its stories at home and abroad. And finally, because of commercialization and the high revenues sponsors engender (Payne 2006; Schmitz 2005), increasingly it is the sponsors who have a stake in creating a platform (or using an already-created one) to advance their goals, whether they are selling soda, burgers, or large scale perceptions about citizenship, consumption, and identity.

Because ownership of the platform is multiple and ambiguous, so too is the question of dominant or accepted narratives (Morgan 1995; Hoberman 1997; Barney, Wamsley, Martyn, and MacDonald 1998). It is not fully transparent how potential conflicts in narrative or even differences in emphasis on narrative are negotiated among these competitors for the accepted narrative. The IOC, for example, must monitor for over-commercialization, for proper conduct of participants during the Games, for coverage, and even for the architecture of the venues themselves, to ensure its continued control over a particular representation of the Olympic ideal.

I also distinguish among various efforts to appropriate the platform. Such uses can be merely complementary (indeed reinforcing), in competition with or in contradiction to the accepted narrative (assuming that narrative can be specified). I use the term *complementary* for uses in which the appropriator gains benefits, but those who built the platform bear no additional costs. For example, cities other than Beijing in China may wish to use the Olympics to promote their value as tourist destinations, rather than Beijing. Large commercial entities—including Johnson & Johnson and other major sponsors—may wish to propagate a vision of China (or a particular sense of "One World, One Dream") that is slightly different from that of BOCOG or the regime, though not in conflict with it. They may wish, for example, to emphasize China's advances in health technology or in science as opposed to achievement in athletic prowess or, subtly, in military power. Or commercial sponsors may seek to integrate their product with the Olympic dream, propagating a message that is a variant on what the state seeks to propagate, or slightly (but not very) subversive of it. And finally, The Olympic Partner Programme (TOP) sponsors as a group may have messages that subtly or less subtly reinforce attitudes toward consumption, or the increased power of China and the pride that that should engender. Johnson & Johnson's theme as a TOP Partner within China is "Golden Touch, Golden Mom," an idea that strongly ties the Olympics to motherhood in Chinese society.

Alongside these complementary narratives, there are major and minor efforts to throw off the dominant narratives of the Beijing Olympics and, via a kind of jujitsu, turn global competition to images of China that are less favorable, or to use the Olympics for some wholly different purpose. The 1999 World Ministerial Conference of the World Trade Organization was a hallmark recent event, not Olympics related, exemplifying the exploitation of a platform created for one general narrative (furthering one vision of world trade relationships) to convey quite another. Just as China is using the 2008 Games to influence public opinion at home and abroad, many advocacy groups and other interests—both inside China and internationally—are using the occasion to deflect this official representation. These groups fight for space in U.S. and global media, mainstream and not, to reinforce China's flaws and weaknesses, all issuing body jabs against the depiction of the new Colossus. The Olympics magnifies the attention given to the repeated reports of manufacturing defects in China.

But from the point of the view of the Olympics there is little difference between a complementary and a competitive user (where the dominant and alternate use are in more of a zero-sum game). Both are "free riders"—sometimes involved in what might be more gently called piggybacking, rather than hijacking, the platform. Free riders threaten the exclusivity of the platform and the underlying marketing theory that yields compensation for the IOC. Even where the free rider does not damage the Games or its family of participants, the IOC has an interest in capturing the economic benefit to the appropriator, thus internalizing the benefit of the Games and protecting those who pay for the privilege. It is a widely told tale that at the 1984 Olympics, Fuji was an official sponsor, but Kodak was a principal advertiser of both U.S. television broadcasts of the Games and named supporter of the U.S. track team. In 1992, at the Barcelona Olympics, official sponsors including Reebok paid $700 million, but when the U.S. basketball team won a gold medal, Nike sponsored the press conference. Increasingly, legislation, at the behest of the IOC, restricts and bans such practices. For the London Olympics, there is already legislation preventing any business making reference to the 2012 Olympics in its promotions, unless it is an official sponsor (House of Commons 2005–6). There is a specific rhetoric that captures the commercial appropriation of the endorsed and official narratives. "Ambush" or "parasite" marketing refers to efforts by a company, not an official sponsor of the Olympics, who, by centering its advertising campaign around the event, appears to have that status (Vancouver 2010). A nonsponsoring company, barred from the use of official logos and other trademarks associated with the sporting event, seeks to inveigle itself by sponsoring an individual athlete or in other ways (Schmitz 2005; Davis 1996).

These commercial appropriations are a way of thinking about the greater stories of the Olympic platform: because so much is spent, because the economy of the Olympics depends upon controlling them, and because there are lawsuits with extensive explanations, struggles in this sphere are better articulated than they are in connection to more substantial areas of competition. More is written about a sneaker manufacturer who is not an official sponsor trying to obtain market share, than about competition over the generalized narratives established by the IOC or the Organizing Committee. Dayan's emphasis on hijacking moves toward the effort to promote contrary or contradictory uses subversive of the principal narrative. The most-cited "hijack" of the Olympics, the frightening presence in the Olympic past, was the terrorist attack in Munich. Each Olympic Organizing Committee is haunted by Munich and its planning is to some extent about mechanisms for avoidance.

The Problem of the "Base Narrative"

To have a category of the subversive, there must be an idea of what constitutes the dominant. Hijacking assumes a legitimated base narrative that is displaced. And that raises the question of who owns or controls the platform—for example, whether it is the platform of the IOC or, in 2008, of the Beijing Organizing Committee of the Olympic Games (BOCOG) or of China, or of the commercial sponsors, or of the great transnational broadcasters, like NBC. A more radical perspective, with respect to the Olympics, is that all claimants have only relative primacy or ownership of the platform. One could go further and argue that the Olympic platform has been seized from a purer Olympic past by commercial interests (since 1984) or by various incarnations of the IOC which, it has been argued, has not always been a true bearer of the Olympic torch. John Hoberman, who has used "amoral universalism" as a descriptor of IOC's approach in the past, has written, in an interview for this chapter, that:

> I have read Coubertin's major works and analyzed them in *The Olympic Crisis* (1986), and I have no doubts about the authenticity of his ideal-

ism and his good intentions about achieving world peace through international sport. The problem, from my perspective, is that a lot of the wrong people have wielded power over the "movement" from even before Coubertin passed from the scene in 1937—viz. the Nazi Olympics and my account in "Toward a Theory of Olympic Internationalism" of who played influential roles in 1936 and how they acquired them. So the question here is whether the IOC has played politically wholesome roles in international diplomacy in the past, and whether, in the light of this past, they are capable of doing so now as 2008 approaches. (e-mail exchange with the author, June 12, 2007)[1]

For Hoberman, it is precisely an absence of understanding of history that renders the current acceptance of the dominant narrative of Olympism possible. Only an absence of understanding allows the positive glow in which NBC and corporate sponsors, who underwrite the Games, can thrive.

It is clear that the Olympic ideology satisfies a deep yearning for globalism (in the key of sentimentalism). The Olympic "movement" (along with Esperanto and the Red Cross) is one of the late 19th-century internationalisms that has actually survived and succeeded. The difference is that ceding the Olympic Games to the sports entertainment industry has inevitably resulted in multiple forms of corruption from which the Esperantists and the Red Cross people—shielded from temptation—remain happily immune. (e-mail exchange with the author, June 10, 2007)

It is against this perspective that one might examine more traditional views of the IOC and its efforts to affect and control the narrative. Here, and elsewhere in this book, one major area for examination is the use of the Games to advance specific goals of civil society. Before I turn to specific areas of competition with respect to Beijing, it is useful to look at expectations that the history of the Games sanction efforts to legitimate pressures for change, and are not just an occasion for measuring athletic performance. In this regard, I borrow from James Nafziger (1992) in his analysis of the traditional interplay between the Olympics and the processes of legal and political change.

Scholars such as Nafziger argue that political activity to this end should be encouraged as strongly consistent with the Olympic ideal. They invoke the Olympic Charter and its aspirations that render, for example, as incompatible with the Olympic Movement "any form of discrimination with regard to a country or person on the grounds of race, religion, politics, gender or otherwise" (IOC 2007). Here the dominant Olympic narrative is the promotion of harmonious interaction between peoples and states and the cultivation of international dialogue. Advocates of this approach point to the role of the IOC in the decision of the North and South Korean teams to march together at the opening ceremonies of the 2006 Torino Olympics. This event was trumpeted as a symbol of a renewed effort to cooperate and was commended as being representative of the Olympic goal of camaraderie and peaceful relations. Olympic officials encouraged North and South Korea to use the Asian Games as a chance to mend diplomatic relations, despite a growing rift between the two over the communist regime's recent missile launches and nuclear test. When the two countries announced their intentions to forge a joint team for 2008, the political decision was applauded by the IOC. A spokesperson announced: "Today marks a milestone in the completion of this important project for the two Koreas and the Olympic movement" (*People's Daily Online* 2006).

Coursing through Olympic history are more aggressive notions of intervention, for example using international sporting events as a bargaining tool to criticize behavior of certain states. The prevailing example of the embrace of international sport to advance the cause of human rights is the IOC's campaign to abate racial discrimination and apartheid in South Africa. Between 1964 and 1991, the IOC not only precluded South Africa from competing in the Olympic Games, it urged all International Federations to do the same until South Africa abandoned apartheid. The IOC recognized that apartheid was "in contravention of the Olympic Charter" (ANOC 1984) and by imposing penalties for its practice, "the IOC rightly subordinated the Olympic goal of widespread international sports participation to the more fundamental principles of international human rights law" (Mastrocola 1995).

Individual states also use the platform of the Games for purposes that can be easily classified as propagandistic and certainly are intended to enhance national prestige: the decision of the USSR to absent itself from the Games until 1952 because of the "bourgeois and capitalist" nature of the event is one well-known example. Intractable regional or international conflict can shift the meanings of, and the narratives expressed during, the Games, and underscore the importance of the IOC to provide control. The 1936 Berlin Olympics was a misuse of the Olympic ideal, exploited by the Nazi regime to strengthen its hold at home while providing foreign spectators and journalists with a picture of a peaceful, tolerant Germany. By rejecting a proposed boycott of the 1936 Olympics, the United States and other Western democracies acted in a way that skirted international obligations (Large 2007).

Nafziger recalls that "At the end of the Cold War, the Olympic Movement helped end a sort of negative ping-pong in the form of reciprocal boycotting by the United States and the Soviet Union, joined by their national allies, of each other's Olympic venues. With governmental support initiated by the IOC, the national committees of the two countries signed an antiboycott and cooperative agreement that was adopted by their Governments in an early hint that the Cold War was drawing to a close" (Nafziger 1992, 497). And the IOC played a key role in conflict between North and South Korea during and around the Seoul Games. It proposed that some of the scheduled events be held in North Korea; though this was eventually rejected (and North Korea boycotted the Seoul Games after it was refused status of co-organizer), mediation encouraged competition that remained peaceful—and ultimately encouraged negotiations to explore ending four decades of near conflict between the two Koreas.

Upon the establishment of the People's Republic of China in 1949, the International Olympic Committee ruled that Taiwan's Olympic committee would represent China; after the PRC gained the Chinese seat at the United Nations in 1971, the IOC recognized Beijing's Olympic committee. The conflict over representation gained another level of complexity when Taiwanese athletes were allowed to compete, but only as part of the "Chinese Taipei Olympic Committee." Under the formal arrangement, the Taiwanese entrants were prohibited from using Taiwan's national symbols, such as Taiwan's flag; the national anthem of Taiwan would not be sung when its athletes won medals.

In this sense the dominant narrative of the IOC hurtles between a more positive notion of Olympian harmony and global cooperation, and a claim of interventionist achievement and the "amoral universalism" in Hoberman's term. The IOC affirms a role in forwarding Olympic goals that seeks, rhetorically and in practice, to avoid the political. But a broad perspective—linked to the history of the IOC—asks whether the IOC sees the Olympics as a mode for moving a society, and the host city itself, "forward" along a number of dimensions. If that is part of the legitimated narrative, civil society groups and others consider advocacy not only an ethical use of the Olympics moment, but wholly consistent with historic Coubertin-like objectives. There are those, including the IOC itself at times, who hew to the notion that the principal overt purpose or intended narrative of the Olympics should only have to do with sports and performance, and any attempt to inject broader social or political meaning and impact is an intrusion, a side effect of the extravaganza. Soon after China was awarded the Games, Jacques Rogge, president of the IOC, said, "The IOC is not a political body—the IOC is a sports body. Having an influence on human rights issues is the task of political organisations and human rights organisations. It is not the task of the IOC to get involved in monitoring, or in lobbying or in policing" (BBC Sport 2001). And in 2006, Rogge's chief of staff wrote a letter to a protesting Tibetan group, the International Campaign for Tibet, rejecting the Tibetans' appeal that the IOC bring pressure to bear on China. Of course, the spokesperson said, a Beijing Olympics would play a positive role "in China's changing social and economic fabric," but "We believe your demands fall unquestionably well outside the remit of our organization" (Hutzler 2006).

These expressions underscore the IOC's reluctance to respond to petitions and letters demanding action from a plethora of civil society groups and others. In contradistinction, the Olympics' capacity to promote positive political, economic, and social change is almost always an element of the bid award process. Before the Games were awarded, the IOC was less reluctant to tie the Games to China's human rights record: in April 2002, Rogge told BBC-TV, "We are convinced the Olympic Games will improve human rights in China . . . However, the IOC is a responsible organisation and if either security, logistics or human rights are not acted upon to our satisfaction, we will act" (*Australian* 2002). One might argue that the Olympic Bid is the occasion for setting forth competing narratives and that after the award, the role of the IOC is reduced, but this would be an odd reading of intentions. The conflict among these views undergirds the extraordinary global interest in what might be called "shaping China" from a variety of perspectives. Thus, it is important to look at the way the International Olympic Committee is being perceived, hectored, influenced, and pressured to alter its sense of mission and how this is done by countries, interest groups, and corporations within and outside China.

Competing Narratives, Civil Society and the Beijing Olympics

What makes the 2008 Olympics different from these previous experiences is the increased complexity of issues and players involved in the process. Beijing is not only the most expensive Games and the Games with the largest potential audience, it is also the Olympics with the most substantial geopolitical consequences. It is about shifts in power toward Asia and shifts in China's role in the global imagination. It comes at a time when every event, including the Olympics, has a transforming environmental agenda. For China it is about the PRC's ability to promote itself as a harmonious society, both at home and internationally. In a not atypical comment, Qin Xiaoying, in *China Daily* (2007), wrote that "Comparing the Olympic spirit and China's quest for a harmonious society, one sees clearly that the aspirations of the Chinese people and the ideas of the Olympic movement have so much in common with respect to interactions between people, between people and society and between man and nature." The official slogan for the Games—"One World, One Dream"—encapsulates this theme of harmony, and renders older competing narratives of China jarring. In the run-up to the games, Chinese scholars have been scouring the foreign press to determine what is written about the PRC, and whether the Games are being portrayed as a moment of potential glory or as symptomatic of larger social and economic flaws and political differences.

The 2008 Games are precariously poised between the zeal and sophistication of NGOs and builders of global civil society on the one hand, and the many complex issues raised by the evolution and development of China on the other. What in the past constituted a debate among governments and national groups has been further transformed and complicated as the battle over representations in the Olympics has expanded and intensified. The major players in this new world are the increasingly global NGOs, a group distinguished by notably more sophisticated means of leveraging power. With their political acumen and reach, these civil society groups have become important entrants in the struggle over the way Beijing is interpreted. In short, the 2008 Olympics are taking place at a moment when an expanding civil society sphere more effectively organizes and communicates globally, and the event provides an ideal opportunity for the relevant actors to mobilize support for their various causes and appeals. The civil society organizations taking up the issue of the Olympics include general human rights advocates and groups specifically concerned with issues of religion and press freedom. There are groups involved in China's relationship with Tibet, and entities with specific public agendas such as environmental organizations and opponents of China's one-child policies. This emerging global society uses a variety of venues to mobilize, to generate support and achieve prominence. They set up BOCOG, the IOC, China, and the advertisers and sponsors of the 2008 Games as foils. They enlist their national parliaments. And in so doing, these civil society actors have become the functional equivalents of the official sponsors, seeking the looming billboard of the Games to attract audiences and loyalties for their views and to reshape the Olympics as an agent for change.

Though it is impossible to chart the various modes of shifting the agenda of the IOC (and through it China) completely or exhaustively, some examples should help to convey how these groups have aggregated to form a kind of global civil society, and how, in competing and different ways, they seek to shape an agenda around the Olympics. Most of these efforts to open up a kind of public sphere—whether coordinated or isolated—involve individual NGOs, some of which were designed especially to bring pressure to bear on the IOC and China. These groups use a variety of techniques and address them to a wide variety of individuals and entities. They use sample letters and electronic petitions to activate their members as intermediaries. They attempt to assert pressure on groups, including the IOC, directly and through sponsors such as Coca-Cola and other companies with vested interests in the country. They act as clearinghouses of information on human rights abuses, keeping track of developments and reporting on the activities of other human rights groups regarding China and the Olympics. They stress continued media pressure on China as a way to directly embarrass or shame the CCP into improving its record and also to prompt the IOC to influence China.

Among the various Christian groups seeking to make their claims part of the Olympics agenda is the Cardinal Kung Foundation, which asserts its ties to and advocates for the underground Roman Catholic Church in China, detailing China's record of religious persecution in an attempt to include religious freedom on the Olympic change agenda. In testimony to the U.S. Congress and in letters to President Hu Jintao, the Foundation has sought to invoke the Olympic aura, describing the "current Chinese government religious policy" as the direct opposite of the Olympic goal of friendship, decency and solidarity, and calling on China to prove that the country "is honoring the spirit of the Olympic Games" (Cardinal Kung Foundation, n.d. and 2005). Groups concerned with issues in Tibet have been particularly active. In 2006, a group of Tibetan cyclists held a freedom rally in New Delhi to protest Chinese rule and appeal to the Indian government to help resolve the Tibet issue for its own security. The rallyists were also garnering support for an Olympic boycott because of China's poor human rights record and in particular, the jailing and disappearance of the 11th Panchen Lama, Tibet's second-ranking religious figure. A small group of Tibetan monks and Tibetans held a hunger strike in Turin, Italy during the 2006 Winter Games to pressure the IOC to pressure China to improve human rights in Tibet. It is not just NGOs that are involved, but a wide variety of organizations, tribal entities, and other political forces. When an Uyghur activist (and Canadian citizen) was extradited from Uzbekistan to China and jailed, lawyers and family members attempted to exert pressure on the Canadian government to influence China by invoking the Olympic values. In cases such as these, the Olympic spirit becomes a kind of symbolic or disembodied code which is invoked as an instrument of rhetorical power.

Some of the themes or tropes of these entities can be identified in a letter issued on August 7, 2006, by an international coalition of human rights organizations, including Olympic Watch (a human rights monitoring association created especially to focus on the Games), Reporters Without Borders, the International Society for Human Rights, Solidarité Chine, and Laogai Research Foundation. The letter maintains that "The IOC has the obligation to protect the Olympic ideals of 'harmonious development of man,' 'human dignity' and 'peace,' and to prevent the political propaganda abuse of the Games." And it alleges that "the IOC has refused to face the reality in which Beijing 2008 is to take place," charging current IOC leadership with being "either too cynical, or too incompetent, or both, to protect the Olympic ideals and take a clear stance on the continuing human rights abuses in China." The group called on National Olympic Committees and individual athletes "to start discussing ways how they can protest the conditions under which the 2008 Games are to take place." As to implementation, the letter suggests that "At a minimum, the IOC could demand that the Beijing Organizing Committee of the Olympic Games not be personally linked to the perpetrators of human rights violations, the Chinese Communist Party." It recommended that National Olympic Committees organize boycotts, stage peaceful protests in Beijing during the Games, include Chinese, Tibetan, and Uyghur exiles in their teams and delegations and visit human rights defenders in prison. Corporate sponsors were urged to "show their commitment to corporate social responsibility by making it clear to the IOC and to BOCOG that their business philosophy does not condone propaganda abuse of the Games and human rights violations" (Olympic Watch 2006). The Human Rights Watch Olympic campaign sought to open the narrative by focusing on three questions. One was "How will China's pervasive censorship and control of domestic and international media and the Internet play out when thousands of international journalists descend on Beijing?" The implication here is of course that there will be necessary consequences when the legions come to cover the Games. Their second question was posed as follows: "How are the Olympic Games being used to justify the violent forced evictions of thousands of people from their homes?" And a third question, revisited later in this chapter, asks ". . . how do China's restrictions on labor rights affect workers on the ground?" (Human Rights Watch n.d.).

Two Case Studies

I want to close this chapter by focusing on two specific efforts of civil society, one involving domestic policy in China and labor standards, and the other involving foreign policy, in particular, China's relationship with Sudan and Darfur. The first example involves a campaign that stretches across several Olympics, and the second involves one that is targeted specifically at 2008. Each example shows civil society mobilizing to use the Olympics platform to gain global attention and change China's behavior.

PlayFair Alliance

An important case study involves the PlayFair Alliance, a group with foundations in the international labor movement (among other bases) which has been engaged in a long-term effort to improve working standards for children and others. Begun before Athens, as the "Play Fair at the Olympics Campaign," it claimed to be one of the "biggest ever global mobilisations against inhuman working conditions" (Play Fair at the Olympics 2004). Somewhat reconstituted for the 2008 Olympics, the PlayFair Alliance demonstrates modes of highlighting a subversive narrative—the exploitation of child labor—and legitimating its claims by bringing them into of the world of the IOC's own documents. PlayFair has skillfully used the rhetoric of the Olympic movement, including the IOC Code of Ethics, and has gained advantage by mastering the intricacies of the IOC and national licensing agreements.

In short, it appropriated an officially proclaimed narrative of Olympic decency and then sought to hold those involved to their articulated high standard.

Their efforts resulted in a report that was published in June 2007 and that documented the illegal use of child labor in China's manufacture of the Olympic-related mementos that were under license to BOCOG. The report was well-documented and provoked an instant reaction from Chinese authorities, always prepared for crisis management, in which they announced that local officials would be punished, businesses closed, and the contracts immediately terminated.

One of the striking features of the report is the way in which it shows how traditional IOC rhetoric can be deployed to create a frame for altering narratives. Quoting directly from extracts of the IOC's Code of Ethics, PlayFair invoked the following principles:

1. Safeguarding the dignity of the individual is a fundamental requirement of Olympism.

   . . .

5. The Olympic parties shall use due care and diligence in fulfilling their mission. They must not act in a manner likely to tarnish the reputation of the Olympic Movement.

6. The Olympic parties must not be involved with firms or persons whose activity is inconsistent with the principles set out in the Olympic Charter and the present Code.

The report details the Alliance's efforts, since 2003, to discuss with the IOC the conditions under which Olympic-branded sportswear is produced. In response to requests for meetings, the IOC commented "that it condemns the practice of unfair labour practices, which are contrary to the spirit and ideals of the Olympic movement," but that day to day licensing is managed by the 202 National Olympic Committees around the world, and "The IOC has no direct involvement with regards to such contracts." PlayFair's report also referenced a 1998 cooperation agreement signed between the IOC and the International Labour Organisation (ILO) that focused on respect for social justice in the labor field. In that agreement, "the IOC and the ILO undertake to encourage activities in pursuit of this objective, particularly those which contribute to the elimination of poverty and child labour . . ." (PlayFair 2008 2007, 6).

Invoking this history, PlayFair urged the IOC to "Adopt a clear and public statement, including inclusion into the Olympic Charter, in support of labour standards and in particular in sporting goods supply chains; Incorporate into IOC licensing/sponsorship contracts, binding language on labour standards issues throughout the supply chains(s) of the company(s) concerned; Establish an effective mechanism through which cases of violations of labour rights in such supply chains can be dealt with, in cases where it has not been possible to remedy these through direct contact with the company(s) concerned; Take concrete steps to ensure that national Olympic committees and games organising committees adopt and implement equivalent provisions." (PlayFair 2008 2007, 6).

The Beijing 2008 Olympic Marketing Plan overview describes an official Olympics Games License as "an agreement that grants the rights to use Olympic marks on products for retail sale. In return, licensees pay royalties for the rights, which go directly toward funding the Olympic Games. The program aims at promoting the Olympic Ideals and the Olympic Brand, providing quality consumer touch points for the inspiration of the Games" (BOCOG n.d.) Thus, PlayFair's style of argument made the IOC's policies on merchandise licensing much more transparent than they had previously been.

PlayFair understood the implications not only for the IOC story, but for the China narrative as well. For China, much was at stake in terms of the relationship between the Olympics and changing global perceptions of the quality of domestically produced goods. The stated "mission" of the Beijing 2008 Licensing Programme is to promote the brand image of the Beijing Olympic Games and the Chinese Olympic Committee (COC), that is, to "express the unique culture of China and Beijing by offering an array of traditional cultural products; make a strong effort to involve Chinese enterprises in Olympic licensing; showcase Chinese products and build the brand image equation that conveys a quality message, i.e. 'Made-in-China = High Quality;' and raise funds for the Beijing 2008 Olympic Games." (Chinese Olympic Committee 2004).

The "Genocide Olympics"

There is no gold medal for the NGO narrative that comes closest to hijacking, usurping or piggybacking on the immense investment in the Olympics. But if there were, one of the competitors for the 2008 award might be Eric Reeves, an English professor at Smith College, who created the accusatory concept of the "Genocide Olympics" as a way of altering China's dealings with Sudan. Reeves's was a classic effort to seize the platform, and to use the social and financial capital invested in the Olympics in order to turn it to the advantage of an NGO policy advocate "free rider." It is useful to trace the intense history of this effort and its implications for the earlier discussion of platforms.

Many have remarked on China's close relationship with countries of marginal stability and democracy, seen to be partly an imperative of the country's growing domestic economy and need for oil reserves. A prominent actor in this arena is Sudan. Since the mid-1990s, China National Petroleum Corporation (CNPC) has been the dominant player in both exploration and production in Sudan's oil reserves. Human Rights Watch and others have charged that China's involvement in oil exploration has been marked by complicity in gross human rights violations, including clearances of the indigenous populations in the oil regions and direct assistance to Khartoum's regular military forces. In addition, China has purchased a great share of Sudan's oil exports, and these revenues are a major source of financial support for the Sudanese government. These policies have undermined the effectiveness of sanctions imposed by other global players.

Most important and relevant to the subject of Reeves's use of the Olympics platform has been international concern about widespread killing and displacement in the Darfur region, and the specific role of China in this crisis. In September 2004, the UN Security Council adopted a resolution threatening Sudan with oil sanctions if it did not stop atrocities in the Darfur region. China abstained. In August 2006, China abstained again in a vote on Resolution 1706 which provided for the transfer of responsibility in Darfur to the United Nations from the African Union (United Nations 2006). Many advocates felt that China was shielding Sudan in its refusal to consent to the entry of UN forces.

The public efforts to pressure Sudan, and countries that can influence Sudan, have, of course, been massive. What was particularly novel however was the leveraging of the 2008 Olympic Games as a method of bringing such pressure to bear. Eric Reeves's "rebranding" of the Beijing events as the "Genocide Olympics" was a kind of asymmetric image warfare, which also proved to be a highly effective mode of mobilizing support for his position. Various elements distinguish Reeves's counternarrative from those of the NGO advocacy projects described earlier in this chapter. But there are also similarities. From the outset, the most salient characteristic was Reeves's rhetorical strategy, deploying the evocative and immediately understandable phrase, "Genocide Olympics." This elegant and powerful formulation effectively juxtaposes two complex worlds that are not readily associated with each other. It is a phrase that assaults and awakens the reader, and invites further inquiry. It is a phrase that, for some readers, plays on deep and abiding concerns about China and 2008 that could not otherwise be easily summarized and compressed. The brilliance of this two word phrase was what gave the project its initial momentum.

Reeves was able to build on Beijing's own contribution to the notion of multiple sorts of Olympics. As part of its expansive claims for the Olympics, BOCOG chose the "One World, One Dream" motto to convey the idea of simultaneous and overlapping Olympics, Olympics that asserted and followed certain themes: a Green Olympics, a People's Olympics and a High-Tech Olympics. The Green Olympics would emphasize harmony and mutual promotion of man and nature, and China's commitment to sustainable development. The People's Olympics would promote an internally harmonious society, facilitate the formation of a peaceful international environment and emphasize solidarity between East and West.[2] The High-Tech Olympics would, according to BOCOG, "be a window to showcase [China's] high-tech achievements and innovative capacity" (BOCOG 2005). In another, slightly more worrisome interpretation, however, the High-Tech Olympics provides an "arena to exhibit the comprehensive power and the highest level of the scientific and technological development of China" (Hua 2004). Playing against the quasi-hyperbole of Beijing's claims, the coining of Reeves's phrase was a small act of jujitsu.

The second reason the phrase was so striking was that it broke through the dense layers of complexity about Darfur, atrocities, geopolitics, oil, and weapons trading. The phrase "Genocide Olympics" was issued and introduced to a global audience that understood something horrible was proceeding in Darfur and that there had been numerous seemingly ineffectual attempts to resolve the crisis. There was, as is often the case, a generalized hope for a new solution that could be understandable and workable. By fixing responsibility on China and suggesting a potential solution, the concept of "Genocide Olympics" had staying power. It gathered, under a single banner, much of the accumulated discontent, anxiety, and suspicion about China and human rights.

Strategy and the Launching of the Narrative

Reeves's public and transparent campaign makes it possible to document and analyze what he proposed to do and how his small campaign played off of great platforms such as the Games. The campaign is an interesting example of diffusion of an idea. Reeves has long experience as a Sudan activist; his Web site, www.sudanreeves.org, carries many of his writings and analyses on this subject. He has spent eight years fully devoted to Sudan related-questions. And he has always had the ability to use newspapers, radio, and other means to keep his views in the public eye. When Reeves turned to the Olympics as a platform for mobilization, he met with the *Washington Post* editorial board and convinced them to write an editorial (2006) that had "Genocide Olympics" in its title (the first such publication of the term). He wrote an opinion piece in December, 2006 in the *Boston Globe* about his proposed campaign. In March, Reeves appeared again in the *Boston Globe*—this time as a subject of a story—with an account of his campaign (Cullen 2007), which he launched with an e-mail manifesto sent in February, an "Open Letter to Darfur Activists" (Reeves 2007a).

The manifesto is interesting for its differing modes of achieving the goal of hijacking the Olympics for secondary purposes. The letter starts by challenging current NGO techniques for citizen actions regarding Darfur:

> Enough of selling green bracelets and writing letters. . . . It's time, now, to begin shaming China—demanding that if the Beijing government is going to host the premier international event, the Summer Olympic Games of 2008, they must be responsible international partners. China's slogan for these Olympic Games—"One world, one dream"—is a ghastly irony, given Beijing's complicity in the Darfur genocide. . . . The Chinese leadership must understand that if they refuse to use their unrivaled political, economic, and diplomatic leverage with Khartoum to secure access for the force authorized under UN Security Council Resolution 1706, then they will face an extremely vigorous, unrelenting, and omnipresent campaign to shame them over this refusal.

In opposition to the established means of exploiting the Olympics platform, Reeves suggested that a boycott of the Games would not be the most effective technique:

> It is important to remember that this should not, in my strongly held view, be a campaign to boycott the Olympics: a boycott would defeat the whole purpose of the campaign, and be deeply divisive. Moreover, if a boycott were successful (extremely unlikely) the political platform from which to challenge China would disappear.

Reeves's aspiration, rather, was for the Olympics platform to foster a global, grassroots movement. He intuited the bigger the platform (and the Olympics is certainly among the biggest), the greater the room for major uses by the appropriator:

> There is tremendous scope for creative advocacy here, and for the deployment of diverse skills and energies: linguistic, internet, communications, graphic design, advocacy writing, and organizational. What happens, for example, if 1,000 students and advocates demonstrate before the Chinese embassy in Washington, DC, declaring with banner, placards, and T-shirts that China will be held accountable for its complicity in the Darfur genocide? What happens if such demonstrations are continuous, and grow, and take place outside China's embassies in other countries? in many other countries? What happens if everywhere–everywhere–Chinese diplomats and politicians travel they are confronted by those who insist on making this an occasion for highlighting China's role in the Darfur genocide?

Diffusion and Losing Control of the Narrative

Almost immediately, there was rapid diffusion of the idea. Reeves gave interviews to NPR and other broadcast outlets. On March 22, 2007, in a stump talk barely noted in the United States, one of the candidates for president of France, François Bayrou, called for a potential boycott of the Olympics if China did not assist in altering Sudan's stance (Keaten 2007). Even at this early stage, other candidates for the French presidency seemed to concur in the idea of a Darfur-related Olympics action.

But the most noticeable step occurred when Mia Farrow and her son, Ronan, published an opinion piece in the *Wall Street Journal* (2007). Reeves had had long discussions, as a kind of tutor on Darfur, with the actress, a goodwill ambassador for UNESCO and a committed Sudan activist before the essay's publication. The essay, not surprisingly titled "The 'Genocide Olympics,'" repeated much that was in Reeves's campaign manifestos and analyses. "[S]tate-owned China National Petroleum Corp.—an official partner of the upcoming Olympic Games—owns the largest shares in each of Sudan's two major oil consortia. The Sudanese government uses as much as 80% of proceeds from those sales to fund its brutal Janjaweed proxy militia and purchase their instruments of destruction: bombers, assault helicopters, armored vehicles and small arms, most of them of Chinese manufacture. Airstrips constructed and operated by the Chinese have been used to launch bombing campaigns on villages."

Then the Farrows introduced a new point—one that also likely originated with Reeves—that turned the rhetorical heat up by more than a few notches. They aimed a verbal volley at the producer Steven Spielberg who had been contracted to orchestrate and produce the opening and closing ceremonies for the 2008 Olympics. "Does Mr. Spielberg really want to go down in history as the Leni Riefenstahl of the Beijing Games? Do the various television sponsors around the world want to share in that shame? Because they will. Unless, of course, all of them add their singularly well-positioned voices to the growing calls for Chinese action to end the slaughter in Darfur."

Bringing Spielberg into the frame seemed to instantly alter the dynamic of the campaign. In a sense, it meant, for Reeves, a slight loss of control of the narrative. All of a sudden, this was now a Hollywood celebrity campaign. A great reputation (Spielberg's) seemed on the line. Diffusion spiked as more and more newspapers carried elements of the story. The *Washington Times*, a frequent critic of China, found the Olympic platform a suitable vehicle for their views. Nat Hentoff wrote for them as follows:

> It astonishes me that the same Mr. Spielberg so admirably founded the Shoah foundation that records the testimony of the survivors of the Nazi Holocaust. How can he fail to make any connection with Shoah and the holocaust in Darfur?
>
> The Farrows also ask whether "the various television sponsors [of the Beijing Olympics] want to share in that shame" of the host's complicity in genocide along with such American corporate sponsors of the games as Johnson and Johnson, Coca-Cola, General Electric and McDonald's. (Hentoff 2007)

By mid-2007, the campaign sparked by Reeves and reinforced by Farrow was beginning to be visible in many contexts. The world's largest mutual fund, Fidelity Investments, slashed its stake in PetroChina amid pressure to sell shares in companies doing business in Sudan (*Wall Street Journal* 2007). In May, more than 100 members of the United States' House of Representatives sent a joint letter to China's President Hu Jintao, urging him to use his influence with the Sudanese government. The letter concluded on a Reeves-like note: "It would be a disaster for China if the Games were to be marred by protests . . . Already there are calls to boycott what is increasingly being described as the 2008 Genocide Olympics" (U.S. House Committee on Foreign Affairs 2007).

Athletes also joined the campaign. A reserve player on the National Basketball Association's Cleveland Cavaliers, Ira Newble, inspired by an article about Reeves in *USA Today,* convinced his teammates to join in a plea to the government of China: "We, as basketball players in the N.B.A. and as potential athletes in the 2008 Summer Olympic Games in Beijing, cannot look on with indifference to the massive human suffering and destruction that continue in the Darfur region of Sudan" (Beck 2007). And in July, Joey Cheek, a speed-skating medalist from the 2006 Winter Olympics, delivered to the Chinese Embassy in Washington 42,000 signatures on a petition from the Save Darfur Coalition. He proposed leading a group of American and Chinese athletes on a trip to Sudan. A column in the *New York Times* celebrated his idealism (Araton 2007).

In July 2007, two scholars from Harvard, one of whom had previously worked with the Chinese government, wrote an op-ed piece for the *Boston Globe,* later reprinted in the *International Herald Tribune,* criticizing "some in the West" who were labeling Beijing 2008 as the Genocide Olympics (Qian and Wu 2007). "Is China really turning a cold shoulder to the humanitarian crisis in Darfur," they asked, or, as they suggested, "has the explosive charge of complicity in genocide blinded observers to China's aid and quiet diplomacy in Sudan?" "In the face of increasing pressure from the international community, China may consider bolder options," but "China's principle of exerting influence but not interfering and imposing is consistent with African practice, and the final political decision will have to be made by Africans." A few days later Liu Guijin, China's special envoy to Darfur, criticized American politicians who, he suggested, had "unfairly played up the Darfur issue to burnish their moral credentials amid the presidential election campaigns." Those who linked Darfur with the Olympics "were either ignorant of reality or steeped in obsolete cold war ideology" (Dickie 2007). And the same week, Steven Spielberg made it known that he might resign his appointment as artistic director of the opening ceremonies if he did not receive a satisfactory response to the letter he had earlier sent to China's president (BBC News 2007).

Controlling the Narrative

I mentioned earlier in this chapter that a platform is defined in part by the modes available to defend it from appropriation. Copyright and trademark laws offer a fierce and aggressive way to protect the Olympic platform from certain contenders who are usually but not exclusively commercial "parasites," as is discussed earlier. I have suggested as well that enhanced physical security (protecting Web sites from hacking) also serve this function. Far more intriguing and interesting, however, are efforts by the dominant players (the IOC, China or BOCOG and the sponsors in this case) to control the discourse and discourage counternarratives. Here again the case study of the "Genocide Olympics" is illustrative.

The consequences of the *Wall Street Journal* essay by the Farrows demonstrated that the launching of a campaign does not guarantee control of how it will be carried and diffused. Reeves's narrative was carefully constructed and phrased, with specific objectives and specific means of persuasion. It was to be a "grass roots"-supported narrative, with a broad international base. It would engage and energize people around the world concerned with Darfur (and the relationship between Sudan and China). The option of boycott as remedy would be sidelined. However, the publication of the *Wall Street Journal* piece subtly shifted the campaign. Mia Farrow's fame launched the concept of tarring 2008 as the "Genocide Olympics" to a wider audience, as indicated by the examples I have given. But despite (or perhaps because of) the success of Reeves and others who initiated the campaign, control of the narrative had been weakened. At the outset they could influence almost every related element in seizing the Olympics platform. Now the platform of Darfur and the Olympics had plural authors.

A different tale began to be told, and, in a way, the shaming seemed to begin to have consequences. China (and Steven Spielberg) sought to regain control of the narrative for themselves. In mid-April 2007, Spielberg's spokesperson, Marvin Levy, announced that the producer had written a four-page letter to the Chinese president, Hu Jintao, urging him to take further action regarding Sudan and Darfur. At the same time, China—while denying any connection to the Genocide Olympics campaign, or to Spielberg's letter—announced that they were sending a special ambassador to Sudan.[3] These events led to a journalistic denouement—at least a temporary one—on the front page of the

New York Times, in an April 13 story by Helene Cooper that realigned the Olympics narrative, placed Steven Spielberg in a good light, and also shifted the dynamic from the perspective of the government of China by suggesting political movement.[4] The story was entitled: "Darfur Collides with Olympics, And China Yields." The following day, it was republished in the *International Herald Tribune,* with the headline "China acts on Sudan after Hollywood push." According to one observer, Cooper, instead of writing about the complexities of the issue, "chose instead to write what seemed a jazzier story: 'Hollywood vs. Hollywood,' with a happy ending in which Steven Spielberg ends up wearing the White Hat and with a single letter to the Chinese government does what no one else in the world can do, with little Mia Farrow by his side."

Two days later, Sudan agreed to allow UN support for African Union troops. This was by no means the end, hardly even the beginning of the end. For Sudan had not yet agreed to the entry of UN troops, which many believed to be necessary for any possibility of resolution. The monitoring of China, of Spielberg, and the rest would no doubt continue. Whether the narrative of a Genocide Olympics would survive— or how it would continue to diffuse—remained to be seen.[5]

There is hardly a more important set of narratives for the twenty-first century than those concerning the role of China in the world and as an internally-governing power. And, as a consequence, there are few narratives that so many actors seek to shape with such fervency. In this chapter, I have concentrated on global civil society groups as actors in this narrative-shaping effort, but it is clearly a process in which multiple other bodies have a stake as well: states, regions, corporations, and large scale movements. For all of these, the 2008 Olympics represents a great opportunity—and both the IOC and China are mindful of this fact. Russell Leigh Moses, professor of politics and international relations at Renmin University of China, put it as follows: "Beijing is spending as much effort on controlling the environment for the Olympics as it is on construction. For the sports authority this is about gaining as much gold as possible. For the party, it is about the greatness of their rule. For the construction team, it is about image and showcase" (Marquand 2006).

The drama of constructing representations of China have underscored what might be called the jurisprudence of platforms: who constructs them and who has access; the mode of controlling their use or defending them; and the modes of seeking access. Over decades, the way of thinking of traditional platforms has been well articulated. There are ways of conceptualizing the structure of broadcasting and the press, thinking about certain public spaces and even zones of transnational discourse. In all these instances, beneath notions of rules and practices, there is the issue of who has what degree of control over the narratives that define our lives. As advocacy groups seek new platforms to advance their messages, understanding of mechanisms by which this takes place becomes crucial. The Beijing Olympics is a site which can aid in this understanding, one in which the role of civil society groups in the shaping of narratives and the effort to seize control of them has been a sign of the increasing role of these groups on the global stage.

NOTES

1. See Hoberman 1986.

2. Before 2006, the People's Olympics was called the Humanistic Olympics. However, the awkward phrasing of this term, as well as its semantic signals to related concepts, such as humanitarianism, resulted in a change to the People's Olympics. The problems might have been even greater without this change.

3. The Press Trust of India (2007) reported that "China's latest attempts to pressurise Sudan to allow UN peacekeepers in Darfur is [sic] partly a result of the efforts of Hollywood actress Mia Farrow and film-maker Stephen [sic] Spielberg . . ."

4. Reeves sought to keep the pressure on Spielberg. See Reeves (2007b): "What are the obligations of artists in the face of genocide? Spielberg and the others are at two removes from the ethnically targeted killing in Darfur; they are helping with the Olympics that China's government cares so much about, and China is helping Khartoum. But how do we assess degrees of complicity in the ultimate human crime?"

5. Cooper's story was republished in abbreviated form in Scotland. There were editorials in the *Austin American-Statesman* and in Syracuse, New York, and New York *Newsday*; Daniel Schorr discussed Spielberg's role on National Public Radio's *Weekend Edition*.

REFERENCES

ANOC. 1984. Mexico Declaration.

Araton, Harvey. 2007. Good Guy Is Forgotten in Bad Week for Sports. *New York Times,* July 31, Sports section, D1.

Australian. 2002. IOC warns China on Human Rights Pledge. April 26.

Barney, R. K., K. B. Wamsley, S. G. Martyn, and G. MacDonald. 1998. *Global and Cultural Critique: Problematizing the Olympic Games. Fourth International Symposium for Olympic Research.* London, Ontario: International Centre for Olympic Studies, University of Western Ontario.

BBC News. 2007. Spielberg "May Quit Olympic Role." July 27.

BBC Sport. 2001. New Boss to Cut Olympic Growth. Available at http://news.bbc.co.uk/sport1/hi/front_page/1511685.stm (accessed May 29, 2007).

Beck, Howard. 2007. Cavalier Seeks Players' Support for Darfur. *New York Times,* May 16.

BOCOG. n.d. Beijing 2008 Olympic Marketing Plan Overview. Available at http://en.beijing2008.cn/bocog/sponsors/n214077622.shtml (accessed July 24, 2007).

BOCOG. 2005. Concepts of the Beijing Olympic Games: Green Olympics, Hi-tech Olympics, People's Olympics. Available at http://en.beijing2008.cn/32/87/article211928732.shtml (accessed July 2, 2007).

Cardinal Kung Foundation. n.d. Collected Testimony of Joseph M. C. Kung before Federal, State, and City Legislative Bodies. Available at http://www.cardinalkungfoundation.org/testimony/index.htm.

Cardinal Kung Foundation. 2005. Petition to China to Release All the Imprisoned Roman Catholic Religious and Faithful and to Exonerate All Their Criminal Charges, Living and Deceased. Available at http://www.cardinalkungfoundation.org/articles/petition2.htm (accessed May 30, 2007).

Chinese Olympic Committee. 2004. Beijing 2008 Olympic Games Licensing Programme. March 27. http://en.olympic.cn/coc/marketing/2004-03-27/121867.html (accessed July 24, 2007).

Cooper, Helene. 2007. Darfur Collides with Olympics, and China Yields. *New York Times,* Washington, diplomatic memo, April 13.

Cullen, Kevin. 2007. Genocide Games. *Boston Globe,* March 25, D1.

Davis, Robert N. 1996. Ambushing the Olympic Games. *Villanova Sports and Entertainment Law Journal* 3 (2): 423–42.

Dayan, Daniel. 2005. A Systematic Approach to Expressive Events. Annenberg Scholar's Lecture. Annenberg School for Communication, University of Pennsylvania, November 8.

Dickie, Mure. 2007. China Defends its Stance on Darfur. *Financial Times,* Asia edition, July 28, 4.

Farrow, Ronan, and Mia Farrow. 2007. The Genocide Olympics. *Wall Street Journal,* March 28.

Hentoff, Nat. 2007. Khartoum's Enablers in Beijing. *Washington Times,* April 16, A21.

Hoberman, John M. 1986. The Olympic Crisis: Sport, Politics, and the Moral Order. New York: Aristide Caratzas.

Hoberman, John M. 1997. Darwin's Athletes: How Sport Has Damaged Black America and Preserved the Myth of Race. Boston: Houghton Mifflin.

House of Commons. 2005–6. London Olympics Bill. Available at http://www.publications.parliament.uk/pa/cm200506/cmbills/045/06045.i-iv.html (accessed July 2, 2007).

Hua, Meng. 2004. An Analysis of the Role of National Culture in 2008 Beijing Olympic Games. Available at http://www.c2008.org/rendanews/english_te.asp?id=876.

Human Rights Watch. n.d. Introduction: China Olympics Watch. http://www.hrw.org/campaigns/china/beijing08/intro.htm (accessed July 24, 2007).

Hutzler, Charles. 2006. Hunger Strike Sends IOC into Tough Situation. Associated Press, February 26. Available at http://www.tibetanyouthcongress.org/news/newsupdate/italy11.htm (accessed May 29, 2007).

IOC. 2007. Olympic Charter. Available at http://multimedia.olympic.org/pdf/en_report_122.pdf.

Keaten, Jamey. 2007. Olympics Boycott Call Made at Rally, 3 Candidates in France Seek to Pressure China. Associated Press. In *South Florida Sun Sentinel,* Broward edition, March 22, 17A.

Large, David Clay. 2007. *Nazi Games: the Olympics of 1936.* New York: W.W. Norton.

Marquand, Robert. 2006. Hopes for Change Hung on '08 Olympics. *Christian Science Monitor,* August 7. Available at http://www.csmonitor.com/2006/0807/p06s02-woap.html.

Mastrocola, Paul. 1995. The Lord of the Rings: The Role of Olympic Site Selection as a Weapon against Human Rights Abuses: China's Bid for the 2000 Olympics. *Boston College Third World Law Journal* 15:41–70.

Montgomery, Kathryn C. 1990. Target, Prime Time: Advocacy Groups and the Struggle over Entertainment Television. New York: Oxford University Press.

Morgan, William J. 1995. Cosmopolitanism, Olympism, and Nationalism: A Critical Interpretation of Coubertin's Ideal of International Sporting Life. *OLYMPIKA: The International Journal of Olympic Studies* 4:79–92.

Nafziger, James A. R. 1992. International Sports Law: A Replay of Characteristics and Trends. *American Journal of International Law* 86 (3): 489–512.

Olympic Watch. 2006. Two Years until Beijing 2008: IOC Fails, Activists call on Athletes, Sponsors to Act. August 7. Available at http://www.olympicwatch.org/news.php?id=100.

Payne, Michael. 2006. *Olympic Turnaround: How the Olympic Games Stepped back from the Brink of Extinction to Become the World's Best Known Brand.* Westport, CT: Praeger.

People's Daily Online. 2006. One More Step towards Joint Korean Team. September 7.

Play Fair at the Olympics Campaign 2004. 2004. Background. Available at www.fairolympics.org/background.html.

PlayFair 2008. 2007. No Medal for the Olympics on Labour Rights. Available at http://www.playfair2008.org/docs/playfair_2008-report.pdf.

Press Trust of India. 2007. China's "Turnaround" on Darfur Links to Spielberg: Report. April 13.

Qian, Jason, and Anne Wu. 2007. Playing the Blame Game in Africa. *International Herald Tribune,* July 24.

Qin Xiaoying. 2007. Harmonious Confluence of Ideas at Olympics. *China Daily,* July 18.

Reeves, Eric. 2006. Push China, Save Darfur. *Boston Globe,* December 17, K9.

Reeves, Eric. 2007a. An Open Letter to Darfur Activists and Advocates. February 11. Available at http://www.sudanreeves.org/Article152.html.

Reeves, Eric. 2007b. Artists Abetting Genocide? *Boston Globe,* April 16, A11.

Schmitz, Jason K. 2005. Ambush Marketing: The Off-Field Competition at the Olympic Games. *Northwestern Journal of Technology and Intellectual Property* 3 (2): 203–8.

United Nations. 2006. Security Council Expands Mandate of UN Mission in Sudan to Include Darfur, Adopting Resolution 1706 by Vote of 12 in Favour, with 3 Abstaining. Security Council, 5519th Meeting, August 31. Available at http://www.un.org/News/Press/docs/2006/sc8821.doc.htm (accessed May 30, 2007).

U.S. House Committee on Foreign Affairs. 2007. Lantos, House Colleagues Send Strong Message to Chinese President, Demand Action on Darfur. May 9. Available at http://foreignaffairs.house.gov/press_display.asp?id= 345 (accessed July 24, 2007).

Vancouver 2010. Frequently Asked Questions about the Olympic Brand. Available at http://www.vancouver2010.com/en/LookVancouver2010/ ProtectingBrand/OlympicBrandFAQs/.

Wall Street Journal. 2007. Fidelity Prunes Its Stake in PetroChina. May 17.

Washington Post. 2006. China and Darfur: The Genocide Olympics. December 14, A30.

II

Precedents and Perspectives

The Public Diplomacy of the Modern Olympic Games and China's Soft Power Strategy

Nicholas J. Cull

In 1965 a retired American diplomat turned college dean named Edmund Gullion unveiled a new piece of terminology to help his countrymen conceptualize the role of communications in foreign relations. That term was *public diplomacy.* He and his team fleshed out the concept in a brochure for their new Edward R. Murrow Center for Public Diplomacy at Tufts University's Fletcher School of Diplomacy as follows:

> Public diplomacy . . . deals with the influence of public attitudes on the formation and execution of foreign policies. It encompasses dimensions of international relations beyond traditional diplomacy; the cultivation by governments of public opinion in other countries; the interaction of private groups and interests in one country with another; the reporting of foreign affairs and its impact on policy; communication between those whose job is communication, as diplomats and foreign correspondents; and the process of intercultural communications. (Publicdiplomacy.org n.d.).[1]

It took more than forty years, the transformation of the world as a result of the end of the Cold War, the global communications revolution, and the crisis following September 11, 2001 for the term to gain real currency outside the United States. Today it is ubiquitous. Most states and many nonstate international actors either use the English term or have a close equivalent to signify the task of seeking to advance foreign policy by engaging foreign publics. The concept is frequently linked to a second American addition to the international lexicon—Soft Power—which is Joseph S. Nye's term (2004) for the contribution that attractive culture and values can make to an actor's ability to operate in the world. This chapter will look at the evolution of a key venue of contemporary public diplomacy—the modern Olympic Games—and the soft power policies deployed in recent years by the People's Republic of China, and consider how they have converged in relation to the Beijing Olympics of 2008.

While Ed Gullion's use of the term *public diplomacy* was new in 1965, the phenomenon he described was not. International actors have sought to engage foreign publics for as long as publics have had any impact on statecraft. A simple taxonomy of public diplomacy divides its practice into five distinct and well established activities: listening to foreign publics and refining policy accordingly; advocating to promote a particular policy before a foreign public; engaging in cultural diplomacy to export particular practices and build good feeling abroad; exchanging diplomacy and building networks to develop links and facilitate mutual knowledge; and finally, using international broadcasting to provide news to foreign publics who might otherwise be denied access to balanced information.

Sports can figure in all areas of public diplomacy. Sports events are branded by hosts to represent particular meanings, and the stars of these events are regularly used as advocates for particular messages. Sports can be a cultural export in their own right and the spectacle of hosting or winning at a major sporting event can raise or maintain the profile of an actor. Sports are an ideal subject of exchanges; the shared experience of viewing or participating in an event with foreign publics is a powerful tool for people-to-people relationship building in world affairs. The transmission of sports by international broadcasters is a time-honored way to attract audiences. Finally, the wise practitioner of public diplomacy listens to world opinion, notes the extent to which his target audience cares about sport, identifies the specific sports which capture the collective imagination, and develops his sporting diplomacy accordingly. As will be seen, all these dimensions of public diplomacy have played a part in the development of the modern Olympic Games, though not always in the way that the International

Olympic Committee (IOC) or the host of any particular Games might wish. In fact, the entire modern Olympic project may be conceptualized as an exercise in public diplomacy.

The Olympics as Public Diplomacy for Peace

In the beginning, Pierre de Coubertin conceived his revival of the ancient Olympics as a form of diplomacy through culture with the hope that nations might compete in peace and thereby overcome their differences. His International Olympic Committee would be a foreign policy actor in its own right, advocating international brotherhood. The games would be above politics and ideology. Chapter five of the Olympic Charter holds that: "No kind of demonstration or political, religious or racial propaganda is permitted in the Olympic areas" (IOC 2007). Symbols, flags, and invented traditions accreted around Coubertin's original idea creating what might be a resource for any state wishing to demonstrate its attachment to universal values of sportsmanship and peace (Espy 1979).

As the Olympic Games evolved, a number of practices were added to try to underline the international peace building intent of the Games, including a new format for the closing ceremony—first seen in the Cold War Games in Melbourne in 1956—in which the athletes mingle freely together rather than parade in national groups (IOC n.d.). A second strategy was the creation of the Coubertin medal to recognize true sportsmanship and a value above the prize of simply being "faster, higher or stronger" than other competitors. The first winner was Eugenio Monti, an Italian bobsledder at the Innsbruck Winter Games of 1964, who selflessly loaned a bolt from his own sled to repair that of a British competitor, Tony Nash. Nash went on to win the gold (*Washington Post* 1964; IOC 2006).

The idea of restoring international brotherhood, the rubric of the ancient Olympic Truce, and new ideals of global citizenship were prominently featured in the host's rhetoric during the Athens Games of 2004—the first Games of the post-9/11 era (Roche 2006). But appeals to brotherhood and internationalism, while present at every Olympic Games and an essential part of the athletes' experience, are usually drowned out by more dominant stories, the foremost being the quest for national prestige.

The Olympics and the Public Diplomacy
of Prestige

It is ironic that simply by emphasizing the coming together of *nations* Coubertin also ensured that national prestige would be at stake. The games he imagined as an antidote to war soon became its analogue, as the display of national physical prowess was used to increase the prestige of a country and gain influence in the world as a result. The first modern Games—the Athens Olympics of 1896—have in fact been blamed for *provoking* a war. Greek diplomat Demetrius Kaklamanos argued that the heady experience of his country's hosting the Games and especially the surge of nationalism sparked by Sprio Louys winning the marathon led directly to its launching of the ill-starred war with Turkey in 1897.[2]

In the aftermath of the Great War, nationalist and revolutionary societies like Mussolini's Italy and Lenin's Soviet Union emphasized sport and physical culture as symbols of the virility of their political system, and achievement in Olympic competition became a profound concern of governments.[3] Similar attitudes could also be found in more democratic cultures. In the run-up to the Antwerp Games of 1920 the British Olympian and war hero A. N. S. Strode-Jackson declared:

> If the war has taught us anything it has proved the value of propaganda: knowing this, we should remember, always, that there is no British propaganda so valuable as the perpetuation of the old idea that, on the field of sport, British prestige is supreme, and that none can outrank us in stamina and virility. (Jackson 1919)

As the emphasis on national prestige increased, so the Games suffered. The Paris Games of 1924 were marred by a series of incidents which suggested that the spirit of international sportsmanship was in jeopardy: anti-American booing and fist fights in the crowd at the Olympic rugby match; a French boxer, Roger Brousse, biting his British and Argentine opponents; and an extraordinary fracas between an Italian swordsman and a Hungarian judge, which culminated in a challenge to a duel. The London *Times* responded by proclaiming the doom of the entire Olympic movement. But for all the bad sportsmanship the movement survived (*Times* 1924a; 1924b; 1924c).

Notable examples of the Olympic competition becoming a stage to display the prestige of a nation include the various appearances of

Hungarians at the Melbourne Games of 1956, which followed hard on the Soviet crushing of the Hungarian uprising. Each event became a celebration of national pride and defiance of the Soviet Union, culminating in the notorious "blood in the water" water polo match between Hungary and the USSR. To the enduring delight of the Hungarian people, their team not only beat the Russians but went on to win the Gold medal in that sport (*New York Times* 1956).

However, the prestige of victory in an Olympic event was soon held as nothing against the kudos of actually hosting the Games. The Olympics became a major mechanism to make or remake the reputation of a city, region or entire country. When in 1920 a small group of Southern Californian businessmen set out to Europe to bring the Olympics to Los Angeles (the Games finally came in 1932), they found it necessary to produce a globe and point out the location of their city.[4] Their Olympic bid quite literally put their city on the map. The 1976 Summer Games in Montreal were planned to provide a boost for the province of Quebec through an exercise in regional public diplomacy. Whatever their contribution to the international standing of the city and its region, however, the costs outweighed the benefits. Montreal did not finish paying its Olympic debt until December 2006. Local branding has been especially apparent in bids to host the Winter Olympics, which in only one case—Oslo 1952—have been held in a national capital.[5] The Summer Games are routinely used not merely to promote a particular city but to rebrand an entire nation.

The classic case of a national agenda emerging in an Olympic bid is that of the Berlin Olympics of 1936. IOC awarded Berlin the Games in 1931 as a gesture to mark Germany's return to the community of nations following the Great War, which had prevented the Games scheduled for Berlin in 1916. They came as an invaluable windfall for Adolf Hitler who, on coming to power in 1933, swiftly redirected plans for the Games to showcase his regime. While in modern lore the big story of the Games was the success of the African American athlete Jesse Owens and the attending disruption to Hitler's narrative of Aryan supremacy, Germany still won more medals than all other nations present combined (Mandell 1987). The prestige associated with the mounting of the Berlin Games gave sufficient boost to the regime's image at home and abroad that Hitler planned to establish Germany as a permanent site for the Games. This said, the Olympics—like the lavish musicals that played in Nazi movie theaters—may have advanced Hilter's purposes only by providing a welcome distraction. At a deeper level their fundamental message of sportsmanship and competition in peace played against his strategy of readying his nation for war and intimidating Germany's potential adversaries. Other totalitarian regimes have also queued up to host the games. In 1935 Japan won the right to host the 1940 event as part of the celebration of the 2600th anniversary of their royal house, and would have done so but for the outbreak of war in Asia. Mussolini's Italy made an unsuccessful bid to host the Games in Rome in 1944.[6]

Following World War II each of the Games seemed conceived to serve a transparent public diplomacy agenda. Both London in 1948 and Helsinki in 1952 presented their Games as gestures of national recovery. Recovery was relative in the case of London, as athletes were asked to bring their own food because of the persistence of wartime rationing (Danzig 1948). The 1956 Games in Melbourne were intended as a coming out party for Australia, and international press coverage about behind-schedule buildings in the run-up to the games gave ample evidence of that country's need to update its sheep-and-bush-hats image in the world. Fortunately, the Games hit their mark. Both the 1960 Rome and 1964 Tokyo Summer Games allowed nations of the wartime Axis to showcase their postwar societies. In Japan, the symbolism was underlined by the selection of Yoshinori Sakai, an athlete born in Hiroshima on the day the atomic bomb dropped, to light the torch at the opening ceremony (*New York Times* 1964). Mexico City planned its 1968 Games to showcase a newly modernized nation with an emphasis on exotic "Op Art" designs and monumental structures, while the Munich Olympics of 1972 were intended to introduce postwar, post-Nazi West Germany, with a sunshine logo and *freundlichspiel* (Happy Games) motto (Zolov 2004; *New York Times* 1972).

Moscow in 1980 and Los Angeles in 1984 asserted rather than rebranded their host nations, which added to the Cold War logic of each superpower boycotting the other's event (Hazan 1982). The Seoul Olympics of 1988 and the Barcelona Games of 1992 returned to the motive of rebranding a society in transition. In the case of Barcelona the transition was at a rather more advanced stage. The IOC awarded the Games to Barcelona in 1986, the same year that Spain joined the European Community. The Games provided an excellent pretext to invite the world to meet the new Spain. Atlanta's bid for the 1996 Games became a gesture to mark the achievement of the American South in transcending its history of racial bitterness. The legacy of Martin Luther King was cited everywhere in the publicity materials, which included abundant allusions to "the dream" of King's "I have a dream" speech (Reid 1990). In a similar vein the Sydney Games of 2000 provided a stage on which Australia could present a new multicultural image and, in its opening and closing ceremonies, pay tribute to the heritage of its indigenous people (Waitt 1999).

The prospect of being an Olympic host tempts every emerging power sooner or later, and it did not take long for China to catch the Olympic bug. At the start of their very first Games since the Cultural Revolution, the Los Angeles Games in 1984, the People's Republic of China called a press conference and announced its intent to host the Games in 2000, thereby beginning the chain of events that would lead to Beijing 2008 (Miller 1984). Yet there is much in the actual experience of hosting the Games that should worry China.

The Olympics and Competing Public
Diplomacy Agendas

As the Olympics emerged as a spectacle to which a diplomatic objective could be tied, so opponents of that objective (and adherents of any objective seeking world-wide publicity) had a mechanism to advance their agendas also. As in the case of national prestige, the Berlin Olympics showed the way. Hitler's persecution of German Jews sparked a boycott movement which split the U.S. athletic establishment and prompted many Jewish athletes from around the world to stay away. The Nazi regime made some concessions to world opinion by removing many anti-Semitic posters and playing down the increasing military presence in German life, but the Games had drawn attention to negative aspects of life in the Third Reich.[7]

Politics swirled around the Games of the Cold War, and the Melbourne event was especially badly hit. China stayed away to protest the participation of Taiwan; Egypt, Lebanon and Iraq stayed away because of the Anglo-French invasion of Suez; while the Netherlands, Switzerland and Spain boycotted the Games to protest the Soviet invasion of Hungary.

From the early 1960s and for thirty years thereafter the issue of the participation of South Africa rubbed raw, prompting boycotts by many African nations. Boycotts were threatened to keep Rhodesia out of Munich and—unsuccessfully—to exclude New Zealand from Montreal (a punishment for a rugby tour of South Africa). The tit-for-tat boycotts of

1980 and 1984 represented the high-water mark of nonparticipation as a form of Olympic public diplomacy (Hoberman 1986).

On occasion domestic political agendas have seized the Olympic spotlight. The run-up to the Mexico Games saw an abortive attempt by African American athletes to organize a boycott of the U.S. team as a protest against American racism. The debate led directly to the famous incident in which American 200 meter runners Tommie Smith and John Carlos performed their black power protest on the winner's rostrum (Fradkin 1967; Allen 1967). Within the host nation, Mexican students sought to take advantage of the presence of the world's media to present their own message of opposition to their authoritarian government. Their protests in the months leading up to the Games culminated in the so-called Tlatelolco massacre of October 2, 1968, during which the Mexican army opened fire on student protestors and bystanders alike. Deaths numbered in the hundreds (Weiner 2004). Domestic pressure for reform also played a role in the Seoul Olympics, though in this case the government accelerated the reform process to head off a major incident around the Games. The country that hosted the Games in 1988 was very different from that which had planned the bid at the end of the 1970s (Manheim 1990).

Munich 1972 brought the most blatant and brutal attempt to piggyback an alternate agenda on the organizer's party when Palestinian terrorists kidnapped and murdered members of the Israeli Olympic team. The disaster was not wholly unconnected to Germany's hopes for the Games. Arguably, the lack of security at the Olympic village and bungled police response to the crisis were by-products of West Germany's eagerness to live down its authoritarian stereotype (*One Day in September* 1999).

The Cold War was fought out in rival propaganda and public diplomacy operations from Moscow and Washington. In the Soviet case these could be quite blatant: for example, their effort to appropriate the Games in Helsinki 1952 when a festival operated by the Communist front organization—the World League for Democratic Youth—sought to spread propaganda among Olympic crowds and athletes (Axelsson 1952). In 1984 the KGB ran a covert campaign to undermine the Los Angeles Games. KGB disinformation operations included circulating a story that security in Los Angeles would include surveillance by Israel's *Mossad* and the anonymous mailing to twenty African and Asian Olympic committees of faked Ku Klux Klan leaflets threatening nonwhite athletes who attended the games. One read: "African Monkeys! A grand welcome awaits you in Los Angeles! We have been training for the games by shooting at black moving targets." Thanks to speedy countermeasures, none of the nations targeted by the Soviet campaign withdrew from the Games.[8]

For its part, the United States has always been ready to use the Olympic story to haul public diplomacy freight. In 1952 the State Department, eager to counter the United States' reputation for racism, ensured that black American athletes figured prominently in U.S. international publicity around the Games (National Archives ca. 1951). In a similar vein, during the Oslo Winter Olympics U.S. diplomats sought to embarrass the Communist world by emphasizing the presence of one official minder for each Eastern bloc athlete (National Archives 1952). The United States managed to piggyback on Tokyo in 1964 by using the opening ceremony to showcase its communications satellite, Syncom 3, and mounting the first trans-pacific telecast (Gould 1964). During the Munich Games the U.S. government's Voice of America reported Soviet achievements only by crediting the home republic of the particular athlete—billing sprinter Valeri Borzov as Ukrainian and gymnast Olga Korbut as Byelorussian—to show support for the claims of constituent nationalities and as a gesture of defiance against the claims of the Soviet state (National Archives 1972). In 1984 the United States sought to counter the impact of the boycott by boosting its efforts to help poorer nations compete in the Olympics. The CEO of Madison Square Garden, David "Sonny" Werblin, chaired a Private Sector Sports Committee for the United States Information Agency, which raised nearly $1 million in donations to bring African athletes to the Games (Ronald Reagan Presidential Library 1984). The most recent U.S. use of the Olympics in public diplomacy is its employment of Michelle Kwan as a special "public diplomacy envoy" (Armour 2005).

By the turn of the millennium it had become clear that even if an Olympic Games dodged attempts by others to piggyback, any number of associated events could disrupt the intended meaning of the Games. Scandals around doping, cheating, and lack of sportsmanship among participants or their respective national media all posed threats to the planned message of the official event. Revelations of malpractice within the process of selecting Olympic venues—specifically a bribery scandal associated with the successful bid by Salt Lake City to host the 2002 Winter Olympics—posed further problems (*Olympic Review* 1999; Roche 2002). The run-up to the Athens Olympics of 2004 was reported as a suspense story focused on whether the Greeks would be able to cope and deliver their buildings on time. Athens made its deadlines but the city's pollution problems became a significant negative story to undermine the Greek government's agenda of national self enhancement. On the eve of the Games the Worldwide Fund for Nature pointed to extra pollution arising from the Olympic construction effort (Environmental News Service 2004).

All of the foregoing should be enough to set Coubertin spinning in his grave and give pause to any potential host. That China would advance its bid regardless can be seen either as rank hubris or admirable self-confidence in its own ability to confront the Olympic challenges head-on and still deliver a Games that fulfills national and international goals. But the onrush of China's public diplomacy has been such that it is all but unimaginable that China could resist the chance to host so prestigious an event.

The Roots of Chinese Public Diplomacy

The Beijing Olympics is merely the latest phase in a sustained Chinese government campaign to woo the world and engage foreign publics, which writer Joshua Kurlantzick has dubbed China's Charm Offensive (Kurlantzick 2007). While this policy is new in its full-blown form, its roots lie deep in Chinese political culture. Many elements of public diplomacy have great antiquity in China. Confucius spoke of attracting through virtue: "It is for this reason that when distant subjects are unsubmissive one cultivates one's moral quality in order to attract them, and once they have come one makes them content" (*Analects of Confucius*). He argued that an image of virtue and morality was the foundation of a stable state. The emperors of old certainly understood the importance of maintaining their image at home and maintaining the "tributary" relationships with the satellite kingdoms around their borders (Qing 2001). At an interpersonal level, the Chinese concepts translated in the west as "face" (*Lian*, a concept of personal honor and moral worth, and *Mianzi*, a concept of social prestige), echo the enduring concern of nations for their prestige and the contemporary discovery of soft power (Ho 1976). These cultural concerns are fertile soil for a contemporary effort to improve the nation's international standing by projecting or maintaining a favorable image. The traditional term for such work is *dui wai xuan chuan* or *wai xuan,* meaning "external propaganda." The term has none of the negatives attending to western usage of propaganda (Wang Y. forthcoming).

Historically China has learned the importance of public diplomacy and "external propaganda" the hard way. In the late nineteenth and early twentieth century the country was targeted by masters of the art including the European empires, American churches, Bolshevik agitators, and the Japanese Empire. Would-be leaders in post-Imperial China soon recognized the value of modern communication methods to establish their legitimacy both at home and abroad. The nationalist regime of Chiang Kai-shek became adept at appealing to American public opinion during World War II, while the seasoned revolutionary Mao Zedong understood the value of international propaganda even during his time at bay in Yan'an province, using foreign journalists such as Edgar Snow to take the story of his Long March to the outside world (Hamilton 1988).

Mao's launch of the People's Republic of China in 1949 can be compared to a rebranding, with dramatic claims of a new era—most famously that "the Chinese People have stood up" (1949)—coupled with rigid control over access to information about life within China for domestic and foreign audiences alike. Favored journalists were allowed to view China—selectively—and the state published a number of journals such as *Beijing Review* to showcase its achievements. Major international campaigns of the Mao period included a perennial battle to undermine the reputation of Taiwan, and various activities designed to extend the revolution overseas, first around East Asia and then, in the 1970s, in Africa and Latin America. Radio Beijing was an archetypal propaganda station, haranguing the world about the Chairman's monopoly on virtue. The opening of China in the 1970s saw a transition from carefully stage managed events, such as Nixon's visit to China or the gift of a succession of pandas to assorted heads of government, to a more recognizable participation in regular public diplomacy. The diplomatic tussle between China and Taiwan around the Montreal Olympics gave witness to a Chinese desire to establish a presence on the international sporting stage (Wang H. 2003).

In the wake of Mao's death, Deng Xiaoping swiftly opened China's doors to international exchange and tourism. In September 1981 the Reagan administration signed a new cultural exchange agreement with China, and interaction gathered pace (Sterba 1981). In 1983 the Ministry of Foreign Affairs opened an Information Department appointing one Qian Qicheng as its first spokesman (Wang Y. forthcoming). The following year, as the Chinese state placed increased emphasis on its international reputation, the world learned of that nation's desire to host the Beijing Olympics for the first time.

In 1989 the house of cards that was China's international reputation came crashing down with the negative images that issued from the repression of the protests in Tiananmen Square. In the aftermath of the crisis Beijing engaged the international public relations firm Hill and Knowlton to begin the process of rebuilding China's reputation (d'Hooghe 2005, 92). The parallel process of consolidation followed at home included the reconfiguration of domestic and international information work under a single State Council Information Office (SCIO), founded in 1991. Its declared purpose was to "promote China as a stable country in the process of reform, a China that takes good care of its population, including minorities, and works hard to reduce poverty." It was a foundation for future work (d'Hooghe 2005, 98–99).

Zhao Qizheng and Chinese Public
Diplomacy Since 1998

As the 1990s progressed, Beijing placed renewed emphasis on its international image, a process which included the revival of the Olympic bid. SCIO flourished under the dynamic leadership of Minister Zhao Qizheng, who led the office from 1998 to 2005. A former vice mayor of Shanghai (and hence part of the "Shanghai-clique" around Jiang Zemin), Zhao was unafraid to confront his country's international critics head on or to concede national error (Eckholm 1998). His international appearances included addressing the National Press Club in Washington in September 2000. From an early stage Zhao sought to avoid using the term *xuan chuan*, which would be translated with negative spin in the west as "propaganda," and described his work as "explaining" China [shuo ming] (Crowell and Hsieh 2000).[9] Zhao's determination to present China to the world was supported at the highest level, and in February 1999 President Jiang Zemin called for China to "establish a publicity capacity to exert an influence on world opinion that is as strong as China's international standing" (Kurlantzick 2007, 39). This led directly to a number of parallel policies, coordinated through the duel structure of the Communist Party and SCIO.[10]

One key problem facing Zhao Qizheng and his colleagues was the need to find an overarching concept to define China's approach to the world and to puncture talk in certain Western quarters of the Chinese threat. He found his answer in the term *peaceful rise* (*heping jueqi*), a phrase coined by thinker Zheng Bijian in 2003 and swiftly embraced by the Beijing government. The term was not ideal for translation—as China-watcher Joshua Cooper Ramo has noted, its coining sparked a brief debate over whether the concept of *jueqi* was best rendered as "surge" or "emergence," while the ideogram for the first part of the word suggested an earthquake—but peaceful rise stuck (Ramo 2007; Zheng 2005). By 2007 it had nevertheless been largely displaced by discourse focused not so much on China as on the international context it wished to promote: the concept of "building a harmonious world" (Li and Wang 2007).

The core of Chinese public diplomacy lies in deeds rather than words. China has developed a keen eye for prestige events and showpiece policy initiatives. One such event was the launch in October 2003 of China's first manned space flight. The achievement certainly played well at home—the primary audience—and in many locations overseas, although as *Times of India* noted, the launch used essentially forty-year-old technology. Its editorial dubbed the flight the "Great Creep Forward" (Banke 2003). More significantly China has launched major international aid and development initiatives, all couched in the rhetoric of "win-win" cooperation. China has already delivered much to Latin America, the Middle East, and most especially Africa, but claims to need nothing in return (Kurlantzick 2007, 44). It has been swift to build links with nations that are isolated from Western diplomacy. Its policy of "nonintervention" has enabled partnerships with Iran, Venezuela, and even Zimbabwe. And, in the last case, Chinese aid has included instruction in how effectively to jam opposition radio signals (*BBC Monitoring* 2006.) Despite the enmity these activities have sparked in the west, they have also played a role in advancing the country's international reputation, as have China's efforts to take a leadership role in the diplomacy around North Korean nuclear weapons (Shirk 2006).

Policies need to be publicized to have an impact, and Zhao Qizheng was swift to move to maximize their reach. Zhao, his colleagues and successors launched initiatives across the range of the five activities that characterize classic public diplomacy practice: listening, advocacy, cultural diplomacy, exchange, and international broadcasting. Zhao's whole approach and much of his rhetoric was couched as a response to what the world was saying about China. In June 2000 the minister solemnly warned a conference on Tibet that "the enemy is strong and we are weak."[11] China used polls to track its relationships. Innovations included a poll in 2005 jointly designed and administered with Japanese counterparts to survey the state of mutual opinion, which revealed that much work needed to be done to build trust between the two populations (Xinhua 2005b). Global polls suggested positive trends for China, as with the BBC/PIPA poll of late 2004 and early 2005 across twenty-two nations, which found that almost all believed China to be playing a more positive role than the United States in world affairs (Kurlantzick 2007, 9). But Beijing is not complacent. Recent fine-tuning of China's public diplomacy included a meeting of the Party Propaganda Department in early 2007 that emphasized the need to avoid offending Islamic nations when celebrating the year of the pig and inflaming domestic anti-Japanese feeling when marking the 60th anniversary of the Marco Polo bridge incident and Japanese invasion of China (Rawnsley 2007).[12] Yet more significantly, in the spring of 2007 international anger around China's support for the regime in Khartoum in the face of the Darfur genocide brought modifications of Chinese foreign policy in this region (*Boston Globe* 2007).

Zhao Qizeng's institutional reforms included upgrading China's ability to address the foreign media. In December 2004 he astonished a gathering of journalists at Beijing's Kunlun hotel by presenting them with the names and phone numbers of the seventy-five spokespersons of every ministry and commission under the State Council. This, he promised, would be an annual event. Xinhua hailed a step toward transparent government (Xinhua 2004; *BBC Monitoring* 2005b). Other advocacy initiatives included the launch of an overseas edition of the *People's Daily* and a number of English language Web sites (*China Daily* 2004). In parallel, as Kurlantzick has noted, the Foreign Ministry increased its investment in regional expertise within its diplomatic corps, sending thousands of its best students overseas to study their target state and society firsthand. Given that the Chinese Foreign Service allows its officers to work entire careers in their specialist geographical area, the rising generation will be well placed to learn from experience and provide advocacy nuanced by local knowledge for years to come (Kurlantzick 2007, 65–66).

Qizheng's tenure at SCIO saw legion Chinese initiatives in the field of cultural diplomacy including major exhibitions, "China Weeks" and tours for artists. The centerpiece of these initiatives was the rapid expansion of the Confucius Institutes—culture and language teaching institutes located within world universities—in an effort to create a network of more than one hundred institutes within five years (Xinhua 2006b).[13]

China has also invested in its exchanges, concluding new bilateral agreements with partners around the world from Austria to Zimbabwe. Institutions that claim to manage people-to-people exchanges, such as the Chinese People's Association for Friendship with Foreign Countries, have flourished. China has also expanded its recruitment of international students, bringing 20 percent more with every passing year. The Ministry of Education expects rolls to top 120,000 by 2008 (Kurlantzick 2007, 118).

Exchanges have been used to promote international study of the Chinese language, lately targeting younger groups of students, providing a stream of foreign language teachers for overseas service and wooing foreign school principals through trips to China, as priorities shift from the university to the secondary and even the primary school sector. In June 2007 the Office of the Chinese Language Council declared that 30 million people around the world were now learning Chinese and predicted that this figure would hit 100 million by 2010 (Xinhua 2007c).[14] In February 2007 the premier of the State Council, Wen Jiabao, paid tribute to the value of exchanges in presenting China's best face to the world, noting that they have "fostered an image of China as a country that is committed to reform and opening-up, a country of unity and dynamism, a country that upholds equality and values friendship, and a country that is sincere and responsible" (Wen 2007).

China's newest resource in its approach to the world is the first generation of truly international Chinese stars. Individuals who have represented China in the world include basketball player Yao Ming and actress Zhang Ziyi. Both have been associated with international children's charities, as goodwill ambassadors for the Special Olympics. China's reputation is doubly enhanced as a result (PR Newswire 2006; Xinhua 2006a). Both figured prominently in pre-Olympic publicity.

Chinese international broadcasting has also been upgraded in recent years. In September 2000 China Central Television launched its twenty-four hour English language service CCTV 9 (Xinhua 2000). It immediately began negotiations to place the service on carriers around the world and succeeded in brokering deals with carriers as diverse as Rupert Murdoch's Sky satellite in the United Kingdom and Fox services in the United States, Vanuatu in the mid-Pacific, and terrestrial channels in East Africa (Gittings and Borger 2001; *Australian Financial Review* 2003; Xinhua 2005a; Powell 2005). The content of CCTV 9 has reflected a need to present something closer to real journalism than the wooden litany of achievements and upcoming cultural events which once typified broadcasts. From 2003 onward a new openness has been evident, with CCTV 9 presenting stories about China's pollution problems and its energy crisis that would have been swept under the carpet in previous eras. In the spring of 2004 CCTV 9 announced a major re-launch to include the employment of foreign anchors and a consultant from the Murdoch stable, John Terenzio. The station's controller, Jiang Heping, told the *South China Morning Post* that "We are taking great efforts to minimize the tone of propaganda, to balance our reports and to be objective. But we definitely won't be reporting as much negative domestic news as the Western media" (*BBC Monitoring* 2005a). New CCTV services in Spanish and French followed. The network also organized a conference on the theme of selling China overseas, while China's media regulators have finally given permission for Chongqing Television to launch an international service (Rawnsley 2007).

Chinese public diplomacy seems poised to engage the same issues of the boundary between news and advocacy that have loomed so large in the history of western international broadcasting and similarly now has to consider how domestic negatives should be treated in public diplomacy. In February 2007 an article in the *People's Daily*, under the byline of Wen Jiabao, declared in its conclusion:

> We should conduct public diplomacy in a more effective way. We should inform the outside world of the achievements we have made in reform, opening-up and modernization in a comprehensive, accurate and timely manner. At the same time, we should be frank about the problems we have. We should be good at using flexible and diversified ways in conducting public diplomacy programs. We should use persuasive ways to communicate with the international community to ensure that our message is effectively put across. We should work to enable the international community to develop an objective and balanced view on China's development and international role, so as to foster an environment of friendly public opinion for China.

It was a clarion call for a still more sophisticated approach to public diplomacy.

China's Image Problem

Despite such efforts, China's international image still faces severe problems. The reputation of China is hostage to the reputation of its exports. When, as in the spring of 2007, America's news carried stories of well-loved pets dying after eating poisonous Chinese dog food or toddlers' health endangered by playing with toy trains painted with lead-based paint by their Chinese manufacturer, China's image suffers. As the SARS crisis of 2003 showed, the government's first instinct may be denial, but only honesty and action can prevent a public relations catastrophe. Some image problems are yet more intractable. A visit from the terracotta warriors cannot blot out the cause of Tibet in the Western mind, or erase the memory of the repression of the Tiananmen protests, or counterbalance stories of censorship and religious persecution, or bury news stories leaking out of major undercurrents of unrest in China's cities. All Beijing can do is try frantically to distract attention from these issues by presenting alternative stories and rebuke the world's media for accentuating the negative. The 2008 Olympics are perhaps the ultimate distraction story.

One fascinating and underanalyzed aspect of Chinese public diplomacy is its relationship to the domestic audience. The relationship is reflected in the fact that the Chinese first used the term *public diplomacy* to refer to the process of explaining their foreign policy at home (the task of public affairs in American parlance). This has been clear in the case of other superpowers. In the heyday of Soviet Communism the Brezhnev regime ached to present its own people with the spectacle of the rest of the world admiring the Soviet way. The KGB soon became adept at staging pro-Soviet demonstrations around the world to maintain the illusion. In George W. Bush's America public diplomacy has plainly been skewed by the administration's desire to be seen to be winning hearts and minds rather than actually building real relationships for the long term. Outsiders can only speculate on the scale of the domestic imperative in the Chinese case and the domestic advantages that the regime must expect from hosting the Olympics. Certainly much of the organization of the Beijing Olympics can be seen as a process of managing domestic opinion in order to deliver the spectacle of the world coming admiringly to the Central Land. Success would give the regime enhanced credibility, and the image of China standing up promises to make the rhetoric of 1949 real. By the same token, a public relations disaster at the Olympics would be a massive humiliation. Interestingly, the organizers have sought to limit domestic expectations around the Games, publicly aiming for what the secretary general of the Organizing Committee, Wang Wei, called "a high level Olympic Games" rather than the traditional target of the "best games ever." It is better to exceed expectations and delight the home audience than to disappoint (Wang 2007).[15] This wider point again underlines China's vulnerability: the fate of China's international reputation has significant domestic consequences.

Part of China's soft power opportunity has been grounded in the hard power aspect of America's reputation. China is welcomed in some quarters of the globe simply because it is not the United States. As China's strength grows and it closes distance on the United States this advantage is diminished. The symptoms of this were apparent in the Pew Global Attitudes Survey released in July 2007 (Fram 2007; Pew Global Attitudes Project). Were China to surpass the United States it would swiftly find that global leadership brings an immediate crop of resentment. In the nearer term China's international image depends on its ability to deliver on its promises. The Soviet Union bought many friends in the middle years of the Cold War and lost them swiftly when its economy could no longer deliver, though if the Chinese economy were ever to collapse the disgruntlement of Malawi would be the least of Beijing's worries.

Even assuming sustained growth and a strong economy, it is unlikely that China will be able to deliver on the enormous promises that it has made as part of its soft power approach. Soft power, in Nye's conception, is based neither on brute force nor financial leverage. In terms of the metaphorical donkey, soft power is neither the carrot nor the stick but the reputation for being nice to donkeys. China seems to doubt—perhaps rightly—that its reputation or the ethical strength of its values will win the day with foreign publics. It has been much easier just to offer to build a sports stadium for a target state or a new office for its ruling party.

The public diplomacy around the Beijing Olympics suggests that China is all too aware of its image problems and is seeking moreover to fine-tune its Olympic experience to counter some of them and thereby reposition the Chinese brand.

Beijing Olympics as Public Diplomacy for China

The Chinese government has approached the organization of the Beijing Olympics with a conviction that the Games can be used to educate the world about modern China. The heart of the plan is a blending of ancient Chinese culture, which seems to strike a positive note around the world, with images of modern China and the ideals of the Olympic movement. China's revolutionary history, with its red flags, stars, and photos of "the Great Helmsman," is nowhere to be seen. The priorities are plain in the official logo for the Games: an image that doubles as both a seal written in ancient script showing the *jing* (Chinese character meaning "capital") from Beijing and the outline of an athlete breaking the victory tape (conversation with Wang Wei, May 15, 2007).

The ideas and agendas that the Chinese government wishes to associate with the Beijing Games are clear in the clutch of videos that it has produced to promote the event (Promotion Video for the Beijing 2008 Olympic Games). The official Olympic video curtain-raiser from 2005—One World, One Dream—has a more complex purpose and plainly aims to make visual the theme of "building a harmonious world" while making use of the famous faces and views of China. Over a soaring soundtrack it cuts from dawn over great monuments around the globe to images of Zhang Ziyi wafting through the dawn and eventually leading an international phalanx of children and athletes as they run with torches. Athletes from around the world perform amid China's great monuments: pole vaulting on the Great Wall and weight lifting in the Temple of Heaven. The climax is a montage of crowds, fireworks, and Olympic events. We see Yao Ming and, among other shots, an athlete in a wheelchair and a token elderly person. At the end Zhang Ziyi only remains, contemplating an ancient Chinese historical sight before melting into thin air, part of the dream of the spectacle that is to come. There are no flags and no politicians (*Beijing Olympic Games: One World One Dream* video).

The video that most obviously seeks to sweep away old images of China is that created by the China National Tourism Administration entitled *Welcome to China—Beijing 2008*. The film illustrates the sensory experience that is China with images that emphasize the vast scale of the Chinese landscape, the history of Chinese culture, and the diversity of China's population. Colorful costumes and smiling children abound, but the landscape is populated by single figures or small groups. Crowds are nowhere to be seen, and cities figure only at the end, apparently as a convenience awaiting the visiting Westerner. The message is that China is friendly and somehow empty. It clearly aims to be an antidote to pictures of streets teeming with blue-suited cyclists familiar from the 1970s. Needless to say, the video glosses over the centrifugal forces in contemporary China—regional minorities, including Tibetans, appear happily integrated into the harmonious whole, performing their culture on cue. One of the film's final images is of two young Tibetan monks jumping for joy in slow motion. It was as if Mexico City had promoted its Olympics with film of happy students or Berlin with pictures of dancing rabbis.

The Challenge: Competing Agendas
at the Beijing Games

From the moment of the Chinese bid it was clear that the Beijing Olympics would be an occasion for competing agendas; a focus of criticism against the regime, and an opportunity for its opponents to emphasize the extent to which China had not changed and remained a repressive one-party state. The Games seem set to be used by Taiwan as an opportunity for its own message. President Chen Shui-bian has promised a referendum on independence to coincide with the run-up to the games, while Beijing and Taipei have exchanged angry words over the route to be taken by the Olympic torch, and associated implications regarding the status of Taiwan (Ford 2007). Beyond such national agendas, by the summer of 2007 there was already a formidable lineup of groups tying long-running protests against China to the Games, each with their own parody of the Olympic logo. Reporters Without Borders began their campaign in 2001 with a striking image of Olympic rings made out of handcuffs.[16] The Free Tibet campaign has chosen Olympic rings formed by bullet holes (Free Tibet n.d.). Other artists have the rings serving as the wheels on a tank or made out of a pile of skulls or stitched in cloth and floating above a child laborer's head (No Beijing Olympics 2008 2007). Protests of some description

seem set to form an antiphony throughout the Games and the organizers are braced for this.

A second potential challenge could come from the internal agendas
around the Games. One paradox that every host with a sporting reputation to protect and a home crowd to impress must face is the problem
of competing gracefully. The display of one's own national strength
and skill craved by the home audience and the sporting bureaucracy is
not necessarily compatible with hospitality or the interests of public
diplomacy. At a time when the world is growing wary of Chinese
strength, China's best interests would probably not be best served by a
run of Chinese victories, but rather by sportsmanlike gestures and displays of comradeship between athletes.

Conclusion

With more than a century of experience, what can be assumed about
the Beijing Games from the point of view of public diplomacy? First,
that the Olympics is a high-risk mechanism, but probably one that any
major power has to tackle at some point in its history. In the world of
the Internet and global satellite news, the days of Potemkin villages
and deceit are fast fading—like it or not China will be known as it is,
not as it wishes to be. It can only hope that these two intersect somehow. Second, for all the meanings, images, and slogans contrived by
the organizers of an event like the Olympics, the event can be used by
an actor with its own public diplomacy agenda seeking to piggyback on
the global news coverage. Third, much hangs on the unfolding of the
competition, the experience of foreign athletes, spectators and their
media, and their interaction with locals. The problems are redoubled
when the Paralympics (scheduled for Beijing) are added to the mix.
Chinese culture has many virtues, but sympathy toward the disabled is
seldom considered one of them.[17] Beijing must be able to host guests
with special needs whose discomfort would play exceptionally badly in
their home countries. The organizers can at least draw comfort from
the success of the Special Olympics in Shanghai in the fall of 2007,
which successfully insulated guests from the difficulties of life for the
differently abled in modern China. Finally, Beijing must be braced for
contradictory agendas as the enthusiasm of the home crowd threatens
to subvert the need to be a good host.

The interests of Beijing will not be best served by amassing a pile of medals but rather by creating an environment in which sportsmanship can flourish and the athletes themselves provide the meaning of the Games. The best public diplomacy strategy for China, having set its frame for the Beijing Games, is to step back from the agenda of national promotion which so begs challenge, to focus on affirming the shared ideals of the Olympic movement, and to have enough confidence to allow the world to draw its own conclusions about the new China.

NOTES

I am grateful to Iskra Kirova and Carrie Walters for bibliographical research and sharing their own ideas around Olympic public diplomacy; to Barry A. Sanders for talking me through the maze of contemporary Olympic diplomacy; to Wang Yi We and Garry Rawnsley for their comments on my draft; and to Niels Kjær Therkelsen, my companion for boyhood Olympic TV viewing and impromptu political criticism.

1. On Gullion and the evolution of the term *public diplomacy,* see Cull 2006.

2. This argument was made in a letter to the London *Times* on Coubertin's death by the Greek ambassador M. D. Kaklamanos. See Caclamanos 1937. (The contemporary transliteration of this name is *Kaklamanos*. The *Times* used the older spelling *Caclamanos*.)

3. As an international pariah, the Soviet Union was initially excluded from the Olympics and so, from 1928, organized its own rival series of "Spartakiads" for workers from around the world.

4. Barry A. Sanders, chairman, Southern California Committee for the Olympic Games, to author, June 12, 2007.

5. The perennial loser in Olympic place-branding is Detroit, which bid unsuccessfully for every Games from 1952 to 1972.

6. When Japan resigned as host, Helsinki stepped in as an alternative to Tokyo, but the outbreak of European war killed that plan also. The 1944 Games were actually awarded to London in 1939. See Olympic Games Museum (n.d.)

7. This boycott is the focus of the Berlin Olympics exhibit mounted by the U.S. Holocaust Memorial Museum, which is preserved online at the Nazi Olympics Berlin Web site.

8. The U.S. attorney general, William French Smith, personally denounced the forgeries, while the United States Information Agency broadcast a special program over satellite in which the African American mayor of Los Angeles, Tom Bradley, and the Games' organizer, Peter Ueberroth, answered questions from African journalists about the Olympics. See Snyder 2005, 108–11 and *Active Measures* 1986, 22–24, 54–56.

9. In 2005, an anthology of Zhao Qizheng's speeches appeared with the

title *Xiang Shijie Shuoming Zhongguo* (Explain China to the World). See also *BBC Monitoring* 2005b.

10. On May 15, 2007 the author and others at University of Southern California met Wang Guoqing, vice minister in China's SCIO, who spoke of his own position as the equivalent to Karen Hughes in the United States. His minister (Zhao Qizheng's successor) is Cai Wu.

11. The Tibet conference was reported by the World Tibet Network News.

12. Similarly, in February 2007, when soft power was the focus of the annual conferences of both the National People's Congress (China's parliament) and the National Committee of the Chinese People Political Consultative Conference (CPPCC), participants acknowledged the scale of the challenge that still lay ahead. See Li, Cheng, and Wang 2007.

13. The institutes are reassuringly titled to emphasize the classical Chinese past, not its tumultuous present. In some poorer countries Chinese aid ensures that it is cheaper to be educated at a Chinese-funded school than within the national system (Kurlantzick 2007, 67–69).

14. See also Xinhua 2007a, 2007b.

15. The organizers seem also to be on guard against accusations of building for the world but ignoring the future of their own people, and hence the domestic audience has also been a key target for publicity around the long-term benefits for the Games. They are swift to point to the four major venues that will become part of universities around the capital and the thirty year contracts to maintain Olympic facilities for the public good.

16. As of July 29, 2007, the handcuffs were the opening image at the site http://www.rsf.org/. See also http://www.rsf.org/rubrique.php3?id_rubrique =174.

17. For recent comment on Chinese attitudes toward mental and physical handicap, see Hallett n.d. On preparations for the Olympics see Hallett 2006.

REFERENCES

Active Measures. 1986. U.S. Department of State, August 1986.

Allen, Neil. 1967. Olympic Boycott by Negroes Uncertain. *Times* (London), November 25, 8.

Analects of Confucius (Lun Yu), XVI, 1 (434).

Armour, Nancy. 2005. Kwan's New Routine: School, Diplomacy, Skate. *Washington Post,* June 26.

Australian Financial Review. 2003. Murdoch Gets Approval for Chinese TV Service, March 7, 63.

Axelsson, George. 1952. Communists Defy Truce Tradition to Spread Propaganda at Classic. *New York Times,* July 22, 30.

Banke, Jim. 2003. China Launches its First Piloted Spacecraft. Space.com, October 15. http://www.space.com/missionlaunches/shenzhou5_launch _031014.html.

BBC Monitoring. 2005a. CCTV International to Re-launch, Add New Languages. April 6.

BBC Monitoring. 2005b. Hong Kong Daily Analyses Official's Role in Improving China's Public Image. June 7.

BBC Monitoring. 2006. Zimbabwe Uses "Chinese Technology" to Disrupt VOA Radio Signal. July 5.

Beijing Olympic Games: One World One Dream. Video posted at http://www
.youtube.com/watch?v=Xhxh3expV10.

Boston Globe. 2007. Shaming China on Darfur. *Boston Globe,* May 31, 2007.

Caclamanos, M. D. 1937. Baron de Coubertin, the Olympic Games and After. *Times* (London), September 7, 14.

Central Tibetan Administration. n.d. http://www.tibet.net/en/flash/flash_
archive/2001/0701/images/noolym.jpg.

China Daily. 2004. English Web Platform Opens. September 17. http://en
glish.sohu.com.

China National Tourism Administration. Welcome to China—Beijing 2008.

Crowell, Todd, and David Hsieh. 2000. Beijing's Spin Doctor. *Asia Week,* September 22.

Cull, Nicholas J. 2006. Public Diplomacy before Gullion, the Evolution of a Phrase. USC Center on Public Diplomacy, April. Available at http://uscpublicdiplomacy.com/index.php/newsroom/pdblog_de tail/060418_public_diplomacy_before_gullion_the_evolution_of_a_ phrase/.

Danzig, Allison. 1948. Strong American Contingent Will Leave This Week for London . . . Food to Be Taken Along. *New York Times,* July 11, S3.

d'Hooghe, Ingrid. 2005. Public Diplomacy in the People's Republic of China. In *The New Public Diplomacy: Soft Power in International Relations,* ed. Jan Melissen, 88–105. London: Palgrave.

Eckholm, Erik. 1998. China Admits Ecological Sins Played Role in Flood Disaster. *New York Times,* August 26, A1.

Environmental News Service. 2004. WWF Gives Athens Olympics No Green Medals. Environmental News Service, July 16. http://www.ens-newswire.com/ens/jul2004/2004–07–16–05.asp.

Espy, Richard. 1979. *The Politics of the Olympic Games.* Berkeley: University of California Press.

Ford, Peter. 2007. Olympic Torch May Stall at Taiwan Strait. *Christian Science Monitor,* June 20.

Fradkin, Philip. 1967. Tommie Smith Tells Negro Threat to Boycott Olympics. *Los Angeles Times,* September 23, A1.

Fram, Alan. 2007. Poll: Distrust of U.S., Bush Growing around World along with Wariness of Russia, China. Associated Press, June 28.

Free Tibet. n.d. http://www.tibet.net/en/flash/flash_archive/2001/0701/im ages/noolym.jpg.

Gittings, Danny, and Julian Borger. 2001. Homer and Bart Realize Murdoch's Dream of China Coup. *Guardian,* September 6, 3.

Gould, Jack. 1964. Sharp TV Pictures of Olympics Relayed Live to U.S. by Satellite. *New York Times,* October 10, 1.

Hallett, Stephen. http://www.bbc.co.uk/ouch/writers/stephenhallett/.

Hallett, Stephen. 2006. One Eye on China: Mainly for Show. BBC, August 28. http://www.bbc.co.uk/ouch/closeup/china/280206.shtml.

Hamilton, John Maxwell. 1988. *Edgar Snow: A Biography.* Bloomington: Indiana University Press.

Hazan, Baruch. 1982. *Olympic Sports and Propaganda Games: Moscow, 1980.* New Brunswick, NJ: Transaction.

Ho, David Yau-Fai. 1976. On the Concept of Face. *American Journal of Sociology* 81 (4): 867–84.

Hoberman, John M. 1986. *The Olympic Crisis: Sport, Politics, and the Moral Order.* New Rochelle, NY: Caratzas.

IOC. n.d. Melbourne/Stockholm 1956. http://www.olympic.org/uk/games/past/index_uk.asp?OLGT=1&OLGY=1956.

IOC. 2006. Angel or Demon? The Choice of Fair Play, April 12–November 5. http://www.olympic.org/uk/passion/museum/temporary/exhibition_uk.asp?id=41&type=0.

IOC. 2007. Olympic Charter. http://multimedia.olympic.org/pdf/en_report_122.pdf.

Jackson, Strode. 1919. The Olympic Games—National Effort Needed—Propaganda in Sport. *Times* (London), September 22, 8.

Kurlantzick, Joshua. 2007. *Charm Offensive: How China's Soft Power Is Transforming the World.* New Haven: Yale University Press.

Li Baojie, Cheng Yifeng, and Wang Mian. 2007. Soft Power a New Focus at China's Two Sessions. Xinhua, March 14.

Mandell, Richard D. 1987. *The Nazi Olympics.* Urbana: University of Illinois Press.

Manheim, Jarol B. 1990. Rites of Passage: The 1988 Seoul Olympics as Public Diplomacy. *Western Political Quarterly* 43 (2): 279–95.

Mao Tse-Tung. 1949. The Chinese People Have Stood Up! Mao's Opening Speech to the Chinese People's Consultative Conference, September 21. Available at http://marxists.org/reference/archive/mao/selected-works/volume-5/mswv5_01.htm.

Miller, David. 1984. Smiling Diplomacy Wins First Gold Medal of the Games for China. *Times* (London), July 25, 19.

National Archives. ca. 1951. Washington, DC, RG 306, IIA Office of Administration, 1952–55, box 4, file "Private Enterprise and Co-op," Walsh to Barrett, "1952 Olympics Progress Report No. 4," ca. December.

National Archives. 1952. Washington, DC, RG 306, IIA Office of Administration, 1952–55, box 4, file "Private Enterprise and Co-op," Walsh to Compton, April 3.

National Archives. 1972. Washington, DC, RG 306, 87.0018, director's subject files, box 28, file "1972 DRO-Issuances," Shakepeare to Towery (IOP), March 17.

The Nazi Olympics Berlin Web site. http://www.ushmm.org/museum/exhi
bit/online/olympics/.

New York Times. 1956. Hungarians Beat Russian Team, 4–0. December 6, 62.

New York Times. 1964. Boy Born on Day A-Bomb Fell Chosen to Light Olympic Flame. August 23, 8.

New York Times. 1972. The Gasman Cometh—Six Days Late. September 11.

New York Times. 1981. American Art Goes to China. August 19, C16.

No Beijing Olympics 2008. 2007. China Still a Communist State—Food Poisoning. June 17. http://noolympics.blogspot.com/2007/06/china-still-se cretive-communist-state.html.

Nye, Joseph S. 2004. *Soft Power: The Means to Success in World Politics.* New York: Public Affairs.

Olympic Games Museum. *Official Olympic Reports, Tokyo 1940* and *Helsinki 1952.* Available at http://olympic-museum.de/.

Olympic Review. 1999. The Salt Lake City Crisis. 26 (25): 33.

One Day in September. 1999. Directed by Kevin Macdonald.

Pew Global Attitudes Project. http://pewglobal.org/.

Powell, Adam Clayton, III. 2005. Chinese TV Extends Its Reach into Africa. USC Center on Public Diplomacy Web Site, December 19. Available at http://uscpublicdiplomacy.com/index.php/newsroom/journal_de tail/051219_chinese_tv_extends _its_reach_into_africa/.

PR Newswire. 2006. Chinese Sensation Ziyi Zhang Joins Special Olympics as Newest Global Ambassador. November 16.

Promotion Video for the Beijing 2008 Olympic Games. As posted at http://www.youtube.com/watch?v=-QgU5iUYTUY&mode=related& search.

Publicdiplomacy.org. n.d. What Is Public Diplomacy. http://www.public diplomacy.org/1.htm (accessed November 20, 2007).

Qing Cao. 2001. Selling Culture: Ancient Chinese Conceptions of the Other in Legends. In *The Zen of International Relations: IR theories from East to West,* ed. S. Chan, P. Mandaville, and R. Bleiker, 178–202. New York: Palgrave.

Ramo, Joshua Cooper. 2007. *Brand China.* Foreign Policy Center, London. Available at http://fpc.org.uk/fsblob/827.pdf.

Rawnsley, Gary D. 2007. A Survey of China's Public Diplomacy. USC Center on Public Diplomacy blog, May 2. http://uscpublicdiplomacy.com/in dex.php/newsroom/pdblog_detail/070502_a_survey_of_chinas _public_diplomacy/.

Reid, T. R. 1990. Atlanta Is Awarded '96 Summer Olympics: Civil Rights History Is Key Selling Point. *Washington Post,* September 19, A1.

Reporters Sans Frontières. http://www.rsf.org.

Roche, Maurice. 2002. The Olympics and Global Citizenship. *Citizenship Studies* 6 (2): 165–81.

Roche, Maurice. 2006. Mega-events and Modernity Revisited: Globalization and the Case of the Olympics. *Sociological Review* 54 (2): 25–40.

Ronald Reagan Presidential Library. 1984. Simi Valley, CA; Ryan, Fred, files, CF OA 753, USIA private sector committee, June 21.

Shirk, Susan. 2006. China Gets Tough with North Korea. *YaleGlobal On-line,* October 26. Available at http://yaleglobal.yale.edu/display.article?id=8341.

Snyder, Alvin. 2005. *Warriors of Disinformation.* New York: Arcade.

Sterba, James P. 1981. China and U.S. Sign Pact on Cultural Exchanges. *New York Times,* September 6, A3.

Times (London). 1924a. Olympic Games Doomed, Failure of the Ideal, Disgraceful Scenes. July 22, 14.

Times (London). 1924b. No More Olympic Games. July 22, 15.

Times (London). 1924c. The Olympic Games, a Cause of Ill-Will, More Evidence. July 23, 14.

Waitt, Gordon. 1999. Playing Games with Sydney: Marketing for the 2000 Olympics. *Urban Studies* 36 (7): 1055–77.

Wang, Hongying. 2003. National Image-Building and Chinese Foreign Policy. *China: An International Journal* 1 (1): 46–72.

Wang Wei. 2007. Presentation at University of Southern California, May 15, 2007.

Wang Yiwei. Forthcoming. Public Diplomacy and the Rise of Chinese Soft Power. *Annals of the American Academy of Political and Social Science.*

Washington Post. 1964. Italian Bobsledder Shows Sportsmanship. February 1, C4.

Weiner, Tim. 2004. When Games Turned Political; In 1968, Violence in Mexico Changed Olympics and a Nation. *New York Times,* July 24, D1.

Wen Jiabao. 2007. Our Historical Tasks at the Primary Stage of Socialism and Several Issues Concerning China's Foreign Policy. *People's Daily,* February 27. (Trans. Xinhua, March 5, 2007.)

World Tibet Network News. http://www.tibet.ca/.

Xinhua. 2000. China to Launch All-English Channel Tomorrow. September 24.

Xinhua. 2004. China Makes Public Names of Government Spokespersons for the First Time. December 28.

Xinhua. 2005a. China's English International Channel to Air in Vanuatu. August 10.

Xinhua. 2005b. Chinese, Japanese NGOs Release Poll on Bilateral Relations. August 24.

Xinhua. 2006a. Yao Ming Appears as Ambassador to the Special Olympics. July 22.

Xinhua. 2006b. Confucius Institute: Promoting Language, Culture, and Friendliness. October 2.

Xinhua. 2007a. 110 British Headmasters Visit China for Language Teaching Co-op. May 27.

Xinhua. 2007b. Foreign Headmasters Follow Chinese Language Teaching Trail. June 20.

Xinhua. 2007c. Overseas Craze for Chinese Spreads from Universities to Schools. June 26.

Zheng Bijian. 2005. *Peaceful Rise: Speeches of Zheng Bijian, 1997–2005*. Washington, DC: Brookings Institution Press.

Zolov, Eric. 2004. Showcasing the Land of Tomorrow: Mexico and the 1968 Olympics. *Americas* 61 (2): 159–88. http://www.tvmyworld.com/links/templates/coming_soon_travel.htm#.

"A Very Natural Choice"

The Construction of Beijing as an Olympic City during the Bid Period

Heidi Østbø Haugen

"**B**eijing has succeeded!" (*Beijing chenggong le!*) President Jiang Zemin's declaration on July 13, 2001 brought the enthusiastic crowd gathered at Tiananmen Square the news they had hoped for. Millions of others heard the announcement through TV and radio broadcasts in China and abroad. This chapter examines how the Beijing Olympic Bid Committee and Chinese media presented Beijing to a foreign audience in the period leading up to the selection of the 2008 Olympic host city. It will show that Beijing was presented in a way that not only won the city the right to host the Olympic Games, but also strengthened the modernist ideologies of the Chinese Government and the Olympic Movement. Finally, Beijing's bid will be discussed in light of the incentives to host the Olympic Games as well as the institutional context for the production of the bid material.[1]

An Olympic bid provides an interesting opportunity to study the process of assigning meaning to places. The limited duration of the bid period, the large amount of textual material produced, the relatively well-defined goal of the bid campaigns, and the focus on an international target audience are all features that make bids different from most other processes of place construction. The Olympic Games take place within narrow spatial and temporal confines, during which the hosts are subject to intense international attention. During this period, the host cities try to project certain images, themes, and values (Hall 1992). As an organizer of the Albertville Winter Olympics put it, "There will only be 16 days of television coverage, but we will have to live with the image for fifty years" (Larson and Park 1993, 246). The place identity constructed during the bid period exerts a powerful influence over how the Games are organized, and is therefore of great practical consequence.

Hallmark events such as the Olympic Games are important in confirming, strengthening, and undermining power relations in the places they are hosted. Their scale and nature necessitates a break with the normal planning procedures. This may create opportunities for new groups to assert their power. The break in routine can also be used by established elites as an opportunity to push their own agendas and to marginalize alternative opinions. The Olympic host selection process—the International Olympic Committee (IOC) selection criteria give extra points in the initial bid round to candidate cities with no demonstrable popular opposition to the bid—and the fierce competition to host the Olympics may combine to deter critical public debate during the bid period. In the case of Toronto's 1996 Olympic bid, for example, it was speculated that the public debate surrounding the bid may have destroyed the city's chances of hosting the Games. The discussion had led to a compromise in which the organizers promised to provide low-income housing, environmental assessment, and employment for unionized workers in return for support for the Games (Hiller 2000). While attaching importance to public support for the Olympics, the IOC does not require local public involvement, either directly or through elected city governments, in the preparation process for the Games.

The Stakes in the Bid Process

The stakes for the Chinese Communist Party were high in the 2008 Olympic bid round. Under Mao Zedong, China's development model represented an ideological alternative to capitalism, both to the rest of the world and to its own citizens. Such an alternative was no longer offered after Mao's death and the reorientation of the national development strategy toward "socialism with Chinese characteristics." The legitimacy of the Chinese government today rests largely on its ability to create economic growth. Chinese leaders have attempted to fill the ideological vacuum in the post-Mao era by reviving Chinese nationalist spirit (Ko 2001). Previous Olympic Games and bids had demonstrated to Chinese leaders that the Olympics could be an avenue both to economic growth and to fostering a form of nationalism that is not hostile to the outside world.

In most cities, economic growth is the primary rationale offered for bidding for the Olympic Games (Hiller 1998). The Olympics are an important means for cities to build an appealing and progressive image and enhance their position in a largely postindustrial economy by attracting investments, residents, and visitors. Bidding for the Games has itself become a promotional act, as the prolonged choice process can ensure considerable publicity even for unsuccessful cities (Waitt 1999; Ward 1998). Beijing has become one of the many Asian cities with a strategic orientation that goes beyond the national space (Douglass 2000; Jessop 1999). In order to become hubs of global and regional economic activity, these cities pour money into urban megaprojects, theme parks, and events with high symbolic value: World Expositions (Expos), the Miss World final, the World Soccer Cup and, the biggest of all, the Olympic Summer Games. Both political and economic motivations drive the transformation of Asian metropolitan regions into "world cities." There is political credit to be gained when a city is internationally recognized as not only a major economic player, but also a creator of cultural symbols (Douglass 2000; Kelly 1997).

The Olympic Games' ability to incite patriotism is lauded as a positive quality in Chinese newspapers (Xinhua 2001b). Beijing's Olympic bid material furthers an official patriotic ideology in which aspirations for national greatness and an internationally openminded optimism are central features (Unger 1996). Such patriotism includes a vision of Chinese national unity that the bid material promotes through a selective representation of multicultural diversity. When writing about minority cultures, emphasis is put on art and cultural performances rather than on differences in systems of meaning and values. The diversity represented is thus nonthreatening to Chinese national unity.

The harmonious nationalism promoted through the bid material stands in contrast to the antiforeign popular nationalism triggered by Beijing's failed bid for the 2000 Olympics. The United States in particular was blamed for the loss, partly because the U.S. House of Representatives had adopted a resolution against Beijing hosting the Games (Xu 1998). Antiforeign demonstrations were arranged by people who accused Western countries of trying to hamper China's development (Zheng 1999). Such sentiments constituted a threat to China's national development strategy, and ultimately to the ruling regime, which derives legitimacy from economic growth (Renwick and Cao 1999). There was also the threat of antiforeign demonstrations turning against the Chinese government itself for acting submissive in the face of foreign interests. The government eventually banned such demonstrations and organized official campaigns to contain antiforeign nationalism after the loss in 1993 (Xu 1998; Zheng 1999). For the 2008 Olympics, in order to contain the damage if the bid were lost, the Chinese nation was no longer presented as the unit bidding for the Games. The slogan of the first bid—"A more open China awaits the 2000 Games"—was exchanged for one that put Beijing at the center—"New Beijing, Great Olympics." The Olympic bid process was presented as an open and fair competition from which all candidates gained something. A Beijing Olympic Bid Committee (BOBICO) representative said that while the Chinese people "calmly and wholeheartedly supported the bid," a loss would have been gracefully accepted because "if the bid were unsuccessful, it would nevertheless have increased Beijing's 'celebrity rating,' made even more people understand Beijing, improved Beijing's image abroad, increased the interest in investing here, and enriched Beijing's cultural life. The bid had many advantages for the development of Beijing and the daily building of culture and civilization" (interview January 2002).

The Olympic Games have also been used to demonstrate the superiority of a certain political ideology. The first example of this was the 1936 Berlin Games, which saw the introduction of certain elements, such as the Olympic torch relay and a spectacular opening ceremony, that we take for granted today (Byrne 1987). The Games were as spectacular as they were well organized, and they were presented as proof of the superior performance of the Nazi ideology. During the Olympic opening ceremony, German officials announced that their country had become the center of world civilization, just as Greece had been during antiquity. Similarly, the 1980 Olympic Games in Moscow attempted to exhibit the success of state Marxism to the western world, just as those in Los Angeles in 1984 were a celebration of American capitalism (Hall 1992). One main reason why the Olympic Games are a useful tool for promoting political ideologies is their perceived neutrality and universality. The Olympics are claimed to be about games and sports rather than politics, and Olympism is purportedly above ideology (Killanin 1983; Hoberman 1995). When national ideology—be it fascism, communism, or capitalism—is tied to allegedly universal Olympism, the gap between nationalism and universalism is bridged.

While the Olympic hosts benefit from tying their political values to Olympic universalism, the International Olympic Committee is increasingly aware that it is in its interest to keep strict control over the symbolic aspects of the Olympics. In the past, countries have boycotted the Games over objections to the ideologies the host nations promoted through the event. In addition to the losses directly incurred, boycotts pose a threat to the IOC's long-term finances. The brand name "Olympic"—together with the Olympic rings—is worth billions of dollars and is the IOC's greatest asset. The brand would lose much of its value if it became associated with a particular group or ideology. Juan Antonio Samaranch, IOC president from 1980 to 2001, had ambitions that went far beyond finances, including becoming a Nobel Peace Prize laureate and raising the status of the IOC to that of the United Nations (Wamsley 2002). An example of a conflict between the IOC and the Olympic host nations over symbolic uses of the Games took place during the Salt Lake City 2002 Winter Olympics. President Bush wanted to use the opening ceremony as an occasion to commemorate the victims of the September 11 terrorist attack. When the IOC objected to what they perceived to be a display of American nationalism, Bush responded that the ideals behind the commemoration were *universal* rather than American: "All people appreciate the discipline that produces excellence, the courage that overcomes difficult odds and the character that creates champions" (U.S. Embassy 2002). The universal nature of these values would be confirmed through their incorporation into the Olympic opening ceremony.

The Production of the Bid Material

Beijing's Olympic bid material must be understood with reference to the concrete circumstances within which it was produced. The most important document presented to the IOC during the bid process is the Candidature File. The bid cities are required to present their practical arrangements for the Games in the Candidature Files, but the format gives ample opportunity to set the bid apart symbolically. Beijing set the tone by presenting the document to IOC members in golden silk boxes closed with traditional Chinese locks. IOC guidelines, former bids, and advice from international consultants and PR firms all influenced the making of the Candidature File and other BOBICO promotion material. The administrative structure of the Beijing bid team is complex and difficult to map, partly because of what one senior official termed a Chinese system of "one organization, two names"; one could simultaneously be the head of the Chinese Communist Party Propaganda Department's Sports Section, the section chief of the China Olympic Committee News Committee, and a leading official in the Chinese Sport Correspondents' Association (interview January 2002).

In addition to the material published by BOBICO, English-language texts about Beijing's Olympic bid were published in Chinese newspapers and magazines. Chinese media displays some distinct characteristics, and the circumstances under which news stories on the Olympic bid were produced therefore merit special attention. Many of the articles written by journalists from the state news agency Xinhua or the newspapers *People's Daily* or *China Daily* were judged suitable for publicity purposes in their original form and republished on BOBICO's Web site. Chinese journalists were under the influence of different, and at times contradictory, sets of journalistic conventions. At the National Forum for Propaganda and Ideological Work in 1994, Jiang Zemin charged the Chinese press with four major tasks: "arming people with scientific theory; guiding people with correct opinion; educating people in high moral standards; and using outstanding works to inspire people." Chinese introductory journalism textbooks later added "being profitable" as a fifth goal (Li 2001). This intertwining of Chinese Communist Party logic with market logic has resulted in a journalistic style dubbed "popular journalism with Chinese characteristics" (Li 1998).

The degree to which the Chinese government exerts control over editorial content depends both on the type of publication and on the topics covered. National newspapers are generally more restricted than provincial and local publications (Lynch 1999). The English editions of Xinhua news agency reports, *People's Daily* and *China Daily* are important to the Chinese government as channels for communications with a foreign audience. They are therefore tightly controlled and have largely been shielded from demands to make a profit. While the Western media claims to be based on objectivity, the Chinese government's attitude toward objectivity as a guiding principle for journalism has varied over time. In 1948, *People's Daily* was upbraided by the government for displaying an "objective tendency not to be allowed in our propaganda work" (Li 1994, 228). During the liberalization period in the late 1980s, on the other hand, top Party officials stressed the informational and watchdog role of the press. The news industry again became more restricted after the Tiananmen crisis of June 1989. However, employees of the Chinese Communist Party Propaganda Department and media institutions cited independence and objectivity as important journalistic ideals (interviews January 2002). Reporters who write for English national media are exposed to foreign ideas about journalism, both through the Internet and through Western journalists hired by their employers to help adjust the writing style to suit a foreign audience. Despite this exposure, articles published by the Chinese media are often different from what Western readers are used to. In the bid material, descriptions of individuals—including residents of Tibet—who go to great length to support the bid come across as especially foreign. The following report about four farmers from Shanxi, for example, takes on an almost religious character:

> Four farmers rode donkeys from the hometown in Shanxi province in Northwest China to BOBICO headquarters in Beijing to express their support for Beijing to bid to host the 2008 Olympic Games. The four farmers could have taken a train or bus, but instead, they decided to make their pilgrimage by riding a donkey all the way to Xinqiao Hotel where BOBICO's headquarters is located. (BOBICO 2001)

The different sets of writing conventions to which journalists are exposed were sometimes reflected in stylistic inconsistencies in their articles about Beijing's Olympic bid. An example is Xinhua's 2000 "Sport Yearender." While the piece generally portrays the bid for the 2008 Olympics in a very positive light, it includes one critical comment from a foreign researcher based in China. In the next sentence, however, the journalist dismisses the researcher's concerns as "unnecessary" (Xinhua 2000b). When questioned about this article, the journalist who wrote it said that he included the critical commentary to give a balanced view and follow his "consciousness and the ethical rules of the reporter." But he also said he served another role as a Chinese journalist, one that obliged him to discount the criticism: "I think BOBICO believes in us. Everything we do is to make Beijing's bid more appealing. We share something; we both want to make Beijing's bid successful. Therefore, when we report, we need to know what should be reported and what should not be reported" (interview January 2002).

The preceding incident is an example of how control over the Chinese media often relies less on direct intervention than on self-censorship on the part of the journalists. While the Chinese journalists I interviewed in 2001 and 2002 all said they had a duty to be objective, they also said they wanted their writing to help Beijing win the Olympics. For example, one journalist commented that negative reporting could cause conflict with BOBICO, and he might be told that "such things are a little inappropriate [to include in your article]; I think you'd better omit it or just put it outside" (interview January 2002). When asked to cite such an occurrence, however, he said that BOBICO had never actually needed to correct him because he anticipated such comments and edited the articles himself. This example brings to mind a description given by a Polish poet writing in the 1950s of how social norms conditioned his writing: "I can't write as I would like to. . . . I get halfway through a phrase, and I already subject it to Marxist criticism. I imagine what X or Y will say about it, and I change the ending" (Milosz 1990, 14–15). Another journalist said that BOBICO did once suggest that he change an article they thought was too negative. He altered it but stressed that the change was also something he *personally* wanted: "I complied because from the bottom of my heart, I don't want to . . . let somebody put their finger on the bid. So I just revised my plan, and they [BOBICO] accepted it. You know, it is right for me to write the things I want to mention" (interview January 2002).

Although the relationship between BOBICO and Chinese journalists was characterized for the most part by such mutual cooperation and lack of dissent, the plan to host the Olympic beach volleyball games in Tiananmen Square caused discord. The foreign press interpreted the plan as an attempt to cover up the tragic events surrounding the 1989 student revolt and described it as an initiative that would "strike many human rights campaigners as grotesque" (*Financial Times* 2000). However, Chinese journalists had very different reasons for being offended by the idea of playing volleyball in Tiananmen Square. While in the West the word "Tiananmen" invokes the strong televised images from June 1989, the Chinese consider the square as the center stage of the country's modern national history. Chinese journalists were upset because the government planned to fill the square they perceive to be the embodiment of China's national dignity with sand and people in swimsuits, and they put pressure on BOBICO to release more information about the plans. BOBICO claimed that Tiananmen was chosen as a venue solely because the International Volleyball Federation had pressured them to choose a prestigious site to promote their sport. BOBICO complied, but they were as uncomfortable with the plans as the Chinese journalists were, according to one BOBICO representative (interview January 2002). The decision was later reversed. This incident is an example of how the same event can be interpreted very differently in China than it is abroad.

Situating the Beijing Olympics
Within Space and Time

The material produced for Beijing's Olympic bid combines to present a worldview in which Beijing becomes "a very natural choice" to host the Games (Xinhua 2000b). Certain notions of time and space are central in this construction. The bid *derives* meaning from existing conceptualizations of time and space by placing itself within a wider discourse on modernization and development. It also *attaches* meaning to these notions by reproducing and reworking them. Our understandings of time and space affect how we view the world—we approach and make sense of the world through certain temporal and spatial perspectives. In most circumstances these perspectives are taken for granted rather than being objects of critical reflection.

In presenting Beijing's candidature, the Chinese government needed to convince the IOC that Beijing possessed the qualities of an "Olympic city." Analysis of how meanings are attached to places is informed by Jacques Derrida's concept of "différance," which holds that definitions do not rest on the entity that is defined, but on the positive and negative references made to other definitions (Rosenau 1992). The perceived essence or identity of a place can only be constructed vis-à-vis a different and deferred Other, and the attribution of meaning is thereby endlessly deferred. While pairs of opposites may be widely circulated and accepted as legitimate ways to categorize places, meanings are never entirely fixed. This is what makes deconstruction, that is, undermining the binary oppositions by revealing their underlying assumptions and contradictions, possible. Two binary oppositions related to time and space are central themes throughout the body of texts about Beijing's Olympic bid—the division between the Orient and the Western world, and between the modern and nonmodern. The bid material, in referencing these dichotomies, makes bidding for the Olympics appear to be a natural choice.

Strategic Self-Orientalization

One of the most influential works on the relational nature of identities is Edward Saïd's "Orientalism," which outlines how "the Orient" is defined in relation to and opposition to the West (Saïd [1978] 1995). Saïd argues that Western academics, artists, and colonial administrators have constructed the Orient as timeless, feminine, despotic, savage, and irrational. Conversely, they present the West as modern, masculine, democratic, civilized, and rational. The resulting worldview, Saïd claims, made colonial rule both possible and desirable. Subsequent work on the relationship between the construction of places and the exercise of power raises two points of criticism against Saïd's "Orientalism." First, the Orientalist system of power-knowledge was more heterogeneous than Saïd depicted it, and the European and American writings on the Orient did not contain one, singular essence (Gare 1995). Second, Saïd is criticized for incorrectly assuming that the power over representations of the Orient lies entirely with the colonizer. The colonized are presented as passively accepting that the Orient is an inferior mirror image of the West (Gregory 1994). Diminishing and devaluing of the voices of opposition against Orientalism can serve a conservative rather than a progressive purpose.

The way meaning is ascribed to a specific term or action depends on its context. Arguments made with reference to Saïd's "Orientalism" in China are examples of such a reappropriation of meaning. Chinese debates about national identity in the 1990s were often cast in terms of binary oppositions between East and West. "Orientalism" was used to restore a Chinese discourse of Western hegemonic imperialism and interpreted in ways that supported reactionary nationalist rather than progressive forces within Chinese domestic politics (Zhang 1998). Saïd's work, created with the intention of challenging the dominant powers in the West, was thereby employed to consolidate the dominance of certain groups in China. The term *Occidentalism* has been coined to describe the stereotyping of the Western world for political purposes in China (Chen 1995). Chinese "official Occidentalism" essentializes the West in ways that justify restrictions on personal and political freedoms. In "anti-official Occidentalism," in contrast, the Western "Other" is used as a metaphor for political liberation from domestic ideological oppression. The official and the antiofficial Occidentalism are influenced both by Western constructions of Asia and China and by previous Chinese constructions of the Western Other (Chen 1995).

Beijing's Olympic bid material placed heavy emphasis on the city's Oriental identity through text and images. The terms *Asia, the East* and *the Orient* are used interchangeably to describe a part of the world that shares a set of essential qualities. Eastern cultures are depicted as being founded in tradition and history, as opposed to the modern, developed West—very much in keeping with Saïd's "Orientalism." In the words of one Chinese journalist: "Beijing [is] more appealing to others because we have such a long history. We have something you have never seen, something very native, something very Oriental" (interview January 2002). Perceptions of Oriental culture as being rooted in the past were reinforced by the bid material's frequent references to historical buildings, traditional costumes, and traditional lifestyles. Asians are described as being committed to ideals such as hard work and the promotion of a common good and a harmonious social order. Authority is sometimes added to such descriptions when they are presented as quotations by Westerners. For example, the opera singer José Carreras, who held a concert in the Forbidden City to promote Beijing's Olympic bid, was quoted in *China Daily* as saying: "China has a very good tradition such as the respect to the old people. I think it is where the West could learn from you" (*China Daily* 2001c; grammar mistake in the original). The chosen director for the Beijing Olympic bid presentation video was Zhang Yimou, whose previous movies, including *Red Sorghum* and *Raise the Red Lantern,* had been instruments of collective Chinese cultural self-assertion (Zhang 1997). The choice indicated a desire to focus on the subjectivity of the Chinese nation and its roots in the past.

Beijing is not alone in constructing itself as essentially different from the West in an Olympic bid. Istanbul—another contender for the 2008 Games—used a similar strategy by pointing out that bringing the Olympics to Turkey would bring Olympism to the Islamic world. The bid material of both cities described Olympism as fully developed in the West, while having unrealized potential in the Orient and the Islamic world. These arguments must be viewed in relation to the Olympic movement's global aspirations. The IOC claims to be the representative of a global community that is united by Olympic ideals. As former IOC president Juan Antonio Samaranch declared, "The Olympic Games belong not to the IOC, but to humanity. The Olympic Games are the whole world's dream and the IOC's role is to perpetuate that dream" (IOC 2002). Beijing's bid material confirms the Olympic movement's universalist claims, and uses them to argue its case. The differences between the East and the West are *discursively created in order to be transcended through Olympism.* If Beijing were to host the Olympic Games, Olympism becomes increasingly universal, and difference is turned into sameness as the Eastern world adopts Olympic values already endorsed by the West. A quotation of Beijing's mayor Liu Qi summarized the argument: "A chance for Beijing to host the Games would provide a closer link between the Eastern and Western worlds, bring fresh blood to the Olympic Movement and a true meaning of universality—which the Olympics represent" (*China Daily* 2001a). Symbolic references to how the Beijing Olympics will unite the East and the West abound in the bid material. The Olympic torch relay was planned along the Silk Road, the ancient trade route connecting China and the Mediterranean (*China Daily* 2001d). In a less subtle symbolic gesture, it was proposed that Beijing's mayor, who is an engineer, should construct a steel bridge to represent the East meeting the West (*China Daily* 2001d).

Olympic Revival of a Mythical Past

Time is a central organizing concept in Beijing's Olympic bid material. The bid was placed within a temporal framework from the opening line of the Candidature File: "Beijing, with its ancient past, dynamic present and exciting future, has the honor to present its second bid to host the Olympic Games." The bid material depicted time in a way that ascribes inevitability and purpose to China's development process and the hosting of the Olympic Games in Beijing. The passage of time was represented as an unbroken process of progress, a unidirectional movement from worse to better, and from lower to higher levels of development.

Since it was assumed that conditions necessarily improve with time, the adjective *new* became an intrinsically positive characterization. The word was used in Beijing's main bid slogan—"New Beijing, Great Olympics"—and was trumpeted even more loudly in the Chinese version—"New Beijing, New Olympics" (*Xin Beijing Xin Aoyun*). The motto of the bid's promotional program—"New Century, New Culture and New Technology"—was yet another example of the use of "new" to indicate an intrinsically desirable quality (Xinhua 2000a). The bid material employed the concepts of "development" and "modernization" to describe both material and cultural changes for the better, and no essential distinction was made between the two. China's *Report on National Economic and Social Development Plans 2000* exemplifies how the material and the social were viewed as parts of the same development process:

> Radio coverage reached 92.1% of the population and TV coverage, 93.4%. The target for controlling natural population growth was

reached. Major advances were made in reform of the drug and health management system. Socialist spiritual civilization and democracy and the legal system further improved. At the XXVII Olympic Games, Chinese athletes scored their best achievements since China began participating in the Games, greatly stirring the patriotic feelings of the people all over the country and stimulating them to unite and work hard. (Xinhua 2001b)

As the passage illustrates, the Chinese people, working under the guidance of the Chinese Communist Party (CCP), were presented as the key engines of China's progress. Technological advances combine with the Chinese people's indefatigable struggle for a better future to move China along the path of development. Through newspaper articles, CCP officials outlined which roles different groups of people were expected to play in the Olympic bid campaign and Beijing's modernization drive (Xinhua 2001a; *People's Daily* 2001). This continued a tradition of instilling in the Chinese people a sense of their responsibility in furthering the country's progress. Another example came several years earlier, when a patriotic education program was launched to teach students where China was strong and where it lagged behind in order to enhance their sense of responsibility and historical mission (Zhao 1994).

Within the ongoing progress, there is a timeless and unitary subject that stays essentially the same—the Chinese nation. One of the symbols used for this constant is the Great Wall. In Beijing's presentation video to the IOC, the Great Wall tied China's past and present together. The video images of the Wall were accompanied by a voice-over suggesting that the past and present were in harmony: "The Great Wall. A monument to the survival of a vibrant culture that has been able to combine the greatness of the past with ever-changing economic, social and technological advances of the present" (IOC 2001). Emphasis on the historical continuity of the Chinese nation, as well as on the need to develop and strengthen the country, have been important features of Chinese postcommunist nationalism (Unger 1996). The way in which the bid material provided meaning and direction to the passage of time is an example of how nationalism can turn "chance into destiny" and "contingency into purpose" (Anderson 1991, 12).

Both Beijing's Olympic bid material and texts produced by the Olympic movement were marked by a certain ambiguity toward the project of modernization. While the texts conveyed a sense of inevitable progress and faith in modernization, they also endorsed myths of a distant past. Frequent references to Beijing's long history were accompanied by images of physical remnants of the distant past. The restoration of the past in the creation of a glorious future, termed "restoration nationalism," was central to official Chinese discourse in the 1990s (Ko 2001). This stands in contrast to the tendency in the second half of the 1980s to blame remnants of traditional Chinese culture, such as Confucianism, for socioeconomic problems (Wang 1996). While the desirability of traditional Chinese values has been questioned within China for a long time, both through intellectual discourse and popular culture, such as the TV series *River Elegy* (*He Sheng*), they were constantly evoked and presented as admirable in the material directed at a foreign audience. China's ancient history is not depicted as an earlier stage in the present development process, but as a golden age that illustrates the potential of China as a nation. The future holds the promise for realizing this potential, and is thus as mythical as the past. This resonated with IOC material describing the Olympic Games as a revival of past greatness and virtue. The founder of the modern Olympic Games, Pierre de Coubertin, contrasts the anxiety of modern life with the happiness of the past and claims that sport has the ability to return mankind to its origins: "O Sport, pleasure of the Gods, essence of life, you appeared suddenly in the midst of the gray clearing which writhes with the drudgery of modern existence, like the radiant messenger of a past age, when mankind still smiled" (Coubertin [1912] 2002). The IOC often draws upon such mythological imagery in explaining its behavior. The establishment of the so-called Olympic Truce Foundation in 2000, for example, was claimed to be the revival of an ancient Greek tradition.

In Beijing's bid material, the present time was described as a period marked by dizzying technological, economic, and social advances. The city is undergoing a transition from underdevelopment to being a modern "world city." When the IOC Evaluation Commission visited Beijing, the mayor expressed hope that the committee members would see the *potential* in Beijing as well as its current achievements (*China Daily* 2001b). The Olympic Games were assigned several roles in this transition process. The first was to speed up the pace of development. As the state news agency Xinhua wrote, "Chinese economists have said that Beijing's successful bid to host the 2008 Olympics will help the city achieve modernization ahead of schedule" (Xinhua 2001c). Such statements reconfirm the Olympic Movement's claim to be a universal force for modernization. In addition to adding momentum to Beijing's modernization process, the Olympic Games were expected to be a *rite de passage*—a dramatic event marking Beijing's transition from one state to another. The term was originally used in anthropology about ceremonies endowing a person with a new status, while simultaneously reconfirming the social order (van Gennep [1909] 1960). The Olympic bid material asserted that the time was right for the world to recognize that Beijing and China had changed. Hosting the Olympics would mark China's transformation from outsider to insider in the international community, and from underdevelopment to modernity. Importantly, the bid material did not express any ambitions to reform the system itself. While Mao aspired to make China an alternative model for development and to overthrow the existing world system, his successors sought to restore China to its historical greatness *within the existing* international economic and political order (Moore 1999).

Conclusion

The presentation of an Olympic candidature goes far beyond organizational issues. Constructing Beijing as an Olympic city was as much about creating and naturalizing certain world views as it was about presenting practical arguments. The variety of topics brought up in the bid material reflects the wide range of objectives that inform decisions to bid for the Games. Beijing managed to strengthen the legitimacy of the IOC by confirming the universality of the Olympic ideals, presenting Olympism as a force for uniting the East and the West, and promoting modernization. IOC president Juan Antonio Samaranch favored Beijing's candidature both in 1993 and 2001 and played an important role in bringing the Olympic Games' civilizing mission in Asia to the forefront of the debate within the Olympic movement (Booth and Tatz 1993–94). Although both the Chinese government and foreign proponents of Beijing's Olympic bid stressed the positive effects the Games would have on China's development, they may have had different kinds of influence in mind. The government expects the Olympics to bring economic growth and international recognition, while the Western press expresses hopes that the Olympics will promote freedom of expression, political reform, and human rights.

The focus of the chapter has been the presentation of Beijing's candidature in official Chinese discourse. However, meanings attached to places are always potential terrains of contestation, never fixed. Different agents resist and redefine the dominant constructions of places for their own purposes, and thereby reconfigure power relations. When a construction is moved from one social context to another, it may take on new meanings and become the tool of new personal and political objectives. A study of how the official narrative of Beijing as an Olympic city was received, contested, reworked, and reproduced by other actors is an intriguing extension of the analysis presented in this chapter. The Olympic bid initiated social and physical changes in Beijing, and influenced the image foreigners have of the city. As the plans for hosting the Olympics are brought to life, the stakes grow ever higher in the struggle to control the narratives through which these Games are understood.

NOTE

1. The expression "bid material" in this chapter refers to promotional texts and videos produced by the Beijing Olympic Bid Committee, as well as articles about the Olympic bid published for an international audience in Chinese electronic and print media.

REFERENCES

Anderson, Benedict. 1991. *Imagined Communities*. London: Verso.

BOBICO. 2001. Farmers Ride Donkeys All the Way to Xinqiao Hotel. Beijing 2008 Olympic Bid Committee Web site press release, January 18, 2001.

Booth, Douglas, and Colin Tatz. 1993–94. Sydney 2000. The Games People Play. *Current Affairs Bulletin* 70 (7): 4–11.

Byrne, Moyra. 1987. Nazi Festival: The 1936 Berlin Olympics. In *Time out of Time. Essays on the Festival,* ed. A. Falassi, 107–22. Albuquerque: University of New Mexico Press.

Chen, Xiaomei. 1995. *Occidentalism. A Theory of Counter-discourse in Post-Mao China.* New York: Oxford University Press.

China Daily. 2001a. City Pledges "Unprecedented" Games. Beijing, January 2.

China Daily. 2001b. Beijing Promises Unique Olympic Games. Beijing, February 7.

China Daily. 2001c. Beijing Betting on Three Tenors Concert to Boost Its Olympic Bid. Beijing, June 14.

China Daily. 2001d. Beijing to Fulfill Dreams of Billions. Beijing, July 10.

Coubertin, Pierre de. [1912] 2002. *Ode to Sport.* www.olympic.org/upload/news/olympic_review/review_ 20021913257_UK.pdf.

Douglass, Mike. 2000. Mega-urban Regions and World City Formation: Globalisation, the Economic Crisis, and Urban Policy Issues in Pacific Asia. *Urban Studies* 37 (12): 2315–35.

Financial Times. 2000. Editorial: Olympic Games. March 11.

Gare, Arran E. 1995. Understanding Oriental Cultures. *Philosophy East and West* 45 (3): 309–28.

Gregory, Derek. 1994. *Geographical Imagination.* Cambridge: Blackwell.

Hall, C. M., ed. 1992. *Hallmark Tourist Events. Impact, Management, and Planning.* London: Bellhaven Press.

Hiller, Harry H. 1998. Assessing the Impact of Mega-Events: A Linkage Model. *Current Issues in Tourism* 1 (1): 47–57.

Hiller, Harry H. 2000. Mega-events, Urban Boosterism and Growth Strategies: An Analysis of the Objectives and Legitimations of the Cape Town 2004 Bid. *International Journal of Urban and Regional Research* 24 (2): 439–58.

Hoberman, John. 1995. Towards a Theory of Olympic Internationalism. *Journal of Sport History* 22 (1): 1–37.

IOC. 2001. Video from 112th IOC Session, Moscow, July 12, 2001. Transcripts made from recording viewed at the Olympic Museum in Lausanne, Switzerland.

IOC. 2002. Olympic Charter. http://multimedia.olympic.org/pdf/en_re port_122.pdf.

Jessop, Bob. 1999. Reflections on Globalisation and Its (Il)logic(s). In *Globalisation and the Asia-Pacific: Contested Territories,* ed. K. Olds et al., 19–38. London: Routledge.

Kelly, Philip F. 1997. Globalization, Power and the Politics of Scale in the Philippines. *Geoforum* 28 (2): 151–71.

Killanin, Lord. 1983. *My Olympic Years.* New York: William Morrow.

Ko Sunbing. 2001. China's Pragmatism as a Grand National Development Strategy: Historical Legacy and Evolution. *Issues and Studies* 37 (6): 1–28.

Larson, James F., and Heung-Soo Park. 1993. *Global Television and the Politics of the Seoul Olympics.* Boulder: Westview Press.

Li Liangrong. 1994. The Historical Fate of "Objective Reporting" in China. In *China's Media, Media's China,* ed. C. C. Lee, 225–37. Boulder: Westview Press.

Li Lirun. 2001. *Xinwenxue gailun* (An introduction to journalism). Shanghai: Fudan Press.

Li Zhurun. 1998. Popular Journalism with Chinese Characteristics. From Revolutionary Modernity to Popular Modernity. *International Journal of Cultural Studies* 1 (3): 307–28.

Lynch, Daniel. 1999. *After the Propaganda State.* Stanford: Stanford University Press.

Milosz, Czeslaw. 1990. *The Captive Mind.* New York: Vintage International.

Moore, Thomas G. 1999. China and Globalization. *Asian Perspective* 23: (4): 65–95.

People's Daily. 2001. Premier Urges Beijing to Rev up Development. Beijing, January 20.

Renwick, Neil, and Qing Cao. 1999. China's Political Discourse towards the 21st Century: Victimhood, Identity, and Political Power. *East Asia* (winter): 111–43.

Rosenau, Pauline Marie. 1992. *Post-modernism and the Social Sciences: Insights, Inroads, and Intrusions.* Princeton: Princeton University Press.

Saïd, Edward. [1978] 1995. *Orientalism.* London: Penguin Books.

Unger, Jonathan. 1996. Introduction. In *Chinese Nationalism,* ed. J. Unger, i–xi. New York: M. E. Sharpe.

U.S. Embassy in the United Kingdom. 2002. President Bush Calls Olympics a Celebration of Peace and Cooperation. February 9. http://www.usembassy.org.uk/bush148.html.

van Gennep, Arnold. [1909] 1960. *The Rites of Passage.* Chicago: University of Chicago Press.

Waitt, Gordon. 1999. Playing Games with Sydney: Marketing Sydney for the 2000 Olympics. *Urban Studies* 36 (7): 1055–77.

Wamsley, Kevin B. 2002. The Global Sport Monopoly. A Synopsis of 20th Century Olympic Politics. *International Journal* 57 (3): 50–65.

Wang Jing. 1996. *High Culture Fever: Politics, Aesthetics, and Ideology in Deng's China.* Berkeley: University of California Press.

Ward, Stephen Victor. 1998. *Selling Places.* London: E. and F. N. Spon.

Xinhua. 2000a. "Countdown Clock Set up to Support." Beijing, December 22.

Xinhua. 2000b. Sports Yearender: New Beijing Benefits from Great Olympics. Beijing, December 28.

Xinhua. 2001a. Beijing Rounds off Bidding Report for 2008 Olympics. Beijing, January 11.

Xinhua. 2001b. Report on National Economic Social Development. Beijing, March 18.

Xinhua. 2001c. Olympic Games to Rev up Beijing's Modernization Drive. Beijing, July 30.

Xu Guangqiu. 1998. The Chinese Anti-American Nationalism in the 1990s. *Asian Perspective* 22 (2): 193–218.

Zhang Longxi. 1998. *Mighty Opposites. From Dichotomies to Difference in the Comparative Study of China.* Stanford: Stanford University Press.

Zhang Xuedong. 1997. *Chinese Modernism in the Era of Reforms: Cultural Fever, Avant-Garde Fiction, and the New Chinese Cinema.* Durham: Duke University Press.

Zhao Suisheng. 1994. "We Are Patriots First and Democrats Second": The Rise of Chinese Nationalism in the 1990s. In *What If China Doesn't Democratize?* ed. E. Friedman and B. McCormick, 21–48. New York: Armonk.

Zheng Yongnian. 1999. *Discovering Chinese Nationalism in China.* Cambridge: Cambridge University Press.

Dreams and Nightmares

History and U.S. Visions of the Beijing Games

Jeffrey N. Wasserstrom

In 1936, the United States participated in the Berlin Summer Olympics, despite Adolph Hitler's scheming to make the Games a Nazi showcase. . . .

Should we go [to Beijing] in 2008?

I think not. How can memories not be considerable of the Tiananmen tanks of 1989 . . . ? (Mizell 2001)

This will be the first time that China has hosted the Olympic Games, and this historic occasion will be a landmark in the rest of the world's discovery of this wonderful and fascinating country . . . [And] greater exposure of China to the world will undoubtedly help promote increased openness and understanding over the coming years. (*People's Daily Online* 2006)

Get ready. Over the coming months, before and during the Beijing Olympics of 2008, you will be bombarded with stereotypes about China that have accumulated over hundreds of years. (Mann 2007)

The Western discourse on the 2008 Olympics, which has periodically reached high levels of intensity ever since the news broke in 2001 that Beijing would get to host the Games, cries out for historical analysis. Or, rather, as the preceding quotes suggest, it cries out for several different kinds of analysis that relate to history. For this discourse has been one in which *historical analogies* (see the Beijing 2008 equals Berlin 1936 reference in quote 1 at the beginning of this chapter) and *historical allusions* to the Chinese past (see the same quote's reference to the 1989 massacre) have figured prominently. This discourse has also featured the suggestion that the Games will mark a *historic turning point* (see quote 2) and been shaped by a long *history of Western commentaries on China* (see quote 3).

This chapter will have something to say about all of these kinds of historical relevance, but will focus primarily on situating some of the comments that have been made and are likely to be made soon about the 2008 Games into long-standing patterns in Western media coverage of and thinking about China. Insofar as this analysis will also touch on other ways in which history figures in this discourse, I will stress the extent to which analogies, allusions, and references to turning points often come naturally to mind or take on a special power as a result of being refracted through the lenses through which Westerners have tended to view China.

For example, Westerners have long been accustomed to view China as a land given to despotic rule. And for a shorter period (but still several decades) some commentators have stressed similarities between Germany's Nazi regime and China's Communist ones. The notion that the Beijing Games should be compared to the Berlin Games—a 1936 event disparaged now for having given Hitler more international legitimacy than he deserved—should be understood as fitting within the context of the general Chinese rulers equal despots and specific Communist leaders equal Fascist leaders patterns.

Conversely, the idea that has been invoked in various IOC pronouncements, including the statement by Rogge quoted previously, that China is finally on the right track and about to turn a historic corner, in terms of both its openness to and place in the world, is by this point a familiar one—especially in the United States. The claim that China was about to undergo a historic shift, which would make it easier for Americans to understand and deal with the Chinese people, was put forward when Sun Yat-sen (1866–1925) was inaugurated as president of the new Republic of China in 1912; when Chiang Kai-shek (1887–1975) ruled the country (1927–1949); and when Deng Xiaoping (1904–1997), governing what by then had been rechristened the People's Republic of China, launched his policies of *kaifeng* and *gaige* (openness and reform) just a few years after the death of Mao Zedong (1893–1976).

One reason for my decision to focus here on long-term historical patterns in commentary on China is that while I disagree with some arguments in Mann's *The China Fantasy*—differences I will not spell out here, as they can be found in my *World Policy Journal* review of his book—I think he was right on target about one thing: we will be "bombarded" between now and the end of the 2008 Olympics by variations of "the same clichéd phrases" and "standard China graphics" that are always trotted out to refer to or represent the world's most populous country when it is in the global spotlight (Mann 2007).[1] We have, in fact, already undergone such a bombardment. It began when the IOC announced in 2001 that Beijing would host the 2008 Games. Indeed almost a decade before, in the early 1990s, the first Olympic-related volleys in this bombardment were fired during the raging debates over whether the 2000 Games should be held in China.

Before trying to place into long-term perspective the resurrection in coverage of the Olympics of old "clichéd phrases" and familiar "images," which present China as either trapped in age-old patterns or rapidly leaving all tradition behind (Mann provides an amusing list of visuals we can expect to see during the television broadcast of the Games),[2] let us look quickly at some examples in the Western discourse on the Olympics of historical analogies, historical allusions, and visions of China having reached or about to reach a historic turning point. In doing so, it will be useful (for heuristic purposes) to divide up commentators into what might be called "pessimistic" and "optimistic" camps (keeping in mind that many commentators walk a line between the two positions or alternate between taking a pessimistic or optimistic view of where China is heading). In the pessimistic camp are those who are doubtful that the 2008 Olympics will have any positive effect for China or for the world. They were in 2001 and remain to this day critical of the IOC decision to award the Games to Beijing. In the optimistic camp, meanwhile, are those who have been and remain hopeful about what the event will or at least might accomplish.

As we will see, each group turns at times to history to buttress their stance. But the analogies and allusions they favor differ markedly, with the best example perhaps being the way in which optimists prefer to think of Beijing 2008 as more analogous to Seoul 1988 (an Olympics that helped democratize an authoritarian society) than to Berlin 1936. And though both groups sometimes suggest that 2008 may be seen by later generations as having marked a historical "turning point" for China and the world, the pessimists imagine it as a turn for the worse (signaling full international acceptance of a brutal regime), not for the better (continuing China on the road to openness and freedom).

History and the Pessimists

Since the 1989 massacre . . . the People's Republic of China has thumbed its nose at world opinion of its degraded human rights practices. . . .

Now the international community—or that segment of it represented by the International Olympic Committee—has administered some long-overdue discipline to China's dictators.

Beijing will not host the Olympic Games in 2000. In a surprise move, the IOC chose Sydney, Australia, as the site of those games.

This year, Congress passed a resolution opposing Beijing's bid. "I do not believe we should allow the Chinese government a huge propaganda victory when it routinely tortures [and] severely restricts freedom of assembly and expression," said U.S. Senator—and Olympic basketball gold medalist—Bill Bradley (D-N.J.).

Not everyone saw it that way. Giving the games to China would "influence a change in behavior," remarked IOC board member Dick Pound. Some people have short memories. Moscow had the games in 1980, but spent almost the rest of the decade engaging in butchery in Afghanistan. Berlin hosted the 1936 Olympics, three years before Hitler made war on the world and initiated the Final Solution.

Den [sic] Xiaoping and his gang are just as merciless. (*Boston Herald* 1993)

As we saw in the first quote used to open this chapter, the two main ways that critics of the IOC's decision to award China the 2008 Games have brought history to bear on the issue are via analogies to the 1936 Games and allusions to Chinese repression in 1989 (*Independent* 2001; *Houston Chronicle* 2001).[3] As the long excerpt from the *Boston Herald* editorial just provided illustrates, these two kinds of uses of history belong to a tradition that predates 2001—for analogies to the Games that Hitler hosted and allusions to 1989 were common in the Western press while China made its failed bid almost a decade earlier to host the 2000 Games.[4] The Berlin 1936 analogy and backward looks to Tiananmen have been and continue to be a mainstay in pessimistic commentaries on China's current condition and future prospects, put forward by people who argued before 2001 that the IOC should not let the Beijing regime host the Games and have since then criticized the IOC's decision on 2008.

Commentators in this camp tend to stress certain basic points. They emphasize the degree to which the PRC has failed to move forward in specific areas (particularly the protection of human rights). They are doubtful about the prospects of meaningful transformation coming soon if the country is left to its own devices (and if the CCP retains control). And they have been skeptical of any suggestion that the Olympics might have a positive impact on China (some think it could even be harmful, either because of the way it will affect the lives of ordinary Chinese or because of the international legitimacy having the Games held in its capital city will give the current regime).

It is important to note that new wrinkles have continually been added to this by now well-established approaches, and we should expect still other ones to be added by the time the Games take place. One example of a recent novelty within a general framework of continuity is that the Berlin 1936 analogy is now (as I write this in June 2007) often reinforced by references to Chinese complicity in the Darfur genocide (Farrow and Farrow 2007; Chu 2007). When efforts were made to tie Beijing 2008 to Berlin 1936 prior to 2007, this typically tapped into the tradition (alluded to earlier) of equating Communist leaders to Fascist ones. This tradition was given a new boost as recently as 2005, with the publication of Jung Chang and Fred Halliday's biography, *Mao: The Unknown Story*, which some scholars (myself included) criticized as sensationalistic and sloppy but which received a great deal of positive media attention and became a bestseller in several countries. Chang and Halliday (2005) link the Chinese Chairman to the German Fuehrer at several points, and they claim that as long as a giant portrait of this bloodthirsty Nazi-like tyrant continues to stand above Tiananmen Square, the PRC cannot be said to have really changed.[5] Now, however, a more specific Holocaust referent has been added to the Berlin 1936 analogy via the use Mia Farrow and others have made of the "Genocide Olympics" phrase.[6]

Another shift over time has been that those critical of the decision to award the 2008 Games to China have begun to put more emphasis on specific things that have been done in and to Beijing to prepare the metropolis for the Games. The destruction of old neighborhoods, forced relocations of residents, and the tough measures taken to keep the central districts free of beggars and migrant workers when foreign observers come to town, for instance, are often now cited as evidence that the regime did not deserve to get the nod in 2001 (Yardley 2007; Sheridan 2007; *New Zealand Herald* 2007; Gu 2007). Still, the basic thrust of pessimistic commentary remains much as it was when the IOC made its decision to grant Beijing the 2008 Games (and before that debated whether to allow China to host the 2000 ones), with the Berlin 1936 analogy in particular playing a central emotional part, conjuring up discrediting memories of a time the world community gave legitimacy to an abhorrent regime.

History and the Optimists

The question of human rights will be an important factor in deciding the site of the 2000 Olympics, International Olympic Committee President Juan Antonio Samaranch said yesterday. . . .

"Human rights is important. . . . To have the Games in a country also is quite important, if you study what happened in 1988, for example," Samaranch said. "Maybe the Olympic Games in Seoul pushed the change in this country quicker." (*Washington Post* 1993)[7]

I think Beijing's hosting of the 2008 Olympics Games could be a great opportunity to help promote democracy and openness in China. If there is [a] democratic movement in China at that time, would the Beijing authorities dare to strike it down by force at a time when the world's spotlight is fixed firmly on it? . . .

Student movements in South Korea used the 1988 Seoul Olympics as a chance—coupled with international pressure—to push for a democratic government.

If Korea can do it, why can't China? (Wang Dan 2003)

On the other side, meanwhile, as indicated in the preceding quotations, there have for years been and continue to be those who stress the Olympics' potential either to start China off, or help it to continue, in a positive direction—and here, too, history is invoked. When optimists turn to international history, their favorite point of reference since the early 1990s has been and continues to be 1988, the year that the Games were held in Seoul, the capital city of an authoritarian state that had just begun to become more democratic and would soon afterward move decisively in that direction.[8] Optimists sometimes pair this with a nod to China's own past, occasionally even invoking the same year,

1989, that figures so prominently in texts calling for a boycott of the 2008 Games. Thus we see some commentators suggesting, as Wang Dan did in his 2003 *Taipei Times* interview, that there is the potential for a revival down the road of the sort of democratic activism that fueled the inspiring Tiananmen protests, and that the global coverage of the Olympics could aid this process. Other optimists bring history into play in a different fashion, as noted in one of the quotes used to open this chapter. Namely, they stress, as IOC President Rogge did in 2006, how far the PRC has come in recent years in terms of opening to the world and modernizing the economy. They emphasize in particular the historical distance that China has traveled since the era of Mao Zedong (1949–76) and even that of Deng Xiaoping (1978–97).[9]

The Seoul analogy is sometimes paired with looks backward to other past Olympics. Some optimists, for example, remind readers of what happened as a result of the Moscow 1980 Olympics. Even though we have seen an example already of this analogy being used in a negative fashion (in the previous quote that referred to Soviet repression continuing after 1980), those Moscow Games have sometimes been given credit for starting the chain of events that ended in 1991. The Olympics are said to have helped bring about the demise of the Soviet Union, since through the Games, despite the American boycott, the Russian people were brought into close contact with far more foreign visitors and generally received far more information about foreign lands than they had for decades. This led them to draw comparisons between their government and their country's stage of economic development and those of other lands that were very unflattering for Moscow. In addition, as noted earlier, optimists sometimes point to the 1964 Tokyo Games. They do so not to suggest that hosting the Olympics pushed Japan onto a new path, but rather that it served as an appropriate recognition of how far that country had come in recent decades; China, optimists suggest, has made similar progress.[10]

Looking Backward

Even though many different kinds of positions are staked out in the media discourse on China and the Olympics, it is striking how prevalent the two stances just sketched out have been and continue to be in rhetorical clashes linked to the 2008 Games. It is also interesting that the clash of viewpoints outlined here, which will doubtless persist through the summer of 2008 (albeit with new wrinkles added over time), is not just one in which references to history have played and will continue to play important roles, but also one in which echoes of past debates about China can easily be heard.

We have already seen that the early twenty-first century debate was prefigured, rhetorical move for rhetorical move, by the late twentieth century one surrounding Beijing's failed attempt to get the nod for the 2000 Olympics. Then, too, some international commentators insisted that China's regime was too brutal to be allowed to host the Olympics, especially in light of its then-recent crushing of peaceful student-led demonstrations in 1989. Then, too, there were those who thought that allowing China to host the Games would push the country in the right direction, making it more likely that it would follow the path to democracy that had recently been taken in countries such as South Korea that had shed their authoritarian ways.[11] And so on.

There are, of course, specific ways that the 1990s differ from the present, as China's stage of development and role in world affairs was not the same then as it is now—and this had an effect on the discourse of the time. For example, the fact that China is now seen as a rising economic power has added novel dimensions to commentaries on the 2008 Olympics as opposed to the bid for the 2000 Games, as has the fact that it is seen as a country with increasing influence in Latin America and Africa. Prior to 2001, the tendency was still to present China as a developing country with ambitions of becoming a world power, and to ask whether its achieving that goal was something that was worrisome or welcome and would be helped or hindered by hosting the Games. In the 1990s, there were more doubts raised about the regime's ability to create a modern urban infrastructure of the kind that the Olympics needs, whereas recently the focus has been on the social costs of the creation of that kind of infrastructure. Still, it makes sense to think of the debates of the 1990s as a dress rehearsal of sorts or prequel to the contemporary debate.

It is not just echoes of that relatively recent debate, though, that can be heard in the early twentieth-century arguments about China focusing on the Games, for James Mann is correct when he refers to "stereotypes about China that have accumulated over hundreds of years" coming into play. In the pages that follow, I will focus on two such "stereotypes," one of them a comforting sort of stereotype, the other of a more menacing type, and each of them misleading in its own way. I will refer to them as stereotypes that feed the "American China Dream" and the "American China Nightmare"—the intertwined fantasies invoked in this chapter's title.[12]

To understand fully the story of the 2008 Olympics, as it is told by and told to international audiences and Americans in particular, it is important to appreciate the role that these two fantasies have played and continue to play. They are fantasies that can be traced back to many starting points, but one of the most plausible is the Boxer Rebellion of 1899–1901. This was a complex series of events but it is remembered mostly now for two things. In the United States, what is remembered is that insurgents (whom Westerners called "Boxers," due to their use of martial arts techniques) killed Chinese Christians and missionaries and then laid siege to Beijing's Legation Quarter for 55 days in the summer of 1900, before foreign troops marched in to free the hostages. In China, while these actions are remembered, so too is something else: after the siege was lifted, foreign troops (marching under the flags of eight nations) looted Chinese national treasures, wreaked havoc on the Chinese countryside, and imposed an enormous indemnity on the Chinese state. What is perhaps most important about the Boxer Rebellion for our purposes here, and what makes 1900 a fitting point of reference, is that the siege of the Legation Quarter was one of the first events (perhaps the very first event) that put China in something that deserves to be called the global media spotlight, thanks to the fact that, because of the marvels of telegraphy (the breakthrough "new" medium of communication of an earlier day) and undersea cables, it was followed in many parts of the world in something very close to real time.

What is intriguing about moving forward from the Boxer Rebellion to the present is that even though the China of today is in many regards a very different country than it was in 1900, the groundwork for the interplay of dream and nightmare in coverage of contemporary stories about China, including the Olympic one, was laid in the violence of that time. The coverage of China in 1900, a year when the American press romanticized the Chinese Christian martyrs slain by Boxers as paragons of virtue, while painting the Boxers as inhumanly savage, was unusual in its intensity. Still, this would not be the last time that American ideas about China would be colored by a love-hate relationship defined by visions of conversion and savagery. Both positive and negative images already in circulation before 1900, but given added power by the events of that year, have continued to shape American ideas about the world's most populous land.

The Dream and the Nightmare Defined

It is time now to flesh out these comments on the Boxers and provide a brief summary and backward look at the evolution of what I have labeled the American China Dream and the American China Nightmare, since their influence on coverage of the Olympics can only make sense if we know more about what they are and how they arose. In a nutshell, the Dream has always been and still is predicated on a vision of the Chinese as people who want to embrace our ways and who live in a land poised on the brink of shedding vestiges of worrisome old ways. The Nightmare is predicated on a contrasting vision of the Chinese as people who are helping to keep in power or have become the unwilling victims of a vicious state that threatens all we hold dear.

It would be a mistake to argue that, just because both the Dream and Nightmare have been in play for more than a century, there has never been and is not now anything new under the sun where American ideas about China are concerned. This is because, as already indicated, there are always shifts taking place within an enduring general framework defined by the poles of the two fantasies. The details of both the American China Dream and the American China Nightmare have continually changed in subtle but sometimes very important ways from period to period, just as they are currently shifting again, as China is being seen as an economic threat (a novelty, at least in modern times), a country capable of competing with Western countries and Japan for a position as a great economic power. This means that versions of the American China Dream and American China Nightmare that took for granted the "backward" nature of the Chinese nation are being re-tooled for an era characterized by high growth rates and rocket launches in the PRC.

Another kind of shift, which is not unprecedented but has some novel features, has to do with the relative power of the Dream and the Nightmare. There have been particularly optimistic moments when the Dream predominated (e.g., midway through the 1989 protests), and pessimistic ones when the Nightmare held sway (e.g., just after 1989's June 4 massacre). There have also periodically been ambiguous points in time when elements of each fantasy were fully in play, and the Dream and Nightmare jostled for supremacy. These third types of moment are, not surprisingly, the most interesting to analyze, and it is in one of these that we currently find ourselves.

One of the interesting features of these moments of ambiguity is that they enable us to see how much the American China Dream and American China Nightmare have in common. They also add new shadings to each fantasy. History suggests that such new shadings are especially likely to come when any one of the following things happens: unexpected events suddenly put China in the global spotlight (as was the case when the Boxers laid siege to the foreign legations in Beijing); orchestrated media events take place (e.g., Nixon's first trip to China in the 1970s and Deng Xiaoping's first trip to the United States in the 1980s); or international phenomena not directly tied to China occur that make Americans particularly hopeful or fearful about a different distant country, thereby indirectly minimizing hopes and fears associated with the Chinese (e.g., the China Nightmare almost disappeared completely in the wake of Pearl Harbor).

The six-year period bracketed by the quotes with which I began has been one that has added new shadings to both old visions. This is not surprising, for not only were updated versions of both the Dream and the Nightmare in play throughout, but all three types of fantasy-altering developments occurred. In April 2001, for example, the "spy plane incident" (the collision of American and Chinese military jets that led to mutual recriminations and a brief period when U.S. servicemen were held on the PRC island where their craft had made an unapproved emergency landing) was an unexpected event that breathed new life into the old Nightmare. In October 2006 (when North Korea carried out a nuclear test and Beijing worked to rein in that neighboring Communist state), an unexpected international political development cast China in a positive light. And during those years, media events held in China, such as the APEC Summit that brought Bush to Shanghai in October 2001, made their mark.

We can also expect the near future to be a fascinating one to watch insofar as the two fantasies are concerned. Leaving aside the always present possibility of unexpected international events that bring China and the United States closer together or push us further apart, modern Olympics involve orchestrated media events (such as the opening and closing ceremonies) and are often accompanied by unexpected dramas of an inspiring or tragic nature, with the multiple 1936 victories of Jesse Owens that undermined Hitler's goal of showcasing Aryan greatness falling into the former category, and the tragic violence of the Munich Games, into the latter.

Scratches on Our Minds

One of the best places to begin a discussion of the long-term evolution of the American China Dream and American China Nightmare is with a book that was published in 1958 (exactly five decades before the Beijing Games), yet remains eerily relevant. It is called *Scratches on Our Minds: American Views of China and India,* and its author, Harold R. Isaacs, worked as a journalist in China before World War II and then went on to have a second career teaching political science at MIT and writing books on various subjects.[13] *Scratches on Our Minds* was based on extended interviews with a variety of influential Americans (journalists, politicians, business leaders, etc.), all of whom Isaacs asked during the interviews (conducted in the early to mid-1950s) to describe their ideas about China and India, and also to reflect upon the readings, movies, and experiences (stories told by relatives, travel, interactions with people from the two countries and so forth) that helped shape these ideas.

The treatment of India in *Scratches on Our Minds* has had some impact, but it is the book's treatment of China that has tended to get the most attention.[14] And it is the book's compelling vision of the peculiar love-hate relationship between America and China that was responsible for the appearance of two updated editions of the book, published at notable junctures in U.S.-Chinese relations. A second edition appeared in 1972, around the time of Nixon's famous meeting with Mao, while a third appeared in 1980, just after Deng had introduced reforms that promised to open the PRC up to international influences.

Notably, while Isaacs wrote new prefaces for the second and third editions of *Scratches on Our Minds,* in which he presented interesting new information about recent trends in American thinking about China (e.g., Nixon's meeting with Mao would add new twists to old motifs), he insisted that the basic framework of the 1958 edition had not been made obsolete by developments of the 1960s and 1970s. In the preface to the 1972 edition, for example, he summarizes his vision of America's peculiar mixture of passionate concern with and ambivalence toward China, and the tendency of Americans to alternately romanticize and vilify the Chinese, as follows:

> Down through time, from Marco Polo to Mao Tse-tung [Mao Zedong], the Chinese have appeared to us as superior people and inferior people, outrageous heathen and attractive humanists, wisely benevolent sages

and deviously cunning villains, thrifty and honorable men and sly and corrupt cheats, heroically enduring stoics and cruel and sadistic murderers, masses of hardworking persevering people and masses of antlike creatures indifferent to human life, comic opera soldiers and formidable warriors. (Isaacs 1980, xxi)

Isaacs then goes on to quote at length from a "key passage" in the first edition. This passage begins by referring to the way that, throughout "the long history of our associations with China," "two sets of images," one strongly positive and the other strongly negative, continually "rise and fall, move in and out of the center of people's minds over time, never wholly displacing each other, always co-existing, each ready to emerge at the fresh call of circumstance, always new, yet instantly garbed in all the words and pictures of a much-written literature." It ends by summarizing American feelings about the Chinese as having "ranged between sympathy and rejection, parental benevolence and parental exasperation, affection and hostility, love and a fear close to hate" (xxi–xxii). In his 1980 preface, he stresses that, while much has changed, "our assorted positive and negative images and feelings about the Chinese flicker in and out of the immediate scene and many of both kinds remain in view together" (xvii).

Scratches on Our Minds does not take a straightforward chronological approach to the subject of the formation of American images of China, but it does flag key moments in the past that helped to solidify or breathed new life into a positive or negative idea about the Chinese. The rise of the Boxers and the appearance of the Fu Manchu books and films soon after that, for example, are cited as developments of the early 1900s that contributed greatly to American fears of China. And the publication of Pearl Buck's *The Good Earth* and that novel's subsequent transformation into a popular Hollywood film, meanwhile, are linked to the circulation of a much less threatening sense of the Chinese in the 1930s.

What comes across most strongly in *Scratches on Our Minds*, though, is the sense of the interplay, at each stage of the twentieth century, of strongly charged positive and negative ideas about China and its people. Isaacs sees this as contrasting with the more dispassionate views that Americans often had of people of other distant lands, including India. It also sets American visions of China off in an important way from the Western visions of the Middle East criticized in Edward Saïd's influential and controversial study of that topic, *Orientalism*

(1979). Some of the forms that negative American images of China have taken can be fit into Saïd's framework. The same cannot be said, however, of the recurring American positive fantasies about China, which are tinged with admiration and present the United States and China as being destined to become, and on the brink of becoming, close friends.

The China-Japan Seesaw Effect

Isaacs adds an intriguing twist to the story of American images of China in a section of the preface to his 1972 edition that brings the Japanese into the story. He presents data taken from Gallup polls to suggest that, while American ideas about China and Japan have each followed a distinctive trajectory, there is also, at times, a strong inverse correlation between our images of the people of the two countries. To put it crudely—more crudely than he does—it sometimes seems that when one country's people are admired, those of the other are distrusted, and vice versa.

The obvious case in point is that American stereotypes of the Japanese during World War II were nearly identical to American stereotypes of the Chinese during the Korean War.[15] In each case, it was not only that the alleged cruelty of the people in the enemy country was stressed, but also that much was made of their alleged tendency toward conformity. The rise and fall of other traits (being considered "hardworking," "brave," "honest," etc.) has not flip-flopped quite as neatly, but with those too, Isaacs argues, the question of whether they are most aptly applied to the Chinese or to the Japanese has shifted from decade to decade, due in large part to changes in international politics. T. Christopher Jespersen, in a book that is particularly good at showing how Song Meiling (Madame Chiang Kai-shek) came to embody the American China Dream, makes a similar point about this China-Japan seesaw pattern in *American Images of China, 1931–1949* (1996). And Sheila K. Johnson's lively and insightful 1988 book, *The Japanese through American Eyes*, sheds light on the same phenomenon (what she calls the "Migrating Asian Stereotype") as well.

To simplify things greatly, we can draw upon the material Isaacs, Jespersen, Johnson, and others present to paint the following picture of American ideas about China from around 1900 through around 1980, and the relationship of these to ideas about Japan:

1. The Boxer period—China was feared or despised (though positive images of the Chinese were kept alive by hagiographic accounts of Chinese Christian converts who died at the hands of the Boxers), while Japan was admired due to its rapid modernization.
2. The 1910s–20s—hope for China rose, especially around 1912, with Sun Yat-sen inaugurated as the first president of the new Chinese Republic, though doubt lingered as to whether it could modernize effectively, while Japan was still largely admired, but starting to be feared as a potential competitor.
3. The 1930s–40s—negative images of Japan as populated by savage conformists predominated, while China was seen as either a victim deserving sympathy or a brave ally in the fight against tyranny.
4. The 1950s–60s—a reversal of the 1930s–40s situation, with Japan admired for its ability to bounce back economically from its World War II defeat and apparent readiness to embrace American ways, while China became again a source of fear, imagined as a land of automatons in thrall to a brutal dictator allied to the Soviets.
5. The 1970s—another reversal begins, with the Chinese now seen as people who, under the surface, are much more like us than we had imagined, and concerns about Japanese economic competition beginning to rise.

1980 Onward: Ricochet Effects and Mixed Emotions

Americans always seem to be busy clearing up misconceptions about China. In an attempt to get beyond one set of misunderstandings, however, they often create new ones to take their place. They substitute today's "truth" for yesterday's myth, only to discover that today's "reality" becomes tomorrow's illusion. This is why American attitudes towards China have undergone the regular cycles of romanticism and cynicism so well described twenty-five years ago in Harold Isaacs' classic, *Scratches on Our Minds*. (Harding 1982, 934).

The story of American images of China from the end of the 1970s through the present is a complex one that can only be told in a very sketchy fashion here. It was a period during which orchestrated media events often played a central role in reinforcing or adding new dimensions to the American China Dream or the American China Nightmare. For example, in the first half of the 1980s, when Deng Xiaoping donned a cowboy hat during his visit to the United States, after American newspaper stories stressed his pragmatic approach to economic and political issues and his love of playing bridge, he became perhaps the most powerful high-ranking embodiment of the Dream since the days in the 1930s and 1940s when Wellesley-educated Song Meiling was routinely celebrated in the pages of *Time* magazine. The new twist here, though, was the idea that Deng was a Communist leader who, at heart, was not really so different from the pioneering capitalists whom Americans credit with having made our country great. And throughout the last two decades, periodic trips to China by American presidents have been orchestrated media events that have given new twists to the Dream in particular.

It has not only been orchestrated media events, however, that have been significant image shapers in recent years, for unplanned occurrences have also put China in the spotlight and resurrected or gave new shadings to old positive and negative fantasies late in the last century and during the first years of this new one. The events of 1989, in particular, showed the ability of unexpected developments to alter American perceptions of the Chinese (for the better) and their leaders (for the worse). We should also remember that the events of 1989 came on the heels of not just a burst of positive publicity about China's leaders (due to things such as Deng's celebrated trip to the United States), but also a decade of Japan bashing (that, via the seesaw effect, helped keep images of the PRC relatively positive). The Tiananmen crisis thus had a curious effect, with the American China Dream retaining its hold but going underground in a sense, as hopes for the country were relocated from the leadership to the dissidents, and fantasies of a complete U.S.-China reconciliation placed in an imagined post-CCP future rather than a Deng-led CCP present.

Big Bad China and the Good Chinese

The 1990s and first years of the twenty-first century also saw pendulum swings, which added new twists to but did not fundamentally undermine the basic pattern that Isaacs described.[16] Once again, orchestrated media events (such as Clinton's 1998 visit to China) played a role. And so, too, did unplanned developments (such as NATO bombs hitting the Chinese embassy in Belgrade in 1999, triggering protests in the PRC, and the conflict that developed during the "spy plane" incident of

April 2001). In general, this period saw hopes for China placed not in the leadership but in the people of the country (the "Good Chinese" of this subsection's title)—both dissidents and, increasingly, less explicitly political groups whose members seemed bent on embracing Western lifestyles (eating hamburgers, going bowling, listening to Western pop music, etc.).

This divide was not absolute, however, as the Chinese people were sometimes seen as dangerous, if only because they could still be mobilized by the regime. The anti-NATO protests in 1999 were thus presented in the U.S. press as both a sign that the government could still get people out onto the streets, and, in the most extreme commentaries, a sign that the mentality of the Boxers had never been completely vanquished. American fear and denigration of Japan, which peaked in the 1980s, waned during the 1990s, and talk of a potential "China Threat" (thought of sometimes in military terms and sometimes in economic ones) began—and at times continues.[17]

Looking Forward: What to Expect in 2008

How does this historical tour prepare us for analyzing the Western and particularly American commentaries on China and its 2008 Olympics? One thing worth remembering is that the Games themselves often involve both planned and unplanned elements (choreographed opening ceremonies, but also unexpected things—not just who wins or loses, but things like the 1968 Black Power salute). No matter how tightly controlled the Games are, unexpected things will occur either on the streets of Beijing, in the announcers' booth, or in crowds, and these compete with internationally acclaimed film director Zhang Yimou's choreographed displays when it comes to media attention. Patterns of framing are persistent. Some themes are emphasized in the media whether or not unexpected events take place. For example, if protests against the regime occur during the Games (or at other times), these will be taken by some commentators to be additional proof that the Communist Party is a repressive organization. But if there are *no protests*, this will likely be cited by some commentators as evidence of just how repressive the Communist Party is.

In other words, given both the continued relevance of the patterns that Isaacs described five decades ago and recent developments in ideas about China (e.g., only in the last few years has the idea of the PRC being more of an *economic* and *diplomatic* threat become more pronounced than the idea of it being a potential *military* threat), future narratives will have the very solid markings of the past. We are likely, for example, to see an ongoing division between stories that look at individual Chinese (in this case mostly athletes) through the lens of the American China Dream, and stories that look at the Chinese state (and representatives of it such as the police) through the lens of the American China Nightmare. The way that Yao Ming has been treated gives us a preview of how the "Big Bad China and the Good Chinese" story line can work in the world of sports.

Yao Ming as an individual is often the focus of reports that play up the similarities between the American and Chinese spirit. He is treated as a person who has been able to move easily across national borders, adopting some elements of the American lifestyle, while remaining tied to China culturally and to some degree politically (such as by continuing to play for the PRC national team). These positive reports compete, however, with tales of Yao Ming the product, a manufactured sports star created by a soulless Chinese state (bred from birth to be a superathlete, the product of a state-arranged marriage between two basketball players, etc.).[18]

History also suggests that we need to be aware that, if stories of the 2008 Olympics spin in an unexpected direction, this may have at least as much to do with changes in the international arena as with changes in China itself. In just the last couple of years we have seen coverage of the PRC affected greatly, but in opposite ways, by two international crises: that relating to Darfur, which as noted earlier added a new twist to the Nightmare, and that relating to North Korea's nuclear ambitions, which added a new twist to the recurring Dream motif of Beijing representing a relatively benign version of Communism, and gave us yet another example of the "migrating Asian stereotype," as Pyongyang has come to represent what Tokyo represented during World War II and Beijing represented during the Korean War.

NOTES

1. For my critique of his representation of how China specialists tend to think and write about the PRC, see Wasserstrom 2007b.

2. Mann's list includes everything from shots of mountains shrouded in mist and of the Great Wall to images of Chinese youths carrying cell phones. See Mann 2007, 90.

3. These are 2 of the 121 articles that came up on November 8, 2006, when I ran a Lexis-Nexis database search for pieces in "major papers" from the period January 1, 2001–December 31, 2001, in which the terms *China* and *Olympics* and *Hitler* and *2008* all appeared. These articles were among the many generated by that search that endorsed the value of the Berlin-Beijing parallel (often bringing Tiananmen as an example of the regime's deeply problematic record on human rights), but a smaller number brought up the parallel in order to debunk or at least question it. See, for example, Sullivan 2001.

4. For an illustrative piece from the 1990s, which refers to how common talk of the Berlin analogy and invocations of 1989 had become during the lead-up to the announcement about the 2000 Games, see Todd 1993.

5. Critical reviews that suggest the need to approach the book with a degree of skepticism include Davin 2005; Wasserstrom 2005; and Nathan 2005.

6. Here is a summary of this position: "Concern over [atrocities in] Darfur . . . prompted actress Mia Farrow to pressure director Steven Spielberg, an artistic adviser on the opening ceremony of the Games.

'Does Mr. Spielberg really want to go down in history as the Leni Riefenstahl of the Beijing Games?' Farrow asked in a commentary last month in The Wall Street Journal, referring to the German director who presented the 1936 Berlin Olympics as a triumph for Adolf Hitler. Spielberg promptly wrote to President Hu Jintao, urging Beijing to use its influence to stop the genocide in Sudan." (Fan 2007)

7. For a similar reference to the relevance of Seoul, see also *Toronto Star* 1993 and *New York Times* 1993.

8. See, for example, *New Zealand Herald* 2001, which I discovered via the Lexis-Nexis search described in note 3, in which the Tokyo and Seoul as well as Berlin analogies are discussed; Moscow parallels are mentioned in Sullivan 2001.

9. See, for example, the *Guardian* 2007.

10. For more on analogies to past Olympics, see Wasserstrom 2002, and for an interesting discussion of the relevance of the Seoul and Moscow analogies for Olympic planners in Beijing, see Liu 2007.

11. See, for an early use of the Seoul analogy, *New York Times* 1993, and for an early claim that the right analogy for Beijing hosting the Games was not Seoul 1988 (or Moscow 1980) but Berlin 1936, see the *Independent* 1993—an article that leads with a reference back to the massacre of 1989.

12. This terminology is original, I think, but was inspired by two very different works: Madsen 1995 and Starr 1973, a series of books that includes Starr 1990. Here I will focus on specifically American images of China, which often overlap with but sometimes diverge from the images of China in play in other parts of the West. Readers interested in Western notions about China more generally would be well served by turning to Spence 1999 and two

books by Colin Mackerras (2000a and 2000b), one a survey and the other a collection of translations.

13. All of my citations will be to the 1980 edition of the book, the third, which comes with three prefaces by Isaacs, written to accompany the book's original 1958 publication and 1972 and 1980 reissues.

14. For a fascinating discussion of *Scratches on Our Minds,* by a writer who specializes in U.S. relations with South Asia and pays roughly equal attention to what Isaacs had to say about China and India, see Rotter 1996. Rotter is both critical of some of the methods that Isaacs used (e.g., many of the people Isaacs interviewed were friends, very few were women, no effort was made to be scientific in his sampling, etc.) and appreciative of many of the basic conclusions put forward in the book. Rotter also provides interesting details about what Isaacs did prior to writing *Scratches on Our Minds.*

15. The classic study of American ideas about the Japanese during World War II remains Dower 1987; see also Johnson 1988.

16. This section draws heavily from my chapter, "Big Bad China and the Good Chinese: An American Fairytale" (Wasserstrom 2000); see also, for further relevant background to American views of China in the 1990s, other chapters in that same volume. Throughout this chapter, I have drawn inspiration from Geremie Barmé's gem of a foreword to that volume, in which he argues that, for the Western press, China stories are too often, in effect, written before they happen, with only the details needing to be filled in at the last minute.

17. For details on U.S.-China relations during this period, see Shirk 2007; issues addressed in the preceding paragraphs are also discussed at greater length in Wasserstrom 2007a.

18. See the following books and the stories linked to each that appeared in the American press when they were published: Ming with Bucher 2004; Larmer 2005. In general, stories building upon material in the former publication emphasized themes associated with the Dream, while those building upon material in the latter emphasized themes associated with the Nightmare.

REFERENCES

Boston Herald. 1993. editorial. September 25, 14.

Chang, Jung, and Fred Halliday. 2005. *Mao: The Unknown Story.* New York: Knopf.

Chu Maoning. 2007. Letter to the editor. *Wall Street Journal,* April 10, A17.

Davin, Delia. 2005. Dark Tales of Mao the Merciless. *Times Higher Education Supplement* (UK), August 12.

Dower, John. 1987. *War without Mercy: Race and Power in the Pacific War.* New York: Pantheon.

Fan, Maureen. 2007. Beijing Criticized on Pledges of Reform. *Washington Post,* April 30.

Farrow, Ronan, and Mia Farrow. 2007. The Genocide Olympics. *Wall Street Journal,* March 28, A17.

Gu, April. 2007. Old Beijing Gives Way to Developers, Greed, and 2008 Olympics. *Star Ledger (Newark, New Jersey),* February 11, Perspective section, 1.

Guardian. 2007. Olympic Games 2008: No Panic Here, China's Got Just about Everything in Hand. Sports section, 8.

Harding, Harry. 1982. From China with Disdain: New Trends in the Study of China. *Asian Survey* 22 (10): 934–58.

Houston Chronicle. 2001. 2008 Olympics: China Unworthy of Being Site for International Games. March 24.

Independent. 1993. Peking Falls Short of Olympic Ideal. September 23.

Independent. 2001. Olympic Games: The Discredited Fantasy of the Olympic Ideal. July 14.

Isaacs, Harold R. 1980. *Scratches on Our Minds: American Views of China and India.* Armonk, NY: M. E. Sharpe.

Jespersen, T. Christopher. 1996. *American Images of China, 1931–1949.* Stanford: Stanford University Press.

Johnson, Sheila K. 1988. *The Japanese through American Eyes.* Stanford: Stanford University Press.

Larmer, Brook. 2005. *Operation Yao Ming: The Chinese Sports Empire, American Big Business, and the Making of an NBA Superstar.* New York: Gotham.

Liu, Melinda. 2007. The Olympic Effect. *Newsweek International,* May 14.

Madsen, Richard. 1995. *China and the American Dream.* Berkeley: University of California Press.

Mann, James. 2007. *The China Fantasy: How Our Leaders Explain Away Chinese Repression.* New York: Viking.

Mackerras, Colin. 2000a. *Western Images of China.* 2nd ed. Oxford: Oxford University Press.

Mackerras, Colin. 2000b. *Sinophiles and Sinophobes.* Oxford: Oxford University Press.

Ming, Yao, with Ric Bucher. 2004. *Yao: A Life in Two Worlds.* New York: Miramax.

Mizell, Hubert. 2001. U.S. Should Boycott 2008 Beijing Games. *St. Petersburg Times,* October 14.

Nathan, Andrew. 2005. Jade and Plastic. *London Review of Books,* November 17.

New York Times. 1993. 2000 Olympics Go to Sydney in a Surprise Setback for China. September 24, A1.

New Zealand Herald. 2001. Olympic Gamble Worth Taking. July 17.

New Zealand Herald. 2007. No Olympic Dream for Beijing Poor. May 19.

People's Daily Online. 2006. Rogge Prefaces Beijing Olympic Issue for Civilization Magazine. October 17.

Rotter, Andrew J. 1996. In Retrospect: Harold R. Isaacs' *Scratches on Our Minds. Reviews in American History* 24 (1): 177–88.

Saïd, Edward. 1979. *Orientalism.* New York: Vintage.

Sheridan, Michael. 2007. Olympics Give Developers Excuse to Flatten Antiquities. *Australian,* April 30, 14.

Shirk, Susan. 2007. *China: Fragile Superpower.* New York: Oxford University Press.

Spence, Jonathan. 1999. *The Chan's Great Continent: China in Western Minds.* New York: Norton.

Starr, Kevin. 1973. *Americans and the California Dream: 1850–1915.* New York: Oxford University Press.

Starr, Kevin. 1990. *Material Dreams: Southern California through the 1920s.* Oxford: Oxford University Press.

Sullivan, Jerry. 2001. Chinese People Deserve the Games. *Buffalo News,* July 15.

Todd, Dave. 1993. Is China's Olympic Bid as Disgraceful as Hitler's in 1936? *Montreal Gazette,* June 23, B3.

Toronto Star. 1993. Should China Get Olympics? August 23, A12.

Wang Dan. 2003. Interview. "Wang Dan Says HK at Crossroads." *Taipei Times,* July 20.

Washington Post. 1993. Human Rights a Factor in Picking Olympics Site. May 17, C2.

Wasserstrom, Jeffrey N. 2000. Big Bad China and the Good Chinese: An American Fairytale. In *China beyond the Headlines,* ed. Timothy B. Weston and Lionel M. Jensen, 13–35. Lanham, MD: Rowman and Littlefield.

Wasserstrom, Jeffrey N. 2002. Using History to Think about the Beijing Olympics: The Use and Abuse of the Seoul 1988 Analogy. *Harvard International Journal of Press/Politics* 7 (1): 126–29.

Wasserstrom, Jeffrey N. 2007a. *China's Brave New World—and Other Tales for Global Times.* Bloomington: Indiana University Press.

Wasserstrom, Jeffrey N. 2007b. China Fantasies and China Policies. *World Policy Journal* (spring): 97–102.

Yardley, Jim. 2007. Bulldozers and Thieves Imperil Chinese Relics; In Rush to Develop, Antiquities Are Lost. *International Herald Times,* February 6.

The Fragility of
Asian National Identity in the
Olympic Games

Sandra Collins

But there is neither East nor West, Border, nor Breed nor Birth
When two strong men stand face to face. (Rudyard Kipling, 1895)

Kipling's twain between the "East" and the "West" of the nineteenth century continues to haunt our modern global imagination. Nowhere is the difference between the two made more visible than in the narratives of Asian national identity that are produced for the Olympic Games.[1] These narratives begin with the bids to host the Olympics, continue through both written texts (of pamphlets, media booklets, official receptions and Web sites) and performative texts (of International Olympic Committee [IOC] receptions, marketing videos, and commercial endorsements), are broadcasted during the Olympic Games themselves, and linger long after the Olympic event is over. The common trope of the East-West dichotomy has been evoked in numerous Asian Olympiads precisely because it is a familiar and expected narrative. In the twenty-first century, the Olympic Games may be the single biggest event for "the production of national culture for international consumption" (Brownell 1995, 314), and our global ubiquitous media continues to exploit this divide for profit.[2] Asian cities vying to host the Olympic Games have enthusiastically employed this rhetoric of difference in their bidding campaigns. What may prove surprising is not that this twain continues, but that it retains any cultural resonance for an increasingly commodified Olympic experience in our vastly shrinking globe.

What is unique for Asian Olympic hosts—beginning with the Tokyo bid to host the 1940 Games and continuing with the 1964 Tokyo, the 1988 Seoul, the 1998 Nagano Winter and the upcoming 2008 Beijing Olympics—are the lingering anxieties of participating in the Western hegemony of the Olympic Games. Other Olympic host cities have not carried the burden of representing their cultural heritage as unchanging to the extent that Asian hosts do.[3] While most Western Olympic host cities underscore their modernity and development to promote themselves as world-class cities, Asian host cities distinguish themselves in their deliberate evocation of their *modern hybridity:* the co-existence of modern development with ancient cultural traditions. Asian Olympic hosts display this hybridity as a syncretism of cutting edge–modern technological industry anchored in the rich cultural histories and exotic civilizations of the East.

Why Asian Olympic hosts intentionally celebrate their cultural heritage and modernity as conjoined can only be understood within the historical framework of global capitalism and modern Asian nation-states. Tokyo, Seoul, and Nagano each defined and, in the case of Beijing, are defining their national identity as the unique embodiment of a timeless national culture replete with modern attributes. For the late-developing industrial nations of Japan, Korea, and China, showcasing the idea of a modern hybridity in the Olympic Games functions as a symbolic means of demonstrating that modernization does not equal Westernization.[4] That is to say, Asian nations are capable of modernization, evidenced by their winning of Olympic bids, but retain distinct and traditional national cultures. By fusing their unique traditional culture with their present modern development, Asian Olympic hosts confirm not only that modernization and globalization are not necessarily universal, but also that the forces of modern and global development have different inflections in Asia. In the narratives of Asian Olympic hosts, the modernity of Asian host nations is not a mirror reflection of the modern development of the West but rather a self-conscious remaking of nineteenth century Orientalist discourse.[5] Asian Olympic hosts turn the earlier assessment of Orientalists—that the Orient was frozen and could not evolve—on its head: Asian Olympic hosts' self-orientalism showcases how their cultural traditions exist conterminously with their modernity.

When Japan, Korea, and China host the Olympics, their "Eastern" civilizations are grafted onto the developmental path established and monopolized by Western powers as a result of the rapid expansion of Western colonialism of the nineteenth century.[6] But a boundary continues to function: because relevant sites of global authority (whether the International Olympic Committee or the WTO) continue to be dominated by the West (Chow 1991), the discourses of Asian Olympics reveal the underlying power structures of the encounter between the East and the West. The representational strategies of syncretism and hybridity, which is often a form of self-orientalism, has proven successful for Asian hosts precisely because modernization is often equated with the West. Rather than argue that Asian modernities are different from those of the West, Asian Olympic hosts deliberately construct the dichotomy between the West and East as the normative of Asia entering the IOC world stage.[7] Here, Asian national cultures are being represented as being at the center of the desired synthesis between the East and the West: the ancient civilization and culture of the orient/Asia/East symbolically positions Asian Olympic hosts as being *nearly* as modernized (industrialized, capitalized, or globalized) as the omnipotent West. Beijing 2008 has proven to be particularly interesting, because, as the fear of China looms large in the Western imagination, China's "Two System" government has represented the 2008 Olympic Games throughout its preparation process as a new iteration of the fusion of the East and the West.[8] With the arrival of "China's Century," Beijing has achieved a level of economic power that previous Asian hosts never enjoyed; and, as the West fears the balance of global power tipping toward China and the East, the Beijing Olympic organizers have also begun to employ different rhetorical strategies to represent China's synthesis of the old and new.

Despite their differences, Asian Olympic host cities adopt similar strategies in showcasing their national identity as a modern hybrid within the context of the Olympic Games. And although the historical contexts vary, these Asian candidates are similar in their timing of joining the larger world system dominated by the West. As such, discursive strategies of representing the Asian Olympic candidates' national cultural identity manifest as the harmonious blending of ancient traditions and modern attributes, of fusing the schism between the East and West, implying that all Asian nations peacefully enter the world system monopolized by the West, the dominant power by which Asia has had to define its own modern experience.[9] The hybrid form suspends Asian national identity safely in between the premodern (Orient) and the modern (West). As China's socioeconomic development continues, the Beijing Olympic organizers will continue to play with the established image of the traditional self-orientalized hybrid Asian nation. This is precisely why the fear of the New China resonates so strongly as America watches its trade deficit with New China grow exponentially every year.

These discursive strategies were first articulated in the 1930s, when Japan bid for the 1940 Olympics. As the first Asian industrialized power, Japan sought to commemorate its 2,600th national birthday in 1940 with the Olympic Games. During the bidding process, the Japanese offered the alluring image of Japan as a unique embodiment of Eastern tradition and Western modernity, and argued that a Tokyo Olympics would truly universalize the Olympic movement.[10] The 1940 Tokyo Games were seen as a spectacular ideological production, designed by the Japanese state specifically to challenge the Western powers' conflation of Western with universal values. The success of the Tokyo bid lay in the fact that Japan was, at the time, the only Eastern (or non-Western) industrial, independent nation state. Japan's economic success offered a counter to Western modernity and development, and thus suggested that the modernity espoused by the West was not necessarily universal.

The historical narrative of Asian Olympic hosts could follow the normative arc of modernization and development, and the impulse is to characterize 1964 Tokyo, 1988 Seoul and the upcoming 2008 Beijing Games as examples of how Asian nations entered the world arena as successful beacons of globalization. The 1964 Tokyo Olympics were a stunning spectacle of Japan's normalization and its re-entry into the world system under the careful tutelage of America as the first Asian, industrialized, capitalist, and democratic nation. The Seoul 1998 Olympics continued Tokyo's Olympic legacy in Asia by showcasing the economic and technological achievements of Korea to the world (Manzenreiter and Horne 2002).[11] Awarded to the then largely unknown military state, the 1988 Seoul Games exhibited the permanent reform of Korea as a more democratic and industrial capital nation-state (Ahn 2002). As for Beijing 2008, the predominant theme anticipated by the existing narrative appears to be that of China's successful entrance into—and not dominance of—the world system. In order to address the West's continuing concerns of (among other things) the rapid pace of China's economic growth, the Beijing Organizing Committee of the Olympic Games (BOCOG) has repeatedly chosen themes that emphasize harmony with the existing world system. This may change as the Beijing Olympics unfold.[12] When bidding for the Olympics, the Beijing Olympic Bid Committee (BOBICO) first lauded

"New Beijing, New Olympics" (*xin Beijing, xin aoyun*) as Beijing's Olympic slogan. Under the IOC's concern that this could be interpreted as an effort by China to change the Olympics into something "new," however, the Bid Committee switched the slogan to "New Beijing, Great Olympics" (Forney 2001).

In contrast to this normative narrative of modernization for Asian Olympic hosts, however, lie the failed 1940 Tokyo and the 1998 Nagano Games. Japan canceled the 1940 Games only to embark on a brutal imperialist campaign to ostensibly liberate Asia from the West, and Japan hosted the 1998 Winter Games at the height of its economic collapse after winning the right to host the Games in 1991, just as signs that the Japanese economy was in trouble were emerging. These two Asian Olympiads, "aberrant" in their deviation from the typical narrative of positive development typically employed by Asian Olympic hosts, suggest that the self-orientalizing/mythologizing constellation of Asian national identity in the Olympic Games is ultimately a fragile and symbolic form of resistance to the West.

Narratives of Dislocation (I):
The Canceled 1940 Tokyo Games

The process of constructing Asian national identities within the context of the Olympic Games is an inherently fragile process that must not only negotiate established sport and political channels of Olympic, city, and national officials, but also, navigate the global media communication complex of corporations, media officials, and spectators. By restoring the "missing Olympics" of the terminated 1940 Tokyo Games to the historical narrative of Asian Olympiads, the continued draw of Asian Olympic nations as a modern hybrid may be better grasped (Collins forthcoming).

Well aware of the western bias against Asian nations during Tokyo's bid for the 1940 Olympics, Japanese officials proposed to commemorate the 2,600th anniversary of the founding of the nation. Although the 1940 Tokyo Games were tied to the ideological production of 1930s Japan that promoted the mythical notion of a Japanese national polity *(kokutai)* as based on the unchanging relationship between the Japanese emperor and the Japanese people, the Olympics were also considered a forum for Japanese diplomacy in an era of increasing international isolation. Throughout the bidding and later the planning processes for the 1940 Games, Tokyo's discursive strategy focused on two key tactics: emphasizing that in order for the Olympic Games to be truly universal, they would also need to be held in the East, and representing the national culture of Japan as the unique blending of a distinct "Eastern" cultural heritage with "Western" forms of modernization and industrialization.[13] Photographs were used to display how Japan's ancient, oriental civilization coexisted with new forms of modern Westernization. Emphasizing the key role of visuality, Tokyo/Japan was often referred to as the "rare montage of the old/new and East/West" by those Japanese involved in promoting the Tokyo bid domestically and abroad. Similarly, 1930s Tokyo was often described as "a modern city . . . a metropolis in Western fashion against the panorama of an age-old civilization" (Tokyo Municipal Office 1934, iii). Images of geisha and samurai were often presented to the West as sensational examples of Japan's self-orientalism. Japanese ideologues guided Western readers on how to see the ancient forms of Japanese culture in modern Japan; Tokyo was hailed as the unique embodiment of "the harmonious blending" of the two great cultures of the East and the West (Olympic Organizing Committee for the XIIth Olympiad Tokyo 1938, 22). However, Japanese national culture was represented as existing outside of time—and more amaranthine—compared to the West so that the idioms of cultural contact between "Japan-East-Traditional" and "World-West-Modern" implied a certain incommensurability.[14]

Although the specific dynamics of the harmonious blending were never defined—and remained a somewhat ambiguous encounter between the East and West when the Japanese government canceled the Tokyo Games in 1938—this idea functioned as a significant example of Japan's singular ability to successfully modernize while simultaneously retaining its unique cultural and imperial destiny.[15] However, in spite of calling for the spread of Olympism and peace throughout the Orient, and lauding the Tokyo Games' ability to improve relations between the East and West, the 1940 Tokyo Games were ultimately a form of self-aggrandizement by the Japanese state. Japanese bid officials viewed Japan as uniquely positioned to host the Olympics as the premier colonial and military power of the Orient. After winning the right to host the Olympics, Tokyo Olympic Officials debated for two years over how best to import the Western rituals of the Olympics to Japan as well as how best to package Japanese culture for the world. Ultimately, the Japanese national government canceled the Games in 1938 because of the protracted war between Japan and China. Just as imperialist

Japan once boasted of its unique economic and military might, the colossal growth of its economy now positions modern China as the premier threat to the established global trade network long dominated by the West.

Normative Narrative (I): Tokyo 1964

Despite Japan's path into what many American historians of modernization theory label as the "dark valley" years, Japan emerged from World War II as the benefactor of America's aggressive campaign for containing Asian communism.[16] With the advent of the Korean War in 1952, the United States actively helped establish Japan as a model democratic and industrial power. The Tokyo Olympics were seen as the symbol of Japan's successful re-entry into the international order as a normalized industrial power. Japan's avowed goal in hosting the 1964 Games was "to show the world that Japan is not just a country of cherry blossoms and geishas. The object was to demonstrate that Japan had been rebuilt after the war and that the country was willing to connect itself to the western world" (Lechenperg 1964, 137–38). Repentant of its fascist and imperial past, democratic Japan now wanted to graft its Asian civilization onto the course of Western civilization. Tokyo's bid, supported by IOC president and American Avery Brundage, was easily won, and in the official program for the 1964 Games, Tokyo was hailed as the "ideal site for holding the first Olympic Games to be held in Asia, for it can be said that she serves as a meeting-point of the East and the West" (Organizing Committee for the Games of the XVIII Olympiad 1966, 20). The success of the 1964 Tokyo Olympics made these Games the model to which subsequent Asian Olympic candidates aspired, and thus it is this Olympics that inaugurated the contemporary normative narrative of Asian Olympiads.

The planning of the Games began in 1959, and the face of the city of Tokyo would be changed in what was called "one of the most ambitious urban construction projects of the twentieth century, a five-year, 24-hour-a-day effort" (Slater 2004, 166). More than $2.8 billion was spent on building the Olympic infrastructure which was in fact modernizing the urbanscape of postwar Tokyo itself: the Tokaido bullet train, two new subways, a monorail from Haneda airport, new metropolitan highways and expressways, sewer and water lines, hotels, a broadcasting center and communication facilities. The National Diet passed a measure (Law No. 138 of June 8, 1961) that gave legal support to the State's involvement in hosting the Games (Organizing Committee for the Games of the XVIII Olympiad 1966, 39). The Organizing Committee's official headquarters was located at the Akasaka Detached Palace, once the residence of the Japanese Meiji emperor who modernized Japan. The then Showa emperor of postwar Japan, His Majesty Hirohito, agreed to act as the royal patron for the Games. Both motions symbolized the importance of the event to Japan's solemn nation (Organizing Committee for the Games of the XVIII Olympiad 1966, 39).

When the Games began, the "Japanese atmosphere" in the opening ceremony was decisively understated: the playing of the national anthem *kimigayo,* the large taiko drums for the Olympic Campanology and Hymn, the presence of the Japanese emperor, and the use of "atom boy" to light the Olympic Cauldron were the only true signs of Japanese difference. There were no elaborate cultural performances showcasing Japanese traditional dance, arts or theatre; these were confined to the Arts Exhibit held at various venues in Tokyo (Organizing Committee for the Games of the XVIII Olympiad 1966, 270). During the opening ceremony, Mayuzumi Toshio composed "Olympic Campanology"—a blend of modern Japanese technology and ancient cultural traditions, incorporating electronic sounds with recordings of temple bells in the nationally important shrines from the cities of Nara, Kyoto, and Nikko (Slater 2004, 169).[17] The music was played as the Japanese emperor Showa took his seat in the Royal Box as "the symbols of the soul of the Japanese people, being transmitted to the world" (Organizing Committee for the Games of the XVIII Olympiad 1966, 231). After the emperor declared the Games open, the final Olympic torch runner, Yoshinori Sakai, who was born in Hiroshima on August 6, 1945, the day of the atomic bombing, arrived in the stadium and lit the sacred Olympic Fire, referencing Japan's status as the world's first atomic victim. Jet planes from the Japanese Air Self-Defense Force formed five Olympic colored circles in the Tokyo sky, as a reminder of the military might that Japan still possessed. In addition, the 1964 Olympics featured a color telecast of peaceful Japan's "distinctive culture" exemplified by the kimono-clad women giving Olympic medals to winning athletes.

For the Japanese, the 1964 Games were a reminder that the country had successfully sutured the wounds of World War II and its imperialist past and gotten back on the "correct" path of Western modernity of democracy and industrialization. For the IOC, the Games were a sign that "The Olympic Movement . . . has now bridged every ocean and the Olympic Games at last are here in the orient proving that they belong to the entire world" (IOC 1998). After decades of U.S. Supreme Commander of Allied Powers (SCAP) censorship it is not surprising that both the opening and closing ceremonies did not display any traditional or feudal forms of Japan's national culture, as were expressed during the 1998 Nagano Games, perhaps demonstrating that Japan in the 1960s had not yet put enough distance between its past and its present.

Despite the Tokyo Games' success, Yashiro Yukio, a commissioner for the Protection of Cultural Properties, lamented in 1965 that Japan suffered from a poor reputation abroad due "to a still-thriving Orientalism (*orientarizumu*) born of nineteenth-century exoticism of 'Madam Butterfly. . . .' (Aso 2002, 18). Parallel with the U.S. (SCAP) occupation's scrutiny of Japanese feudalistic traditions that were deemed the source of its imperialist aggression (such as martial arts and notions of a sacred and divine emperor), the Japanese were trying to define and promote their own cultural traditions. Recalling the earlier 1930s hybrid modernity, Japan's modern identity in the postwar era was again likened to the unique combination of a timeless and thus authentic traditional culture that survived amidst the progression of Japan's modernization: "Present day visitors to Japan are interested to find that the old and the new, the traditional and the progressive, are active side by side, and are in good accord mutually in this country" (Aso 2002, 30). Japan succeeded in accomplishing what it had set out to do some twenty years earlier: to reveal to the world its national strength and power in a distinctively Japanese fashion.

Normative Narratives (II): 1988 Seoul

Raising suspicions that he was seeking the Nobel Peace Prize, IOC president Juan Antonio Samaranch was a keen supporter of hosting the Olympics in Asia again, and his close relationship with the IOC member in Korea, Kim Taek-soo, helped Seoul secure the 1988 Games. The Seoul bid was launched in 1981 by the then president of the Republic of Korea, General Chun Doo Hwan, to help promote several economic and political goals. Economically, the substantial growth of the Korean industrial economy (1975 GNP for South Korea was $44.3 billion; 1980 GNP was $63.1 million; Manheim 1990, 281) legitimized South Korea's ability, as a newly modernizing nation, to host the Olympics. The government believed that hosting the Olympics would help to promote its fledgling automotive and electronics industries internationally insofar as it would announce South Korea's successful entry into the world system. Politically, the Seoul bid was designed to cultivate domestic approval from the Korean people, who distrusted governmental authority, as well as "[expand] its relations with Communist bloc countries" (Seoul Olympic Organizing Committee [SLOOC] 1989, 34; Manheim 1990, 282).

The more than fifty-member Seoul delegation used the division of Korea along the thirty-eighth parallel to convince other IOC delegates of the validity of Seoul's candidacy: "The logic focused on the justness of an Olympiad in Seoul . . . an Olympiad in a divided country would be helpful to solidifying peace there" (SLOOC 1989, 39). In keeping with Tokyo's success in showcasing a hybrid Asia that was both traditional and modern, Seoul organizers claimed that the elaborately constructed display hall of Seoul's candidacy "effectively displayed the time-honored culture and spectacular development of Korea . . ." (SLOOC 1989, 40; Manheim 1990, 283). In keeping with the characteristic gendered subservience of Orientalism, Korean Air stewardesses and former Miss Koreas in "elegant traditional Korean costumes gracefully served visitors" (SLOOC 1989, 40). The Seoul bid campaigners also invoked Tokyo's earlier appeal as a universalizing force: "Considering the Olympic principle of universality . . . it is important to share the hosting role among nations and thus spread the Olympic Movement throughout the world. . . ." (SLOOC 1989, 42). The "unique cultural heritage and characteristics" of Seoul and the fact that South Korea had not previously hosted the Olympics helped to cement Seoul's attractiveness.

When the Games were awarded to Seoul in 1981, Seoul Olympic organizers were determined to match Japan's success but in a "distinctively Korean manner," by displaying Korea's cultural heritage as distinct not only from the West but from other Asian nations as well (Larson and Park 1993, 151–55, 162, 169). The 1987 change in the national government of Korea, however, led to a reassessment of the Seoul Olympics by the Korean government; the IOC remained largely unconcerned by the shift in governmental leadership. Korean president Chun Doo Hwan reconfirmed the priority of the Seoul Games to the nation by remarking, "The 1988 Seoul Olympics . . . will be a golden opportunity for national prosperity, thereby placing the country on the road towards becoming an advanced country" (Larson and Park 1993, 162, 169). The IOC was relieved that the second Olympic Games to be held in Asia would continue as scheduled. IOC spokesperson Michele Verdier proclaimed, "The Games have been awarded to Seoul, and there is absolutely no change in our position." The only condition that would change the IOC's view would be an "act of war" (Reed 1987, 1).

The Republic of Korea spent well over $3 billion in preparations for the 1988 Games (Reed 1987). In the most watched of all Olympic broadcasts to date, an estimated one billion international viewers watched the Han River boat parade inaugurate the opening ceremony (Larson and Park 1993, 153). Korean national culture was evoked in the ornate choreographed scenes of the opening ceremony, with traditional music, dress, folklore, and dance orchestrated along modern technological lines. The theme of the ceremony was "Toward One World, Beyond All Barriers," which broadcasters suggested to viewers meant moving beyond the barrier or the cultural gap between the East and the West (Larson and Park 1993, 159, 207–8). Recapitulating the fusion of old and new, the broadcast of the cultural ceremonies made references to Korea's "5,000 year history" along with South Korea's move toward democracy, modernization, and Westernization (Larson and Park 1993, 212–14). The arcane reference to 5,000 years was a self-conscious attempt by South Korean pundits to emphasize that their culture was distinct from other Asian cultures, of China and Japan, boasting 3,000 and 2,600 years of history, respectively.

The distinctiveness of traditional Korean culture was emphasized in other ways during the 1988 Games as well. SLOOC contracted with Polygram for $2.5 million to have the Korean vocal group Koreana sing the Olympic theme song, a song designed to have as much "Korean imagery as possible" (Larson and Park 1993, 108). The result, "Hand-in-Hand," became a top ten song on the pop charts in seventeen countries and the most popular Olympic theme song in history. The Seoul Olympic mascot, *Hodori,* recalled the familiar figure of the tiger from Korean legends and folk art (Larson and Park 1993, 106). All women acting in an official Olympic capacity as hostesses were outfitted in traditional Korean dresses; the medal bearer escorts wore the *wonsam,* the ceremonial robe of ancient Korean queens, and the medal bearers themselves wore *hanbok,* the traditional Korean dress (SLOOC 1989, 144–45).

As a media event in the sense of the term developed by Katz and Dayan, the Seoul Olympics was a strategic opportunity for South Korea to represent its national identity, which had hitherto remained largely unknown to a global audience (Larson and Park 1993, 238; Jaffe and Nebenzahl 1993, 445). The opening ceremony was a striking example of Korea's self-exoticization for the benefit of the foreign gaze. The opening ceremony visualized the "Korean culture characterized . . . in the form of the indigenous dances, sounds and colors" and the Seoul Olympic organizers helped to cement Korea's national hybridity by stating that the event was a "remarkable artistic creation which married the traditional Korean culture and the contemporary senses" (SLOOC 1989, 390). The national identity of South Korea was showcased as a modern hybrid that fused its 5,000-year old traditions with a modern democratic and industrial state. Seoul Organizers devoted tremendous resources to showcasing "the originality of Korean culture," utilizing some 13,625 people in fifteen cultural performance numbers during the unprecedented three-hour-long televised event (SLOOC 1989, 391). The traditional cultural performance of "Greeting the Sun" alone lasted twenty minutes and involved more than 3,300 Korean performers and four different dances and musical events. The Olympic gold medalist Sohn Kee-chung, who competed in the 1936 Japanese delegation to Berlin, brought the Olympic torch into the stadium, a moment loaded with political symbolism insofar as it featured a contemporary Korea, independent of its colonial past (SLOOC 1989, 406). In Korea's efforts to position itself as a successful (yet traditional) nation within the Western trajectory of modernization and industrialization, it did not address the traumatic division between North and South Korea. For a domestic audience, however, the opening ceremonies' complementary and glorious national narrative of a unified, healed, unchanging culture attempted to soothe the painful political boundaries formed by student protests, military coups, and the division with North Korea. Despite the Demilitarized Zone that separated North from South Korea, the opening ceremony constantly underscored the timeless and shared culture of a "Korea" that existed before modern political boundaries and simultaneously highlighted the modern technological advances made by South Korea.

The Seoul Olympics helped solidify the notion that the televised Olympic Games function not only as a media event in and of itself, but also as a point of reference for other discursive events (Larson and Park 1993, 48). Throughout the long years of Olympic planning, the fact that the national identity of the Olympic host will be communicated through global media is taken into account. The construction of this identity involves the dual processes of broadcasters creating the media message and audiences receiving these messages and their separate and often divergent interpretations. Another communicative layer beyond sender and receiver involves the global transcultural communication systems of the IOC, National Olympic Committees, and Olympic Corporate Sponsors (Larson and Park 1993, 48).

The media event, however, involved more than just the Olympic organizers. Local Korean culture was often not elucidated for the American (or global) viewing audience during the numerous cultural performances. In fact, Korean national identity was often simply essentialized as "unique" and as possessing a "5,000 year heritage," demarcating Korean civilization as distinct from Japan and China (Larson and Park 1993, 35). NBC, which had the U.S. broadcasting rights, frequently offered political analyses of contemporary South Korea alongside images of traditional culture. As such, the broadcasters offered little explanation of the encounter between the East and West, and focused on the sensational and troubling aspects of contemporary South Korean society. NBC detailed the recent political history of the nation as a former Japanese colony, the violence of student riots and the military dictatorship, the tumultuous relations with North Korea and the aftermath of the 1952 Korean War, as well as the black market, mistreatment of Amerasian (half-American and Korean) children, and the status of women (Larson and Park 1993, 224). Koreans were able to view NBC broadcasts aired on the U.S. Armed Forces network, and South Koreans, outraged at the nation's portrayal on an American network, staged public protests that resulted in NBC spokesman Kevin Monaghan delivering a public apology on Korean television (Larson and Park 1993, 224).

Narratives of Dislocation (II):
1998 Nagano Winter Olympic Games

The 1998 Nagano Winter Olympics emerged as an outlier to the historical narrative of the Asian Olympiads. For Japan in the 1980s hosting an Asian Olympiad was not a condition of entering the established Western world system since the yen and stock market were already very strong. Rather, the key impetus behind Nagano's bid was developing the infrastructure for local tourism for the Seibu Development Corporation by showcasing the 1980s Japanese discourses on Japan's national uniqueness, which have come to be labeled as *nihonjinron* (translated as discourses on "Japaneseness"). Nagano won the right to host the Winter Olympic Games in 1991 just as signs that the Japanese economy might be in trouble were beginning to emerge. Despite repeated budget cuts, the operating expenses for the Games were estimated to be $792 million, an overwhelming figure for this small regional municipality.[18] For the organizers of the Nagano Games, however, the timely investment in hotels, stadiums, and transportation for the required Olympic infrastructure was to transform the Nagano region, home of the "Japanese Alps," into an attractive tourist destination.

The opening ceremony strategically emphasized Nagano as a regional attraction. Award-winning Keita Asari, chief producer for the opening and closing ceremonies, was chosen because of his intercultural fluency as evidenced by his success in adapting foreign Broadway musicals for Japanese audiences. The goal of the opening ceremony was to unite the world through the use of the latest technology while emphasizing traditional images of Nagano and Japan. Asari commented that he intentionally emphasized traditional Japanese culture in the opening ceremony:

> The Olympics are not something that should be completely done in a Western style. Opening ceremonies should embrace the (host) country's culture and tradition. The cooperation between the sumo wrestlers and the rendition of the *onbashira-tate* festival are examples of unique Japanese culture. We can make it appealing to the international audience. (Kyodo News Wire, October 29, 1997).

The sounds of the bells ringing from Nagano's Zenkoji Temple, which marked the beginning of the 1998 Games, represented a much more traditional approach than the 1964 Tokyo Games' use of the electronic recording of temple bells. Next, the local culture of Nagano prefecture was showcased when 1,000 Nagano residents participated in the erection of sacred Shinto pillars of the Suwa Taisha Shrine. Asari staged an elaborate *dohyo-iri*, the ring entering ritual of sumo wrestlers during the opening ceremony. Led by the 6'8", 500-pound Akebono, the first foreign-born sumo Grand Champion (*yokozuna*) of Japan (Akebono became a Japanese citizen in 1996), the large and nearly naked sumo wrestlers wore *kesho-mawashi* (decorated ceremonial aprons). Akebono alone, as a Japanese citizen, performed the *dohyo-iri* to drive away evil spirits and purify the venue for the Olympic athletes.[19] For Asari,

"There is nothing that feels more like 'Japanese culture' than a sumo wrestler. When everyone sees the wrestlers assembled, they will be left with the strong impression that they have truly visited (seen) Japan" (Kyodo News Wire, December 26, 1997). Ito Midori, Japanese ice-skating gold medalist, was elaborately dressed in a ceremonial kimono and lifted into the air on a platform to light the Olympic cauldron.

Asari did not just seek to portray Japan's uniqueness. The "Westerners," Asari revealed, "see the Japanese as a peculiar people. I want to show (also) that Japanese people have sensitivities that are similar to those people in other places in the world through the chorus of the *Ode to Joy*" (Kyodo News Wire, October 29, 1997). World famous conductor Seiji Ozawa led a worldwide chorus of Beethoven's *Ode to Joy* for the finale of the pageant that featured five choral groups from Beijing, Berlin, Cape Town, New York, and Sydney singing together via a satellite linkup as Ozawa conducted the orchestra from the Nagano Prefectural Cultural Hall. "The significance lies in the fact that people from all over the world will sing the same song at the same time," the Boston Symphony Conductor Ozawa mused (Kyodo News Wire, December 25, 1997). For the global viewing audience, however, the carefully orchestrated "Ode to Joy" also served as a postmodern Olympic performance at a different register: that of displaying an interconnected world based on transnational telecommunication and computerized information networks (Smith 1990, 75).

Despite Asari's best intentions, however, the CBS broadcast often deliberately interrupted the narrative and theatrical flow of the opening ceremony. As the Japan Expert for the CBS Research Team, I had an interesting view of the decisions made by the CBS Producers for the Nagano Games. Jim Nance and other broadcasters often mistakenly referred to Zenkoji Temple, looming in the background of each CBS broadcast, as the "spiritual and cultural center of Japan," even though Japanese would probably refer to Ise as the spiritual center and Kyoto as the cultural center of Japan. The use of traditional images and rituals to represent Japan—or any Olympic host city—is of course not new. What was surprising was the extent to which the visual nature of television determined what aspects of Japanese tradition were selected both to be broadcast by CBS and to be showcased during the Olympic Ceremonies. CBS producers admitted that they liked these traditional images of Japan rather than shots of "modernity" because they were so aesthetically appealing and so consistent with America's imagined fantasy of an exotic and unchanging Japan. Even the executive producer of the ceremonies, Asari, confessed that he created the ceremonies by imagining how the scenes would be represented by both the close-up shots and long pans of the television camera. For the spectacle of Nagano, what became "tradition" for Japan were those visual elements that could be best captured by the television lens and that best referenced the familiar trope of an unchanging cultural aesthetic: the kimono of Midori Ito, the colorful silk sashes against the naked bodies of the sumo wrestlers, and the majestic Zenkoji Temple. The desired orientalism of Japan by CBS producers was enthusiastically satisfied by the complicitous images of Japanese unchanging traditional culture as orchestrated by Asari.

The use of traditional national images by the global media underscores the complex process of the Olympics as a media event. Sensational and stunning images were excavated from the treasure troves of the Japanese past and selected for their ability to be successfully staged as "Japanese tradition," which then determined what kind of "Japan" viewers and spectators were encouraged to celebrate. Local cultural practices were removed by Asari from their specific Nagano regional contexts, inserted into the opening ceremony, and then aestheticized for the Olympic viewing audience as nostalgic reminders of the ancient traces that remain in modern Japan. The Nagano Games showcased the ascent of what Joseph Nye (2004) has characterized as Japanese soft power: the worldwide demand not only for traditional Japanese art but for its modern forms of popular culture as well. Perhaps for the producers of the Olympic Ceremonies and CBS, "Japan" represents a visually stunning symbol of modern hybridity itself: the unchanging traditional culture of a nation can be found in the pockets of one of the world's leading exponents of technology and modernity.

Coda: Locating 2008 Beijing Olympics

By analyzing the discourses that emerged from the bidding and planning process for the Beijing 2008 Games against this backdrop of these other Asian Olympic Games, it is possible to discern the image of China that is being projected thus far. In some respects, the Beijing Games fit within the normative narrative of showcasing the successful entry of a developing Asian nation into the globalized world. During the bidding process, BOBICO adopted the 1930s Japanese and subsequent Asian

Olympiad strategies of positioning the Asian candidate as a modern hybrid and as a vehicle by which the Olympic Movement is diversified.

In competition with the final round candidate cities of Toronto, Paris, Istanbul, and Osaka, Beijing accentuated its cultural traditions as an ancient, Oriental city. BOBICO officials stated that displaying the ancient culture of China was a key element to the Beijing bid, which the Mayor of Beijing, Liu Qi, also affirmed by stating that the long, 3,000 year history of Beijing would provide a truly remarkable spectacle (*People's Daily* 2001). One Beijing journalist professed, "Beijing [is] more appealing to others because we have such a long history; we have something you have never seen, something very native, something very Oriental" (Haugen 2005, 223). In the Beijing candidature video for the IOC, famed Chinese director Zhang Yimou, who was also contracted to help produce the opening ceremony with Steven Spielberg, presented the Great Wall as a monument "to the survival of a vibrant culture that has been able to combine the greatness of the past with ever-changing economic, social and technological advances of the present" (Haugen 2005, 219). Given Zhang's expertise with visually appealing depictions of Chinese culture—his film's "orientalist" and exotic representations of "China's antiquated, folkloric and superstitious cultural past" have attracted a global audience (Liu 1998, 166; Chow 2007)—one can only imagine a continuation of such self-exoticization.

Mimicking earlier Asian Olympiads as the harmonious blending of the East and West, the Beijing Olympics were also hailed as bringing "the East and West together" (*China Daily* 2001). The oriental heritage of Beijing "gives the city a strong and rich culture, which can make the 2008 Olympics unique" (*China Daily* 2001). Beijing's "otherness" is often presented visually through the traditional forms of culture that position China as simultaneously unchanging and modern. As a rapidly developing nation, Chinese bid officials were eager to stress how China wanted to enter the community of Olympic hosts and the promise of progress that would follow. Although Haugen contends that the Olympics will be a catalyst for Beijing to transcend its differences with the West by mimicry, China scholar Liu counters that China will embark on an alternative path of development (Haugen 2005, 225; Liu 1998, 182). Another Chinese scholar, Xin Xu, takes a more centrist position, claiming that "[T]he People's Republic of China (PRC) is determined to turn this sporting mega-event into the celebration of a Chinese renaissance and the harmonization of world civilizations . . ."

precisely because state policy and Beijing Olympic themes highlight "efforts to redefine China's political identity in line with traditional and universal values of greater appeal" (Xu 2006, 90, 97).

The Beijing bid, Haugen notes, detailed China's "faith in a glorious past, combined with images of a great future" and recalled the "restoration nationalism" promoted by official Chinese discourse in the 1990s (Haugen 2005, 222). As Japan confronted the threat of Western colonialization, the Japanese nation state also formulated a "renaissance discourse" by which Japan called upon its ancient past in order to modernize without Westernizing for the good of the nation's future (Oguma 2002, 334). As the countdown to the Beijing Olympics nears and the repercussions of the exponentially expanding Chinese economy grow transparent, it will not be surprising if China ultimately defines its own, distinctly Chinese, path. China has evaded any appeal to universal human rights by the West, including those concerning China's ongoing involvement in Darfur, acknowledgment of the independence of Tibet or Taiwan, or the role of a critical and independent press. In the end, the universalism espoused by the West is tainted by the history of the declaration of human rights as a power construct developed by the West for the globe. As China's economic power grows its confidence in defining its own path will also.

Other texts on the Beijing Olympics offer insight into the developing national narrative. During the closing ceremony of the 2004 Athens Olympic Games, the Chinese created a twenty-minute performance to define the country's national culture. Despite the brutal repression of tradition that occurred during the Cultural Revolution only decades before, the film resurrected this traditional culture, pristine and unscathed by its earlier destruction. The ceremony opened with a Chinese instrumental ensemble's rendition of the folk song "Mo-li-hua" (Jasmine Flower) infused with a modern techno beat that then slowed to an unaccompanied version of the song sung by a child. Attempting to mask the vast developmental unevenness and ethnic differences within China, symbolic erasures of difference within China have emerged in BOCOG's plan: one of the five Olympic mascots is the Tibetan antelope, which can be interpreted as an attempt to subsume a separate Tibetan culture into the dominant Han culture and erase the ongoing political conflict. There are plans for the Olympic Torch relay to traverse the historic Silk Road, including the Northwestern province of Xinjiang, a region of ethnic, religious, and political contestation. Tensions have also emerged over Beijing's proposed inclusion of Taiwan in the Torch relay route. Taiwan reacted negatively to this announcement and declared that Taiwan was not consulted with BOCOG's proposal. The National Council on Physical Fitness and Sports issued a public statement protesting being included as "Taipei China":

> China will most certainly publicize the transfer of the torch from Taiwan to Hong Kong as being from "Taipei China" to "Hong Kong China" and "Macau China" and then onward to other cities in China. This is an attempt by China to engineer the relay route so that Chinese Taipei is included in China's domestic relay route, *thereby obviously undermining our sovereign status.* We resolutely reject this. We therefore take this opportunity to declare to the IOC and the Beijing Organizing Committee our rejection of the relay route arrangement. (Taiwan Government Information Office Web site, April 27, 2007; emphasis added).

Tsai Chen-wei, chairman of Taiwan's Olympic Committee, also voiced his criticism that the relay route is "an attempt to downgrade our sovereignty" (BBC 2007). It would seem that the PRC is pushing a political agenda that regards Taiwan as the PRC's "foremost and vital national interest" (Xu 2006, 102). BOCOG also announced that the flame relay would pass from Mount Everest through Tibet, seen by some critics as the IOC's approval of China's military occupation of the region (Whelan 2007). IOC president Jacques Rogge announced at the unveiling ceremony that "the Beijing Torch Relay will, as its theme says, be a 'Journey of Harmony,' bringing friendship and respect to people of different nationalities, races and creeds" (BOCOG 2007). If the symbolic erasure of Taiwan and Tibet's national difference in the Torch Relay is any indicator of what China deems as a "harmonious" celebration of Chinese renaissance, many should take notice of how the New China's national identity will be projected as the Beijing Olympics plays out to a global audience.

The Beijing Olympics is shaping up to be the most sensational hybrid to date; Beijing is being marketed as a "dynamic modern metropolis with 3,000 years of cultural treasures woven into the urban tapestry" (BOCOG Web site). As for the East-West encounter, IOC member He Zhenliang reiterated the familiar theme concretized by 1930s Japan:

> In 2008, it will be the first time for the Olympic Games to be celebrated in China, one of the birthplaces of Oriental Civilization. It will also be

an exceptional opportunity for the Olympic Movement to enrich itself with the Oriental Culture, thus enhancing the multicultural nature of the Olympic Movement and contributing to the exchange and symbiosis of the Oriental and Western cultures. (BOCOG 2006, 6).

The preceding discourse is subtly different from previous strategies adopted by Asian Olympic hosts: unlike previous hosts who were under the tutelage of America, Beijing is confident that the Olympic Movement will also adopt aspects of China's Oriental culture. Beijing's optimism is perhaps warranted given its exponential growth and continued unhindered development.

China represents a new challenge to the established balance of power in the current global (read: Western dominated) economy. The United States has maintained a strong military presence in both Japan and Korea since the 1950s. When Japan and Korea hosted the Olympics, Japan and Korea were firmly under America's dominance, but China, while operating within a global system of interdependence, is more independent from America (Harootunian 1993). The world system remains unsure as to how much China will attempt to accommodate itself to the established global order. Depending on how the "Two System" government of China evolves, China threatens to change the arc of development characterized by Western global capitalism. The potential of global capitalism has always contained elements of struggle, as Richard Sennett aptly reminds us in his discussion of Max Weber's trenchant analysis of the military rationality inherent in capitalism itself (Sennett 2006). Whether Samuel Huntington's predicted clash between Eastern and Western civilizations emerges or whether China forges a new reconciliation point between the East and the West remains to be seen. The flow of global capital toward New China is, as Walter Mignolo observed, the significant crossing of the colonial difference of the East/the Orient from the West (2002, 179). The new globalism of rising China will undoubtedly rework this colonial difference but how it will do so is uncertain. What is certain, however, is that the Beijing Olympics will be historically significant not only in providing a platform for the New China's national cultural identity but also for actively engaging with the IOC to rework the paradigm of Olympic political communication that has been dominated thus far by the West. In this sense, the Olympics must be seen within the heritage of defining Asian national identity extending from Tokyo in 1940 to Tokyo in 1964, to Seoul, Nagano and beyond.

NOTES

1. For further reading of the significance of sports and the Olympic Games for nation-states, see Brownell 1995; Maguire 1999; and Roche 2000.

2. See Hobsbawm 1983; see also Huntington 2003 for the clash of world civilizations.

3. As Haugen has recently pointed out, these terms (*Asia, Orient,* and *East*) are used interchangeably to describe an imagined area that references nineteenth century's Orientalist discourse. For further reading, see Saïd 1994 and Young 1990.

4. The seminal collection of essays, *Postmodernism and Japan* (ed. Miyoshi and Harootunian 1989) addresses this issue, especially Naoki Sakai's work "Modernity and Its Critique: The Problem of Universalism and Particularism."

5. Immanuel Wallerstein (1990) asserts that the central tenet of Orientalist discourse was that only the civilizations of the West had evolved into modernity. Edward Saïd also discusses the role of how the West institutionalized various discourses of the difference between the East and the West as a form of Orientalism (Saïd [1978] 1994, 2–3).

6. Although Samuel Huntington (2003) refers to the post–Cold War break as pitting the West against the rest, he separates Japan from other Asian nations. This separate status of Japan mirrors the treatment Japan received by the political agenda of American modernization theory to posit Japan as a separate and successful example of non-Western, noncommunist, democratic, and capitalist nation in the immediate post–World War II era. Also see Bradshaw and Wallace 1996, especially 96–101.

7. H. D. Harootunian (2000) has written about how various intellectuals in 1930s Japan self-consciously attempted to view modernity as not a Western monopoly.

8. The "Two System" style of government refers to how China is currently defining its modern nation-state. In 1992, under Deng Xiao Ping, China changed its constitution and defined itself to be a "socialist society intent on creating a social market economy with Chinese characteristics" (Collins 2002, 135). Ong comments that the reference to a unified "Chineseness" is an attempt to elicit support from the Chinese people by the Chinese state as it imposes specific reforms to benefit the state (Ong and Nonini 1997, 173).

9. For other readings on defining Asian modernity vis-à-vis the West, see Chow 1991 and 2007; Ivy 1995; and Miyoshi and Harootunian 1989 and 1993.

10. The history of the 1940 Tokyo Olympics is detailed in the forthcoming *The 1940 Tokyo Games: The Missing Olympics: Japan, the Asian Olympics and the Olympic Movement* (Collins forthcoming).

11. Jeffrey Wasserstrom (2002, 126) warns against using 1988 Seoul as an analogy to 2008 Beijing.

12. The bidding slogan for Beijing 2008, "New Beijing, Great Olympics,"

was retired when Beijing won the right to host the Games in 2001. The current BOCOG slogan, "One World, One Dream," is meant to emphasize the common and shared dream by the world of the Olympics, although some may speculate that the Chinese characters for "one" could be also read as "the same" leading one to conclude that it is "The Same World (i.e., China's), The Same (i.e., China's) Dream."

13. The most typical example is the 1933 booklet produced by the Tokyo Municipal Office, *Tokyo: Sports Center of the Orient,* which outlined specific features of the Tokyo bid and presented numerous black and white photographs of Tokyo and Japan. See Collins forthcoming.

14. This interpretation is similar to Wolfgang Iser's notion of "dual coding" in which categories of same/different are constructed and mutually constituted.

15. My upcoming book, *The 1940 Tokyo Games: The Missing Olympics,* details this history especially in chapter 2.

16. Post–World War II American historians, typified by the work of E. O. Reischauer and A. W. Craig (1978), labeled Japan's 1930s militarism as an aberration to its overall successful path of Westernization and modernization in order to support the United States' political agenda of stopping the spread of communism in the East.

17. Nara was the first permanent imperial capital of Japan, established in 710. The imperial capital was later moved to Heian (today's Kyoto) in 794, where it remained for several centuries. Nikko is the location of one of the most lavishly decorated shrines and the national mausoleum to Tokugawa Shogunate, established in 1617.

18. Atsuji Tajima states that the debt structure of the Nagano Games left the Nagano municipality with an average debt of $45,000 per household. For further reading, see Tajima 2004.

19. Akebono was born in 1969 in Oahu, Hawaii, as Chad Rowan. He became a Japanese citizen in 1996 and retired from sumo in 2001. For further reading, see Panek 2006.

REFERENCES

Ahn Min-Seok. 2002. The Political Economy of the World Cup in South Korea. In *Japan, Korea, and the 2002 World Cup,* ed. John Horne and Wolfram Manzenreiter, 162–73. London: Routledge.

Aso Noriko. 2002. Sumptuous Re-past: The 1964 Tokyo Olympics Arts Festival. *positions: east asia cultures critique* 10 (1): 7–38.

BBC News. 2007. Everest Climb for Olympic Torch. April 26. http://news.bbc.co.uk/2/hi/asia-pacific/6595235.stm (accessed May 30, 2007).

BOBICO. 2000. Beijing 2008 Olympic Candidature File. Beijing.

BOCOG. 2006. *Beijing 2008,* no. 1 (March): 6. Electronic copies of the official Beijing 2008 Magazine are available at http://en.beijing2008.cn/34/41/column212014134.shtml.

BOCOG. 2007. Beijing 2008 Olympic Torch Relay Planned Route and Torch Design Unveiled. April 26. Available at http://torchrelay.beijing2008.cn/en/news/headlines/n214042288.shtml (accessed May 30, 2007).

Bradshaw, York W., and Michael Wallace. 1996. *Global Inequalities.* Thousand Oaks, CA: Pine Forge Press.

Brownell, Susan. 1995. *Training the Body for China: Sports in the Moral Order of the People's Republic.* Chicago: University of Chicago Press.

China Daily. 2001. Olympic Bidding: Beijing Mayor Pledges Best Games Ever. February 19.

Chow, Rey. 1991. *Woman and Chinese Modernity: The Politics of Reading between West and East.* Minneapolis: University of Minnesota Press.

Chow, Rey. 2007. *Sentimental Fabulations, Contemporary Chinese Films: Attachment in the Age of Global Visibility.* New York: Columbia University Press.

Collins, Michael. 2002. China's Olympics. *Contemporary Review* 280 (1834): 135–41.

Collins, Sandra. Forthcoming. *The 1940 Tokyo Games: The Missing Olympics: Japan, the Asian Olympics and the Olympic Movement.* London: Routledge.

Forney, Matt. 2001. Eyes on the Prize. *Time,* February 19. http://www.time.com/time/world/article/0,8599,99900,00.html (accessed July 27, 2007).

Friedman, E. 1995. *National Identity and Democratic Prospects in Socialist China.* Armonk, NY: M. E. Sharpe.

Harootunian, H. D. 1993. America's Japan/Japan's Japan. In *Japan in the World,* ed. M. Miyoshi and H. D. Harootunian, 196–221. Durham: Duke University Press.

Harootunian, H. D. 2000. *Overcome by Modernity.* Princeton: Princeton University Press.

Haugen, Heidi. 2005. Time and Space in Beijing's Olympic Bid. *Norwegian Journal of Geography* 59 (3): 217–27.

Hobsbawm, Eric. 1983. *The Invention of Tradition.* Cambridge: Cambridge University Press.

Huntington, Samuel. 2003. *The Clash of Civilizations and the Remaking of the World Order.* New York: Simon and Schuster.

IOC. 1998. *The Olympic Review.* 26, no. 19 (February–March).

IOC. 2001. *Report of the IOC Evaluation Commission for the Games of the XXIX Olympiad in 2008.* Lausanne: IOC.

Ivy, Marilyn. 1995. *Discourses of the Vanishing: Modernity, Phantasm, Japan.* Chicago: University of Chicago Press.

Jaffe, E. D., and I. D. Nebenzahl. 1993. Global Promotion of Country Image: Do the Olympics Count? In *Product-Country Images—Impact and Role in International Marketing,* ed. N. Papadopoulos and L. A. Heslop, 433–52. New York: International Business Press.

Kipling, Rudyard. 1895. The Ballad of East and West. In *A Victorian Anthology 1837–1895*, ed. Edmund Clarence Stedman. Cambridge: Riverside Press.

Larson, James, and Heung-Soo Park. 1993. *Global Television and the Politics of the Seoul Olympics*. Boulder: Westview Press.

Lechenperg, Harald, ed. 1964. *Olympic Games 1964: Innsbruck-Tokyo*. New York: A. S. Barnes and Co.

Liu, Kang. 1998. Is There an Alternative to (Capitalist) Globalization? The Debate about Modernity in China. In *The Cultures of Globalization*, ed. Fredric Jameson and Masao Miyoshi, 164–90. Durham: Duke University Press.

Maguire, Joseph. 1999. *Global Sport: Identities, Societies, and Civilizations*. Cambridge, UK: Polity Press.

Manheim, Jarol B. 1990. Rites of Passage: 1988 Seoul Olympics as Public Diplomacy. *Western Political Quarterly* 43 (2): 279–95.

Manzenreiter, Wolfram, and John Horne. 2002. Global Governance in World Sport and the 2002 World Cup Korea/Japan. In *Japan, Korea and the 2002 World Cup*, ed. John Horne and Wolfram Manzenreiter, 1–25. London: Routledge.

Mignolo, Walter D. 2002. The Many Faces of Cosmo-polis: Border Thinking and Critical Cosmopolitanism. In *Cosmopolitanism*, ed. Carol A. Breckenridge, Sheldon Pollock, Homi K. Bhabha, and Dipesh Chakrabarty. Durham: Duke University Press.

Miyoshi, Masao, and H. D. Harootunian. 1989. *Postmodernism and Japan*. Durham: Duke University Press.

Miyoshi, Masao, and H. D. Harootunian. 1993. *Japan in the World*. Durham: Duke University Press.

Murakami, Takashi, ed. 2005. *Little Boy: The Arts of Japan's Exploding Subculture*. New Haven: Yale University Press.

Nye, Joseph. 2004. *Soft Power: The Means to Success in World Politics*. Cambridge, MA: Perseus Group.

Oguma, Eiji. 2002. *A Genealogy of "Japanese" Self-images*. Trans. David Asket. Melbourne: Trans Pacific Press.

Ong, A., and D. M. Nonini. 1997. *Ungrounded Empires: The Cultural Politics of Modern Chinese Transnationalism*. New York: Routledge.

Panek, Mark. 2006. *Gaijin Yokozuna: A Biography of Chad Rowan*. Honolulu: University of Hawaii Press.

People's Daily. 2001. Beijing Aims at Lively, Cultural 2008 Olympics. July 10. http://english.peopledaily.com.cn/200107/10/eng20010710_74616.html (accessed July 10, 2007).

Polumbaum, J. 2003. Capturing the Flame: Aspirations and Representations of Beijing's 2008 Olympics. In *Chinese Media, Global Contexts*, ed. Chin-Chuan Lee, 57–75. London: RoutledgeCurzon.

Reed, J. D. 1987. A Symbol of Pride and Concern. *Time Magazine*, June 29. http://www.time.com/time/magazine/article/0,9171,964778-1,00.html (accessed July 8, 2007).

Reischauer, E. O., and A. M. Craig. 1978. *Japan: Tradition and Transformation.* New York: Houghton Mifflin.

Roche, Maurice. 2000. *Mega-Events and Modernity.* London: Routledge.

Saïd, Edward. [1978] 1994. *Orientalism.* New York: Random House.

Sennett, Richard. 2006. *The Culture of the New Capitalism.* New Haven: Yale University Press.

Slater, John. 2004. Tokyo 1964. In *The Encyclopedia of the Modern Olympic Movement,* ed. John E. Findling and Kimberly D. Pelle, 165–73. Westport: Greenview Press.

SLOOC. 1989. *Official Report of the XXIVth Olympiad Seoul.*

Smith, Anthony D. 1990. Towards a Global Culture? In *Global Culture: Nationalism, Globalization, and Modernity,* ed. Mike Featherstone, 171–92. London: Sage Publications.

Taiwan Government Information Office. http://www.gio.gov.tw/ct.asp?xItem=33043&ctNode=2462.

Tajima, Atsuji. 2004. Amoral Universalism: Mediating and Staging Global and Local in the 1988 Nagano Olympic Winter Games. *Critical Studies in Media Communication* 24 (3): 241–60.

Tham, G. J. E. 2005. Jasmine Flower in Three Different Lights. GRASP, 1st Annual Symposium, Wichita, KS.

Tokyo Municipal Office. 1933. *Tokyo: Sports Center of the Orient.*

Tokyo Organizing Committee for the XVIII Olympiad Tokyo. 1966. *The Official Report of the Games of the XVIII Olympiad Tokyo 1964,* vol. 1. Tokyo.

Wallerstein, Immanuel. 1990. Culture as the Ideological Battleground. In *Global Culture: Nationalism, Globalization, and Modernity,* ed. Mike Featherstone, 31–56. London: Sage Publications.

Wasserstrom, Jeffrey N. 2002. Using History to Think about the Beijing Olympics: The Use and Abuse of the Seoul 1988 Analogy. *Harvard International Journal of Press/Politics* 7 (1): 126–29.

Weber, Max. 2001. *The Protestant Ethic and the Spirit of Capitalism.* London: Routledge.

Whelan, Charles. 2007. Taiwan, Tibet among Controversial Leg Proposed for Beijing Olympic Torch Relay. Agence France-Presse, April 25. http://www.phayul.com/news/article.aspx?id=16314&t=1&c=1 (accessed May 30, 2007).

Xu, Xin. 2006. Modernizing China in the Olympic Spotlight: China's National Identity and the 2008 Beijing Olympiad. *Sociological Review* 54 (s2): 90–107.

Young, Robert. 1990. *White Mythologies: Writing History and the West.* London: Routledge.

Journalism and the Beijing Olympics

Liminality with Chinese Characteristics

Briar Smith

On December 1, 2006, Beijing released a significant declaration concerning foreign media professionals traveling to China to report on the 2008 Beijing Olympics. Ostensibly keeping promises to the International Olympic Committee (IOC) that it would allow journalists to report on the Games in a free media environment, Beijing announced that it would temporarily relax restrictions on foreign reporters in China from January 1, 2007, until October 17, 2008. This development was part of a long discourse concerning the impact of the Beijing Olympics on ideas of freedom of speech and journalistic practices. In the several years before 2008, a formulaic approach to discussing "emerging China," in which debates about China, human rights and particularly freedom of expression have been central, established itself. In keeping with this discourse, one frequently asked question concerned how China would respond to thousands of foreign journalists on its soil, especially in light of the promises it had made in its Olympic bid and afterward to allow unrestricted reporting during the Games. The relaxed foreign press reporting guidelines issued in preparation for the 2008 Beijing Olympics can be seen as part of a conversation between China, the IOC, the Beijing Organzing Committee of the Olympic Games (BOCOG) and global civil society groups.

In this chapter, I argue that although China's desire to nurture a more positive international image and present a confident and benevolent China is the impetus behind these new regulations, their implementation is problematic, both for China itself as it struggles to negotiate its continued need for media control, and for foreign journalists in China as they operate within this unstable new climate. I also illustrate the ways in which the temporary nature and uneven application of the regulations mitigates China's presentation of itself as a full participant in the globalized, "modern" world.

Background

When China narrowly lost its 1993 bid to host the 2000 Summer Olympics by two votes, its record on human rights violations was often cited as a reason. Four years later, China was the clear favorite, trouncing second-place Toronto, but again, it was criticized for its human rights abuses (and an Olympic history rife with doping scandals) (Gamesbids.com). The International Olympic Committee (IOC) Evaluation Commission and its members were ultimately reassured by many elements of the government-driven bid, by the depth and breadth of public support within China, and by China's ability to provide the IOC with a viable balance between public and private financing (Polumbaum 2003). China's proclamation of its ability to meet the significant environmental challenges and "leave a unique legacy to China and to sport" (BOCOG 2001) illustrated the nation's sensitivity to the implications the Olympics might have for China's geopolitical position and economic security. Still the human rights issues were haunting, especially those concerning freedom of the press.

Despite Beijing's infrastructural overtures of friendliness and sophistication, China's successful bid has been a lightning rod for speculation about the ability of an authoritarian country to host an Olympic Games in line with the IOC's charter, which, among other things, "seeks to create a way of life based on the joy found in effort, the educational value of good example and respect for universal fundamental ethical principles" (IOC 2007). China's dismal human rights record, as well as its historically dismissive attitude toward press freedom, attracted international press attention as the media debated the capacity of the Olympics to provide a positive legacy in a country like China. With a history of increasing controls and reversing hard-won liberties in response to controversies and politically damaging events, (i.e., Tiananmen), a tendency colloquially referred to as the "two steps forward, one step back" policy,[1] the Olympics could ameliorate human rights conditions, including press freedoms, or encourage China to tighten its fist further if Beijing deems the results of its foray into increased press freedom threatening or damaging in any way. Beijing is acutely aware that the world's eyes are closely watching its every move and its national image in the foreign press has become of paramount importance. BOCOG has even commissioned university research to assess the foreign media's coverage of the Beijing Olympics. Although they were hoping otherwise, an analysis of foreign media reports on the Atlanta, Sydney, Athens, and Beijing Olympics revealed that in contrast to coverage of the other three Games, most articles on the Beijing Olympics were concerned with political issues instead of less sensitive topics like economics, preparations, and sport. In a particularly revealing statement about China's conceptions of state involvement in the media, the report suggests that "Beijing should adapt a more integrated strategy to promote the city image and [have more opened policy] in communicating with western media in order to be more active and influential in transferring her international image in the world" (Dong 2006).[2]

As soon as the Games were awarded to China, the question of how China's tight media environment and restrictions on foreign journalists would be handled when the estimated 20,000 foreign media professionals descend on the Middle Kingdom generated intense speculation (Armitage 2005). International media organizations have not been comfortable with China's commitment to ensuring journalists' ability to freely cover the Games. BOCOG has been aware of the IOC's expectations that the media, particularly U.S. and European organizations with large budgets and consuming audiences, have unfettered access to report on the Olympics, since media-related enterprises make up a significant portion of IOC revenue. In their 2001 bid, Chinese officials gave assurances of "complete media access for all journalists in 2008" (Committee to Protect Journalists [CPJ] 2006b), but what the government meant by "complete media access" and its relation to journalistic practices on the ground was left undefined for almost six years until its December announcement.

China's Media System

In order to understand the regulatory alterations, it is important to have some grasp of the extraordinarily complicated Chinese media context in which the regulations are to be operationalized and the system by which the PRC manages foreign media presence within its borders. China's domestic media system, itself, is chaotic in concept. It is too simple to think of it as wholly a system under unitary state and Party control; at the same time, steps toward privatization, decentralization, and technological adaptation run in directions that often seem inconsistent. A typical account addressed by media critics for a Western audience might describe it as the "propagandist/commercial model" of journalism (Zhao 1998, 151), or a form of "authoritarian liberalism—a combination of economic liberalism and political illiberalism" (Hemelryk Donald et al. 2002, 5). The hybrid form of governance constituting the Chinese media scene means that it cannot be reduced to either the Party principle or market forces. Departing from the policy of directly funding or subsidizing the media without regard for economic viability, economic reforms and decentralization in the 1990s meant rapid commercialization for news organizations and an expectation that they become mostly, if not completely, financially independent from government resources even while independent ownership is prohibited. Commercialization resulted in rapid diversification and a reorientation toward the consumer market, relevant content, broadened scope of coverage, and developments in watchdog reporting. The shift to a market economy has led to a large variety of players who find and diffuse information, some not within the traditional concept of press. The rise in defamation cases is an indicator that there are more critical reports in areas such as the environment or business and these may increase as part of an effort to show enhanced attention to quality of production. Still, efforts to protect consumer interests are undermined by corruption and increasingly powerful private corporations that go so far as to threaten and physically rough up journalists for reports that might jeopardize their bottom line. Although the media have gained more freedom in less political areas, the Party still seeks to retain editorial and political control over the news media; the goal that "the power of the Party may not be threatened in the least remains unchanged, or even strengthened in the context of commercialization" (Zhao 1998, 151).

Journalists obviously face threats apart from private interests within China; China has had the dubious honor of being the leading incarcerator of journalists since 1999 (CPJ 2007)[3] and reports of journalists facing harassment, abuse, and detention are well documented by press watchdog groups. As is true in many contexts, journalists and editors frequently engage in self-censorship to avoid offenses. The relocation and demotion of editors is not uncommon and they can be held responsible for their employees' reporting on controversial issues, such as news of infectious diseases, Party corruption, protests, and disasters.[4] PRC journalists often have a different conceptualization of their profession from those of journalists in more liberal political contexts, though the gulf may be narrowing. The Chinese media tend to be patriotic toward the state, receptive to patronage from superiors and advertisers (in many cases turning into outright bribery and corruption) and "paternalistic and elitist in self-expression . . . Journalists are both integrated into the system as part of the cultural elite and treated as part of an ideological instrument" (Lee 2001, 247). Zhou He qualifies the evolution of Chinese media and journalists as a more complicated movement away from acting as simple mouthpieces of the Party and toward a more nuanced role between the political-economic "tug-of-war," frequently promoting and legitimating the Party in what he calls "Party Publicity Inc" (He 2000). Important developments have occurred in pushing the boundaries of "free speech" in recent years, both because of shifts in policy, market competition, and the sheer amount of publications as the result of commercialization and diversification, which makes wholesale monitoring much less possible.[5] However, even while geared toward catering to market demands, avoiding official violations remains paramount in maintaining the viability of any news organization. As Chin-Chuan Lee has put it, "the Western bourgeois-liberal concept of 'neutral journalism'—let alone the development of an oppositional culture to the state—is officially rejected" (Lee 2001, 247).

Foreign journalists are a significant source of anxiety for image-conscious China. Sensitive to criticism and wary about its citizenry's access to foreign reports, China has sought, in the past, to curtail access to news that is produced by non-Chinese nationals and has not been internally vetted. With the 1990s economic reforms, increased foreign trade, and the opening of the stock market have necessitated improved access to financial reporting by Chinese business organizations and government departments. Foreign news services such as Dow Jones and Reuters have established a profitable presence in China's financial news environment, selling up-to-the-minute financial data to banks and investment firms. Xinhua, the PRC's official press agency, retains at least symbolic oversight of these companies to filter sensitive content that might jeopardize national interests. The imperative to retain a monopoly in the information market also prohibits Chinese companies from setting up joint media ventures with foreign ownership. The Internet has, of course, immensely complicated this task.

Foreign journalists operating within China have been required to follow what could be considered a draconian set of regulations. Applicable to resident foreign correspondents, short-term correspondents, and the permanent offices that employ foreign journalists, any journalist entering China must submit an application to the Information Department of the Foreign Ministry in Beijing or the equivalent office if they are stationed in any other province and must show up in person to receive a foreign press permit. Reporters on short-term stays are under the supervision of "host organizations" that are to assist them with their activities. Article 14 of the "Regulations Concerning Foreign Journalists," which is worth quoting at length, is indicative of the circumspection with which the PRC approaches foreign journalists:

> Article 14: Foreign journalists and permanent offices of foreign news agencies shall conduct journalistic activities within the scope of business as registered or within the mutually agreed plan for news coverage. Foreign journalists and permanent offices of foreign news agencies shall observe journalistic ethics and shall not distort facts, fabricate rumors or carry out news coverage by foul means. Foreign journalists and permanent offices of foreign news agencies shall not engage in activities which are incompatible with their status or tasks, or which endanger China's national security, unity or community and public interests. (Ministry of Foreign Affairs 2003)

The most physically restrictive of the regulations requires foreign journalists to submit a written application to the relevant governmental authorities in any province or municipality outside of Beijing in which the journalist wishes to conduct journalistic activities. This is widely considered to be a means by which the government monitors foreign journalists within the country and prevents their sanctioned travel to parts of China that might result in the publishing of sensitive reports, such as reports out of Tibet or Xinjiang. Travel approval can take days, weeks, or possibly years to obtain, placing journalists in the position of either being too late to cover timely topics in other provinces or traveling without permission. Journalists' violations are usually overlooked for routine reports, but if they are caught covering protests, epidemics, or anything else the government deems unflattering, they risk being arrested, interrogated, and having notes and footage confiscated. Journalists are also required to seek permission for interviews in Beijing and are discouraged from conducting street interviews, and there have been incidents of interviewees being beaten or arrested for talking to foreign journalists (McLaughlin 2006–7). Even sanctioned interviews often involve the presence of an official, further dampening the environment in which journalists operate. The often ill-defined and ambiguous regulations can have the effect of curtailing independent reporting, and tactics like roughing up correspondents, aggressively monitoring and tailing correspondents "surprise, anger and frustrate visiting journalists from the United States and other free-press countries" (McLaughlin 2006–7).

Adding to the doubts that Beijing cared to at least present the semblance of a press-friendly environment to the world, China announced in September of 2006 that it would impose broad new restrictions on the distribution of foreign news within China. These restrictions would have positioned Xinhua to act as the "de facto gatekeeper" (Kahn 2006) for foreign news reports, photographs, and economic data leaving China and to act as the middleman between foreign news providers and their clients. Following complaints by powerful news agencies like Reuters and Bloomberg, the plan was soon scrapped. In June 2006, Beijing announced plans to impose fines on domestic and foreign journalists who reported on sudden events, such as riots, disease outbreaks, or natural disasters without authorization.[6] Combined with increased censorship of Web sites, blogs, relocation or firing of editors and journalist arrests in previous months, these steps were interpreted through the lens of the impending Olympics and Beijing's desire to increase media control prior to the Olympics, regardless of world or IOC opinion (Watts 2006).

Announcement of New Regulations

For a number of months, the negative press attention garnered by the backward trajectory didn't appear to bother the PRC but its December 2006 announcement came in the wake of vigorous criticism and advocacy by groups like Reporters Without Borders, Amnesty International, the CPJ, Foreign Correspondents Club of China (FCCC), and even the European Union. The *Wall Street Journal* described the changes as "reflecting pressure by the IOC and human-rights groups for China to provide an atmosphere of greater freedom and openness for the

Olympics, as well as the Chinese government's desire to be seen as an increasingly powerful, but benevolent global power" (Fong 2006). Possibly hoping that promoting a more comfortable operating environment for foreign reporters would positively influence reporting on China during the Games (and beyond), the Foreign Ministry held a press conference to declare that the restrictions on foreign journalists covering the Olympic Games and "related matters" would be relaxed temporarily, for the time period beginning January 1, 2007, and expiring October 17, 2008, which encompasses the lead-up to the Games and a couple of months after they end. The most notable article in the regulations allows media professionals to travel within China without prior approval, as long as they have an Olympic Identity and Accreditation Card. Another article states that "to interview organizations or individuals in China, foreign journalists need only to obtain their prior consent" (*BBC Monitoring Asia Pacific* 2006). The regulations permit foreign news organizations to hire Chinese citizens to assist them in their reporting activities, as long as they are hired through organizations that provide services to foreign nationals. Aware that journalists will not limit their coverage to sports, the Foreign Ministry is broadly interpreting the new rules and Spokesman Liu Jianchao predicted that the media "will also cover politics, science, technology, and the economy. The 'related matters' . . . actually expands the areas on which foreign journalists can report" (*Taipei Times* 2006). However, Liu warned that authorities would still have the authority to intervene, "especially during emergencies, protests, and other incidents that suddenly arise," revealing the degree to which the government is fearful of spontaneity and free access to cover events. Allowing travel to Tibet and Xinjiang was also ambiguously defined, with the caveat that some control for security reasons was possible. He also acknowledged that implementation would not be friction-free and that foreign journalists must still comply with Chinese law, evidencing China's ambivalence toward wholesale commitment to these relaxations. Adding more reservations about the success of implementing the rules outside of Beijing, vice-minister of the State Council Information Office, Wang Guoqing, said that he was "not quite optimistic about their implementation outside of major cities" (*China Daily* 2007) and that he wouldn't be surprised if reporters encountered some difficulties in obtaining news.

However, there have been several encouraging signs that Beijing is honoring the spirit of its recent foray into a more liberal handling of the press. Explained as part of a policy shift toward "serving the media" instead of managing it, Vice-Minister Wang stated that there are "a hundred advantages and not a single disadvantage" in dealing with the press in a forthright and friendly manner, adding that "besides informing the public, the media act as a watchdog of government activities." Although it appears he was only talking about the foreign press at the time, it is rare to hear this kind of rhetoric coming from the main governmental information office.[7] A specially designed master's program in Media Management was instituted at the University of Bedfordshire in the United Kingdom with the help of Beijing's municipal government. Equal parts coursework and projects, there are journalist guest lectures and site visits to UK media organizations. Wanting to be prepared for the onslaught of foreign media and their foreign expectations, the students, made up of Chinese government and media workers, are learning how to be more effective communication partners during the Olympics. Commenting that Beijing's feedback has been positive and without complaints about "liberal democratic values," one lecturer said, "We are just here planting the seeds. It's brave of the Chinese government and brave of the university—it is widening participation . . . and giving the students ideas, techniques and skills they otherwise wouldn't have access to" (Corbyn 2007).

In another effort toward transparency, the National People's Congress (NPC) and Chinese People's Political Consultative Conference (CPPCC), both held annually in March, allowed overseas journalists to directly contact and interview lawmakers and political advisors after they filled out an online journalist registration. Past regulations mandated that journalists contact the "Two Sessions" Press Center, who would then contact the committee members on their behalf. For the first time in more than 50 years, the Two Sessions Center released the names, addresses, and background information of all NPC delegation members and deputies on its Web site and translated the work reports into six languages (*BBC Monitoring Asia Pacific* 2007). In late January 2007, Reporters Without Borders was allowed to visit China for the first time, and government officials told the group they might be ready to reconsider the situation of journalists and Internet users who are being held in prison, more than a little ironically adding, "China hopes to see comprehensive, objective and fair assessment of its development and human rights conditions" (*Press Trust of India* 2007).

However, since the new rules took effect on January 1, 2007, many incidents concerning foreign journalists seem to contradict Beijing's creation of "an enabling environment for foreign journalists" (Hutzler

2006), and a continuing confining atmosphere for the domestic media has dampened enthusiasm for China's "courageous" new policy. Perhaps not surprisingly, a recent special report released by CPJ and a survey conducted by the FCCC evaluate China's pledges to the international community concerning press freedoms for the Olympics and find ultimately that the PRC is failing on many fronts. The FCCC reported that 40 percent of foreign correspondents working in China have experienced some form of interference, such as source intimidation, detention, and even violence since the rules took effect. Refracting the findings through the prism of the Olympics and its entailments, FCCC President Melinda Liu cautioned, "A nation where citizens who speak to foreign correspondents face threats, reprisals, and even bodily harm does not live up to the world's expectations of an Olympic host" (FCCC 2007). According to the CPJ report, one of the most serious problems is treatment of domestic journalists who are subject to the "full force" of domestic censorship and are still bound by restrictions on their travel and reporting practices in other provinces (CPJ 2007). Further complications arise for the Chinese nationals who are hired to assist foreign media professionals and press organizations with interviews, translations, and other services that help overcome the tremendous language barrier in China. It remains unclear what protection, if any, will be afforded to Chinese citizens who assist foreign journalists with writing anything offensive to the government. CPJ is concerned about the double standard inherent in the rules and the post-Olympic implications: "once the closing ceremonies are held and international attention fades, Chinese journalists will bear the brunt of official retribution for reporting any news that the government deems unfavorable" (CPJ 2006b). CPJ provides international media organizations with comprehensive lists of precautions and recommendations on ways to protect themselves, as well as sources and assistants, from punishment and suspicion while working in China. Treatment of Chinese nationals remains one of the most problematic aspects of this regulatory turn, and the report calls on China to abandon "archaic systems of media control" and "end violent retribution meted out by local officials angered by critical reporting" while urging the IOC to insist that China extend the new press freedoms to domestic journalists (CPJ 2007, 8).

Even with the restrictions lifted on interviewing Chinese citizens, Chinese authorities have implemented creative mechanisms by which to further control the flow of information. In a fascinating glimpse into the PRC's conception of politics and journalism, when foreign reporters attempted to interview Zheng Enchong, a former human rights lawyer who served three years for illegally providing state secrets abroad, they were turned away by police. Although he was released last year, he is serving an extra year of "deprivation of political rights," which means he is "not suitable for taking interviews" (Ching 2007) raising intriguing questions about the right to meet with foreign journalists as a condition of citizenship, a privilege that has been effectively denied all citizens under the old policies. Denying interviews based on deprivation of political rights is also a convenient mechanism by which officials can circumvent the new interview rules since some citizens can have their "right to be interviewed" revoked. In February 2007, the Central Propaganda Department banned news reporting on twenty specific issues in order to promote a "conducive atmosphere" in the lead up to the 17th Chinese Communist Party Congress. Mandates that only "ethically inspiring" programs be aired during primetime have also been imposed (Feuilherade 2007).[8] The local government in Shandong province issued a document that urged all departments, organizations, and officials to "use all measures to downsize the impact of negative reporting to a minimum level" (*BBC Monitoring International Reports* 2007) in preparation for the challenge posed by relaxed media restrictions. Noting that measures to "block malicious information that might intensify social conflicts or uneasiness" has been a long-standing practice by local officials, a Chinese editor warned that reporters can't expect full transparency when the specter of negative news endangers their position (*BBC Monitoring International Reports* 2007) and provincial authorities (often with the cooperation of local business) often work together to prevent investigative reporting on potentially embarrassing issues.

Although the CPJ and FCCC reports find that foreign journalists have had an easier time since the rules were relaxed (FCCC 2007, 1), travel and interview access is far from unproblematic. One day after the rules were announced, *New York Times* Beijing bureau chief Joseph Kahn and *International Herald Tribune*'s Roger Cohen were detained and made to write "confessions" after interviewing a businessman in Hubei province (CPJ 2006a). While attempting to report on toys with possible lead contamination, *New York Times* reporter David Barboza, his translator, and his photographer were detained by the factory's private security officers, necessitating hours of negotiations before their release. A

BBC crew was arrested in Hunan province for investigating a rumored student death in a protest over increased public transportation fares. Police criticized the reporters for not obtaining permission to visit the city, and when one journalist explained that new regulations allowed them to move freely within China, the officer replied, "That is just for stories linked to the Olympic Games and I don't think you came here for the Olympic Games" (Reporters Without Borders 2007). China's vast and decentralized bureaucracy presents troublesome challenges for any consistent application of the new regulations. The regulations out of Beijing are not necessarily taken seriously at the local level; provincial officials have little retribution to fear from Beijing since any inconsistencies can be explained away as accidents or miscommunications. Second, the regulations are temporary, belying the sincerity that a permanent rule change might express.

In order to assess the situation on the ground for a foreign reporter stationed in China, I contacted Howard French, Shanghai-based senior reporter for the *New York Times*.[9] As a longtime reporter in China, Mr. French has spent much of his career operating under the previous press regulations and said that he had been detained from time to time for being an unauthorized visitor in another province. Although it has not happened to him since the relaxations, he said he had not yet fully tested the new rules. When asked how he interpreted the changes as a media professional, he answered, "I think it is a positive step, generally speaking. It will need to be tested thoroughly through real-world experience, but the authorities should be praised, at least provisionally, for removing anachronistic controls." French also stated that the temporary nature of the rules "struck [him] as the way the Chinese government does a great many things. They introduce economic reforms in a province or two, to see how things go before rolling them out on a broader, more permanent scale. It is perfectly possible, of course, that there is no intention to make these changes permanent, and that it is essentially meant to give political cover during the Olympics." He expects the Olympics to present an intense media situation in China, with "millions of journalists running around China, running the entire gamut of knowledge and sophistication." In his opinion, the nature of the stories written and the degree to which they are seen as affecting China's image in the world will largely determine whether the government makes the rules permanent.

Regardless of whether or not the new rules are made permanent, the

PRC's media climate is still troubling for both foreign and domestic media alike. With a built-in expiration date, China is truly doing "liminality with Chinese characteristics." The Olympics represents an important rite of passage in which new approaches to media freedom, government transparency, and environmental stewardship could lead the way to a new, more globally participatory Chinese era. Instead, the rules are conceived as transitory, allowing China to revert to its previous policies and behavior if it chooses, eschewing the permanently transformative element of liminality.[10] Conceived as a temporary rapprochement with a more liberal press model, it is not necessarily borne of a self-reflexive or organic progression toward lasting freedom of the press for foreign or domestic media. Moreover, the difficulties journalists encounter on the ground and the government's hesitancy to put its full muscle behind the new regulations is indicative of the awkward and ill-conceived notion of sudden, wholesale importation of a "Western" model of journalism into a non-Western context that is ill-equipped to accommodate the model.

The discontinuity of journalists' experiences speaks to the rather clumsy and half-hearted institution of the regulations as well as the heavy hand of provincial authorities who have no real reason to take Beijing seriously. Possibly just a gesture of compliance to the IOC and a consequence of pressure from global civil society groups, the foreign media rule changes are often described in terms of other Olympic infrastructural improvements designed to comfort and impress tourists. Even while remaking itself in the image of a responsible and ascendant nation, Beijing seems unaware that while its efforts are an important step, they might do even more damage to its international image. A temporary and domestically hypocritical press policy reifies China as an authoritarian "other." If liberal press freedoms and transparency are endemic to the type of globally influential, politically stable, "first-world" nations in which China is asserting its membership, the double standard of disallowing their own journalists from engaging in the practices that they bestow on foreign journalists belies China's self-presentation as a confident nation.[11]

Following a well-practiced strategy of *neijing-waisong* (internally tight and externally loose), China can be comfortable with allowing foreign journalists to report freely during this period only as long as it retains (or retains the illusion of retaining) a domestic grip on information. Whether it is by curtailing permissible reporting in the internally influential domestic press, firing and jailing journalists and dissidents, or maintaining a purposefully ambiguous and uneven application of the new regulations, it is clear that the desire to establish the presentation of a respectable, open, and responsible nation in time for the Olympics is not a seamless task. Countering the skepticism that China can fully commit to and maintain an environment in which international media organizations feel unencumbered in their journalistic activities cannot be achieved simply through lip service and grandiloquent press conferences. It necessitates a pervasive examination of habituated behavior and attitudes toward both domestic and foreign media, and a home-grown, sustainable approach to increased press freedoms.

NOTES

1. This phrase was discussed by the students in a class taught at Beijing University as part of the Penn-in-Beijing 2007 Summer School, which was comprised of both Chinese and American students.

2. Dong's presentation at a July 2006 symposium, "Global Olympiad, Chinese Media," held in Beijing, was an interesting window into the way in which media research is conducted in China. Her report suggests that the way China's national image is portrayed will improve as the result of Beijing's interceding strategies with respect to Western media.

3. According to this report, twenty-nine journalists are currently in jail because of their work, held on vague "antistate" charges.

4. In discussing media freedom at Beijing University in the summer of 2006, a student told me the following story. A newspaper had published an article that concerned the Uighurs, an ethnic Muslim minority within China. The report contained a description of the reason that Muslims do not eat pork, which was criticized later by Uighurs for its inaccuracy and offensive tone. The editor of the newspaper was fired almost immediately for allowing the article to be printed. This anecdote underscores both how terrified China is of its Muslim minorities and the ease with which editors' careers are terminated.

5. According to 1999 statistics in Gunaratne's volume *Handbook of the Media in Asia,* there were some 2,000 newspapers in China, not to mention magazines and other industry publications, which can only have increased since then. What remains truly off limits, however, is questioning the legitimacy of the CCP and/or promoting political regime change.

6. This proposed law was rewritten in the summer of 2007 to remove the fines for journalists, but still bars reporting on whatever the government classifies as "false information." See *People's Daily Online* 2007.

7. Vice-Minister Wang also commented that part of the ideological and practical shift toward serving the media has included the development of a "reporter's assistance project," which is a compilation of information about people and places they may want to cover. Each region is responsible for coming up with a general handbook and pamphlets for reporters with information about projects that might be of interest to journalists. It also requires the foreign affairs offices at the provincial level or local level to ease the way for foreign journalists when they come to town. This idea of regionally produced pamphlets and compilations of people and places of interest is indicative to me of China's complete inability to understand how absurd this appears. Their idea of not managing the press entails a new "helpful" and "friendly" management by way of not-so-subtle nudges to cover certain topics and interview certain people (and steer clear of others). This is also emblematic of the way China conceptualizes the press as operating at the behest of governmental suggestions and influences instead of providing independent coverage and independent research. This approach was echoed at last summer's Olympic conference in Beijing when the head of BOCOG's media affairs office outlined its future plans for handling the media when it came to report on the Olympics. He said that information packets on all the athletes would be made in advance, minimizing the need to conduct interviews; a plush new media center was being created with everything they would need at their fingertips; and transportation would be provided for journalists, along with suggested restaurants and hotels. The international participants at the conference were listening to his description with barely concealed shock and cynicism at the implications while he appeared extremely earnest and pleased with the "progressive" plan.

8. This includes a ban on foreign-produced cartoons during prime time and a crackdown on "vulgar" reality shows.

9. All quotes in this section are from personal communication with Howard French.

10. The subtitle of this chapter, "Liminality with Chinese Characteristics," is meant to be a play on the term *Socialism with Chinese Characteristics,* which is the term used to describe the PRC's economic reforms in the 1980s, encompassing a mixed form of private and public ownership competing within a market environment, creating a system that is in essence identical to capitalism but where the state dominates large parts of the economy and it is pointedly not called capitalism.

11. I do not mean to argue here that a free press is necessary in a "first-world" nation, although I'm sure the argument can be and has been made. I only mean to say that China wants to present itself on par with countries like the United States, Australia, Europe, and so on, where other successful Olympics have been held and in which a positive image of the host nation was sustained. These countries all have variations of an independent press, which is sometimes synonymous with politically influential, modern nations.

REFERENCES

Armitage, Catherine. 2005. Countdown to a Crisis. *Australian,* August 8. LexisNexis (accessed March 30, 2007).

BBC Monitoring Asia Pacific. 2006. Text of China's Regulations on Foreign Media's Reporting of Beijing Olympics. December 1. LexisNexis (accessed March 21, 2007).

BBC Monitoring Asia Pacific. 2007. China to Allow Overseas Media to Interview "Two Sessions" Deputies Directly. March 1. LexisNexis (accessed March 21, 2007).

BBC Monitoring International Reports. 2007. China Cadres Told to Block Negative News Reporting ahead of Beijing Olympics. March 20. LexisNexis (accessed March 21, 2007).

BOCOG. 2001. Statement of the Beijing 2008 Olympic Games Bid Commission. Beijing Organizing Committee for the Games of the XXIX Olympiad, May 15, 2001. Available at http://210.75.208.182/eolympic/news%20room/news%20release.5-15.html.

China Daily. 2007. Serve the Media, Not Manage Them. January 4. LexisNexis (accessed April 23, 2007).

Ching, Frank. 2007. Free the Press. *South China Morning Post,* January 10. LexisNexis (accessed February 26, 2007).

Corbyn, Zoe. 2007. In Pursuit of Media Gold: China Is Sending Journalists to Study in Britain ahead of the Olympics. *Guardian,* March 27. LexisNexis (accessed April 23, 2007).

CPJ. 2006a. Cases 2006: U.S. Reporters Detained while Interviewing Source. December 2. Available at http://www.cpj.org/cases06/asia_cases_06/china02dec06ca.html.

CPJ. 2006b. At International Olympic Committee Headquarters, CPJ Raises Concerns about Press Freedom in China. November 15. Available at http://www.cpj.org/news/2006/asia/china15nov06na.html.

CPJ. 2007. Falling Short: As the 2008 Olympics Approach, China Falters on Press Freedom. Available at http://www.cpj.org/Briefings/2007/Falling_Short/China/china.pdf.

Dong Xiaoyong. 2006. Beijing Olympic Games and the Promotion of National Image: Subject Analysis of the Foreign Media's Reports in Four Olympic Holders. Paper presented at the "Global Olympiad, Chinese Media" International Symposium, Beijing, China, July 28–29.

FCCC. 2007. FCCC 2007 Survey on Reporting Conditions. Available at http://www.fccchina.org/when/FCCCSURVEYAUG2007.PDF.

Feuilherade, Peter. 2007. China's "Media Transparency" Has Limits. *BBC Monitoring International Reports,* March 5. LexisNexis (accessed March 21, 2007).

Fong, Mei. 2006. China to Relax Limits on Media for '08 Olympics. *Wall Street Journal,* December 4. LexisNexis (accessed March 21, 2007).

Gamesbids.com. Archive—Beijing 2008 Olympics Bid. Available at http://www.gamesbids.com/english/archives/beijing.shtml.

He, Zhou. 2000. Chinese Communist Party Press in a Tug-of-War: A Political-Economy Analysis of the *Zhenzhen Special Zone Daily*. In *Power, Money, and Media: Communication Patterns and Bureaucratic Control in Cultural China*, ed. Chin-Chuan Lee, 112–51. Evanston, IL: Northwestern University Press.

Hemelryk Donald, Stephanie, et al. 2002. *Media in China: Consumption, Content, and Crisis*. London: RoutledgeCurzon.

Hutzler, Charles. 2006. China Relaxes Rules on Foreign Reporters but not for Chinese Reporters. Associated Press, December 1. LexisNexis (accessed March 21, 2007).

IOC. 2007. Olympic Charter, Fundamental Principles, Paragraph 2. http://multimedia.olympic.org/pdf/en_report_122.pdf.

Kahn, Joseph. 2006. China Puts Stricter Limits on Distribution of Foreign News. *New York Times,* September 11. LexisNexis (accessed March 1, 2007).

Lee, Chin-Chuan. 2001. Servants of the State or the Market? Media and Journalists in China. In *Media Occupations and Professions: A Reader,* ed. Jeremy Tunstall, 240–52. Oxford: Oxford University Press.

McLaughlin, Kathleen E. 2006–7. Letter from China. *American Journalism Review*. Available at http://www.ajr.org/article_printable.asp?id=4233.

Ministry of Foreign Affairs of the People's Republic of China. 2003. Regulations Concerning Foreign Journalists and Permanent Offices of Foreign News Agencies. Available at http://www.mfa.gov.cn/eng/xwfw/jzfw/3635/Part%20V/t25155.htm.

People's Daily Online. 2007. China Adopts Emergency Response Law. August 30. Available at http://english.peopledaily.com.cn/90001/6251540.html.

Polumbaum, Judy. 2003. Capturing the Flame: Aspirations and Representations of Beijing's 2008 Olympics. In *Chinese Media, Global Contexts,* ed. Chin-Chuan Lee, 57–75. London: RoutledgeCurzon.

Press Trust of India. 2007. China Asks Western Media to Be "Fair" Regarding Human Rights Issues. January 26. LexisNexis (accessed March 21, 2007).

Reporters Without Borders. 2007. Disturbing Lapses in Application of New Rules for Foreign Media. Asia Press Releases, March 22. Available at http://www.rsf.org/article.php3?id_article=21394.

Taipei Times. 2006. China Announces "Laxer" Foreign Media Restrictions. December 2. LexisNexis (accessed March 26, 2007).

Watts, Jonathan. 2006. Civil Liberties Crackdown Casts Long Shadow over Chinese Leader's Visit to Britain. *Guardian International,* September 13. LexisNexis (accessed March 31, 2007).

Zhao, Yuezhi. 1998. *Media, Market, and Democracy in China: Between the Party Line and the Bottom Line*. Chicago: University of Illinois Press.

III

Theaters of Representation

"All Under Heaven"— Megaspace in Beijing

Carolyn Marvin

Staging the 2008 Olympics is heady stuff for the modern descendants of the Middle Kingdom. Though its emperor once possessed a divine mandate to rule "All Under Heaven," China's international role has been far more circumscribed during the last century and a half. Now the Chinese believe their luck has changed. Playing host to the largest of all modern peacetime extravaganzas perfectly suits the current Chinese political imagination, succinctly if not subtly expressed in the Beijing Olympic slogan, "One World, One Dream." Through the magic of media, the 2008 Games will certainly reach all under heaven, a scale the Chinese have embraced by sending an Olympic flag to orbit the earth for five days in 2005 aboard China's second manned space mission, Shengzhou VI (Zhao 2005).

The image of the world as China's sphere of influence could be seen in talk about the Olympic torch relay, the most ambitious ever. The "Journey of Harmony" would, according to Beijing Organizing Committee of the Olympic Games (BOCOG) head Liu Qi, be the most territorially extensive ever, crossing 85,000 miles and five continents, tracing the ancient Silk Road and ascending Mt. Everest (nailing down China's claim to Tibet), before reaching the capital (Channel NewsAsia 2007). When state television broadcast "Rise of the Great Nations," presenting the histories of nine world-dominating modern nations including the United States, the Netherlands, and England (Beijingmike

2007), there was scant need for the series to name China as the coming tenth to ascend to greatness for its domestic audience. Many citizens are said to believe their leaders have a secret strategy that will make this century China's. Meanwhile, visually lush programs about the history of ancient China are endlessly recycled on the West-directed English-language channel.

Architecture has long been at the heart of Chinese statecraft, so it is no surprise that built form has a special role to play in the XXIX Olympiad. The character of Olympic public space is part of the effort to change the subject from protests about China's human rights record, its role in Darfur, its labor practices, and the lingering memory of the 1989 massacres of protesters in the streets near Tiananmen Square by giving expression to "the firm belief of a great nation, with a long history of 5,000 years and on its way to modernization, that it is committed to peaceful development, harmonious society and people's happiness," as the BOCOG Web site insists (BOCOG 2005). Always just offstage, the past is a resource for reinventing not only the Maoist legacy recent leaders have been at pains to go beyond, but less savory elements of the current regime as well.

Taken as a whole, Olympic construction, emblematized in Olympic Green and its venues, is the latest in a series of contemporary public works projects including the Tibet-Qinghai railway (the world's highest) and the Three Gorges Dam (the world's largest) that form a stately procession forward from the Great Wall, the Forbidden City, and Tiananmen Square, all of which will greet Olympic visitors in newly restored splendor. The massive coordination of people and resources that produced each of these works in times past hints of a historically preordained sweep to the "harmonious society" invoked by Hu Jintao as a national goal. As well, it deflects concern for the several millions who have borne the brunt of Olympic development directly, either as laborers without rights or protection, or citizens who have lost homes and livelihoods in this latest wave of urban redevelopment (Watts 2005). The harmonious society also appeals to newly resurrected Confucian values of respect for authority and stability. Maligned during the Maoist era, this most venerable of Chinese political traditions has reemerged as an invented tradition for legitimizing the considerable domestic social burdens created by a rising China.[1]

According to the social theorist Henri Lefebvre every society produces its characteristic material spaces (1991). Lefebvre posits a trialectic of contending and contradictory forces that can go some way to plumb the multiple material layers of the current Olympic drama, though any such framework for such sociospatial complexity must be suggestive at best. Lefebvre's first layer is the space conceived by rulers, architects, planners, and bureaucrats. It expresses what Amos Rapoport has called designers' values (1982). This officially authorized spatial imagination of Beijing 2008 seeks to project, above all, the image of a sophisticated modern country open to a world that will be enthusiastically receptive in its turn. For this purpose, Olympic planning and execution have been shared out among the State Council, the Beijing Municipal Government, the Beijing Olympic Organizing Committee, the Chinese Olympic Committee, the International Olympic Committee, and a collaborating army of sponsors, developers, architects, and construction crews. The same could not be said for many of the people most directly affected by it. Still, Olympic goals occupy a prominent place in the 10th and 11th Five-Year Plans and all supporting texts addressing the development of specific spaces and projects. These goals are publicly articulated on BOCOG's Web site, which offers official commentary on Olympic preparation and will be the authorized site for the festival itself.

Lefebvre's second layer emerges as those whose lives unfold in the effort to bring "conceived" space to life struggle to shape it to their own symbolic and material uses. Here are manifest all the desires and passions of users' values of reception, resistance, accommodation, and revision. Debates about the character of particular uses and structures, struggles over building and implementation decisions, and responses to their impact on urban life occur here. In Beijing such debates have generated new vocabularies and rhetorical resources for surrogate discussions about the political future of China itself. Concrete practices of construction and use, the third layer of the Lefebvrian trialectic, tack back and forth between officially "conceived" and vernacularly "lived" levels to produce actualized structures and spaces that in the present case will contain the activities of athletes, officials, and luminaries, and will anchor the large and animated crowds without which no Games can be considered successful. The realized spaces and the communities (including the crowds!) that are thus created will continue to modify their new spaces when the Games are done. Briefly sketched, this is how space for Lefebvre is the unending work of a whole society, an oeuvre.

Meanwhile, the Chinese have officially and informally embraced the Games as a moment of national history. Newspaper coverage of the bidding process riveted public attention while posters and slogans appeared everywhere in the run-up to the announcement of the 2008 Olympic host city. When word came, Beijingers pulled out the stops for a dazzling "flag-waving, horn-honking, music-jamming, firecracker-exploding" party. Millions of citizens have since been enthusiastic participants in Olympic preparation, though not everyone has been equally swept up. There have also been protests, riots, and the occasional suicide. Organized resistance to the sharp elbows of planners has come from improvised and shifting alliances of artists, intellectuals, and professionals. Whatever their views, all Beijingers have picked their way through the dizzying pace of small and large changes and their aftershocks in the dramatic transformations under way.

The ongoing demolition of what remains of the old, often dilapidated republican city reflects the regime's desire to remove every obstacle to China's modernizing vision of itself and to make Beijing a contemporary showcase. The urban renewal of Beijing has been a project of every regime since the collapse of the Qing dynasty.[2] The period of post-1978 reforms has engendered especially great social strains. Citizens have endured intense urbanization, growing inequalities between the wealthy and ordinary workers, the displacement and impoverishment of agrarian peasants by industrialization, and massive environmental degradation. To contain the resulting pressures for accountability and democratization simmering just beneath the surface, there are strong pressures to vindicate the post-Mao direction of Deng Xiaoping and his market-oriented successors with an iconic Olympic success.

Since 1960 host cities have counted on the Games to jump start lagging urban economies (Hanwen and Pitts 2006; Owen 2005). Beijing's economic miracle needs no fanning. Government figures recorded more than 12 percent growth in 2006 (*Economist.com* 2007a). By melding globalization, local needs, and cultural tradition the regime hopes to transform Beijing from a major regional city to a full-fledged world capital on a par with Singapore, Tokyo, and Hong Kong. That effort stands behind the official presentation of the Games as a "Green, Hightech, Olympics for the People." Mindful of international anxiety about the pace of China's development for resource competition and the environmental pollution (China produces 17 percent of global carbon emissions, second only to the United States' 22 percent) (*Economist.com* 2007b), the "Green" Olympics aims to present China as an ethically and technologically responsible environmental steward. The "Hightech" Olympics will promote a China possessed of first-world communications, transportation, and building technologies. For the "People's" Olympics, China hopes to demonstrate a level of domestic and ethnic enthusiasm that will impress visitors and its own populace. To accomplish all this, the Chinese claim to be spending in the range of $30 to $40 billion, up from $14 billion for Sydney, the previous record (*Economist.com* 2007a).

Olympic Challenges

For a country whose economy is not as large or sturdy as those of first-tier industrial nations, this is a high stakes, risky undertaking. Olympic deadlines, however, are certain. For a month in 2008 a city of 15 million permanent residents and 4 million from elsewhere in the country will receive more than 2.5 million visitors, among them some 17,600 athletes and officials and at least as many members of the press. For the Games to succeed, Beijingers know that this influx must be greeted with seamlessly functioning communications and transportation infrastructure, comfortable and plentiful accommodation, ample food and water, clean enough air and streets, a courteous and able service population, and a level of public order that is effective without being threatening to tourists, some of whom may have more than sports on their minds—all under the acute observation of foreign journalists.

Since 2001 herds of bulldozers, cranes, and scaffolds have chewed up huge swathes of the city in order to raise hundreds of multi story buildings generated by Olympic planning. New maps of the city have been issued every three months (Harris 2006). By 2008 there will be a total of 800 hotels with 130,000 rooms compared to 458 hotels with 84,812 rooms in 2005 (Owen 2005, 13–14). Thirty-one sports venues are mandated for Beijing and six more for the host cities of Qingdao, Hong Kong, Tianjin, Shanghai, Shenyan, and Qinhuangdao. Sixteen of these will be completely new; all but three will be upgraded. Some $3.6 billion is earmarked to crisscross Beijing with fiber optic cable for information and telecommunications infrastructure. Olympic Green, the main venue of the Games, will have full access to broadband, Wi-Fi, and networking technology (Ness 2002).

Beijing has undertaken dramatic new transportation initiatives. Existing satellite airports have been renovated. A new $1.9 billion terminal designed by Norman Foster in the shape of a flying dragon, the totem animal of Beijing, will make Tianjin International Airport the world's largest at a million square meters. Three new ring roads have been built along with new interurban rail links to surrounding cities. On tap for 2008 are 1,000 kilometers of new highways and 84 kilometers of new train lines (Harris 2006). Eight new subway lines will stretch across the city, including two special lines connecting the airport with Olympic Green. Beijing's original two lines have been renovated for automated ticketing.

Olympic construction has made a significant contribution to China's double-digit economic growth. In 2004 the *Economist* reported that national spending on construction was 16 percent of GDP, growing 8 to 9 percent annually, just behind America and Japan. China consumes more than half the world's cement production, a bit more than a third of its steel, a bit less than a third of its coal. It is second only to the United States in consuming wood and petroleum. It builds an average 2 billion square meters of floor space annually, roughly half the world's total. Twenty to thirty billion more are planned by 2015 (Jakes 2006).

In 2006 Beijing hosted an Olympic dress rehearsal in which thirty-five leaders of developing nations came to the China-Africa Forum while 810,000 police, public officials, and retired party members directed traffic and kept public order. Out of town vehicles were banned; government workers stowed their car keys and walked or biked to work. When an IOC inspection team visited Beijing in 1993, police sweeps removed street children, the unemployed, beggars, and street vendors from view (Broudehoux 2004, 198). Similar measures to cosmeticize public space are doubtless in place for the 2008 Games. In 2006 officials were forced to deny rumors that a million migrant laborers would be expelled from the capital before the Games, and the mentally ill confined to hospitals (*Economist.com* 2006). Public plans to create frictionless space for visitors include selective traffic bans, sending workers away from the city on well-timed vacations, and energetic campaigns against spitting, smoking, line-jumping, and foul language. Classes to teach tourist-friendly English to police, taxi drivers, and ordinary citizens are in full swing (Marquand 2004).

Less publicly visible, but logistically critical, are adequate water supplies for Olympic visitors, hotels, and the new greenbelts springing up all around the city. Deep in a seven-year drought, Beijing's average per capita water availability is 300 cubic meters annually, far below the

1,000 cubic meter international benchmark (Xinhua 2006c). The city's current maximum daily consumption of 2.42 million cubic meters will swell to 2.7 million during the Games. To meet this demand the municipal government plans to divert 400 million additional cubic meters from reservoirs in neighboring agricultural provinces. This is a point of regional contention since these areas also suffer from water shortages as a result of drought, population increase, and industrial overuse (Hornby 2006).

Organizers have vowed to make Beijing's air as clean as Paris's by the beginning of the Games. Such an achievement seems unlikely. Prosperity, geography, and coal make Beijing one of the most polluted cities in the world. Lung-damaging nitrogen dioxide and sulfur emissions spew from a disproportionate number of coal-burning power plants and factories across China, much of which ends up in the north, where Beijing is (Sheridan 2006). Fierce dust storms from the Gobi Desert blow into the city, blinding traffic and delaying flights. Three and a half million cars are expected to clog city streets by 2008. A pall of dust from 24-hours-a-day, year-in and year-out construction hovers over the city. Not only residents and tourists are at risk, but alarmingly, marathoners who will run along streets where particulate levels exceed U.S. safety standards three and four times (Li 2006; Watts 2005). To scrub the air, Beijing has invested $5.4 billion (Owen 2005; Ness 2002). More than 100 of the worst-polluting textile, pharmaceutical and chemical factories have relocated beyond the city, among them two major polluters, the Capital Iron & Steel group and the Chemical Industry Area (Xinhua 2006b). Other factories and construction sites will halt work or follow reduced schedules weeks before the Games. Furnaces of less than 20 tons, including a number of home furnaces, are being converted to clean fuels. In addition to imposing new emission standards on automobiles, 90 percent of the city's 20,000-odd public buses and 70 percent of its 67,000 taxis will convert to natural gas (Xinhua 2006b). During the Games clouds will be seeded to induce rain, and roads sprayed daily to dampen down particulate matter. The planned installation of 8,000 public toilets for the Games (USA Commercial Service 2004) will require 4,700 new restrooms and the demolition of 2,800 hutong-alley public toilets (Marquand 2004). Four hundred miles of sewage pipes will be renovated or added to city streets (Watts 2006) to treat 90 percent of Beijing's sewage in modern plants by 2010, compared to 60 percent in 2002 (Ness 2002).

Olympic Space

Nearly half of Beijing's competition venues are sited on Olympic Green, the purpose-built 2,800-acre park where the major festival venues will be located. The Green sprawls in a rough T-shape across the fourth and fifth ring roads in Chaoyang district. Additional venues are spread out among eight universities in the Haidan district of northwest Beijing; the so-called Northern Scenic Area of Shunyi district and the Ming dynasty tombs; and the Western Community area in Shijingshan district. The dominant Western aesthetics of these spectacular structures with which the Chinese mean to present themselves to the world has sparked a contentious civic debate. The most passionate controversies involve the National Grand Theater, which occupies politically charged real estate just off Tiananmen Square, and the new China Central Television (CCTV) headquarters that will launch its new institutional home by broadcasting the Games from start to finish. Though neither building is officially an Olympic venue, both occupy a prominent role in the campaign to display a glamorous urban face to international visitors. The National Grand Theater is intended to showcase the high culture of Beijing, and the close association of CCTV with the Games signals the regime's focus on China's image for the duration.

The National Grand Theater

The National Grand Theater is a giant silver ellipsoid dome set on an artificial square pool and entered through an underwater tunnel. As Beijing's preeminent performance venue, it will be home to a 2,416-seat opera house, a 2,017-seat concert hall and a 1,040-seat theater. At night its semitransparent skin will offer a glimpse of the performances within it, staging a very public spectacle for passersby (Rjorr 2006). The theater stands just off Chang An Avenue, west of the Great Hall of the People in Tiananmen Square. It is a dramatic stylistic departure from the sacred architectural legacy next to it.

The theater began as Zhou Enlai's dream of completing Mao Zedong's legacy of Ten Great Buildings around Tiananmen Square. Diverting economic resources to build it was politically out of the question during the Great Leap Forward and the Cultural Revolution. Subsequent Party infighting about what kind of monument was most suitable for the space caused more delay, a debate that grew sharper after the 1989 democracy protests made the regime wary of drawing people to Tiananmen Square. While interest in stimulating an active arts culture or creating a distinguished modern cityscape like that of long-time rival Shanghai was slow in coming to this city of ceremonial and administrative tradition, the rivalry with Shanghai ultimately moved the project forward. After Shanghai renovated its centrally located People's Square in the 1990s, adding the Urban Exhibition Hall, the National Museum, and the Grand Theater to general architectural and urban planning acclaim, the National Grand Theater was reimagined as a prestigious Beijing icon able to stand tall next to both Shanghai's Grand Theater, an elegant modernist structure by the French architect Jean-Marie Charpentier, and the Sydney Opera House, a galling reminder of Beijing's failed 2000 Olympic bid.

The National Theater was designated as the most important cultural project in the 10th Five-Year Plan. Because of, or in spite of, this fact, five rounds of domestic competition failed to produce a design acceptable to the State Council. International architects were solicited and, after a hasty show of public consultation, the Council settled on Paul Andreu, designer of the Pudong International Airport and the innovative Charles de Gaulle Airport (*Volume 5* n.d.). Andreu had also been the finishing architect for the Grande Arche in Paris following the death of Johann Otto von Spreckelsen, its original architect. Modern and gracefully monumental, the arch is an homage to the nearby Arc de Triomphe. If the Chinese had hoped for something as historically sensitive, this was not what they got. Andreu's selection, widely reported abroad, was not announced at home for nearly a year. This was apparently to avoid embarrassing the fiftieth anniversary celebration of the founding of the PRC with the news that after forty years of deliberation, a Westerner had been chosen to erect a resolutely futurist landmark in hallowed Chinese national space.[3]

When the plan for the giant glass and titanium egg and artificial lake finally surfaced, forty-nine members of the Chinese Academy of Science and Academy of Engineering petitioned Jiang Zemin demanding a reversal. They were followed by 109 Chinese architects denouncing its aggressively avant-garde appearance and "illogical" interior (*China Daily* 2004). Critics charged that the $536 million cost—more than the Sydney Opera House, four times the Lincoln Center in a country with one quarter the GDP of the United States—would raise ticket prices to a level only the most privileged could afford (*China Youth Daily* 2004). Also of concern was the symbolism (and maintenance costs) of a large pool in a city of scarce water resources. Official descriptions of the design—sparkling drop of water, silver tear, pearl and eggshell—did battle with popular insults: theater as alien egg, big tomb, boiled egg, French opera house, flying saucer. Xiao Mo, an architectural historian from Tsinghua University, memorably charged that the red desert dust constantly blowing through Beijing would give the dome the look of "dried dung" (Kahn 2004). In an unprecedented move, even the state-sponsored *China Daily* sided with the project's opponents. Several construction halts and the unrelated collapse of an Andreu-designed terminal at Charles de Gaulle finally provided face-saving safety reasons to scale back the project and trim its cost by $200 million.

Despite its avant-garde style, the theater does gesture strategically to tradition. Building and lake together evoke the square earth and round heaven of ancient Chinese cosmology. An earth-red masonry wall at the theater entrance echoes the color of the walls of the Forbidden City. The 46-meter height of the building exactly matches the elevation of the nearby Hall of the People, thus respectfully observing the ancient imperial taboo forbidding any structure to stand taller than the footrest of the Emperor's Throne.

CCTV

In imperial China the only exceptions to this taboo were the royal Bell and Drum Towers, visible at every point as the tallest structures in the ancient city. From these public monuments issued the loudest communal noise as well, clanging and beating as the city gates were locked each night and unlocked at dawn. In a society where commoners were forbidden to behold their rulers, imperial power daily penetrated domestic life by imposing dominion over space and time. Something of this ancient role is reprised by a new skyline topper, the 750 foot (230 meter) headquarters of the CCTV broadcasting system, ceaselessly beaming the presence of the twenty-first century state into domestic space. Though not the tallest structure in Beijing, it is by any cultural measure the loudest. Designed by Rem Koolhaas for the Office of Metropolitan Architecture, the trapezoidal square-looped building occupies its own 10-hectare site at the heart of a new Central Business District east of the Forbidden City. The first of 300 planned towers planned for the CBD, the CCTV "Twisted Donut" consists of two vertical sections leaning toward one another at 60-degree angles and bent at right angles into horizontal connectors at top and bottom to form a continuous Möbius-strip loop. The architect has mischievously suggested that the irregular patterning visible on the structure's face traces the forces traveling through it. This, says a reviewer,

> raises the question of why a Chinese media conglomerate would want to express the structural forces of its building. The juxtaposition of the fully glazed, hence transparent, building surface with an irregular grid would seem to symbolically reveal the hidden institutional power struggle in a large state-owned organization. It is safe to assume that the Chinese authorities do not interpret this symbolism as a general cry for independent journalism, otherwise the project would not have received the green light. (Horsley n.d.)

With a straight face Koolhaas also argues that his colossal edifice does not point to the sky and so is not a skyscraper but an "earthbound structure" (Leonard 2004). Regardless, it houses the complete apparatus of the state system—administration, news, broadcasting, program production, and studios. More than 10,000 employees will circulate through the continuously communicating, self-contained site complete with its own hotel, shopping, and parking facilities.

Critics have been harsh. Ian Buruma (2002) has deplored the unseemly tussle among Western "starchitects" for the privilege of erecting a temple to state information control:

> There is nothing reprehensible about building an opera house in Beijing, or indeed a hotel, a hospital, a university or even a corporate headquarters. But state television is something else. CCTV is the voice of the party, the centre of state propaganda, the organ which tells a billion people what to think.

Having warmed up, Buruma piles on the criticism:

> [I]t is true that architects are often drawn to power. Le Corbusier tried to interest the Vichy regime and Stalin in his projects. Philip Johnson was a bit of an amateur black-shirt. Before leaving Germany, Walter Gropius and Mies van der Rohe were too close to the Nazis. One can see why. To build on a grand scale you need authority and a lot of money. And architects with a utopian bent, who dream of transforming not just skylines but the way we live, are natural suckers for totalitarianism. And, indeed, suckers for capitalist excess.

In a similar vein Spanish critic Luis Fernández-Galiano (2003) writes that the tower conveys "the communicatory ambition of China's totalitarian capitalism and its determination to adapt to the symbolic codes of western economies." Koolhaas's response is that the final answer on China's future is not in. Offering his own communicative take on the tower, he likens its appearance to that other imperial message medium of choice, ancient calligraphy (Leonard 2004).

Nor has the tower escaped criticism for its $750 million price tag. Wu Liangyong, cofounder of the architecture department at Tsinghua University and a director of early feasibility studies for a number of Olympic venues, publicly deplored the tower's original $5 billion yuan ($603 million) estimate as outrageously extravagant, writing: "I'm not against novel ideas, or unconventional or unorthodox designs, as that is what the art needs . . . But we cannot put aside engineering and structure, we cannot overlook our culture, or the cost. China is not rich enough not to care about 5 billion yuan" (*People's Daily Online* 2004).

The partly completed tower has been the focus of grassroots dissent as well. The demolition of a nail house standing in the way of site construction in April 2007 became an emblematic story of local resistance to the tower in particular and the ruthless pace of urban redevelopment in China generally (Reuters 2007). In China a "nail" is a stubborn troublemaker who refuses to be flattened. A nail house is the last house left standing on a tract marked for demolition because its owners refuse compensation from developers and hold out against eviction orders by the courts. Several nail houses across China have brought national and international publicity to street protests, several suicides, and other desperate efforts by local residents with few legal remedies and no say in the fate of their homes and neighborhoods in spite of energetic efforts by the regime to block press coverage.

Olympic Green Venues

Set down in the heart of the city, both the National Grand Theater and the CCTV tower provide highly visible targets for vigorous civic debate around officially "conceived" and vernacularly "lived" space. By contrast, Olympic Green has been largely shielded from public view by the high construction fence that surrounds the site. The final look of the Green will remain something of a mystery until the opening of the

Games, and there is reason to believe it will differ in important details from the layout presented in the winning master plan by Sasaki Landscape Architects of Boston. Three parcels comprise the Green. Northernmost is Forest Park, a squarish 1,680-acre plot three times the size of Manhattan's Central Park but likewise intended to reduce urban heat and noise with vast expanses of green. The abutting second parcel, the 1,000-acre (405 hectare) Central Area drops vertically toward the fourth ring road along the imperial spine of old Beijing. Here are celebrity venues for the major athletic contests and ceremonies, and open areas for containing Olympic crowds. To the south and east of the Central Area is the third parcel, the site and stadium complex of the 1990 Asian Games, the first mega sporting event in China. More modestly sized than Forest Park, this parcel is formally integrated by an axis running northwest from the Asian Games stadium through the Central Area.

The entire Green is tethered by a seventeen-mile (twenty-four km) path that extends the north-south boulevard running through the Central Area of the Green to the north gate of the Imperial City and beyond to the enormous new train station connecting Beijing to the rest of China. The design, which features trees and grand esplanades, is the work of Albert Speer, Jr., and has been compared to the axis envisioned for Adolf Hitler's Berlin by Speer's father. Speer demurs, calling his boulevard "a philosophical and religious axis. . . . We transformed the Chinese character *zhong,* which means middle, into an axis surrounded by an ecological garden" (Bernstein 2003). He adds, "This is not an axis representing power. It's an axis that looks back to two and a half thousand years of Chinese history." Maybe. But *zhong* invokes *Zhongguo,* the name of the kingdom that claimed as its rightful domain "all under heaven," which meant, roughly, the center of the civilized world for most of those two and a half millennia. No Chinese citizen would miss the allusion.

National Stadium

The glamorous showpiece of the built Olympics is the National Stadium. This dazzling confection will be the setting for the Steven Spielberg–choreographed opening and closing ceremonies and all major track and field competitions and football finals. The 91,000-seat stadium is the biggest commission ever undertaken by Jacques Herzog and Pierre de Meuron, of Tate Modern and de Young Museum fame, who have aspired to make it "the most visible icon in contemporary China." Their original structure was a daring structural response to the problem of concealing the retractable all-weather roof insisted on by the Chinese. Its solution was an arrangement of mutually supporting curved steel rods crisscrossing in apparently random fashion to create a huge basketlike structure that appears visually weightless. In the words of the competition document (Bejing Municipal Commission of Urban Planning n.d.):

> The stadium is conceived as a large collective vessel, which makes a distinctive and unmistakable impression both when it is seen from a distance and from close up. It meets all the functional and technical requirements of an Olympic National Stadium, but without communicating the insistent sameness of technocratic architecture dominated by large spans and digital screens. The spatial effect of the stadium is novel and radical and yet simple and of an almost archaic immediacy.

At the same time the gray outside, red inside color scheme paid tribute to Chinese building tradition by repeating the color scheme of an archetypal Beijing courtyard. The roof that occasioned the original design problem was eventually discarded, partly in response to a report by the Chinese Academies of Science critical of the stadium's "outlandish visual effects" and questioning its seismic safety, and partly to an across the board cost-cutting order imposed on all Olympic-related construction in 2004 (Marquand 2004).[4] The look of the stadium improved, a number of construction and maintenance headaches were eliminated, and $37 to $40 million was saved.

Hoping to kick-start the popular naming tradition that is a sign of beloved Chinese buildings, the architects strategically compared the look of the stadium to the crackled glaze of a ceramic vase and the lattices in a Ming window in their original proposal. What caught the judges' fancy, however, was the Swiss team's casually offered analogy of the steel rods to the delicate twigs of a bird's nest, and the plastic membranes stuffing the openings to the grass and leaves that pack a nest. Instantly, the stadium became the Bird's Nest, auspiciously conjuring up the edible nest of the cave swift, the main ingredient of a prized Chinese delicacy associated with ritual feasting.

The stadium is self-consciously green, housing a natural air ventilation system central to its much-trumpeted sustainable design (Rjorr 2006). A spacious ambulatory between the outer structure and the interior bowl contains a hotel, a shopping mall, and public areas meant to be open at all times. "What we think is the strength of this project is the space in between, the concourse, which is to be filled with life" in a continuous pageant. Even in Beijing's sometimes harsh climate, observes de Meuron, "the people use . . . public space—to dance, to play cards" (Lubow 2006), a prescient nod to the motivating nonpolitical atmosphere of Olympic Green that appears to be its larger national purpose.

Water Cube

Across from the Stadium is the other celebrity building on the Green. The $100 million 7.8-acre National Aquatic Swimming Centre by the Australian firm PTK has been nicknamed the "Water Cube" for its blue skin of irregularly patterned water bubbles. With a floor space of 70,000 square meters, it contains five pools; has room for 17,000 spectators; and will host swimming, diving, synchronized swimming, and water-polo finals. Its rectangular frame is a network of slender steel pipes linked by 12,000 load-bearing nodes that distribute the building's weight. Filling in the exterior cell-like geometry that articulates its shimmering skin are 100,000 square meters of a Teflon-like membrane eight one-thousandths of an inch thick that are state of the art in strength and energy efficiency. The architects claim these panels will let in more light and heat than glass while slashing total energy costs by 30 percent and daytime lighting costs by half (Xinhua 2006b). Green engineering also extends to the reuse of double-filtered, backwashed pool water, and rainwater collected in subterranean tanks to fill the pools.

The architects have taken pains to impose meaning on form by publicly linking the pipe and node structural geometry to natural systems like crystals and molecules. They point to water as an ancient symbol of tranquility and happiness and connect the bubblelike clusters of the outer skin to the circular heavens and the shape of the building to the square earth of ancient Chinese universe.

Discontent and Disgruntlement

Embedded bows to traditional cosmology aside, the assertive Western look and feel of the most visible Olympic structures has been a contin-

243

uing source of civic grumbling. Forced to accept the program of the Games as a showcase of Occidental sport, dependent on Western media to frame the festival for much of the global audience, many Chinese expected that the major landmarks of Olympic built form, visual stage sets for media images of the Games, would certify their Chinese, or at least Asian, character. Instead, a celebrity stable of foreign superstars has made embarrassingly apparent the lack of a distinctive Chinese interpretation of modern architecture for the country's coming out party in its emblematic new national space.

There are certainly enthusiasts, many young and hip, who have embraced the cultural mixing of China and the West (Becker 2004). The syrupy official line puts the best face on it. In stilted English, the *People's Daily* calls Olympic Green "the cream of urban architectural construction and urban planning of Beijing in the history of architectural art at all times in all countries." Describing a promotional marathon race from the Forbidden City to the National Stadium (doubtless meant to stir local enthusiasm and downplay poor air quality), it continues: "One is Oriental and the other Occidental, wholly modern. It is another integration of ancient oriental culture with modern Olympic Games sports and a spectacular scene of harmony of Chinese with Western cultures" (*People's Daily* 2001).

Forests of gleaming skyscrapers designed by Western architects seem to reprise on a grand scale the multistory buildings erected by Western legations at the end of the nineteenth century. In the next century the New Culture Movement embraced Western modernism as the model for reconstructing Chinese society on the ruins of dynastic tradition. Then, too, Western adventurers stood ready to exploit the transition (Dong 2003, 30–31). Today China is "the largest construction site in the world" for Western architects in search of new frontiers. As *Business Week* (Bell 2007) puts it:

> Beijing, in particular, is a city of eggs awaiting a clutch of architectural omelettes, with whole districts razed for redevelopment. And why not? From a western perspective, China represents a colossal opportunity, the physical manifestation of architectural ideas that, until now, had only found their expression in elaborate computer-generated imagery or in small, bespoke projects.

Absent a prominent coterie of Chinese architects to steer the building boom that followed the Deng reforms, many observers regard every new Western-style building as a loss of Chinese identity. It does not help that substandard building quality and aesthetic banality have often come along for the ride. "On the one hand, you have these two projects—CCTV, which could only be built in China, and the stadium," Pierre de Meuron has written, "and you have on the other hand thousands of uninteresting projects, like mushrooms" (quoted in Lubow 2006).

Architectural critic Deyan Sudjic (2005) echoes themes widely voiced in and outside China: "Cars move around disconnected clumps of newly completed towers," and "entire new districts appear arbitrarily as if from nowhere." He adds:

> A city that, until 1990, had no central business district, and little need of it, now has a cluster of glass towers that look like rejects from Singapore or Rotterdam. And these, in turn, are now being replaced and overshadowed by a new crop of taller, slicker towers, "the product of the international caravan of architectural gunslingers that has arrived in town to take part in this construction free-fire zone."

Chinese intellectuals, activists, and architectural professionals have not been hesitant to broadcast similar conclusions. As early as 1999 Wu Liangyong used the annual congress of the Union of International Architects to denounce Western theories of architecture as inapplicable to China's changing and complex environment (Li 2000). Wu called for developing countries to explore their own paths "according to their conditions, rather than copying models of industrialized nations." "The foreign moon is not always better than the moon in China," seconds Ma Guoxin, chief architect for the Beijing Architectural Design Institute (Gluckman 2001).

Returning to Beijing after a year in Europe, journalist Lin Gu described his feeling of disorientation. "This city is increasingly unrecognizable, and it feels alien, all this avant-garde architecture," he writes. "Many people in Beijing have been brainwashed to think big buildings—however ugly—are modern" (Gluckman 2004). "'Overstatement' is now the main approach in design, bold form the main character," writes architect Li Xiaodong (2000, 402). Feng Jicai, an activist working to save the slender remnants of republican Beijing, observes, "In the 1960s and 70s, we destroyed our culture angrily. In the 1980s to now, we're destroying our culture happily" (Meyer 2003). Looking back on a century of unthinking modernization lately kicked into high gear,

Kongjian Yu, founder and dean of the Graduate School of Landscape Architecture at Beijing University, and a principal of the first private landscape design firm in China, ventures this pessimistic diagnosis (*LAND Online* 2006):

> [O]ur cities are now becoming the same. Why? Because we neglected the natural environment, we neglected the cultural heritage, and we destroyed too much. We destroyed the everyday living structures, even people's houses. Things have not been designated as historical sites, and they are all gone; they have all been destroyed. Millions of square meters have been destroyed in every city. And it is the natural landscape and the cultural heritage that make a city different from others. So, when we wiped out all of this cultural heritage and these vernacular landscapes, and when we didn't respect the natural landforms, the natural water systems, the natural vegetation, the whole city became man-made with no meaning or form. Sometimes it looks like you've just dumped an American city in the middle of China.

The dilemma of a culture that cannot return to the past but has not seized its own architectural path to the future is captured by I. M. Pei, who has sought to establish a Chinese interpretation of modern architecture informed by its own tradition:

> Chinese architecture is at a dead end, totally. There is no way for them to go. Chinese architects will agree with me on that . . . The days of the temples and the palaces are not only economically out of reach but ideologically unacceptable to them. They've tried the Russian way, and they hate those buildings. They are trying to take the Western way. I am afraid that will be equally unacceptable. (Li 2000, 393)

In the 1980s Pei, who was born in China, championed a "new vernacularism" featuring the modest white walls and gray tiles of traditional demotic style. Admired by many academics and intellectuals, it nonetheless proved too nostalgic, too delicate, and too technologically backward to prevail against the ambitions of China's modern developers.

Mao's Ghost

China's lack of an identifiable modern architecture goes back, as so much does, to the trauma of the Cultural Revolution. Nor is it of small consequence that China's ancient building traditions had persisted nearly unchanged up to the fall of the Qing. In the wake of that collapse, energies long compressed by imperial enclosure were suddenly drawn out into newly revealed spaces animated by nationalist enthusiasm (Dong 2003, 82). Partly in response to the public park movement gathering steam in Japan and the West, imperial gardens, hunting grounds, and ceremonial sites were opened to vibrant experiments in public life and politics including mass rallies organized by republican activists to express their democratic aspirations (Padua 2006, 33). In time the T-shaped intersection in front of Tiananmen gate became so associated with nationalist and antigovernment protest that Tiananmen Gate was the only conceivable place from which Mao, standing atop it, could declare the birth of the People's Republic. Here, too, the lingering imperial association was propitious since the Chinese characters for Tiananmen may be rendered as "receiving the mandate from Heaven and stabilizing the kingdom."

As it turned out, Mao wielded architecture as ruthlessly as any emperor. His monumentally expanded Tiananmen Square was larger than either Moscow's Red Square or Mexico City's Zocaló, a vast revolutionary plain without walls or gates, the traditional markers of Chinese cosmological and social order. Though Tiananmen visibly rebuked the closed power of the Forbidden City, Mao shamelessly traded on its deeply embedded psychological authority by annexing the square as a kind of giant imperial forecourt. Every architectural gesture associated with Tiananmen was carefully calculated, beginning with the widening of Chang An Avenue into a major traffic artery. Slashing through the ancient inviolable north-south axis, the boulevard severed the walled city from the socialist square, signaling the triumph of socialism over the past and creating a grand promenade for displays of socialist military power. Even before the founding of the PRC, Mao had dreamed of a Monument to the People's Heroes at the center of Tiananmen. Its chief designer wrote, "We . . . recognized that the axis of the present Square is no longer the past Imperial Path. The importance of the Monument will be most effectively accentuated by this central position" (Wu H. 2005, 25). To a later critic the Monument constituted "a revolutionary-proletarian obscenity in the middle of the sacred way" (Leys 1977, 54).

Clearing a fifty-acre open space at the dense heart of a traditional urban patchwork of endlessly articulated walls within walls was no small undertaking. Ancient city ramparts and blocks of tiled-roof courtyard houses that had formed the city's elegant aesthetic since the Ming dynasty were leveled. To celebrate the PRC's first decade, Ten Great Buildings devoted to government and commemorative purposes went up during a ten-month, twenty-four-hour-a-day building frenzy around the borders of Tiananmen and along Chang An Avenue. Their severe Soviet monumentalism implemented with technical help from Moscow was another break with traditional form (though not a complete one—the symmetry, horizontality, and serial columns of socialist neoclassicism recall features of traditional Chinese style) and trumpeted a new antifeudal aesthetic. Their stolid gaze framed the spectacles of mass assent that came to be the legitimizing ritual of twentieth century state power.

During the Cultural Revolution, architects suspected of bourgeois tendencies were unable to publish or get approval for their designs. Access to all foreign architectural texts was strictly forbidden, and training programs started in the republican era were shut down. Not a single architect was trained for a decade. Many that had been working were sent to the countryside, factories, and the army for reeducation (Liu 2003, 45). Beijing's growth was brought to a halt, the better to revitalize the countryside as the privileged space of social renewal. By such means the sustained and patient cultivation necessary to the evolution of any architectural art was deliberately destroyed, another casualty of the Cultural Revolution.

When Deng Xiaoping's Four Great Modernizations shifted resources back to the cities there were, therefore, few practitioners to implement the new program of office complexes, hotels, and skyscrapers (Bezlova 2003). Visiting Western architects and the creation of training opportunities abroad for Chinese architectural students were called on to fill the gap as the profession struggled to reconstitute itself. Aspiring Chinese designers looked to Western postmodern styles with little understanding of their ironist mannerism. The result was a hybrid kitsch of decorative Western-style detail appliquéd on Soviet-style grandiosity.[5] Recoiling from this incoherent mimeticism, the mayor of Beijing briefly required every new tower block to sport a Chinese-style pagoda roof, which were popularly labeled "watermelon rinds."

The 1989 democracy protests marked still another turning point in the regime's relation to space. By effectively seizing Tiananmen Square the June Fourth Protesters challenged state power at its physical and symbolic core. Refusing to play the acquiescent and submissive role demanded of Chinese citizens, they dared the state to reclaim its own space. It did so with a horrific display of force in the surrounding streets that deeply damaged its standing at home and abroad. Defined for centuries by their unquestioned control of space, China's rulers found that monumental space was no longer sacrosanct in a television age, but politically ambiguous and highly vulnerable.

Olympic Green as a Successor to Tiananmen

This brings us to Olympic Green as a monumental successor, or perhaps an antidote, to Tiananmen Square. According to the Confucian understanding that what is superior is northernmost to what is inferior, the Green's northern extension of the fourteenth century imperial axis of earthly and cosmic order "leads" it to completion in the twenty-first. There is also talk of the Green as a "second capital" to relieve pressure on the dense, untidy jumble of central Beijing (*People's Daily* 2001). If the Green is the new living room of the people, Tiananmen Square looks more like the relic of a completed phase of Chinese history. Without overtly rejecting Mao, such a shift at least dislodges him. The gesture is infinitely more subtle than Tiananmen's drastic refocus of public representation away from the Forbidden City.

Open and unwalled Tiananmen was an epochally new kind of Chinese political space where masses of citizens could gather as the corporate body of the nation to affirm the socialist state. In an extraordinary departure, Forest Park and the Central Area are officially imagined as glitzy leisure spaces for public pleasures. The official vision of post-Olympic commercial, exhibition, sports, and entertainment spaces on the Green and elsewhere paints a civic portrait of obedient consumers attuned more to immediate gratification than politics. In Lefebvrian terms the Green is a wholly new conceived space, a cagey gamble by a new generation of rulers who are betting that stripping national space of overt political content will diffuse its potential for "lived" protest. They are likely encouraged by nearly two decades of public response to commercial malls and nighttime strips (Wu H. 2005, 22).

In imperial China the boisterous and varied street life of commoners was crowded into festivals and markets conducted in the narrow *hutongs* between traditional *siheyuan* walls. Cathedrals, stadia, open squares, and other public gathering spaces familiar to the West were unknown since the only great open spaces were royal playgrounds. Lesser parks, temple and monastic gardens, and private scholar gardens were reserved for the gentry. Mary Padua (2006, 31) finds key elements of classical Chinese garden style in the scholar's garden:

> Private scholar gardens represented high culture and were designed for and by the literati—in this case, retired government officials—as places for contemplation. Garden design was influenced by Taoism and the yin-yang principles of harmony, where the garden contained the essence of the world with all things standing in proper relationship to each other. Mountains (artificial rockery) represented yang, the active stimulating force, while still water was intended to induce tranquility, representing yin, the passive principle that stands for darkness and mystery.

The winning master plan of Sasaki Associates for Forest Park alludes to many of these features. Its three-dimensional representation of Kunlun Mountain, a legendary axis mundi connecting Heaven and Earth and the source of the four great rivers of China, references the mythical origin of Chinese civilization. The 277-acre (1,122 hectare) Dragon Lake situated at the foot of the Sasaki Kunlun is in the shape of Ying Lung, the Responding Dragon of water, wealth, and good luck in Chinese lore, its long curving tail sweeping the length of the Central Area below. A peach tree flower forest edging Dragon Lake symbolizes immortality and references the idyllic society created by Tong dynasty poet Tao Qian, the cultural hero credited with inventing Chinese poetic tradition. Tao's wilderness cosmology corresponds with the emergence of the landscape *shan shui* school of Chinese classical painting that may have originated in poetic illustration. Tao Qian is associated with the spiritual refinement of a broadly civilized life (Hinton 2002).[6] Additional references to a grand conception of tradition in the Sasaski plan depict the boulevard descending down the axial spine of the Central Area as serially segmented into thousand-meter plazas, each celebrating the achievements of a millennium of Chinese history.

One looks in vain to the official Web site that tracks the construction progress of the Green for any mention of all this. It briefly explains that Forest Park is divided into north and south parcels by the fifth ring road. It describes the northern portion as a forest of 800,000 newly planted trees. The south is described as a sculpted landform of hills, wetlands, meadows and upland forests of pine and deciduous trees. The whole is touted as a model ecology of indigenously biodiverse plants and animals in a sustainable natural habitat. But Kunlun Mountain and Dragon Lake have now become Main Mountain and Olympic

Lake and have migrated to the southern half of the park below the fifth ring road where they are said to display the art of the contemporary Chinese garden. The landscaped layers of classical mythology have disappeared. There is not a mention of thousand-year plazas. It appears that any whiff of feudal traditionalism has been decisively rejected for a resolutely depthless modernism.

In its simplified surfaces the apparent evolution of Forest Park away from the complexity of the Sasaki master plan also speaks to the experiences of a number of Western architects. Their tale is an opposite iteration of that told by Chinese architects about the flow of design contracts to their better organized, more glamorous Western counterparts. In this alternate tale, Western designers are lavishly courted and pursued by Chinese developers anxious to dangle Western experience and exposure before skeptical investors. Once a design is awarded, however, government overseers have the power to demand severe cost cutbacks if money gets tight. Already working, they claim, for 20 to 30 percent of what they could expect to charge outside China (Gluckman 2001), Western designers of record have found themselves forced aside in favor of their less pricey Chinese partners, with whom all foreign designers are paired by law, who are quick to discard Western-contributed aspects of an original design for less costly alternatives. Facing corruption, construction delays, and endless bureaucratic meddling, many Western architects have been unable to break even (Lubow 2006). Sasaki principal Dennis Pieprz has commented, for example, that the $68.7 million ceiling ultimately imposed on Forest Park was too slender to justify the continued participation of his firm (author, phone interview, December 28, 2006).

Public Space as a Casualty Then and Now

Under Mao, Beijingers lived mostly in decentralized, self-sufficient work unit enclaves to which they were legally tethered for housing, employment, and essential social services. No large public space, mass transportation system, or even a central business district was allowed to disturb the close pattern of walled compounds that encompassed what remained of the republican city. This inherited urban fabric, which has been the sustained target of modernizing efforts since the beginning of the twentieth century, has given way to industrialization, market reform, and growing demands for living space in the post-Mao period.

Regime claims for the positive benefits of this transformation notwith-standing, the quality of travel within the city and space for exercise, play, and beauty have declined sharply for most citizens, swallowed up by endless constellations of glass office towers and gated enclaves whose scale broadcasts a lofty indifference to the texture of public life and whose security personnel manifest contempt for ordinary citizens. A once diverse urban texture has steadily mutated into an aesthetically and socially homogenized cityscape.[7] Neighborhoods in which ex-tended families lived for centuries in close-knit community networks have been lost. In 2005 the Geneva-based Centre on Housing Rights and Evictions (COHRE) claimed to have verified 400,000 cases of forcible relocations of city residents as far as 25 to 60 km (16 to 37 miles) from familiar communities and social networks (COHRE 2005).

While arguing for the necessity of bringing modern sanitation and safe physical surroundings to acres of dilapidated neighborhoods, official statistics concede that roughly 40 percent of the approximately 3,700 hutongs recorded in the 1980s have now disappeared. In re-sponse, critics like Richard Ingersoll (2003) have articulated a strong oppositional rhetoric:

> With the increased pace of development for the Olympic Games, the tightly woven hutongs, narrow alleys that serve the single-story his-toric courtyard houses surrounding the core of the Forbidden City and the Tian Tan temples, face imminent demolition or gentrification. The former will eradicate the memory of architectural form, while the lat-ter will undermine the local class mix that gives these neighborhoods their vitality . . . Right next to the Forbidden City, for example . . . bull-dozers are demolishing everything in sight, scooping out a huge hole in the ground for a multilevel shopping mall. When one realizes that the tens of thousands of people who participated in the demonstra-tions that led to the 1989 massacre filtered through the ancient capil-laries of the hutongs to fill Tiananmen Square, this form of urban lo-botomy does not seem so casual.
>
> The hutongs are the only places left in Beijing that have architectural density and urban vitality. Otherwise, the cityscape—restructured dur-ing the past 20 years on a concentric web of ring roads, 10-lane high-ways, and hundreds of elevated interchanges—is dotted with countless new 15- to 30-story condominiums and office towers. Intense land-scaping succeeds to some extent in mitigating the disturbing lapses in scale, style, and color of these new buildings. Armies of gardeners, it seems, have groomed every intersection and highway viaduct.

The district set aside for the "Olympic Green" will be no exception to this program of agoraphobic vegetation, replacing urban fabric with more easily maintained public spaces.

The use of public funds to transform the deteriorating compounds of the proletariat into leisure enclaves for the rich and the disintegration of the "urban public goods regime" remain contentious issues (Solinger 1995). In light of the government's modest compensation awards (30,000 lawsuits were filed in protest to municipal authorities in 2004) (Lin 2004), many citizens cannot afford the commodity estates that are replacing their old compounds and have been forced to seek housing on the periphery of the city. Critics argue that the privatization of the housing market has created an income-segregated cityscape that has further impoverished public life (Li and Yi 2007). Beyond the city, the industrialization of agriculture and the denial of resources to rural areas have driven nearly 200 million workers and peasants to cities such as Beijing in search of jobs and better lives. These floating workers have no access to state-subsidized goods, services, and opportunities available to legal residents and no entitlement to shelter or medical care. Many lack adequate food. A large number have joined the construction army of the building boom with its punishing working conditions and lack of legal protections. What will happen when these jobs decline is anyone's guess (Liu 2003, 46). Prostitution, homelessness, and petty crime are rising along with tensions between city residents and migrant workers.

Among those who have challenged the emergent spatial order of the regime, some have strategically used it to express their dissatisfaction. They include Zhang Dali, an artist from Harbin, an industrial city northeast of Beijing. Lacking a Beijing *danwei* (work unit) or *hukou* (living permit), he and other "floating" artists occupy an artists' colony near the ruins of the Summer Palace gardens, burned to the ground during the Boxer Rebellion and preserved as a testament to Western rapacity. Since 1995 Zhang has painted more than 2,000 images of his bald profile on freeways, condemned buildings and crumbling walls in the city (Wu H. 2000). He writes, "I go on these walls to enter their life. I open a dialogue with people. I assault them with the knowledge that this city is changing. I don't care if you take part or don't take part, you have to look at me" (Broudehoux 2004, 221). Though hundreds of city workers erased his images in advance of celebrations for the handover of Hong Kong in 1997, the government has not otherwise pursued him.

His mode of public engagement has enlisted positive press coverage, and admiring followers have marked new buildings they deem particularly offensive (Broudehoux 2004, 220–25). It remains to be seen how this Lefebvrian "lived" space will be tolerated for the Olympics. "Destroying Beijing," an artist's photograph from Zhang's "Dialogue Series," is here described by Wu Hung:

> It depicts a large stylized portrait of a man's head chiseled into a broken wall. However, there is a hole in the wall that allows the viewer to peer through the man's head and see the Imperial Palace and the Palace Museum in the distance. . . .
>
> The Imperial Palace is an obvious representation of tradition and the broken wall represents modernity. Tradition, situated in the dimly veiled distance, is in the process of being covered over—forgotten, but in the course of the destruction of memory China must experience an inchoate and broken modernity—broken and incomplete from its very beginning . . . We know that Chinese tradition will remain even after the wall has been completed. But once the hole has been repaired, this tradition will be forever unseen and forgotten. (Zhao and Bell 2005, 498)

Conclusion

From the perspective of the regime, the mission of the 2008 Olympics is to show an ambitious, confident China standing tall among the world's advanced global powers. The stars of this outsized national moment are the grand and gaudy Olympic Green and its companion spaces, which for sixteen days in August 2008 will offer a spectacular visual backdrop for international attention. The newest model of the national patrimony is a carefully designed space that lacks both an obvious center and an explicit political focus. Grand state ceremonies will not take place here. The crowds that visit it will encounter super-sized distractions: splendid architecture, forested groves, shopping, eating, and elite sports spectatorship. The regime is banking on the scale of the Green, which dwarfs Tiananmen, to render it impervious to political appropriation. It is fortuitously segregated from ordinary communities of work and politics. Its extravagant entertainments and tended landscapes have little to offer the poorest and most disenfranchised residents of Beijing, who mostly live at the southern edge of the city, from which the Green is not readily accessible except by systems of transport that lend themselves to state control should the need arise. The regime nonetheless confronts a nascent civil society that has creatively used resistance to the ongoing redevelopment of Beijing, on which the Games have conferred urgency and purpose, to fashion vibrant new networks of association and modes of discourse with a political coloring that may find other uses after the Games.

The message of the Green is that twenty-first century public life in China is a colorful, bustling affair, a green escape, a frictionless territory of upscale consumption and leisure. Its function is less to provide a setting where citizens may gather freely than to assemble and display the harmonious society idealized by the regime, in which consumption equates with culture to trump history, and islands of imperial and republican nostalgia survive if they are pleasing to a domestic and international elite.

Unlike Tiananmen, the visual space of Olympic Green does not belong unquestionably to the state, but it does not quite belong to the people, either. Like Tiananmen it is a triumphalist space that repositions authoritative public representation but speaks most clearly of commodity consumption. It argues that a national vision of harmony nestled within a regime of accumulation can overcome whatever problems arise from the forces that have created it. What Chinese citizens will make of it all when the Games are done, and how to address the growing tensions of postreform urban life gathering in the shadow of Ozymandias, is a continuing story.

NOTES

1. See D. Bell 2007.

2. See, for example, Dong 2003 and Wu H. 2005.

3. Ironically, Andreu's design did address itself to high Chinese building tradition with bridges that provided a ceremonial entry and simple spatial and figural arrangements. See Liu 2003.

4. See also Hawthorne 2004.

5. This comment was attributed to Rem Koolhaas (2000), who, according to Wolf (2000), informed "students, who spend years in school and then more years in grueling apprenticeships, that, in China, 40-story buildings are designed on Macintoshes in less than a week. In the context of this hyperdevelopment, the traditional architectural values—composition, aesthetics, balance—are irrelevant." 2000.

6. See also Yang 2005, 43–45.

7. An excellent discussion of China's changed residential landscape is Wu F. 2005.

REFERENCES

Becker, Jasper. 2004. Seeing Red. *New Republic,* December 9. http://www
.tnr.com/doc.mhtml?i=20041220&s=editorial122004.

Beijingmike. 2007. Beijing Olympics Herald a Return to China's Powerful
Past. February 9. http://bjmike.blogspot.com/search/label/olympics.

Beijing Municipal Commission of Urban Planning. n.d. Presentation of
Competition for the Architecture Design of National Stadium. http://
www.bjghw.gov.cn/forNationalStadium/indexeng.asp.

Bell, Daniel L. 2007. From Marx to Confucius: Changing Discourses on
China's Political Future. *Dissent* (spring): 20–28.

Bell, Jonathan. 2007. Eastern Promise? *Business Week,* April 27.

Bernstein, Richard. 2003. The House of Speer: Still Rising on the Skyline. *New
York Times International,* February 27.

Bezlova, Antoaneta. 2003. Friction Builds over Beijing's Olympic Revamp.
Asia Times Online, March 18. http://www.atimes.com/atimes/China/
EC18Ad02.html.

BOCOG. n.d. The Official Web site of the Beijing Olympic Games 2008.
http://en.beijing2008.cn/.

BOCOG. 2005. Image and Look: The Olympic Slogan, "One World, One
Dream." June 26. http://en.beijing2008.cn/17/74/article212027417.shtml.

Broudehoux, Anne-Marie. 2004. *The Making and Selling of Post-Mao Beijing.*
New York: Routledge.

Buruma, Ian. 2002. Don't Be Fooled—China Is Not Squeaky Clean. *Guardian,*
July 30.

Channel NewsAsia. 2007. Olympics: China to Take Olympic Torch to Everest.
April 27. http://www.channelnewsasia.com/stories/afp_sports/view/272
762/1/.html.

China Daily. 2004. Overseas Architects Challenged by Chinese Culture. October
1. http://www.chinadaily.com/cn/english/doc/2004/10/01/content_3793.

China Youth Daily. 2004. National Grand Theater: Studying the Three Obses-
sions. Trans. Wang Qian for *China through a Lens.* March 15.
http://www.china.org.cn/english/2004/Mar/90340.htm.

COHRE. 2005. Evictions Monitor, Newsletter of the COHRE Global Forced
Evictions Programme 1 (3).

Dong, Madeline Yue. 2003. *Republican Beijing: The City and Its Histories.* Berkeley: University of California Press.

Economist.com. 2004. Cultural Revolution. February 12. http://www.econo
mist.com/cities/PrinterFriendly.cfm?Story_ID=24.

Economist.com. 2006. On Safari: Practising for the Olympics. November 2.
http://www.economist.com/research/articlesBySubject/displaystory.cfm?s
ubjectid=478048&story_id=8113380.

Economist.com. 2007a. Beijing's Olympic Frenzy: Inflated by the Olympic
Spirit. March 1. http://www.economist.com/research/articlesBySubject/
displaystory.cfm?subjectid=478048&story_id=8776275.

Economist.com. 2007b. Grim Tales. May 29. http://www.economist.com/research/articlesBySubject/displaystory.cfm?subjectid=478048&story_id=8880881.

Fernández-Galiano, Luis. 2003. Asia on the One Hand, Europe on the Other. April. http://www.arquitecturaviva.com/News.asp#the%20airport.

Gluckman, Ron. 2001. Architecture at a Juncture. August. http://www.gluckman.com/ArchChina.html.

Gluckman, Ron. 2004. Beijing: Bold? Brazen? *Wall Street Journal Asia,* April. http://www.gluckman.com/BeijingArchitecture.html.

Hanwen Liao, and Adrian Pitts. 2006. A Brief Historical Review of Olympic Urbanization. *International Journal of the History of Sport* 23 (7): 1232–52.

Harris, Nick. 2006. Secrecy and a Shifting Skyline: Changed Nation Relishes the Great Ball of China. *Independent,* March 23.

Hawthorne, Christopher. 2004. Architecture: China Pulls up the Drawbridge. *New York Times,* September 19.

Hinton, David, trans. 2002. *Mountain Home: The Wilderness Poetry of Ancient China.* New York: Counterpoint.

Hornby, Lucy. 2006. China to Divert Water from Dry Hebei to Beijing. *Planet Ark and World Environmental News,* September 11.

Horsley, Carter B. n.d. Elsewhere: New China Architecture by Xing Ruan. *New City Review.* http://www.thecityreview.com/nuchin.html.

Ingersoll, Richard. 2003. The Revisionist Olympics: Beijing 2008. *Architecture* 92 (1): 39.

Jakes, Susan. 2006. A Force of Nature. *Time Magazine,* April 11. Republished in *CRIEnglish.com,* http://english.cri.cn/811/2006/04/11/199@76181.htm.

Kahn, Joseph. 2004. A Glass Bubble That's Bringing Beijing to a Boil. *New York Times,* June 15.

LAND Online (Landscape Architecture News Digest). 2006. Kongjian Yu: Fighting the Emperor's Playground. Interview, October 17. http://www.asla.org/land/2006/1017/yu.html.

Lefebvre, Henri. 1991. *The Production of Space.* Trans. Donald Nicholson-Smith. London: Blackwell.

Leonard, Mark. 2004. Profile of Rem Koolhaas. *Financial Times,* March 6. http://fpc.org.uk/articles/243 (accessed December 26, 2006).

Leys, Simon. 1977. *Chinese Shadows.* New York: Viking Press.

Li, Si-ming, and Zheng Yi. 2007. The Road to Homeownership under Market Transition. *Urban Affairs Review* 42 (3): 342–68.

Li, Zijun. 2006. Filthy Air Choking China's Growth, Olympic Goals. *Worldwatch Institute,* February 14.

Lin Gu. 2004. Letter: Battle over Beijing. *BBC News,* September 15. http://news.bbc.co.uk/2/hi/programmes/3657008.stm.

Liu, Erica. 2003. The Architectural Fairyland of China (1984 onward): Problems and Recommendations. *Global Built Environment Review* 3 (2): 40–48.

Li Xiaodong. 2000. The Celebration of Superficiality: Chinese Architecture since 1979. *Journal of Architecture* 4 (winter): 391–409.

Lubow, Arthur. 2006. The China Syndrome. *New York Times Magazine,* May 21.

Marquand, Robert. 2004. Eye on Athens, China stresses a "Frugal" 2008 Olympics. *Christian Science Monitor,* August 13.

Meyer, Mike. 2003. The Threshold. *WorldView Magazine Online* 16 (2). http://www.worldviewmagazine.com/issues/article.cmf?id=116&iss.

Ness, Andrew. 2002. Blue Skies for the Beijing Olympics. *China Business Review,* March 20. http://www.chinaabusinessreview.com/public/0203/ness.html.

Owen, Jeffrey G. 2005. Estimating the Cost and Benefit of Hosting Olympic Games: What Can Beijing Expect from Its 2008 Games? *Industrial Geographer* 3 (1): 1–18.

Padua, Mary. 2006. Modernity and Transformation: Framing the Park in Post-Mao Chinese Cities. *Landscape Architect, IFLA Conference Papers,* May 2006.

People's Daily Online. 2001. Olympic Park to Become Heart of "Second Capital" to Beijing. October 31. http://english.peopledaily.com.cn/english/200110/31_83599.html.

People's Daily Online. 2004. Time for Chinese Architects to Come off the "Eggshell," June 30. http://english.peopledaily.com.cn/200406/30/eng20040630_148060.html.

Rapoport, Amos. 1982. *The Meaning of the Built Environment.* Tucson: University of Arizona Press.

Reuters. 2007. Chinese Couple Bows to Developers. April 3. http://uk.reuters.com/article/oddlyEnoughNews/idUKPEK21803420070403?pageNumber=1.

Rjorr. 2006. The New China: No Longer a Sleeping Giant. Collaboratory for Research on Global Projects at Stanford University. October 22. http://crgp.stanford.edu/news/global_projects_the_new_china.html.

Sheridan, Michael. 2006. Dirty Great Cloud Hangs over Beijing Olympics. *Sunday Times,* June 25.

Solinger, Dorothy. 1995. China's Urban Transients in the Transition from Socialism and the Collapse of the Communist "Urban Public Goods Regime." *Comparative Politics* 27 (January): 127–46.

Sudjic, Deyan. 2005. The City That Ate the World. *Observer,* October 16.

USA Commercial Service. 2004. Preparation for Olympics Begins in the Restroom. September 9. http://www.buyusa.gov/china/en/hs040909.html (accessed December 30, 2006).

Volume 5. n.d. The Beijing National Grand Theater Competition. http://www.volume5.com/beijingcomp/beijing_national_grand_theater.html.

Watts, Jonathan. 2005. China: The Air Pollution Capital of the World. *Lancet* 366 (9499): 1761–62.

Watts, Jonathan. 2006. Bustling Beijing Gives London an Olympic Lesson. *Guardian Unlimited,* September 5.

Wolf, Gary. 2000. Exploring the Unmaterial World. *Wired,* June.

Wu, Fulong. 2005. Rediscovering the "Gate" under Market Transition: From Work-unit Compounds to Commodity Housing Estates. *Housing Studies* 20 (2): 235–54.

Wu Hung. 2000. Zhang Dali's *Dialogue:* Conversation with a City. *Public Culture* 12 (3). http://www.socialresearch.newschool.edu/publicculture/back issues/pc32/wu.html.

Wu Hung. 2005. *Remaking Beijing: Tiananmen Square and the Creation of a Political Space.* Chicago: University of Chicago Press.

Xinhua News Agency. 2006a. Beijing to Gain Water from Neighboring Province, September 22.

Xinhua News Agency. 2006b. Green Olympics: Pledge to Honor for Beijing. October 4. http://www.china.org.cn/english/sports/182954.htm.

Xinhua News Agency. 2006c. Hebei Builds up Water Resources for Thirsty Beijing. *China.Org.Cn,* August 22.

Yang, Lihui. 2005. *Handbook of Chinese Mythology.* Santa Barbara, CA: ABC-Clio.

Zhao Huanxin. 2005. Olympic Commitment Held Aloft in Space. *China Daily,* October 20.

Zhao Xudong and Duran Bell. 2005. Destroying the Remembered and Recovering the Forgotten in Chai. *China Information* 19 (3): 489–504.

From Athens to Beijing

The Closing Ceremony and Olympic Television Broadcast Narratives

Christopher Kennett and
Miquel de Moragas

It is a characteristic of Olympics broadcasts throughout the world that national distribution systems have a major impact on how narratives are communicated and received. Much of what is written—in this book and elsewhere—deals with efforts by host cities and nations, the International Olympic Committee (IOC), and sponsors to manage the story by scripting and thus affecting what gets transmitted. There are key moments in the course of Olympic rituals when narratives emerge and global impressions are formed, and these are particularly interesting from the perspective of the producer and transmitter. In this chapter, we continue a long research effort by the Centre d'Estudis Olímpics to study modes of transmission and how they relate to intended narratives. We analyze the broadcast, in five countries, of the closing ceremony in Athens, with its "handover" to Beijing.

The closing ceremony and its components form an integral part of the Olympic Games process and contain unique ritual and symbolic value (MacAloon 1989). Central to this ceremony is the handing of the Olympic flag from the mayor of the current host city to the president of the IOC, who then passes it onto the mayor of the next city to host the Olympic Games. This is the precise moment that a new Olympiad begins.

During the closing ceremony of the Athens 2004 Games, the mayor of Athens, Dora Bakoyyanis, passed the Olympic Flag to mayor of Beijing Wang Qishan, signifying the closing of Greece's Olympiad and the beginning of China's. In a stylized and elaborately produced production, Beijing stepped onto the global stage and presented itself to international television audiences through a combination of a sixty-second video and eight minutes of cultural displays. Within the context of complex regional and international geopolitical relations, this ritual handover and cultural display meant far more than the beginning of the Chinese Olympiad. It was meant to reaffirm the emergence of China as an economic, political, and sporting world power (Xu 2006; Ren 2002).

The representation by international television broadcasters of Beijing's presentation as Olympic host is an interesting object of study for several reasons. The structure of the closing ceremony meant that Chinese culture was framed within the wider Olympic context, combining universal messages of Olympism with those of national culture. The broadcast commentators were faced with the challenge of interpreting Chinese cultural displays for their respective national audiences. The handover moment also provided an opportunity to comment on Beijing as an Olympic host and for comparisons to be made with other host cities.

A comparative content analysis of five international broadcasters, including NBC (United States), CBC (Canada), TVE (Spain), Televisa (Mexico), and Eurosport (broadcast in English in Europe), was undertaken for this segment in order to identify how Beijing as host city and Chinese national culture were represented in this context, and what type of narratives were adopted by broadcasters. This limited analysis provides an insight into the complexities of controlling the Olympic narratives. Our focus is on the brief moments of global transmission in Athens in 2004, but from them we gain insight into how the opening ceremony of the Beijing 2008 Olympic Games may be broadcast internationally and the substantial differences and similarities that exist between national broadcasts.

As China approaches a key moment in its long history, the construction and communication of a desirable identity through the international media will play an important role in determining the reception of the Games by the international community. For the pre-Games period, salient features of Beijing as an Olympic host can be observed through its architecture; through the official symbols of the Beijing Organizing Committee of the Olympic Games (BOCOG); and, as we claim, through its cultural presentation during the Athens 2004 closing ceremony.

The Olympic Ceremony as
an International Stage

The Olympic opening and closing ceremonies are signature opportunities for nations to appear favorably on an international stage. Moragas et al. (1995) focused on the athletes' parade during the opening ceremony of Barcelona 1992 to provide an extensive analysis of the presentation of nations by international broadcasters in the context of Olympic rituals and protocol. For some nations, marching into the Olympic stadium can be a defining moment of recognition for a people as the sports arena is transformed into a political arena where the state of international relations and modern nationhood are debated (MacAloon 1989; Brownell 1995). The main conclusions of this analysis were that the broadcasts tended to lack analytical content, focused on the national interests of the broadcaster, and in practice were "not conducive to intercultural learning and understanding" (Moragas et al. 1995, 143). The commentaries of the broadcasters served to reproduce standardized representations of national identity and, more often, national stereotypes.

As the athletes parade into the stadium behind their national flags, sometimes in traditional dress, national broadcasters find themselves in the position of commenting not only on the sporting merits of the respective teams, but also on political and cultural issues. The abstract idea of "our" nation is partly constructed through international comparison with "other" nations, which generally occurs through the interpretations of sports broadcasters.

Many of these broadcasters find themselves outside their commentary comfort zone of sport, and the national lens through which they view the proceedings produces a mix of reactions as the different nations of the world parade past them. This involves responses that range from a combination of reverence and respect for nations that are identified as relatively similar in terms of cultural heritage to "our" nation, to trivialization and misrepresentation of national cultures that are viewed as very different or are little known internationally. In some cases "no representation" occurs as national broadcasters ignore national identities, which happened in the case of Barcelona 1992 when the Chinese state broadcaster did not recognize the representation of Catalan national identity and chose to focus only on the nation-state of Spain in its coverage (Moragas et al. 1995).

While the handover to Beijing occurred in a different context and involved a longer, more complex construction and representation of cultural identity, the limitations and dangers of misrepresentation by national broadcasters were evident. One consequence that we explore in this chapter is increasing effort by the host to establish a presentation in which the risk of missed translation, altered emphasis, or ignoring of significant themes is significantly reduced. In short, the closing ceremony of the preceding Games becomes part of a long-term communication strategy to present the desired identity of the new host.

Planning and Constructing
Olympic Host Identity

The Olympic Games of Barcelona 1992, Sydney 2000, and Athens 2004 highlight the attempts made by Olympic Games Organizing Committees to construct positive identities and break with commonly held stereotypes. Moragas et al. (1995) identified the steps undertaken by COOB 1992 in the development of host identity, and which subsequent hosts have replicated:

1. *Select a geographical reference for the host.* In reality, the idea of a host identity is actually a combination of multiple identities that must be negotiated and represented. While the identity of the host city is central, the Games are generally celebrated in a wider region or throughout an entire country. In some cases different nations exist within the nation-state, which also may require representation (e.g., Catalonia in the case of Barcelona '92; England, Scotland, Wales, Northern Ireland for London 2012).
2. *Define a desired "character" for the host that is realistic but promotes the host's most positive features.* This involves a combination of traditional cultural heritage with contemporary reality and a vision of the future. Combining past, present, and future provides depth to the constructed identity as well as the dynamic notion of change, which is linked to the celebration of the Games and the change this brings.

3. *Choose appropriate symbolic representations of the desired character.* The selection and design of symbolic representations of the desired character for the host has become part of the complex process of establishing a look for an Olympic Games. Typical symbols include an emblem, mascot(s), pictograms, color schemes, etc. In addition, emblematic geographic and urban features that symbolize the host may also be used (e.g., the Sydney Harbour Bridge).

4. *Develop an approach for dissemination of the host identity locally and internationally.* The communication strategies adopted by Olympic Organizing Committees have become increasingly complex and wide reaching. Locally, publicity and media campaigns aim to foster popular support and cement political consensus around the staging of the Games. Internationally, this may include advertising campaigns, media, and public relations activities and strategic cooperation with sponsors and other organizations such as tourist authorities.

5. *Create opening and closing ceremonies that represent the host culture in an accessible and appealing way to international audiences.* The international broadcasts of the ceremony present the interplay between two communications processes. The Organizing Committee has a desired cultural message that it encodes through cultural displays typically involving combinations of sport, dance, music, dress, historic enactments, myth and legend, geographic features etc., and the ceremonies are used as a medium. Television acts as a secondary medium that filters the ceremony, determining camera angles, editing sequences and providing commentary that reinterprets the contents and transforms them into a media spectacle for their national audiences. What emanates is an instantaneously arbitrated version of the encoded presentation as reproduced or altered or neglected by the rights-holding broadcaster.

The desire to communicate a rich traditional heritage combined with a modern contemporary image is central to the Beijing 2008 Olympic Games project and was prefigured in the closing ceremony. At the time of writing, Beijing had moved through all but the last of the five stages of the identity construction process described previously. The geographic reference point for the Beijing 2008 Olympic Games is the city itself, but also China as a nation. The definition of the "desired character" for the host and its symbolic representation has been undertaken through typical Olympic image construction activities. This process has involved constructing national and local cultural messages that can be understood by international audiences. For as Dayan and

Katz (1992) have observed, while the nation is central in the Olympic Games, the Olympic host's ability to construct its image requires that celebrations of nationhood combine with a commitment to internationalism as well.

Narrating the Olympics

The methodology adopted for this limited study closely follows the work of Moragas et al. (1995) in their international research project *Television in the Olympics*. The object of this study was much narrower, focusing on the handover of the Olympic flag to Beijing and its presentation as the new host city of the Games. A limited sample of five international broadcasters were selected to provide diversity in terms of the narrative styles adopted and the cultural interpretations undertaken. This sample provides an indication of the similarities and differences between national broadcast representations of the same phenomenon.

Semantic fields were established to provide systematic comparison between the broadcast segments, and included the representation of: Olympism and universal values; evaluation of the host; the initial presentation of Beijing as host city; and the interpretation of Chinese cultural displays.

The comparative model adopted is based on the integral role that commentators play as primary narrators and interpreters of an event. Not only the content of what is said, but also differing verbal styles, reflect the disparate roles of commentators with respect to their audience. As observed in *Television and the Olympics,* the narrative approach a commentator employs directly influences how an audience perceives what is being displayed visually, and these differences can be used to compare how broadcasters around the world portray international events and the effect this may have on local audiences. All of the broadcasts were transcribed and interpreted by the researchers using semantic fields that enabled direct comparison.

The results of the research were compared with three narrative approaches identified by Moragas et al. (1995)—history, celebration, and entertainment—underscoring the fact that most broadcasts employ a combination of the three, or shift in style and tone during different segments. It is important to emphasize that the broadcasts do not directly represent their country or culture, but because commentators are "chosen" and therefore accepted by their respective national culture, their commentary can offer valuable insights into more general cultural tendencies.

The historical approach views the ceremonies as part of a historical cycle, as a unique event taking place at a specific moment in history. The narrative focuses largely on the importance of Olympic tradition, the symbolic nature of events and rituals, and the transcendent, universal values that sport provides. The commentator adopts the role of an *observer:* their tone and language suggest that an exceptional, unforgettable event is taking place, and that they are lucky to be there as a mere observer of history. Thus, they intervene only to introduce or highlight the importance of events taking place; their solemn, formal style and rare verbal intercession evoke a sense of personal awe, which in turn implies a certain respect for the tradition of the Olympics.

The celebration narrative presents the ceremony as a lively party or festival. The style adopted is less transcendent and more informal; nevertheless commentators continue to pay attention to cultural significance. Broadcasters derive their emotion from "the party of youth, the festival of humanity" inside the stadium. Music and dance become a common language, and the exuberant, superlative tone utilized during art, music, and dance segments reflects an intercultural connection. In order to convey the excitement and happiness taking place inside the stadium, the commentator becomes a participant; through their enthusiastic tone, they encourage viewers themselves to take part in this unique celebration.

The entertainment approach pays less attention to culture, Olympic ritual, and mythology. Commentators, whose job is to amuse local audiences, react to what visually unfolds in the stadium, mirroring the improvisational way in which a sports broadcaster calls a live game. In this manner, sport, not the opening or closing ceremonies, becomes the central spectacle of the Olympics. Commentators tend to describe images that audiences can see themselves, without delving far into their cultural depth or meaning. This approach tends to be characteristic of highly competitive broadcast markets, where stations must attract maximum audience or maintain their reputation as the "best." The commentator plays the role of an insider, presenting the spectacle as "full of surprises" for the audience. Their status as an informed expert, who already knows the events about to take place and hence is never overawed, implies a position of omniscience.

Also characteristic of entertainment presentations is the element of triviality. Commentators tend to distort basic cultural elements and rit-ual meanings through their intended humorous or entertaining com-ments, often coming at the expense of others. Triviality is not neces-sarily synonymous with the informality characteristic of many "celebration" broadcasts, but demonstrates a fundamental lack of con-sideration for certain cultural acts or countries.

In addition, the amount of commentary as well as the narrative's depth and focus can reveal other disparities between broadcasts. The length of commentaries, including duration and amount of comments made, varies considerably and has significant implications for local au-diences. In general, the more "historical" a broadcast, the less talk there is; vice versa, the more entertaining broadcasts tend to be filled with talk. Despite the abundant commentary, not many entertainment broadcasters make analyses with respect to cultural anthropology, or elucidate the significance of cultural elements. In this manner, exces-sive description becomes a way to conceal the inability to interpret cul-ture. Hence the observation of "richness of description, poverty of in-terpretation" emerges, in which commentators present a litany of seemingly irrelevant facts in order to maintain an active commentary when they otherwise do not know what to say.

The systematic comparison of the different broadcasts' content within the context of the existing theoretical framework enabled the researchers to draw some initial conclusions regarding the presentation of Beijing and Chinese culture that may affect the interpretation of the desired identity of the host.

A key part of the mediation process by the television broadcasters occurs with the aid of the official ceremony media guide. The guide is prepared by the Organizing Committee of the Games in collaboration with the IOC and is designed to provide broadcasters with a basic in-sight into the structure and contents of the opening and closing cere-monies. The 1984 Los Angeles Olympic Games marked a watershed moment in the establishment of the opening and closing ceremonies as mediated performances. The heightened cultural complexity and symbolic value of the ceremonies in Seoul 1988 and Barcelona 1992 in-creased the need for more developed materials for broadcasters. The media guide has become an essential tool for both the Organizing Committee and the broadcasters, as the former attempts to inform and to some extent control the contents of the broadcasts, while the latter often rely on the guide in the construction of their narratives.

This document remains a closely guarded secret so as to avoid leaking of the contents, and is only available shortly before the ceremony itself, which provides some challenges in the preparation of the commentary for the broadcast team. Due to the fact that broadcasters from around the world quote directly from it, the preparation of the guide is a key part of the communication process for the host nation and is an opportunity to influence the interpretation of cultural displays.

The Olympic Flag Handover Ceremony and
the Presentation of Beijing as Host City

In order to understand the results of our study of the closing ceremony and its representation of Beijing and Chinese culture by international television broadcasters, it is necessary to provide a more extensive description of events during the handover of the Olympic flag in Athens and the official presentation of Beijing as host city.

The handover of the Olympic flag from host city to new host city is a central element of the closing ceremony of the Games and is characterized by its ritualistic significance. In more recent times, under the presidency of Juan Antonio Samaranch, the handover became perhaps the most eagerly awaited moment of the proceedings, as Samaranch declared the Games in question to be "the best ever." This moment of judgment was interpreted as the seal of approval for the host city and confirmation of its success in staging the world's largest sporting event. Controversially, these magic words were not spoken in the closing ceremony of Atlanta 1996, but were used at Sydney 2000. The new president, Jacques Rogge, has subsequently ended this practice, stating that the Olympic Games is a sporting contest between nations, not between host cities.

The structure of this section of the ceremony forms part of IOC protocol and involved the entrance to the stadium of the mayor of Athens, carrying the Olympic flag, together with the mayor of Beijing. The mayor of Athens then presented the flag to the President of the IOC who passed the flag to the mayor of Beijing and waved it to the applause of the crowd. The president of the IOC then declared the Athens Games closed in accordance with the Olympic Charter: "I declare the Games of the XXVIII Olympiad closed and in accordance with tradition, I call upon the youth of the world to assemble four years from now in Beijing."

These are the only words spoken live in the stadium during the twenty minutes of handover and the presentation of Beijing. The cameras then cut to the giant video screen in the stadium, where a sixty second film of Beijing and its preparations for the Games was shown. The video was directed by the internationally renowned film director Zhang Yimou and contained sequences of traditional and modern Chinese culture underpinned with the central message that Beijing welcomes the world to celebrate the Olympic Games in 2008. The video was the centerpiece of the presentation of Beijing and functioned as an advertising spot for the city that was broadcast live around the world, constituting an unprecedented opportunity to communicate carefully constructed messages about Beijing and the Chinese culture to an international audience. The images moved fluidly between traditional and modern Chinese cultural heritage, which was represented by images of the Chinese opera, the Great Wall of China, temples, traditional dance, and dragon costumes. This was combined with images of modern Beijing's skyscrapers and new cultural spaces. These elements provided a backdrop for the people of Beijing, who were the protagonists of the video. People of all ages appeared, many playing sports, from teenagers with an NBA-style basketball look to a businessman in a suit hurdling bicycles. All of them were smiling and welcoming the world to Beijing.

The cultural display continued into the stadium as the video linked almost seamlessly into a modern dance involving fourteen young Chinese women wearing contemporary dresses and carrying traditional instruments, which culminated in a solo performance of a traditional red-streamer dance. The red-streamer dance provided a link to the Beijing 2008 logo, representing "dancing Beijing" as a symbol with its roots in ancient Chinese civilization but with a modern day application that represents change and the opening up of the city to become an international meeting point of cultures (BOCOG 2005).

While the dancing took place, stilt walkers entered the stadium carrying large red lanterns and moved around the athletes gathered on the track. Lanterns are a relatively easily identifiable Chinese symbol that form part of traditional culture and are used during certain festivals, adding to the sense of celebration for the Olympiad that had just begun.

This was followed by more dancing, this time combining elements of tai-chi, which again would be potentially recognized by an international audience, and the traditional martial art of Wushu. A group of children then entered the stage to perform Beijing Opera in traditional dress and masks.

The final part of the presentation of Beijing was the emergence of a young girl from the center of a giant red lantern who sang "Jasmine," a Chinese folk song whose lyrics talk of blossoming flowers and welcoming friends and families. Two banners were then unfurled to reveal a message of welcome to the world to come to Beijing in 2008 to celebrate the Olympic Games.

This ended the nine minutes that Beijing had to communicate to the world. The combination of tradition and contemporary Chinese culture and references to Zhang's films (e.g., the use of lanterns) appealed to Western audiences, but some critics viewed this as predictable and were looking for content that would surprise international and Chinese spectators (Zhang 2006). Zhang would have to rely on the world's national television broadcasters to interpret the contents accurately and comprehensively, and from a Chinese perspective, positively.

How would the broadcasters interpret the subtle yet complex mix of traditional and modern Chinese culture, the humanistic dimension of the "people's Games," the open messages of welcome to the world and their significance in the wider political and economic context of international relations? Had they done their preparation for this moment and carefully considered how to frame the presentation of one of the world's historically most influential national cultures? Our study suggests some answers to this question and, in so doing, offers a sense of the difficulties that Beijing (or other organizing committees) will face in producing a story for the world.

International Television Olympic Broadcast Narratives: Representing Beijing and Chinese Culture

The analysis of the selected television broadcasts of the handover to Beijing and the new host city's presentation is structured thematically. The handing over of the flag from Athens to Beijing occurred amid highly regulated Olympic protocol providing the broadcasters the opportunity to commentate on the universal messages of Olympism, reflect on the success of Athens as a host city, and look toward 2008 and anticipate the coming Games in Beijing.

Olympism and Universal Values

The commentators from CBC, Televisa, and to a lesser extent NBC made reference to the universal messages of Olympism following on from the IOC president's speech. NBC and Televisa commentators highlighted the importance of Jacques Rogge's message to respect others, referring also to the doping issue and the need to promote clean sport in almost identical words. The CBC broadcasters entered into more depth related to the importance of the athletes, Olympic values, and education:

> [Jacques Rogge wants the athletes] to promote the message of the Games, to promote respect for others, promote clean sport and that's what I believe. Every one of these athletes would go home and schools will want them out to speak to their schools and they'll be able to express the message of what the Games represent. (CBC)

This was combined by an emphasis on tradition, with both NBC and CBC referring to the history of the Olympic flag and the latter going on to discuss the IOC Athletes' Commission and its role.

Televisa, Eurosport and CBC all commented on the use of the phrase "the best Games ever." The Mexican commentators focused on the issues of judging the host city and the fact that president Rogge did not follow the tradition of his predecessor in using "the best ever" phrase but instead had called them the "unforgettable" Games, at which point a co-commentator highlighted the case of Atlanta not being recognized by president Samaranch for "obvious reasons," which were not explained.

The Eurosport commentators picked up on the same issue and then began casting personalized judgments that continued throughout the segment analyzed. There was also some confusion between the IOC presidencies of Rogge and Samaranch, with the former being given credit for closing the Sydney 2000 Games:

> He didn't say they were the best games ever as he has done, did do in Sydney, and for me that was about right. Sydney was the best ever, but this ran a very close second. (Eurosport)

On TVE, there was no discussion of universal values or Olympism during this segment, and the Spanish commentators adopted a celebratory narrative (Moragas et al. 1995). The entrance of the mayors was met with "Here you have them!" which was followed by a somewhat overexcited description of the events as they occurred on the viewers' screens and the exclamation that the handover was about to take place:

C2[1] This is the big moment!
C1[2] The Athens Games are gone!
C2 Goodbye Athens! Hello Beijing!
(TVE)

Moreover, the TVE commentators had problems with the pronunciation of both Greek and Chinese names, which was made light of as part of what seemed to be a private joke made public:

[Mayors enter]
C1 Come on Maria [co-commentator] start to practice. What's his name?
C2 Wan Kim San [written phonetically] and next to him, the mayor of Athens, Dora Vayonakis, Vakoyannis, excuse me, Dora Vaco, Vacoyannis . . .
(TVE)

By way of contrast, the Mexican commentators adopted a much more formal discourse, showing great respect for the mayor of Athens in particular and providing historic factual information about the city and the Greek flag. As in the case of CBC, the fact that the mayor of Athens was a woman was also emphasized.

While the speech of Jacques Rogge and the Olympic rituals provoked general reflection on the values of sport and challenges for the future, the handing over of the flag led into an evaluation of Athens as a host city.

Evaluating the Host

It is interesting to note that the presentation of the "new" host of the Games takes place in the shadow of the "old" host. How the "new" host city steps out of that shadow and into the limelight of the international stage constitute key communication challenges.

It is logical that the handover of the host role should produce moments of reflection, or in some cases judgment, among the broadcasters. These comments can be influential in the opinion forming process, despite their subjectivity. For example, one of the comments made by NBC during the handover noted that Greece had "got it together for 2004":

> For all the concerns about the readiness and the organization and security of Greece, these Games ran as smoothly as anyone could have asked. (NBC)

The Eurosport commentators chose to explain their personal experiences of the "village atmosphere" in Athens from what could be interpreted as a position of superiority, being pleasantly surprised by local population and in particular with security levels:

> C2 People were being extremely friendly, it's remarkable how many of them actually speak English.
> C2 There has been as you said Simon, a solid presence in terms of security . . . it's not been in your face . . .
> C1 I felt safe and I haven't been hassled. (Eurosport)

The areas of evaluation for Athens were their preparedness to stage the Games and security, but the sensation created was that this had been achieved against the odds and that question marks perhaps still existed with regards to the hosts' organizational capabilities. The issue of readiness provided a natural point of comparison with Beijing and the state of preparations for 2008.

The Initial Presentation of Beijing as Olympic Host City

As the flag was handed to the mayor of Beijing, the first comments were made about the new host city and its national culture. NBC, TVE, Televisa and Eurosport commentators all made comments on the Chinese capital's readiness to host the Games. The consensus was that Beijing was well ahead of schedule in preparing for the Olympics, with the Televisa commentators joking that the venues would be ready before 2006, when Germany was to host the 2006 FIFA World Cup. The argument was that, by contrast to the Greeks, the Chinese were somehow overprepared as hosts and this fit with an image of a country that was developing so rapidly:

An impressive push by the Chinese, not only in sports, but also in general. Its growth in recent years has stood out. The Games are going to be everything you could hope to bring together: the latest technology and also the thousands of years of Chinese history. (Televisa)

TVE commentators focused on the importance of hosting the Olympic Games for China and the opportunity for the country to present itself to the world and demonstrate its organizational capacity. China was portrayed as a country that had changed dramatically in recent times. This idea was also expressed by the CBC commentators who identified the 2008 Olympic Games as the "awakening of Asia," using the words of President Rogge to refer to China perhaps as a sleeping giant that was stepping into the international limelight.

The other main area of interest for the commentators was China's sporting potential. NBC stated that China had "tremendous" Games and detailed their medal tally for Athens. CBC stated that China's performance at Athens had been "wonderful," their medals totals were "staggering," and with their largest contingent ever they were "on a mission" for 2008. This mission was likened to Canada's quest to top the medals table in Vancouver 2010 for the Winter Games and highlighted the importance of the hosts' sporting performance on home soil.

The Interpretation of Chinese Cultural Displays

The completion of the handover was followed immediately by Zhang Yimou's sixty-second video, which introduced the cultural display in the stadium. This video was central to the Beijing 2008 Olympic Games communication process and the construction of a desired identity for the hosts.

It was therefore surprising to discover that NBC, as exclusive broadcaster of the Olympic Games in the United States, cut to an advertising break during the entirety of the Zhang video. The opportunity was missed to reach the audience of the world's largest economy and driving force behind globalizing processes. This demonstrated how the representation of the Olympic Games was subject to local editorial decision-making processes that were beyond the control of the organizers of the Games.

Meanwhile, after making a hash of pronouncing his name several times, TVE focused on the prestigious career of Zhang and his contemporary cultural relevance in international cinema. The Eurosport commentators talked throughout the video, highlighting that the contents were designed to show how China wanted to be seen by the world, before returning to reflections on their experiences of the transport system and Greek salads in Athens.

The interpretation of the Chinese cultural displays that followed the video could be described as a challenging experience for some of the broadcast commentators. Heavy use of the official media guide was made as the broadcasters struggled to provide commentary and analysis on the mix of traditional and contemporary Chinese culture on show.

The NBC commentators were perhaps the best example of this struggle as they fumbled through a highly descriptive narrative that was interrupted by occasional cultural insights and more frequent sports references. The lantern was identified by the main commentator as:

> uhhh, a very familiar object. The Chinese embroider lanterns in celebrations of big occasions, and that would certainly be the case here four years from now. (NBC).

The co-commentator tried to embellish upon this, providing an explanation direct from the media guide about the use of the lanterns to decorate homes for festivals or the approaching of dignitaries, which established a pattern of commentary that continued throughout the section.

Indeed, the relative lack of preparation on the part of the NBC commentators became increasingly evident and resulted at times in the trivialization and simplification of the cultural displays. The performers were described as "costumed characters that roll into the stadium" combining with the female dancers carrying traditional instruments that created a "different feel than what we saw at the top of the evening with the way the Greeks go about it" (NBC). The "going about it" would appear to be performing a traditional national custom to inform an international audience about the changing cultural reality of a society.

As the cultural display unfolded the NBC commentators did likewise, but added little in terms of accurate or incisive analysis of the spectacle. Moragas et al. (1995) highlighted the fact that the ceremonies tended to be commented upon by sports broadcasters, which affected the representation of the cultural contents. The comments of NBC were an example of the "sportification" of the cultural displays. The red-streamer dance was observed as follows:

> C1 looks like she could do well in a rhythmic gymnos [gymnastic] competition . . .
> C2 Classical Chinese dance, accompanied by classical Chinese music [13 second pause]. Some pretty good gymnastics too! (NBC)

Both TVE and Televisa described the dancing as "folkloric" with an emphasis on tradition but recognition that "China is also very international," which was also commented upon by NBC. The TVE commentators were the only ones to identify the martial arts display and even commented on the relevance of Zen Buddhism.

During the cultural contents the Mexican commentators chose to reflect again on the changes in Chinese society since they came out from behind the Great Wall of China and "opened their doors" (Televisa). China was identified as an important global economic driving force "that also produces Olympic sportsmen and women" (Televisa). The image of China was again framed in the light of its economic progress and work ethic, emphasizing its productivity in manufacturing terms.

The representation of the Beijing opera by NBC could be described as "carnivalesque" as the commentators seemed to be amused by the performers who were depicted as entertainers in fancy dress:

> C1 looks like they know how to party too!
> C1 They're dressed for it . . . you know who gets best costume tonight (NBC).

These comments trivialized the performance, as events were described in their own cultural terms that the broadcasters perhaps felt that the audience would understand. The aim seemed to be to entertain the viewers rather than inform or challenge them in any way.

During the opera segment and the concluding Jasmine song, performed by a young girl, commentators from NBC, TVE, and Eurosport made frequent use of the official media guide. This often involved reading directly from it, or making literal translations. While this provided some continuity between the broadcasts, it created uncomfortable moments that did not fit with the narratives of some of the commentators.

For example, the NBC co-commentator suddenly used an extract almost direct from the media guide, which was contrasted by the main commentator's mix of nostalgia and basic description:

C2 The song talks about how the Jasmine blooms in Beijing, to welcome friends from around the world to our home. The beautiful Jasmine, fragrant and beautiful, aromatic and clean.

C1 And how could you not want to be there in Beijing after that precious little girl on top of the illuminated red lantern? (NBC)

The Eurosport commentators meanwhile had slightly mixed up the martial arts display and the Beijing opera and began reading from the media guide at the wrong time. The performance of the "dance group" was evaluated as simply "terrific," and the commentators moved on to comments about the Jasmine song before it even began. The British Eurosport presenters ended their commentary with yet more personal reflections, this time with a distinctly national focus (considering this is *Euro*sport) on the how the people from "back home" would travel to China:

C2 It will be a huge adventure for so many back home who actually got on planes and got here [Athens]. Well, they won't be able to do that on a quick, short-haul flight, it may take a bit more planning, but I think it could be really special. (Eurosport)

This is followed by a relatively long comment on the superiority of British fans at the Athens games and a nostalgic description of how "our flag looked terrific last night. Certainly stands out" (Eurosport).

After nine minutes of highly planned and expertly executed cultural displays, the broadcasters shifted their gazes toward the cauldron where the Olympic flame was extinguished as the final Olympic ritual of the night. The Beijing Olympiad had begun, and the experience of standing on the Olympic stage as hosts in front of the world's media would be an important learning experience in preparation for the official opening ceremony.

Findings

The comparative analysis reveals certain common themes could be identified in relation to the representation of Beijing as the next

Olympic host, such as the recognition of China as an emerging sporting superpower and the focus on Beijing's readiness to host the Games. In this sense, while the evaluation of Athens was generally positive but not entirely convincing, Beijing stepped out of Athens's shadow with positive strides. There was consensus that Beijing will be ready not only to host the Games, but to potentially top the medals table.

The cultural analysis undertaken in this study reveals a diversity of narratives, which reinforces the findings of Moragas et al. (1995), highlighting multiple representations of the host rather than a coherent desired identity.

The different narrative styles adopted by the broadcasters produced diverse representations of Beijing and Chinese culture as the new Olympic host took center stage. The NBC broadcast was characterized by its entertainment narrative, dealing awkwardly with the cultural contents and preferring instead to remain in the comfort zone of sports. The commentators made light of the cultural displays, likening the performers to gymnasts or costumed party characters that entertained the crowds.

The Spanish commentators on TVE adopted a more celebratory narrative, adopting the role of observers at a festival. The tone of the comments aimed to provoke excitement and emotion among the viewers, providing grandiose introductions to the displays. In-depth cultural analysis is lost in the process of celebrating the moment: the end of one Olympiad and the beginning of another.

Similar but different historic narratives were adopted by the Mexican commentators at Televisa and their Canadian counterparts on CBC. The Televisa broadcast was characterized by reverence for both Olympic traditions and the figures of authority such as the mayor of Athens and the president of the IOC. Beijing and Chinese cultural heritage were also represented with respect, with one of the commentators referring to China as a "great civilization." The CBC commentators also adopted a more formal approach, signaling the historic significance of China hosting the Games, but they interestingly chose to provide very little commentary on the cultural display. This left the viewers to interpret events for themselves.

Indeed, it is interesting to consider briefly what was not said in the commentaries of the selected broadcasts. For example, Communism was not mentioned, and no overtly Communist symbols were included in the cultural displays. Zhang's video clearly focused on China's traditional cultural heritage combined with contemporary, international

278

messages. There were also no reflections on criticisms of the IOC's decision to award the Games to the People's Republic of China. The "two China's" issue, which has formed part of the Olympic political history, was also not mentioned. The broadcasts were therefore noncontroversial and largely apolitical.

Eurosport was difficult to classify using the narrative framework adopted in this study. The broadcast was not nation-specific and spanned several countries, yet the commentators adopted a more overtly national stance than any of the other broadcasters analyzed. This arguably inappropriate use of the national lens to interpret proceedings was combined with a series of personal evaluations of the broadcasters' experiences in Athens. Beijing was left at the margin of the broadcast and was referred to partially and inaccurately.

Indeed, in terms of the implications for the international broadcast of the Beijing 2008 ceremonies, the issues of most concern to the ceremony organizers were perhaps the inaccuracies in several of the broadcasts, the examples of flippancy and superficial descriptions, and the awkward use of the media guide as a safety net.

While it would neither be possible nor desirable to standardize the broadcasts of the ceremonies, if the organizers of the 2008 Olympic Games want the constructed cultural identities of Beijing and China, both traditional and contemporary, to be represented accurately and comprehensively, there is considerable work to be done in media relations terms to inform and educate international broadcasters. For example, developments in online and multimedia technologies could be used to provide broadcasters with more support in the buildup to the Games to allow more in-depth preparation of the cultural content that is to be included in the ceremonies, without reducing the surprise factor that is necessary in the creation and communication of the spectacle. While it is the broadcasters' right to determine the interpretation and representation of ceremonies' contents, they also have the responsibility to inform audiences. As demonstrated in this chapter, sometimes the broadcasters appeared in certain cases to stray from the message that was being communicated through the ceremonies, which at times resulted in the trivialization of host culture.

The digitalization of Olympic broadcasts through digital television and Internet may provide an important opportunity in some societies for the representation of Olympic traditions and rituals, as well as the representation of nations. Interactive services may provide the opportunity for viewers in some countries to choose camera angles and commentary (narrative) styles, and to access additional information on Olympic history, rituals, and the host's cultural displays.

Indeed, the opportunity for viewers to obtain more information may enable some of the gaps in coverage to be filled. The decision of NBC to cut to a commercial break during Zhang's video demonstrates the importance of commercial content over cultural, but also a missed opportunity for viewers. This could be overcome with replay options and edited highlights content, combined for example with the option of more informed cultural analysis. Interactive television, while altering the "live" experience, could provide viewers with a more personalized experience and the possibility to construct their own narrative.

Conclusions

Only a small minority of the audience will experience the Beijing 2008 Olympic mega-event in person, while the masses will have to rely on the mediated product that is constructed and communicated through the media (Dayan and Katz 1992; Roche 2000).

The mass global appeal of this event means it will be a gauge of societal changes and globalizing processes, contributing, to a limited extent, to a greater understanding of globalization in both "basic" and more "complex" ways (Roche 2006).

In terms of ideas of "basic" globalization, time-space compression may occur around the celebration of the Beijing 2008 Olympic Games. As the world looks to one place at the same time, people will be brought together from diverse cultures around a single event. This will be reinforced by the communication of the universal values of Olympism and its system of rituals and symbols that promote notions of peace, understanding, and unity.

These processes will occur within the wider sports media cultural complex and the interdependent relationships that exist between the International Olympic Committee, the media (in particular NBC as U.S. broadcast rights holder), and the sponsors (global and local) that together provide the majority of funding to stage the Games (Rowe 2003). In commercial terms, the Beijing 2008 Olympics are poised to be the most commercially lucrative Games in history, largely as a result of the increasing speed of globalizing processes, while simultaneously contributing to the acceleration of global economic, social, and cultural exchange.

However, to what extent these exchanges are equal is questionable. Critics of the Games in cultural terms have highlighted the disproportional influence of U.S. and Western European economic power within the Olympic media cultural complex through NBC's contribution to broadcast revenue and long-term multinational sponsors such as Coca-Cola and McDonald's. These developments have furthered the "Westernization" of the Olympic Movement, contributing to the "Disneyfication" of the Olympic spectacle (Tomlinson 2004).

The presentation of Beijing as host city during the Athens 2004 closing ceremony highlighted the challenge facing Zhang Yimou as he attempts to please both Chinese and international audiences through the construction of cultural contents of the opening ceremony. As he codes the messages that will construct a desired identity for Beijing and China, the decoding and reinterpretation will occur through the filter of multiple national broadcasts within the context of the Olympic media cultural complex.

The broadcast of the opening ceremony in 2008 will generate individual and collective memories, affecting attitudes and perceptions of China and its people. Judgments will be cast, heroes and villains created, and history "made" as an Olympic discourse is constructed, communicated, consumed, and reproduced.

Through the national television broadcasts, the Beijing 2008 Olympic Games as a global media event will be subject to local interpretations. What Roche (2006) identified as a more "complex" understanding of globalization can complement the "basic" interpretation of globalization. This complexity is derived from the differentiation that exists between the national broadcasts and the existence of agency in the interpretation of events. The results of this limited study reinforce the importance of these interpretations and the need to research the complex and diverse narratives constructed in broadcasting the Olympics.

The risk of misinterpretation and misrepresentation of the cultural contents of the ceremonies and desired host identity from the Organizing Committee's point of view is high. The official ceremony media guide has become a key tool, and according to this research it forms a fundamental part of broadcast narratives. Despite this, some national broadcasts were still not conducive to intercultural understanding and involved frequent inaccuracies and sometimes trivialization of the host for the sake of entertainment.

The challenge for the Games organizers was how to create a balance between accurately informing broadcasters about the ceremony contents and influencing their interpretation in order to homogenize the message comments. This situation is made more complex as certain broadcasters have increased the number of their own cameras in the stadium, increasing the diversity of the visual images received in different countries around the world, and marginalizing the international broadcast signal produced by the Organizing Committee. Through online broadcasting, hypertext and developments in mobile technologies in the digital era, new technologies will have an increasing role to play in informing broadcasters and audiences about the contents of the ceremonies and their cultural and historic context.

The Beijing 2008 Olympic Games are perhaps the most eagerly awaited mega-event of recent times. While the Games will probably become, albeit temporarily, the most watched sports event in history, they are being staged in a country that has experienced exponential economic, social, and cultural change over the past three decades. While "East met West" at the Olympic Games in Tokyo 1964 and Seoul 1988, the staging of the Games as part of the "opening" of China to globalizing forces is particularly symbolic and will involve a more complex challenge for those broadcasters that are willing to rise to it.

NOTES

1. C2 denotes the co-commentator.
2. C1 denotes the main commentator.

REFERENCES

BOCOG. 2005. The Olympic Emblem. http://en.beijing2008.cn/57/71/arti cle211987157.shtml (accessed May 21, 2007).

Brownell, Susan. 1995. *Training the Body for China: Sports in the Moral Order of the People's Republic.* Chicago: University of Chicago Press.

Brownell, Susan. 2004. China and Olympism. In *Post-Olympism: Questioning Sport in the Twenty-first Century,* ed. John Bale and Mette Krogh Christensen, 51–64. Oxford: Berg.

Dayan, Daniel, and Elihu Katz. 1992. *Media Events: The Live Broadcasting of History.* Cambridge: Harvard University Press.

MacAloon, John. 1989. Festival, Ritual, and Television. In *The Olympic Movement and the Mass Media,* ed. R. Jackson and R. McPhail, Pt. 6, 21–40. Calgary: Hurford Enterprises.

Moragas Spà, Miquel de, Nancy K. Rivenburgh, and James F. Larson. 1995. *Television in the Olympics.* London: John Libbey.

Ren, Hai. 2002. *China and the Olympic Movement: University Lecture on the Olympics.* Barcelona: Centre d'Estudis Olímpics (CEO-UAB). http://olympicstudies.uab.es/lec/pdf/ren.pdf (accessed May 21, 2007).

Roche, Maurice. 2000. *Mega-events and Modernity: Olympics and Expos in the Growth of Global Culture.* London: Routledge.

Roche, Maurice. 2006. Mega-events and Modernity Revisited: Globalization and the Case of the Olympics. In *Sports Mega-events: Social Scientific Analyses of a Global Phenomenon,* ed. John Horne and Wolfram Manzenreiter, 27–40. Oxford: Blackwell.

Rowe, David. 2003. Sport and the Reproduction of the Global. *International Review of the Sociology of Sport* 38 (3): 281–94.

Tomlinson, Alan. 2004. The Disneyfication of the Olympics? Theme Parks and Freak-Shows of the Body. In *Post-Olympism: Questioning Sport in the Twenty-first Century,* ed. John Bale and Mette Krogh Christensen, 147–63. Oxford: Berg.

Xu, Xin. 2006. Modernizing China in the Olympic Spotlight: China's National Identity and the 2008 Beijing Olympiad. *Sociological Review* 54, no. 2 (December): 90–107.

Zhang Xueying. 2006. Beijing's Gift to the World in 2008. Chinatoday.com. http://www.chinatoday.com.cn/English/e2006/e200607/p54.htm (accessed June 17, 2007).

New Technologies, New Narratives

Lee Humphreys and
Christopher J. Finlay

Media events and communication technology are inexorably tied. The success of a media event relies on communication technology as a means of connecting the audience to a live event. For, as Dayan and Katz write: "the power of these events lies, first of all, in the rare realization of the full potential of electronic media technology" (1992, 15). The broadcasting of the same message to geographically dispersed audience members not only connects the audience to the event but also connects audience member to audience member. Audience member awareness of technology-enabled copresence at a mass scale has the potential to galvanize the audience (Dayan and Katz 1992), and endow the event with a grandeur and importance that local events and smaller media broadcasts cannot achieve. Such shared experiences contribute to the power of media events to unite nation-states and, as examples such as Live 8 and Live Earth[1] have demonstrated, to unite, albeit ephemerally, populations across the globe. The Olympic Games unify the audience both within nation-states, as athletes compete for national glory and recognition, and globally, as audiences share in the experience of watching sports competitions and ceremonies, as well as learning about the culture, politics, and heritage of Olympic host cities.

Media events, much like expos in the nineteenth and early twentieth centuries, should be understood not only as being facilitated by technology, but as crucial opportunities for institutions and nations to utilize new communication technologies and technological formats (Roche 2000) to alter their place in the world or their own and others' perceptions of it. Historically, media events have also provided an impetus for technological development as event organizers, sponsors, and broadcasters established deadlines or provided other incentives for accomplishment. This trend can clearly be seen in the Beijing Olympics. In negotiations with the International Olympic Committee (IOC), the Beijing Organizing Committee for the Olympic Games (BOCOG) committed to produce 3G mobile technology for the 2008 Olympics. Established communication technology yields a slightly different pattern as the media event provides the opportunity for greater implementation or diffusion. Beijing appears to conform to this trend as well. Lu Xuewu (2007), associate president of the Communication University of China, has explained that broadcasting key events in the 2008 Beijing Olympics in high definition is expected to spark greater demand for HDTV both within China and internationally.

Like other Olympics before it, the 2008 Beijing Games has created a narrative surrounding the event that emphasizes progressive technology. BOCOG has put a special emphasis on technology via the development of the "High-Tech Olympics" theme. "High-Tech Olympics," "Green Olympics," and "People's Olympics" form the three core themes of the Games. Technology has been a central component of the Beijing Games since the bid was first constructed: in early Beijing 2008 Olympic Games Bidding Committee (BOBICO) promotional material, such as the Beijing Olympic bid films, technology and other elements associated with hypermodernity are presented alongside a mythic or traditional Chinese culture (Haugen 2005). Hogan (2003) found a similar pattern in her analysis of the Japanese Winter Olympics in Nagano. She suggests that the introduction of a traditional/technology binary was an important component of the discursive formation of a narrative constructed for global consumption. This binary seems particularly important for Asian Olympic hosts, as Atsushi Tajima (2004) and Haugen and Collins (in this volume) suggest. These countries use the universal narrative of technology to conform to the globalizing and homogenizing Olympic discourse of progress and peace, while simultaneously including a flare of multicultural color via self-orientalizing representations of the past.

In this chapter, we focus on the "universalizing narrative of technology" component of this binary by exploring aspects of the High-Tech Beijing Games. This is not just about specific advances in communications hardware and software; the High-Tech performance should also be understood as a platform for constructing a new discourse about Chinese technology, and via this new technology discourse, a new discourse about China itself. The Beijing Olympics has the potential to send crucial messages to domestic and international audiences about China's ability to be both a technological pioneer and a producer of reliable technology, and to transform the perception of China from a low-cost industrial support system for the global information economy to a major player. And, though it may not have been planned that way, this sector offers an important means of redefining what it means for something to be Made in China.

Via two case studies, we examine the complexities and challenges of constructing and maintaining a consistent High-Tech narrative with the ability to reform the image of China's technological prowess in the global imagination. In the first case study, we explore the ascension of Lenovo to Olympic TOP sponsor status. Lenovo is one of the top personal computer manufacturers in the world, and the largest in the Asia-Pacific region. The company was founded in 1984 by a group of eleven engineers in Beijing. The former English name of the company was the Legend Group Ltd. and New Technology Developer Incorporated. In 2005, Lenovo's purchase of IBM's PC division transformed the company into a major international personal computer manufacturer. "Lenovo" is a portmanteau of "Le-" (from Legend) and "novo," pseudo-Latin for "new." Since 2005 the company has been working hard to establish its global image and to reinforce its leadership within China.

As the first Chinese company in the IOC's The Olympic Partner (TOP) sponsorship program, Lenovo, though it continues to struggle with poor brand name recognition outside of China (Norton 2007; Li and Yu 2007), is poised to become a global household name in personal and business computing. As Olympic TOP sponsor, Lenovo has pledged to provide equipment and technical support for "virtually every aspect of the management of the Games" (Lenovo 2007). The director of Olympic Sponsorship in Lenovo's Brand Communications Department, Xie Long, has directly linked (2006) success of the 2008 Games to successful performance of Lenovo equipment in their implementation. The fate of Lenovo, whose motto is "New World, New Thinking," is intricately linked to the fate of China as a global technology leader. If the Lenovo campaign and, more importantly, the Games management, succeeds—and this is the Dream—it could usher in a new way of thinking about China's ability to lead on the global stage. Failure will only add to the existing Made in China narrative that positions China as "the global economy's low cost manufacturer" (Loo and Davies 2006, 198).

Similarly, the second case study, which analyzes the impetus behind China's 3G commitment to the IOC, finds that the ability to deliver this technology on time has become a way to measure Chinese innovation and success. This is a narrative about the ability to launch and implement a new system. When Beijing won the bid, China Mobile Communications Corp. (China Mobile), the country's largest mobile operator, suggested that it would be possible to watch live video coverage of the Games on its properly equipped mobile phones, and would radically change the way consumers could access information about restaurants, shopping, and sightseeing. Athletes and staff would also use 3G technology to access information related to the Games. Here—as with the question of whether Beijing will meet air-quality standards—the story is one of nail-biting anticipation: will China meet its aspirations or not?

As both case studies show, Beijing's High-Tech Games may author new narratives about China's role as a global innovator and economic power. However, these nascent Created in China (Su 2007) narratives, part of an overall Brand China emphasizing intellectual and technological leadership over cheap mass production, are delicate and could easily be destroyed if evidence is found that discredits or challenges them via the construction of technology-enabled counternarratives. The Beijing Olympics represents a major gamble for China's technological and political reputation. The goals that have been set are tough and, as the Lenovo and 3G stories unfold, the path to success continues to be tenuous.

Historical Perspective on the Olympics and New Technology

The twentieth century Olympics have been characterized by a modern discourse of technological innovation. They have provided the host country with an opportunity to prove itself to the world as a modern force in a global event. This occurs not only through the host country's athletes, but also through the facilities and technology the local organizing committee uses to host the event. Communication technology's role in the Games is increasingly central because of the importance of audience for financial as well as reputational reasons. Innovative communication technology is used frequently by the host country both to increase the sense of the host's prowess as an innovator and to spread news about Olympic events to the audience at the Games and to a larger broadcast audience.

There are established examples of Olympic host cities associating their country with modernity and progress by using new communication technology to extend the Olympic audience. Through IOC archival data, we learn that the Amsterdam Games of 1928 used state-of-the-art telephone and telegraph systems for immediate transmission of Olympic news (Netherlands Olympic Committee 1928). The Los Angeles Olympics of 1932 used radio broadcasting extensively to distribute news about the Games: "The capacity of radio to enable a mass nationwide listening audience to imagine that they are present at a dramatic and important 'live' event received an early demonstration in the USA through the broadcasts of the 1932 Los Angeles Games" (Roche 2000, 162). And in 1936, Germany experimented with local television transmission of the competition "to transmit pictures of the competition to a paying audience around the city" (Senn 1999, 60). In each of these examples, communication technology was used to create a greater sense of immediacy; extend the Olympic message to an ever-larger audience; and demonstrate the technological capacity, excellence, and modernity of the host city and country.

At the same time, broadcasting dramatically shifted the role of the Olympic audience: "Television provided the crucial complement to the Olympics, adding to the scale and intensity of their dramatic appeal" (Roche 2000, 159). The 1948 Olympics in London, the first Summer Games to be held after Berlin, heavily relied on broadcasting to create a global presence. A 1948 IOC report about communications technology suggests a tone that reverberates through to Beijing:

> The XIV Olympiad was the greatest sporting festival that had ever been staged and the progress and results of the 136 Olympic events were of interest to millions of people throughout the world. As only a small number out of those millions was able to be at the Games in person, radio had to provide the rest with the nearest equivalent to front row seats whenever and wherever anything exciting was happening. Thus,

the listeners of five continents found themselves at Wembley as the competitors of 59 nations marched into the Stadium in brilliant sunshine on the opening day and, thereafter, as record after record was broken, they were able to share in the suspense of each event while it was actually taking place. In fact, they were often better off than the spectator, because he could be in only one place at once, whereas the radio listener could visit half-a-dozen venues in as many minutes and could travel from Empress Hall to Torbay at the turn of a single knob. (The Organising Committee for the XIV Olympiad 1948, 114)

The radio listeners of the 1930s and 1940s, who could "visit" many more events in a day than a spectator who attended the Olympic Games, were the first signs of an Olympic mass media audience that could eventually be sold to sponsors for millions and millions of dollars. In the 1960s, television coverage of the Games became integral to the Olympics as a mega media event (Roche 2000), and the mass media audience became essential to the financial and cultural success of the Olympic Games.

Beijing 2008: The Techno-Narrative

We have already suggested the important association between technological innovation and the Beijing Olympics. BOCOG anticipates that the Olympics will burnish the idea of what it means to be Made in China in the high-tech sphere. With an estimated audience of 4 billion (Lenovo 2007), the Beijing Olympics is expected to provide an opportunity for China to show off its best and brightest technological advancements to the rest of the world. The Olympics is about China as technological innovator, with the 2008 Games furnishing an impetus to develop and innovate information technology to showcase at the event: "The Beijing 2008 Olympic Games will symbolize and spur on the city's commitment to technological advancement and environmental protection for the future benefit of the Chinese people" (BOCOG n.d., 5). Consistent with its claim of inclusion and service to the world, BOCOG explained that technological development in preparation for the Games would benefit not only the Chinese, and not only those who come to visit the Games. Like previous organizing committees, it perceived the Olympics as an opportunity to project the host country's technological advancements onto a world stage.

Case Study I: The Lenovo Sponsorship

Lenovo's sponsorship and the Beijing Games High-Tech theme are interrelated because they give China a way to demonstrate and reinforce its technological advancements at the same time: the Lenovo sponsorship highlights China's information technology, while the High-Tech theme redirects attention to the Lenovo technology created for and used during the Beijing Games. In 2004, Lenovo secured international sponsorship rights to the Beijing Olympics "for an estimated $65 million to $80 million" (Spencer and Fowler, 2007). The securing of the 2008 sponsorship rights allowed Lenovo to enter the IOC's exclusive TOP sponsor program. The program, which was initiated by the IOC in 1985, grants TOP partners exclusive worldwide marketing rights to both the Summer and Winter Games. Partners in this exclusive club include global brands such as Coca-Cola, Kodak, McDonald's, Panasonic, General Electric, Samsung, Visa, and Johnson & Johnson (IOC 2007).

Lenovo's participation in this program marks the first time that a Chinese company has been a TOP sponsor (Liu 2007b). This ascension is an important step for Lenovo, as a company, and Lenovo, as a representative of China (Legend Group Holdings, "controlled by the Chinese government, owns a majority stake in Lenovo" [Lower 2007]). Lenovo, then, must be understood as both an emerging global brand and as an important representative of the Chinese government. Thus, Lenovo's messaging can be understood as messaging from China as well.

While TOP partner status confers significant privileges, it is also an extraordinary responsibility. The pressure to construct successful and mature campaigns that will resonate with both a global and a domestic Chinese audience is immense. If Lenovo's Olympic sports marketing fails to adequately capture the world's imagination, the ramifications of such a failure will only be emphasized via comparison with other IOC TOP sponsors, with significantly more expertise in marketing on a global scale.

Lenovo's difficulties working with the established IBM brand identity since 2005 indicate that the computer manufacturer is still struggling to master global marketing. In 2005, Lenovo acquired IBM's personal computing sector for approximately $1.75 billion (Lower 2007). The terms of the acquisition allow Lenovo to use IBM's logo on established product lines, such as Thinkpad and Thinkcentre, for a period of five years (Lower 2007). In effect, the deal created a five-year period during which Lenovo could focus on branding and product integration before the IBM logo rights become off-limits. Despite this branding agreement, Lenovo has primarily featured the Lenovo brand rather than the IBM brand in recent years. Today, Lenovo is seeking to build brand recognition outside of China and to maintain sales within China. Although it is among the top PC manufacturers in the world, Lenovo has thus far failed to connect with the important North American market and is, in fact, facing a declining market share in this region (Spencer and Fowler 2007). Lenovo is the dominant player in China, with more than 30 percent market share, but Dell and Hewlett Packard are strong competitors, and together "already boast an 18% share in China" (Kleinman 2007, 6). In March 2007, Dell introduced an inexpensive PC in China that was intended to directly challenge Lenovo, whose success in China was largely due to the sales of inexpensive computers (Lower 2007). Dell's recent move has only added to a growing perception among financial analysts that Lenovo is facing serious challenges in its own domestic market (Norton 2007).

To fend off declining domestic brand loyalty and establish global brand awareness, Lenovo has committed significant resources to sponsorship of sporting events, including the Olympics, the National Basketball Association (NBA), and Formula One. Philippe Davy, the head of Lenovo's Worldwide Sponsorship and Alliance Division, has described Lenovo's sports sponsorship efforts as the company's "broadband solution" (Norton 2007, D1). The broadband solution refers to the ability of sports sponsorship to: (a) allow long-term exposure because the brand name is a constant across a season or throughout a global event, as opposed to a short television or radio spot; (b) allow for more cooperative advertising opportunities with other sponsors as sporting events have multiple sponsors; and (c) reach a wide demographic, from "C-level [corporate level] officers to consumers," as Lenovo (2007) suggests.

Olympic sponsorship, unlike that of the NBA and Formula One, allows Lenovo to reach a diverse global audience. While the NBA sponsorship was primarily designed to promote much-needed brand awareness in North America, the Beijing Olympic campaign was designed with a multiplicity of audiences in mind, a significant portion of which are already aware of the Lenovo brand. Thus, the $150 million Olympic campaign is being structured to showcase the technology's ability in real time via the donation of Lenovo equipment for use by event organizers during the Games (Liu 2007a). This is a risky yet important venture that attempts to solidify brand trust as opposed to creating brand awareness. If Lenovo equipment is used successfully in the facilitation of the Games, it will demonstrate Lenovo's technological prowess and dependability, adding credence to both Lenovo and the Created in China narrative.

Lenovo used the same brand trust-building strategy at the 2006 Winter Olympics in Torino in what could be seen as a trial run for the 2008 Games. Lenovo considers its Torino marketing strategy a success because the Lenovo equipment operated error-free, thus promoting Lenovo as a powerful Created in China alternative to other computer manufacturers (Xie 2006). Although Torino was a triumph, Lenovo acknowledges that the Beijing Games represent a far more strenuous test of their products. The Torino Games hosted 2,508 athletes in 84 events at 15 competition sites; the Beijing Games are expected to host 10,000 athletes in 302 events at 39 competition sites (Lenovo 2007). Lenovo states that the "equipment and services provided during the two weeks of the Games are equivalent to that needed for any Fortune 500 company" (Lenovo 2007). The technological infrastructure demands of the Olympic Games, daunting in and of themselves, will be tested in front of a much larger global audience than in the 2006 Winter Games. Whereas only 80 nations participated in Torino, 201 nations are expected to participate in Beijing, and the number of accredited journalists is expected to double, from 10,000 in Torino to 20,000 in Beijing (Lenovo 2007).

Like other multinational corporations, Lenovo must pursue dual strategies. To develop its identity as an "international" corporation, its connection with China must be delicately defined. Within China, and its huge market, the strategy is quite different. The company must touch a personal nerve, making its success relate to the ambition of individuals who see themselves as part of a collective and advancing social whole. It is important to note that Lenovo's Beijing 2008 promotional activities extend beyond the two-week event itself. Domestic promotional activities seek to extend brand awareness from technologically advanced cosmopolitan cities such as Beijing and Shanghai to the rest of China. If the international narrative uses the idea of Created in China, the domestic message may be something like "Lenovo: part of China's global advancement and continued aspiration."

Through associations with state media and state officials, Lenovo has created what it calls the "500 Days of Lenovo Advertising" (Lenovo 2007). On March 27, 2007, Lenovo began airing daily twenty-five-second spots on CCTV channels in advance of CCTV 1's primetime news program and during daytime viewing hours on CCTV 5, China's most popular sports channel (Lenovo 2007). Lenovo has produced "eight sets of commercials [that] feature different phases of the Olympic Games, including preparation of venues, Opening Ceremonies, test events, etc." (Lenovo 2007). These commercials also act as short public information campaigns, thus linking the Lenovo brand to state-controlled news about Beijing's preparations for the Olympics.

Perhaps more interestingly, the domestic campaign also includes a 1,000 town "road show" with the goal of rural outreach. These rural outreach events include full-day events with athletes, government officials, and Lenovo spokespersons, and the donation of personal computers to schools with the goal of giving the "first PC experience to thousands of Chinese" (Lenovo 2007). Lenovo suggests that through this initiative it has "brought [the] Olympic Games to cities outside Beijing" (Lenovo 2007). The linking of the Lenovo brand to the *national* Olympic experience makes Lenovo a key player in promulgating the notion that the Beijing Games are China's moment as opposed to Beijing's moment. Thus, at the domestic level, the Created in China narrative legitimizes Lenovo for millions of rural Chinese by exposing the company to them for the first time with the government and the government's Olympic goals as a key partner. Further, Lenovo's road show strengthens Chinese national pride and challenges regional disparities and discontent by uniting the Olympics with the nation and the nation with the intoxicating effects of modern technologies. In these road shows the nation-state legitimizes Lenovo just as Lenovo legitimizes the nation-state. Finally, as Lenovo's intensive domestic Olympics advertising campaign indicates, the success of Lenovo is as much about the faith of Chinese citizens in their own technology brands as it is about global impressions of Chinese technology products.

The complexity of Lenovo's task—and its relationship to the narrative for China and the Games—can be seen in much of the publicity it generates. *China Daily* reported, "For Lenovo, it will be important to build emotional ties. The firm wants to impress upon its customers and dealers that it is global, innovative and offers high performance products" (Li and Yu 2007, 3). In a company press release, Lenovo representative Philippe Davy stated, "Created in China, headquartered in the United States and with employees worldwide, Lenovo is both a symbol of 21st century business and the Olympic desire to build international understanding" (Lenovo 2005). Indeed, an international event would seem the ideal place to promote Lenovo as a company that has an "international executive team" and "headquarters in Beijing, Singapore and Raleigh, NC" (Lenovo 2007). At the same time, Olympic sponsorship material has focused on Lenovo's identity as a Chinese company attempting to enter the global market and has not framed Lenovo as a multinational corporation that, despite its Chinese roots and ties, has a head office in the United States. In the lead-up to the Beijing Olympics, Lenovo is attempting to present itself as both a Chinese company and as a global company. The two categories are not mutually exclusive. But Lenovo's choice of messaging has implications for the Created in China narrative and Brand China. If Lenovo, the global company with Chinese roots and an American head office, is the most prominent international public face, then the Created in China narrative loses much of its impact. In fact, one could argue that this version of Lenovo would conform more to the Made in China narrative where China is the support mechanism for the innovations that take place in the American head office. If, on the other hand, Lenovo, the Chinese company with global aspirations and global offices, is the most prominent international public face, then the Created in China narrative is strengthened as Chinese ingenuity and quality is shown to have created a global demand that must be met by the construction of multinational bases of operation.

One clue to the thematic direction of the company's promotional intentions can be discerned via a brief analysis of how Lenovo's design for the Beijing Olympic Torch was presented to the global public. The unveiling of this torch—an aluminum torch resembling a scroll of paper—garnered international media attention, and suggests that Lenovo intends to package itself for international audiences at least partly as a Chinese company. A BOCOG press release stated: "The design of the Torch takes advantage of Chinese artistic heritage and technological expertise" (2007). As *China Daily* reported in their story about the torch, "paper is one of the four great inventions in ancient China that was spread to the rest of the world along the ancient Silk Road" (Lei 2007, 15). Thus, the torch represents China's history of technological advancements and innovations. The construction of the torch emphasizes Lenovo's ties to science in China. While the outside of the torch was designed by Lenovo, the internal flame system was designed by the China Aerospace Science and Industry Group. Maintaining a constant flame is particularly important because the Olympic torch route is intended to include the scaling of the highest mountain in the world,

Mount Qomolangma (or Mt. Everest) in Tibet. To scale the mountain successfully, the torch will have to withstand low air temperatures, high wind, and low air pressure (Lei 2007). The torch nicely represents a triad of the techno-narrative simultaneously symbolizing the *historical* inventiveness of China through the scroll design, the *current* inventiveness of China through the Lenovo-created design, and the *future* inventiveness of China through the unprecedented burning mechanism.

Lenovo's association with the torch must also be understood as a national project, again highlighting Lenovo as a Chinese company. Through its explicit cooperation with national scientific organizations and its implicit support of China's planned torch route through Tibet by helping construct a device precisely for this purpose, Lenovo is signaling to the world its clear association with the Chinese government and its prerogatives. The torch route through Tibet has been subject to substantial international criticism, and Lenovo's close association with the torch opens the possibility for the company to be subjected to criticisms related to China's tenuous relationship with the Tibetan people. This linkage between Lenovo and the Chinese government opens the possibility for the promotion of a new Created in China narrative; at the same time, it makes the company vulnerable to international criticism directed at China's political agenda. The Lenovo-spearheaded Created in China narrative is ultimately a fragile narrative that is dependent not only on the technology that Lenovo manufactures, but also on the policies that the Chinese government pursues.

Loo and Davies argue that "the nation brand is an overarching concept with a single positioning that straddles the entire range of outputs a nation has" (2006, 202). In the spring and summer of 2007, concerns about Chinese quality control in products ranging from pet food to toothpaste and toys dominated international media coverage of China. Following Loo and Davies's logic, toothpaste may actually prove to be mightier than technology. This is to say that despite Lenovo's broadband advertising strategy and the importance of becoming China's first TOP sponsor, the company, if understood by international audiences as Chinese, must today also contend with a reinvigorated Made in China narrative that highlights poor workmanship; poor quality; and, now, potential danger. If, as we have argued, the fate of Lenovo's Olympic campaign plays an important role in determining China's image as a player in the global information and technology economy, then it can also be said that China's reputation plays an equally important role in determining Lenovo's fate.

Case Study II: Mobile Initiatives

Mobile technology initiatives are an important component of Beijing's progressive techno-narrative of Created in China. China is one of the fastest growing mobile phone markets in the world. Currently, there are more than 400 million mobile phone users in China, and this number is increasing by 5 million users a month (Bremner 2006; Chandler 2007). The largest mobile phone provider is China Mobile, which is controlled by the Ministry of Information Industry. Originally spun off from China Telecom in 2000, China Mobile has since signed up more than 300 million mobile phone subscribers (Roberts 2006); the company's closest competitor, China Unicom, has more than 100 million mobile subscribers. In 2006, China Mobile's ad spending increased 57 percent to 4 billion yuan in preparation for the Beijing Olympics (Yeung 2007). Third generation mobile (3G) services, including high-speed data and broadband Internet services for mobile devices, are an important technological development within China as well as globally, and are an important component of the country's successful modernization and international integration. Such mobile services have been projected to increase mobile revenues in China from $10 billion in 2006 to $28.8 billion in 2010 (Roberts 2007).

The report that Beijing submitted to the IOC as part of its bid for the 2008 Olympics described Beijing as characterized by "the rapid development and application of leading edge technologies, such as IT" (BOCOG n.d., 3). It boasted that mobile 3G services would be available well before the Games (BOCOG n.d., 85). Xin Xu argues that "the award to host the Olympiad has certainly set the new impetus for China's modernization drive and international integration" (2006, 91). But in mid-2007, with testing of platforms and standards still under way—and no clear end in sight—the narrative implications have changed: Will China be able to fulfill these technological aspirations and permit and achieve the infrastructure for a meaningful advance in the way people receive and experience the Olympic Games?

There have been several technological and bureaucratic hurdles to China's successful development of 3G services. The Chinese Ministry of Information Industry is a key decision maker, but there have been inputs from the State-owned Assets Supervision and Administration Commission (SASAC), which oversees China's state-owned companies. Also involved in restructuring of the sector are the National Development and Reform Commission, the Ministry of Science and Technology, and the State Administration of Radio Film and Television. One question, one narrative outcome, is how China deals administratively with these aspects of technological change.

There is no worldwide standard platform for 3G. The European and Japanese 3G standard is W-CDMA (wideband-code division multiple access), whereas the U.S. 3G standard is CDMA2000. In late October 2006, the Chinese State Administration for Radio Film and Television announced that the national 3G standard would be TD-SCDMA (these initials stand for "time division synchronous code division multiple access," though that hardly makes the standard more understandable). "The TD-SCDMA standard has received the full blessing of the Chinese government and it will surely play a critical role in mobile communication development in China as well as in the world" (Chen et al. 2002, 48).

The initial choice of TD-SCDMA over W-CDMA and CDMA2000 as the national standard in China seemed an important decision because TD-SCDMA was developed by researchers and telecommunications industry leaders *in China*. China is not only competing at the Olympics for gold medals but is also competing with other technological standards for global market dominance. The decision to choose a Chinese-developed standard "reflect[s] government efforts to control core technologies by using domestic rather than international standards" (Yeung 2006, 15). By choosing TD-SCDMA first, the homegrown technology was given an additional six months of testing in China. In addition, much of the core intellectual property of TD-SCDMA is owned by Chinese companies, which means that the licensing fees for China to use this standard will be significantly lower than they would be for competing standards developed outside of China (Bremner 2006). If TD-SCDMA were to be successful, China and its industries would not only benefit financially, but the country's reputation as a world leader in information technology would also improve. "The implications of [China's] TD-SCDMA technologies to other countries will be far beyond technical significance. The success of TD-SCDMA from proposal to operational system will bring China into the world club, which used to be limited to the Western powers only" (Chen et al. 2002, 59). The Olympic Games are, in this sense, a world stage on which to showcase TD-SCDMA and China's technological prowess.

As of a year before the Games, the commitment to 3G and mobile service remained an unsettled question. Industry leaders insist that TD-SCDMA will be ready in time for the 2008 Games. The deputy director of TD-SCDMA at the largest equipment vendor for TD-SCDMA said, "TD-SCDMA will play a critical role during the Olympics and the networks will absolutely be up and running before the Olympics" (*BusinessWeek.com* 2007). Meanwhile, others, including the Chinese government and BOCOG, appear to have realized that the homegrown 3G mobile platform might not be serviceable in time for the Games. The question then became whether it was more important singly to advance the underlying China-developed technology or to demonstrate commitment to having mobile services ready. Jiang Xiaoyu, the executive vice president of BOCOG, indicated that China may "have to go back to the IOC to discuss its pledge to have a third generation mobile phone network available in time for the games" (*Economist* 2007). In a step to encourage further opportunity for 3G development in time for the Games, the Ministry of Information Industry announced in mid-May 2007 that it would place the two other international 3G standards alongside TD-SCDMA as choices for 3G in China. According to the ministry, mobile phone operators in China would be allowed to choose from all three technologies.

This decision to diversify China's acceptable 3G platforms is important for two reasons. First, it increases the chances that 3G services may actually be available during the 2008 Olympic Games. While the mobile services may not be as robust as originally intended, opening its 3G standards will most likely allow China to offer at least limited 3G services during the Games as promised. Second, the decision to include W-CDMA and CDMA2000 as 3G choices allows China to proclaim itself "technologically neutral" in regard to 3G. It is not a coincidence that this announcement was made less than a week before "high-level Chinese delegates visited the US for talks on long-term bilateral issues" (Poon 2007, 30). Internationally, China wants to project an image of fairness in regulating the potentially highly lucrative mobile 3G market in China. Allowing the three 3G platforms not only helps to ensure technological robustness during the Olympics, but can be seen as a positive gesture from China in the information technology global marketplace. Of course, it is important to keep in mind that state-run China Mobile will most likely be the primary service provider of any 3G services during the Olympics. Thus while China may open its standards for 3G services to include W-CDMA and CDMA2000, the Ministry of Information Industry is ensuring its control over the rollout and development of any mobile services.

In addition to the technological challenges of 3G, administrative, political, and economic issues in China have also provided hurdles to mobile initiatives. Once a mobile 3G platform is developed and tested, the Chinese government must decide which mobile phone carriers can provide 3G services in China. China has been reluctant to issue 3G mobile licenses to providers because of a potential major restructuring of the telecommunications industry, which would integrate landline and mobile phone services and determine which operators would receive 3G licenses in China. However, any industry restructuring is immensely complicated, as three competing regulatory agencies must approve any changes (*Economist* 2007). Thus, despite allowing the other international 3G standards to operate in China, by not issuing 3G licenses China continues to inhibit efforts that would allow them to offer 3G services during the 2008 Games. When visitors from around the world come to Beijing for the Olympics, they will likely rely on Chinese mobile services. If China can prove its technological superiority during the Olympics then its technological standards may be adopted elsewhere throughout the world.

In addition, mobile technologies, including 3G and mobile TV initiatives, are important to the success of the 2008 Games because mobile technology provides an additional channel through which spectators can follow the events of the Games. While modern media events were originally viewed on the television at home (Dayan and Katz 1992), digital technology increasingly displaces the home as the site of spectatorship for the Olympics and other media events. Advanced mobile technology like 3G and mobile TV encourages the watching of events from wherever the viewer may be. Increased accessibility to Olympic coverage may encourage continuity in viewing and contribute to viewer attachment and investment in the success of the 2008 Games. NBC's multimodal approach for the 2006 Torino Games—with Olympic content made readily available on the Internet or through podcasts—allowed it to reach a broader audience. "'We found that the more content we make available, the more buzz we create,' said Gary Zenkel, president of NBC Olympics. 'There's an audience for the consumption of media that's super-strong in front of the TV and also strong when people are not. We have to make sure our content is made available to people wherever they are'" (Levingston 2006, D05). If people are no longer sitting in front of their televisions to watch the Olympics, broadcasters and Olympic media planners of the Beijing Games must develop new ways to reach an ever more mobile audience.

Mobile Sousveillance and Potential
Counternarratives

While coverage of the 2008 Olympics through mobile technology may encourage viewership and reinforce the techno-narrative of the Games, the interactive nature of mobile technology also threatens the control of the official narratives surrounding the Beijing Games. Advancements in camera and video on mobile phones make users not only consumers of mobile content, but producers as well. Such technological advancements open up the possibility of counternarratives by noncorporate or nonstate institutions. The new producers may have very different incentives and priorities than Chinese authorities. And because mobile phones are highly accessible and portable, they may be able to record events and situations that were previously obscured from public scrutiny. Information technology also opens up possibilities for different kinds of surveillance. Typically surveillance is the monitoring *of* those with less power *by* those with more power—the use of information technology by bureaucratic and state institutions to monitor the behavior of individuals. However, Mann, Nolan, and Wellman (2003) suggest that ubiquitous information technology can allow for individuals to observe those in authority. Mann et al. refer to this inverse surveillance as "sousveillance," from the French meaning to watch from below.

The power of sousveillance lies not just in the ability to record the behavior of those in authority, but also in the ability to present this behavior back to those in authority so as to confront them with their recorded actions, a process Mann (1998) refers to as "reflectionism." This is partly done through the dissemination of the recorded act to mass media outlets. Probably the most famous example of sousveillance in the United States is the video of the police assault on Rodney King. The power of the video was not that it captured the events unfolding but that it was presented back to the public and to authorities and called on them to account for their abusive tactics.

More recently there have been examples of mobile devices contributing to the sousveillance of corporate and state institutions. Because mobile devices are almost always available to large numbers of people, there are recorded events and situations in which authority figures exert highly disputed examples of power or force over those less powerful. For example, in November 2006 a UCLA student refused to show his student identification to campus police at the library and was subsequently stunned with a Taser gun. Several nearby students caught this exchange with their camera phones and posted it to the Internet. This resulted in a lawsuit and an investigation of campus police practices (*LA Times* Staff 2007).

The power of mobile devices to expose the behavior of authority is recognized within China as a matter of state concern. Chinese authorities have at times inhibited uses of mobile technology so as to impede the dissemination of information by average citizens. For example, on March 28, 2007, six workers died while building an underground railway connecting Beijing to the Olympic Village. The tunnel they were working on collapsed on top of them, and it took several days to recover the bodies of the victims. The *Daily Telegraph* reported:

> The state-run construction company responsible for the work was so concerned to keep details secret it locked workers inside the construction site and confiscated their mobile phones while attempting its own rescue work. Eventually, one man who had managed to keep hold of his phone crept away and called a relative who works for the police. (Spencer 2007, 17)

Beginning in 2005 global news media started to use camera phone recordings by citizens who had captured newsworthy events that the official media could or did not record. Notable examples include the London bombings in July 2005, the coup in Thailand in September 2006, the hanging of Saddam Hussein in December 2006, and the Virginia Tech shootings in April 2007. The potential ubiquity of mobile phones at the Beijing Games increases opportunities for both athletes and spectators to record events and occurrences to which official press may not have access.

Already, mobile technology in conjunction with the Internet and blogs have proved a mobilizing communication tool for activists and citizens in China. For example, a text message campaign was used to raise awareness and fight the construction of a chemical factory in the seaside city of Xiamen (Cody 2007). Demonstrations were held, and demonstrators sent text messages and photos about the event to bloggers throughout China who then posted them on their Web blogs. Thus real-time accounts from the demonstrators and citizen journalists circumvented censorship by the government and could be read throughout the country. Chinese authorities postponed construction of the factory to conduct a review of the environmental impact (Cody

2007). The sousveillance enabled by mobile technology is changing the flow of information among citizens in China and indicating the fragility of the Chinese authorities' official narratives and their control over them. Although the mobile phone–enabled examples of sousveillance in China have only garnered minor international attention so far, mobile services are expected to be heavily promoted leading up to and during the 2008 Olympics, encouraging many athletes and tourists to have mobile phones on hand throughout the Games. When the world's eye is on Beijing during the 2008 Games, such sousveillance incidences may quickly become global news, tarnishing the positive techno-narrative that BOCOG and China have worked so hard to preserve.

Conclusion

The techno-narrative surrounding the 2008 Beijing Olympics is a means through which to foster an association between China and modern technological innovations, while at the same time suggesting that such a relationship has always been there. The High-Tech theme of the Beijing Olympics, the Lenovo sponsorship, and the mobile initiatives each represent a different but complementary facet of this techno-narrative. Central to this High-Tech theme is a Created in China narrative, which can be seen in both the Lenovo and 3G examples. In both cases, the Chinese government is involved in attempting to control the information technology preparation and branding for the Olympics as a means of protecting the potential fragility of this narrative.

While the High-Tech theme of the Olympics may connote Chinese technological progressivism and innovation, the increased adoption and prevalence of advanced information technology, including mobile technology, may provide opportunities for such a narrative to be hijacked and for counternarratives to emerge. Camera and video mobile phones provide a means of sousveillance through which everyday citizens can monitor, record, and disseminate official acts and behaviors of abuse or negligence. No doubt Western media, if their early framing is an indication, will be hungry for Olympic scandals involving the athletes, the events, or the host city and country during the 2008 Games. The ubiquity of mobile phones suggests that practically all of the Olympics including the main stage, side stage, and backstage activities will be captured and recorded one way or another; however, which backstage activities get disseminated remains to be seen. Similarly, as a TOP sponsor and provider of information technology for the Games, Lenovo will be closely scrutinized as being both of China, for China, and for the world. The Chinese authorities will certainly try to control the discourse throughout the Olympic Games, in part by focusing on the High-Tech theme, but recent news coverage suggests that counternarratives can leak into the mainstream press with the help of the information technology itself.

Future research should explore the successes and failures of China to use the 2008 Olympic Games as a stage on which to demonstrate its shift from an economy producing inexpensive goods to a sophisticated information economy and one where Created in China and Made in China gain respect. By harnessing the Olympic discourse of progress, the Beijing Olympics will try to construct itself as a High-Tech Olympics. The computing services by Lenovo and the mobile services promoted for the Games contribute to this techno-narrative. The final year leading up to the 2008 Olympics emerges as a critical time for China to negotiate the tensions between internal regulatory struggles and the desire to project an international image of a technologically progressive country.

NOTE

1. Live 8 was a series of free concerts held on July 2, 2005, in the G8 countries and South Africa to raise awareness of poverty. Live Earth was a series of concerts held on July 7, 2007, around the world (at least one concert was held on each of the seven continents) to raise awareness of climate change.

REFERENCES

BOCOG. n.d. Candidature Files. http://en.beijing2008.cn/65/68/col umn211716865.shtml (accessed May 2, 2007).

BOCOG. 2007. Beijing 2008 Olympic Torch Relay Planned Route and Torch Design Unveiled. Press release, April 26. http://torchrelay.beijing2008.cn/ en/news/headlines/n214042288.shtml (accessed May 2, 2007).

Bremner, Brian. 2006. China's 3G Mobile Marathon: a New Homegrown Wireless Standard, TD-SCDMA, Is Being Rolled out in Time for the Beijing Olympics. Will It Win Gold or Create Headaches for Global Players? *BusinessWeek.com,* November 27. http://www.businessweek.com/technol ogy/content/nov2006/tc20061127_928580.htm?chan=search (accessed August 2, 2007).

BusinessWeek.com. 2007. Beijing's Wireless Olympic Games. June 5. http://www.businessweek.com/print/globalbiz/content/jun2007/gb2007 0605_718837.htm (accessed June 12, 2007).

Chandler, Clay. 2007. China's mobile maestro. *Fortune,* July 31. http://money.cnn.com/magazines/fortune/fortune_archive/2007/08/06/ 100156748/index.htm (accessed August 15, 2007).

Chen, Hsiao-Hwa, Chang-Xin Fan, and Willie W. Lu. 2002. China's Perspective on 3G Mobile Communications and Beyond: TD-SCDMA. *IEEE Wireless Communications* 9 (2): 48–59.

Cody, Edward. 2007. Text Messages Giving Voice to Chinese. *Washington Post,* June 28, A01.

Dayan, Daniel, and Elihu Katz. 1992. *Media Events: The Live Broadcasting of History.* Cambridge, MA: Harvard University Press.

Economist. 2007. Olympic Hurdle. June 14. http://www.economist.com/ busi ness/displaystory.cfm?story_id=9340479 (accessed June 23, 2007).

Haugen, Heidi. 2005. Time and Space in Beijing's Olympic Bid. *Norwegian Journal of Geography* 59:217–27.

Hogan, Jackie. 2003. Staging the Nation. *Journal of Sport and Social Issues* 27 (2):100–123.

IOC. 2007. Olympic Sponsorship. http://www.olympic.org/uk/organisation /facts/programme/sponsors_uk.asp (accessed June 25, 2007).

Kleinman, Mark. 2007. Lenovo Feels the Force of Global Competition. *Daily Telegraph,* May 29, City section, 6. http://www.telegraph.co.uk/money/ main.jhtml?xml=/money/2007/05/29/cnlenovo29.xml (accessed August 2, 2007).

LA Times Staff. 2007. UCLA Student Files Suit in Taser Incident. *Los Angeles Times,* January 18, B4.

Lei, Lei. 2007. Beijing Olympic Torch Designers Strike It Lucky. *China Daily,* April 27, 15. http://www.chinadaily.com.cn/2008/2007–04/27/content_ 861795.htm (accessed August 2, 2007).

Lenovo. 2007. Activation in the City: How Sponsors Make their Investment Pay off in Host Cities and Elsewhere. Powerpoint presentation, available at: http://www.sportaccord.com/vsite/vfile/page/fileurl/0,11040,5035- 183339-200557-120926-0-file,00.ppt (accessed June 28, 2007).

Lenovo. 2005. As Newest Worldwide Sponsor of the Olympic Games, Lenovo Begins 150-Day Countdown to Torino. Press release, Purchase, NY, September 13. http://www.lenovo.com/news/us/en/2005/09/olympics.html (accessed May 2, 2007).

Levingston, Steven. 2006. Olympics Web Site a Winner for NBC. *Washington Post,* February 14, D05.

Li, Bo, Dongliang Xie, Shiduan Cheng, Junliang Chen, Ping Zhang, Wenwu Zhu, and Bin Li. 2005. Recent Advances on TD-SCDMA in China. *IEEE Communications Magazine* 43 (1): 30–37.

Li Weitao, and Yu Yilei. 2007. Olympics to Fuel Lenovo's Growth. *China*

Daily, April 28, 3. http://www.chinadaily.com.cn/cndy/2007-04/28/con
tent_862325.htm (accessed August 2, 2007).

Liu, Baijia. 2007a. Lenovo Logs into Advertising Campaign. *China Daily,* January 12. http://www.chinadaily.com.cn/2008/2007-01/12/content_782118
.htm (accessed August 3, 2007).

Liu, Baijia. 2007b. Lenovo Lifts its Profile Through Sponsorship. *China Daily,*
January 25, 15. http://www.chinadaily.com.cn/cndy/2007-01/25/con
tent_791780.htm (accessed August 2, 2007).

Loo, Theresa, and Mike Davies. 2006. Branding China: The Ultimate
Challenge in Reputation Management. *Corporate Reputation Review* 9:198–
210.

Lower, Josh. 2007. Company Report: Lenovo Group Limited. Hoover's,
Austin, TX.

Lu Xuewu. 2007. The Olympics: Threats and Opportunities for China's Media. Paper presented at the China/East Asia Media/New Media Conference, Brisbane, Australia, July 6.

Mann, Steve. 1998. "Reflectionism" and "Diffusionism": New Tactics for De-
constructing the Video Surveillance Superhighway. *Leonardo* 31:93–102.

Mann, Steve, Jason Nolan, and Barry Wellman. 2003. Sousveillance: Inventing and Using Wearable Computing Devices for Data Collection in Surveillance Environments. *Surveillance and Society* 1 (3): 331–55.

Netherlands Olympic Committee. 1928. *Official Report of the Olympic Games
of 1928.* Ed. G. Van Rossem. Available at http://olympic-museum.de/o-re
ports/report1928.htm (accessed November 12, 2006).

Norton, Frank. 2007. Lenovo Longs for America to Know Its Name. *Seattle
Times,* March 12, D1.

Organising Committee for the XIV Olympiad. 1948. *The Official Report of the
Organising Committee for the XIV Olympiad.* London: McCorquodale.

Poon, Terence. 2007. China Sets 3G Wireless Specifications. *Wall Street Journal Asia,* May 17, 30.

Roberts, Dexter. 2006. BW CEO Forum: China Mobile at Full Speed; The
Mainland's Big Mobile Player Plans to Add Yet More Market Share. *Busi-
nessWeek.com,* November 1. http://www.businessweek.com/globalbiz/con
tent/nov2006/gb20061101_266729.htm?chan=search (accessed August 2,
2007).

Roberts, Dexter. 2007. China Mobile's Hot Signal. *BusinessWeek.com,* February 5. http://www.businessweek.com/globalbiz/content/jan2007/gb2007
0125_650122.htm?chan=search (accessed August 2, 2007).

Roche, Maurice. 2000. *Mega-events and Modernity: Olympics, Expos, and the
Growth of Global Culture.* London: Routledge.

Senn, Alfred E. 1999. *Power, Politics, and the Olympic Games.* Champaign, IL:
Human Kinetics.

Spencer, Jane, and Geoffrey A. Fowler. 2007. Lenovo Goes for Its Own
Olympic Medal. *Wall Street Journal.com,* March 27. http://online.wsj.com/

public/article/SB117493079450849239-EV1aN93UYjV7M3Nd14dy4qSFY
vg_20070403.html?mod=regionallinks (accessed August 2, 2007).

Spencer, Richard. 2007. Fears Rise for China's Olympics Workers as 6 Die. *Daily Telegraph,* April 3, International section, 17.

Su, Tong. 2007. The China Code. Paper presented at the China/East Asia Media/New Media Conference, Brisbane, Australia, July 6.

Tajima, Atsushi. 2004. "Amoral Universalism": Mediating and Staging Global and Local in the 1998 Nagano Olympic Winter Games. *Critical Studies in Media Communication* 21 (3): 241–60.

Xie Long. 2006. Olympic Sponsorship. Paper presented at the Global Olympiad, Chinese Media Workshop, Beijing, July.

Xu, Xin. 2006. Modernizing China in the Olympic Spotlight: China's National Identity and the 2008 Beijing Olympiad. *Sociological Review* 54 (2): 90–107.

Yeung, Frederick. 2007. Games Boost Ad Spend. *South China Morning Post,* February 10, Business section, 2.

Yeung, Frederick. 2006. Shanghai Media Benefits as Mainland Decides Mobile TV Standard. *South China Morning Post,* October 31, Business section, 15.

Embracing Wushu

Globalization and Cultural Diversification of the Olympic Movement

Hai Ren

Homogenization

When the 2008 Olympics were awarded to Beijing, there was some hope that a trend toward homogenization, in terms of Western sport culture, would be altered. Because the sports events are the central aesthetic of the Games, what sports are included, how they are presented, and how they are honored sends a powerful message to the world. In this chapter, I will describe an example of the cultural tensions involved in the selection process by focusing on a debate over the inclusion of the traditional Chinese sport of Wushu.

What do I mean, in this context, by "homogenization?" In order to understand this, I want first to place this phenomenon in the context of globalization—a process of integrating not just the economy but culture, technology, and governance (UNDP 1999). Globalization involves more than the flow of money and commodities; it encompasses the growing interdependence of the world's people as well. Globalization is obviously one of the most important historical processes that human beings have ever encountered. And in the mega-trend toward globalization, the Olympic Movement has been a very active pioneer.

Homogenization in the Olympics means stressing Western sports cultures and, in doing so, leveling local sports cultural differences. Here are some points to keep in mind:

- The sport events in the Olympic Games have been dominated by Western-oriented ones: among the 28 sports and 301 events only very few events, including Judo and Tae Kwon Do, have non-Western roots.
- There is lower participation in the Olympic Games from developing countries. Some 10,960 athletes were accredited for the 2000 Sydney Games, with 10,651 of these athletes actually competing. Nearly half of the athletes were from European National Olympic Committees (NOCs), as table 1 shows.
- Though some measures have been taken to promote and increase the participation of developing countries in the Olympic Movement, the gains so far seem to be mainly symbolic. Seventy-one NOCs had five or fewer athletes compete (International Olympic Committee [IOC] 2001a) in the 2000 Games; the British Virgin Islands had only one participant. These countries and athletes are in the international spotlight for just a few minutes, as the TV camera passes over them during the opening ceremony; the few athletes and officials carrying the national flags signal nothing but "we are here."

TABLE 1. Participation Figures of Sydney Olympics by Continent

Continent	Men	Women	Total	Percentage of Total
Europe	3,325	1,950	5,275	49.5
America	1,211	798	2,009	18.9
Asia	1,006	678	1,684	15.8
Africa	592	277	869	8.2
Oceania	448	366	814	7.6
Total	6,582	4,069	10,651	100.0

Source: IOC, Highlights of the Week 6, February 5–11, 2001.

TABLE 2. Host Cities of Summer Olympic Games

I	1896	Athens	XVII	1960	Rome, Italy
II	1900	Paris, France	XVIII	1964	Tokyo, Japan
III	1904	St. Louis, United States	XIX	1968	Mexico City, Mexico
IV	1908	London, England	XX	1972	Munich, Germany
V	1912	Stockholm, Sweden	XXI	1976	Montreal, Canada
VII	1920	Antwerp, Belgium	XXII	1980	Moscow, USSR
VIII	1924	Paris, France	XXIII	1984	Los Angeles, United States
IX	1928	Amsterdam, Netherlands	XXIV	1988	Seoul, Korea
X	1932	Los Angeles, United States	XXV	1992	Barcelona, Spain
XI	1936	Berlin, Germany	XXVI	1996	Atlanta, United States
XIV	1948	London, England	XXVII	2000	Sydney, Australia
XV	1952	Helsinki, Finland	XXVIII	2004	Athens, Greece
XVI	1956	Melbourne, Australia	XXIX	2008	Beijing, China

- For a variety of reasons, the Olympic Games have been held less frequently in cities with non-Western cultural traditions, which limits the scope for broadening the sports that are included.
- The decision-making circle is dominated by European figures. Among the current 111 IOC members 46 percent are from European and North American countries.
- The European dominance is so powerful that even the young Olympic athletes have been strongly influenced as indicated by the election of the IOC Athletes' Commission during the Sydney Games, in September 2000. A total of 5,216 athletes (47.3 percent of those participating in the Games) took part in the elections. Of 44 candidates (Africa 5, America 6, Asia 9, Europe 22, and Oceania 2), eight athletes (North America 2, Europe 5, and Oceania 1) were elected and none of them belong to developing countries from Asia, Africa, and Latin America. (IOC 2000)

Olympic cultural homogenization disseminates and reinforces the message that modernity entails a rejection of cultural traditions and ethnic sports, and conformity with the dominant sports of the West. The more popular the Olympic Movement gets, the more intense the pressure against these indigenous sports becomes. And, cultural diversity, one of the essential factors of the Olympic ideal, has been threatened as a result. In the long term view, this is a cause for great concern.

While it may be obvious that the Olympic Movement should incorporate more cultural elements from traditional sports—thus resisting homogenization—this is not however easily accomplished. The controversies involved with Wushu's application to become an Olympic sport in 2008 provide a good case study.

Wushu, also known as Gongfu or Chinese martial arts, is an internationally known traditional Chinese sport that has been blended with Chinese philosophical ideas and various theories of traditional medicine during its long historical development. The modern form of Wushu is composed of two disciplines: Taolu (routines) and Sanshou (sparring). Taolu consists of a series of routine movements involving martial art patterns; the players are judged and given points according to standard rules similar to those in gymnastics. Sanshou is a combat sport of free fighting, guided by special regulations. When the IOC granted Beijing the right to host the 2008 Olympic Games on July 13, 2001, many Chinese and Wushu fans believed that the inclusion of Wushu in the Olympic Games was secured. They anticipated that their beloved sport would march easily into the Olympics, following in the footsteps of Judo from Japan (introduced in the 1964 Tokyo Games) and Tae Kwon Do from Korea (introduced in the 1988 Seoul Games).[1] On December 29, 2001—just a few months after Beijing's successful bid—Li Zhijian, president of the International Wushu Federation (IWUF), sent a letter to IOC president Jacques Rogge, applying to include Wushu in the Olympic Games. The letter stated, "Wushu (the martial arts) derived in various martial arts of ancient times in China and based on deep East cultural heritage, endowed with unique values for both contest and fitness and has spread over the world in the past century, attractive to people in different cultural backgrounds." Thus, "to include *Wushu* into the Olympics will enrich the Olympic Movement and bring honor to the Olympic spirit" (enorth.com.cn 2001).

Despite the IWUF's efforts to persuade the IOC, and the support of international organizations and individuals, including a letter written to the IOC president by a group of U.S. athletes, business executives, and elected officials (2008 Trip: Our Support n.d.), Wushu did not succeed in joining the ranks of the official program of the Games.

The size of the Olympics is another possible obstacle to Wushu's success. See table 3.

When Jacques Rogge succeeded Juan Antonio Samaranch as president of the IOC in 2001, he immediately began cutting down the Games' scale. In February 2002, Rogge described the current scale of the Games as "a threat to their quality." An Olympic Programme Commission was tasked with "identifying ways of reducing the cost and size of the Games" (IOC 2002a).

Six months later, the Commission issued a report recommending that Wushu not be admitted to the 2008 Beijing Games, claiming that "statistics reviewed on federation affiliation, nations competing in ma-

TABLE 3.   Growth of the Olympic Games

Host City	Year	Sports	Events	Athletes (accredited)
Moscow	1980	21	203	5,283
Los Angeles	1984	21	221	6,802
Seoul	1988	23	237	8,473
Barcelona	1992	25	257	9,368
Atlanta	1996	26	271	10,630
Sydney	2000	28	300	10,960
Athens	2004	28	301	10,500

Source: IOC, Review of the Olympic Programme and the Recommendations on the Programme of the Games of the XXIX Olympiad, Beijing 2008, Report by the Commission Chairman, Franco Carraro, IOC Executive Board, August 2002.

jor events and broadcast and press coverage of major events for most requested sports did not indicate a higher level of global participation and interest than sports currently in the Programme, and therefore could not be considered to bring additional value." The sports recommended by the Commission for consideration for admission to the Games were golf and rugby 7s. The Commission also suggested excluding baseball, softball, and modern pentathlon from the current Olympic program (IOC 2002b). But Wushu's hopes were still alive. At the end of August, the IOC Executive Board decided not to admit roller sports, polo, surfing, bridge, chess, air sports, billiards, boules, dance sport, bowling, racquetball, water skiing, squash, and underwater sports, but stated that the request from the International Wushu Federation (IWUF) would be further studied (IOC 2002c).

Following further study, IWUF's application was rejected. The IOC president, on his October 2005 visit to the Formula One race of the Chinese Grand Prix in Shanghai, said, "We are not introducing wushu into the Olympic program. It will not be an exhibition. Not at all" (China.org.cn 2005). IWUF still did not give up its effort to make Wushu a part of the Olympics, officially recognized or not. In December 2005, at the 8th IWUF Wushu Congress in Hanoi, the IWUF president stated, "This work has been full of challenges and difficulties, including the barrier from the Olympic Charter. However, we had opportunities to discuss this issue with the IOC several times. Recently we invited Dr. Jacques Rogge, the President of the International Olympic Committee to attend the Opening Ceremony of the 10th National Games of China. We discussed this issue again and have reached a common consensus. The IOC will allow us to organize an international wushu event during the 2008 Beijing Olympic Games, but this event is not one of the 28 official Olympic sports, it is not a demonstration event, either. It will be the 2008 Beijing Olympic Games Wushu Tournament. I am confident in having the opportunity to stage an excellent Wushu performance in 2008. We would keep in touch with the IOC and continue to do our utmost for the bright future of Wushu movement" (IWUF 2005).

Denis Oswald, a member of the IOC Executive Board, explained the reason for the rejection of Wushu in a May 2007 interview by the Chinese media. According to him Wushu is not popular enough to become an Olympic sport as people in most countries of the world do not practice it. Chen Guorong, deputy director of the Wushu Administration Center of China, disagrees; she says that "since the establishment of the International Wushu Federation (IWUF) in 1991 (in Beijing), altogether 112 associations of martial arts from five continents have joined in. You can say that IWUF is qualified as a large-scale international sports organization" (Xinhua 2007). Based on these figures, shown in table 4, Wushu comfortably meets the Olympic Charter criteria for a sport to be included in the program of the Olympic Games, namely that "only sports widely practised by men in at least seventy-five countries and on four continents, and by women in at least forty countries and on three continents, may be included in the programme of the Games of the Olympiad" (IOC 2004).

Then what is the real reason for Wushu being rejected? The Olympic Program Commission states that Wushu's disqualification is because it "could not be considered to bring additional value" to the Olympic Games. However, given the recent trend toward homogenization of Western sport culture and the leveling of local sport culture, discussed earlier in this chapter, the Olympic Movement needs such cultural diversification in order to fulfill its noble goals. This is exactly the "additional value" that Wushu and other influential non-Western sports may contribute to the Movement. The "additional value" may have different meanings when approached from different angles. In the global perspective, to take other cultural elements will surely bring a great deal of benefit to the development of Olympic Games in the long run.

The controversies around Wushu's case also let us reconsider the roles the Olympic Games play. Are the Olympic Games a bridge to connect various cultures in the world together through sports? Or are the Games merely entertainment, such as the World Cup? Will they intensify already dominant cultural forms and further marginalize the weaker ones? Or will they help prevent a distinct cultural heritage from fading away, so as to maintain a culturally rich and balanced human

TABLE 4. International Wushu
Federation: National and Territorial
Member Federations

Continent	Number of Federations
Africa	20
America	18
Asia	35
Europe	37
Oceania	2
Total	112

Source: Data from IWUF Web site.

society? It is interesting to recall that in 2001 the IOC Evaluation Commission predicted that a "unique legacy" would be left after the Beijing Games (IOC 2001b). Though this legacy will not be apparent until the Games are over, Wushu's fate so far has not contributed to the realization of this goal.

Functions of Cultural Diversification

Why should we emphasize the importance of cultural diversity in the Olympic Movement? Some people may say it is because diversified cultural patterns would make the Olympics more attractive. This is true, but there are much deeper reasons, related to the fundamental principles and purpose of the Olympic Movement. The IOC has made it clear that the Olympics are not merely an ordinary sporting event. As the Olympic Charter indicates, the Olympic Movement aims at much higher goals:

> The goal of the Olympic Movement is to contribute to building a peaceful and better world by educating youth through sport practiced without discrimination of any kind and in the Olympic spirit, which requires mutual understanding with a spirit of friendship, solidarity and fair play. (IOC 2004)

The Olympic Movement sets itself an important role as a world peacemaker. It is exactly this noble goal that has made the Movement so valuable. It is not easy, however, for people with different social and cultural backgrounds to live together harmoniously and with respect for each other. The precondition of world peace is international understanding, to which the Olympic Movement is trying to contribute by acting as an agency to bridge the gap between different regions and to facilitate intercultural communication.

In today's world, with ethnic and cultural conflicts playing a conspicuous role in regional and global tensions, intercultural communication is especially important. Globalization has tightened the interrelationships between different cultural regions, but has also permitted an unprecedented assertion of individual identity. The self-awareness and pride that comes from cultural identity is an essential part of empowering communities to take charge of their own destinies. It is for these reasons that respect for the culture and identity of peoples is an important element in any viable approach to people-centered development (World Bank 1999).

Intercultural understanding today plays an important role in world peace. However, one of the great difficulties for international understanding is the lack of proper tools for cross-cultural communication because of the political, economic, and linguistic variety and differences around the world. Here, the traditional sports of various parts of the world offer a much-needed solution. To explain what I mean by this, I want now to consider some of these sports' unique characteristics:

1. Traditional Cultural Value Carriers

Traditional sports, as the result of cultural accumulation in a nation, embody the basic cultural elements that have guided a nation for thousands of years and still significantly influence the lives of citizens. For instance, Chinese Tai Chi not only reflects Chinese social values, such as self-control and benevolence, but is also imbued with cardinal Chinese philosophical ideas such as *Yin* and *Yang; Qi* (vital energy); *Wu Xing* (five basic elements: metal, wood, water, fire, and earth); *Ba Gua* (eight diagrams: *Qian*—the symbol of heaven, *Kun*—the symbol of earth, *Zhun*—the symbol of water, *Li*—the symbol of fire, *Zhen*—the symbol of thunder, *Gen*—the symbol of mountain, *Xun*—the symbol of wind, and *Dui*—the symbol of pond). The same is true for other indigenous sport activities around the world, like Yoga for the people in India. Traditional sports are like great containers filled with abundant and important cultural elements. The richness of the cultural messages is often beyond our imagination.

2. Good Communication Tools

A magnificent feature of traditional sports is their communication value: they are body languages, allowing the expression of cultural meanings through a set of physical movements. Traditional sports, through their integration of diverse philosophical thoughts, can be regarded as physical symbols for those complex conceptual ideas that are often difficult for people outside a particular culture to understand. In other words, traditional sports are the simplified, intuitive, and comprehensive explanation for a nation's thoughts and deep feelings. Those abstract concepts are such an integral and natural part of the physical activity that learners inevitably experience those ideas in the course of doing the exercises. Therefore, to study and learn a nation's traditional sports is to acquire a deep knowledge about the nation. Tai Chi and Yoga provide short-cuts to complex Chinese and Indian philosophies, and serve to facilitate the transmission of cross-cultural messages.

3. Most Popular Cultural Forms

In general, traditional sports are the popular cultural forms recognized and shared by a majority of the people of a nation. There is perhaps no other convenient way to know the ordinary people of a nation, on a large scale, than by investigating their forms of play and sporting activities. Traditional sports thus provide the proper means for ordinary peoples to know each other better.

Moreover, as Pierre de Coubertin indicated in 1929, the direct goal of the Olympics is to draw more ordinary persons to mass sport participation: "For a hundred to engage in physical culture, fifty must engage in sport. For fifty to engage in sport, twenty must specialize. For twenty to specialize five must be capable of astonishing feats" (Coubertin 1967). Diversified sport forms would be more attractive to ordinary people with various cultural backgrounds.

In addition, to keep the Olympic Movement culturally diversified, people must have an opportunity to show the appeal of various patterns of national cultures, thereby setting them on equal terms. Such a solid cultural base would make it possible to appreciate each other in a more rational way.

4. Resources to Enrich the Olympic Movement

Historical evidence has shown that the development of a cultural form depends on its interaction and exchanges with other cultures. The more resources it gets the faster and healthier progress it makes. Taking the Olympics as an example, the fundamental reason for its successful initiation lies in its bridging the barriers that separate, say, English sports from the gymastics practiced on the European continent. Now as the Movement has become globalized, it needs abundant new cultural resources to enrich itself for further development. Obviously, multicultural forms have the ability to meet the new demand of the Olympics and nourish the Movement with fresh cultural resources. The natural environment has taught us serious lessons about how the extinction of a given species diminishes future possibilities. The same is now true of the world of sports. When all traditional sports are gone, the Olympic Movement will be without a significant future. In other words, maintaining a diversified and balanced cultural ecology is necessary to the sustainable development of the Olympic Movement in the twenty-first century.

To summarize, the universality of the Olympic Movement can only be achieved through cultural diversity. Globalization and diversification are dialectically related to each other. Cultural diversification means to introduce different sport cultural forms to the Olympic Movement in order to balance the negative impacts resulting from globalization. However, it should be noticed that the diversified cultural forms that need to be introduced into the Olympic Movement are not the out-of-date and isolated patterns. They have to be mutually respectful instead of critical of each other, open instead of isolated, communicable instead of incommunicable. In a word, they should be diversified but all harmoniously presented.

5. Role of Developing Countries in Olympic Cultural Diversification

There is much to be done in order to achieve Olympic cultural diversity, not least of which is including more non-Western sports; doing this will turn the Games into a magnificent multicultural celebration. But the most important task is to reconsider the role and status of the developing countries in the Olympic Movement. Developing countries are vital to the future of the Olympic Movement: 61 percent of the world's territory—and 79 percent of its population—belong to developing countries, and these areas have a rich cultural heritage. For instance, of the thirty-four countries with a rich multilingual tradition (i.e., more than fifty languages in daily use), two thirds are found among the developing countries of Sub-Saharan Africa, South-East Asia, and Oceania. Sub-Saharan Africa alone is home to fourteen of these countries. There is also great treasure in the sport cultures of the developing world.

Looking at the current Olympic Movement, we see that the developing countries have kept quite a low profile, and this has reinforced an image of them as passive beneficiaries who must depend on the generosity of others. Until now, most discussions about promoting the Olympic Movement in the developing countries have been mainly focused on their less developed economic conditions, and consequently, the Olympics is typically viewed as providing benefit *to* these countries, particularly in economic terms, rather than as a potential beneficiary *of* the sports cultures in these countries. Promotion efforts have primarily focused on the economic aspect in the sense to help them to accept the Western oriented sport culture, while their own sport cultures have been neglected. It is rare for people to think how the Olympic Movement could benefit from the great sport cultures of these countries because the stereotyped Olympic model has been deeply stamped on our minds.

The issue of developing countries, and how to include them, presents a big challenge for the Olympic Movement in the twenty-first century. How to let the Movement take deep root in these countries is a question that demands creative new thinking, such as that of Coubertin nearly a century ago. The developing countries inherited a brilliant sport heritage from the preindustrial era, but their traditional sports need to be modernized in order to make them understandable and applicable for intercultural communication. At the same time, the universally respected Olympic ideas should be localized in their expressing patterns, operational forms, and participating approaches.

In this way, universality and diversity may coexist harmoniously within the Olympic Movement; and globalization and diversification may complement each other in ways that will ensure a prosperous future for the Movement.

Conclusion

Spurred by globalization, the Olympic Movement has experienced fast growth during the last several decades, diffusing modern Western sports and their social values to every corner of the world. Cultural homogenization in many areas has caused social displacement—a lack of continuity with traditions and perspectives that gave life meaning, and producing, for many, a feeling of dislocation and alienation. Some societies have reacted by turning inward, toward isolationism and exclusion. Alerted by the trend, the World Bank has insisted that for development "to be inclusive and sustainable, it must nurture the diversity of belief systems and traditions that enhance people's self-images and give them confidence to act in their own interests while respecting and supporting the traditions of other groups" (World Bank 1999).

The momentum of cultural homogenization that has built up within the Movement is not only threatening non-Western sport cultures but also making it difficult for the Movement to reach its ambitious goals of contributing to "building a peaceful and better world." To address this, it is crucial for the Olympic Movement to take more traditional cultural elements from various parts of the world, especially from the developing countries, to ensure cultural diversification. Obviously it is not easy to integrate different sport cultural forms in the Olympic Movement in general and the Olympic Games in particular, as the case of Wushu has indicated. Pierre de Coubertin, the founder of the Olympic Movement, referred to the Olympic Games as a great symbol that ought to be as colorful as the diversified cultures we have inherited. This idea is clearly expressed in the report of the IOC 2000 Commission for Olympic reform in 1999: "In the Olympic Movement, valuing 'universality' should never mean demanding standardized modernization or cultural homogenization, much less Europeanization or Westernization. Proper Olympic education seeks to explore and to celebrate cultural diversity in the Olympic Movement" (IOC 1999b).

NOTE

1. Tae Kwon Do started as a demonstration sport at the 1988 Seoul Games and became an official Olympic sport in the 2000 Sydney Games.

REFERENCES

China.org.cn. 2005. Rogge Says Wushu No "Olympic Sport" in 2008. Xinhua News Agency, October 16. Available at http://www.china.org.cn/en glish/2005/Oct/145502.htm.

Coubertin, Pierre, de. 1967. *The Olympic Idea: Discourses and Essays.* Ed. Carl-Diem-Institut.

enorth.com.cn. 2001. December 29.

International Olympic Committee. 1999a. The Olympic Charter.

International Olympic Committee. 1999b. Report by the IOC 2000 Commission to the 110th IOC Session, Lausanne, 11 and 12 December. Available at http://multimedia.olympic.org/pdf/en_report_588.pdf.

International Olympic Committee. 2000. IOC Highlights of the Week 39. September 25–October 1.

International Olympic Committee. 2001a. IOC Highlights of the Week 6. February 5–11.

International Olympic Committee. 2001b. Report of the IOC Evaluation Commission for the Games of the XXIX Olympiad in 2008. April 3.

International Olympic Committee. 2002a. Prepared Text for the IOC President, Opening Ceremony of the 113th IOC Session. February 3. Available at http://multimedia.olympic.org/pdf/en_report_271.pdf (accessed July 19, 2007).

International Olympic Committee. 2002b. Review of the Olympic Programme and the Recommendations on the Programme of the Games of the XXIX Olympiad, Beijing 2008, Report by the Commission Chairman, Franco Carraro, IOC Executive Board. August 2002. Available at http://multimedia.olympic.org/pdf/en_report_527.pdf (accessed July 19, 2007).

International Olympic Committee. 2002c. Transcript of Press Conference with the IOC President on August 29, 2002. Available at http://multimedia.olympic.org/pdf/en_report_538.pdf.

International Olympic Committee. 2004. Olympic Charter.

IWUF. 2005. Minutes of 8th IWUF Congress. Hanoi, Vietnam, December 9.

2008 Trip: Our Support. n.d. http://travel.ec-t.com/mall/c101/s26079/olympic_support.aspx.

UNDP. 1999. Human Development Report 1999: Globalization with a Human Face, Overview.

World Bank. 1999. *Culture and Sustainable Development: A Framework for Action.* Washington, DC: International Bank for Reconstruction and Development/World Bank.

Xinhua. 2007. Beijing Olympics to Showcase Wushu in Optimal Way. May 30.

"We Are the Media"

Nonaccredited Media and Citizen Journalists at the Olympic Games

Andy Miah, Beatriz García, and
Tian Zhihui

Narratives about the Olympics arise largely from the stories filed by the mass of journalists—press and broadcasters—who attend the Games and spew forth accounts of what occurs on and off the competition ground. Who those journalists are, what they do, how they are channeled through the Olympics world—each has implications for what is represented and what the billions around the globe see and read. As such, the issue of defining who is a journalist, what rights they have, and how they are served and managed is crucial, since it will play an important role in determining control of the platform. Yet it is increasingly understood that the concept of "the journalist" has changed and, with it, the management tasks of the Olympics and its host cities. Our newly expanded concept of the journalist has nevertheless resulted in more than increased demand for media guidance, information, and facilities. It will likely have important implications for what is covered and how. In this chapter, we look at the processes of change in journalism, using the accreditation process at the Olympics as a lens. We also examine the challenges and opportunities this presents to the construction of narrative(s) about and the management of the Games.

Since the 1980s, the International Olympic Committee (IOC) has established guidelines that determine who is accredited as an Olympic journalist. To be an accredited journalist in this context enables privileged access to Games venues and the exclusive right to report the official competitions. However, new technologies and new sources of supply have highlighted the need for new institutions and new protocols. From the Sydney 2000 Games, *nonaccredited* journalists have become a significant component of the Games' journalistic community. And increasingly elaborate arrangements have been developed for the management of this group at both Summer and Winter Games. These arrangements take the form of specially constructed enterprises, which have come to be called Nonaccredited Media Centers. The term *nonaccredited* refers to journalists who *do* receive recognition—an accreditation of sorts from the established center, so they are not simply unaccredited or completely external to the Olympic organizational framework. However, such journalists do not have an official IOC accreditation and cannot access official venues as journalists or cover the sport competitions. This term is most commonly used by the people who organize facilities for such journalists, so it also coheres with the self-characterization of this community. By studying the origins, functions, and development of the Nonaccredited Media Centers, we can gain insight into the shifting world of journalism and how it puts additional narratives into play.

The emergence of nonaccredited journalists highlights the challenges arising from shifts in traditional journalism since, in the absence of IOC guidelines, the criteria for defining a journalist are more fluid. In the context of the Olympics, these shifts have given rise to at least three categories of journalist. The most obvious is the Olympic journalist who would be labeled "accredited," namely those to whom the relevant authorities have given certain rights to cover the Games. A second category would be journalists, traditionally professionalized, who cannot, because of limitations and contractual rights, be included in the full complement of entitlements for those who are accredited but who will be present at the Games and influence mainstream narratives. A third category, closer to the technological and supply side exposition, are those who self-characterize as journalists; this group has a more tenuous relationship to mainstream media, but through blogs and similar devices, may have a greater impact on public understanding of what the Olympics mean and why. At the Torino 2006 Olympic Winter Games, these Web-based journalists were a strong presence at the Nonaccredited Media Center. This was the first occasion in Olympic history where low-budget journalistic operations could broadcast in an effective manner through the Internet (e.g., the audio-visual file-share Web site, YouTube, came online around the end of 2005). Torino demonstrated the challenge posed by such journalists, given the capacity to publish multimedia content through diverse online platforms. Together, the combination of an increased number of journalists who are not accredited to the main facilities and the emergence of new media suggests that the established mechanisms of media representation at the Olympic Games are being reconstituted.

This chapter is based on research that draws on ethnographic, documentation, and interview data collected at the Nonaccredited Media Centers at four consecutive Olympic Games: Sydney 2000, Salt Lake City 2002, Athens 2004, and Torino 2006. The research entailed participant observations, archiving of materials, and interviews of key management personnel at all of these centers. At each of the Games, except for Salt Lake City, we were present at least three days before the opening ceremony of the Olympics. Our analysis of Nonaccredited Media Centers is also based on documents and interviews with officials affiliated with and working within the Beijing Organizing Committee of the Olympic Games (BOCOG), which we used to ascertain the extent of planning for nonaccredited media two years before the 2008 Games.

In this context, the chapter will undertake three main tasks. First, we will discuss the emergence of much more varied and variously regulated media at the Olympics, offering evidence from the last four Olympic Games and contextualizing it with reference to the broader media framework of the Games. These details help to develop an understanding of the Nonaccredited Media Center's character, function, and outcomes. Second, we consider the immediate context of the Beijing Olympic Games, particularly how its new media landscape might look, given its particular cultural and political circumstances. Finally, we discuss how the notion of nonaccredited media fits within broader discussions about new media studies and the challenges posed by the reprofessionalization of journalism via the rise of the citizen journalist.[1]

The Nonaccredited Media Centers (NAMC)

Media Structures at the Olympics

The official media structures at the Olympic Games are the result of a combination of operational and financial need. Ever since the Games' financial crisis of the 1970s and the subsequent restructuring of the Olympic Movement in the 1980s as a commercially viable enterprise,[2] the IOC has treated the media as a crucial Games stakeholder and a key member of what is termed the "Olympic Family,"[3] which includes international sport federations, the athletes, team officials, sponsors, and IOC guests. To secure full coverage of the extremely diverse and concentrated range of Olympic activity during the sixteen days of competition, the host city is required to provide members of the media state-of-the-art working venues (the Main Press Center and the International Broadcasting Center—sometimes described together as the Main Media Center—as well as Venue Media Centers within each of the sport competition venues); a fully equipped Media Village providing meals and accommodation; transport to all official Olympic venues coordinated with the times of competition; and an extensive network of information points with the latest updates on all sports events and competitor backgrounds.

To control the number of media with access to such facilities, the IOC has set a strict accreditation process following similar patterns to that established for the rest of the Olympic Family (IOC 2004, Rule 55). For press writers and photographers, the IOC has set a maximum quota of 5,600 places per Games since Sydney 2000; numbers are allocated per country, with priority to the "main media organizations" (IOC 2006a), which are determined by respective National Olympic Committees. Broadcasting organizations, as the main funders of the Olympic Movement (providing up to 53 percent of all Olympic revenue sources, while sponsors provide up to 36 percent), are treated differently. Because "Television is the engine that has driven the growth of the Olympic Movement" (IOC 2007),[4] broadcasters are not only treated as accredited media, but also as "Olympic right-holders" with access to the core Olympic properties, such as the rings. The IOC states that "rights are only sold to broadcasters who can guarantee the broadest coverage throughout their respective countries free of charge" (IOC 2007), and they are offered in exclusivity to one broadcaster per geographical area. This means that in any one country, there is only one approved official broadcaster and no competing TV channels can offer images of official Olympic events. Broadcast organizations are allocated a set number of accreditations according to the level of funding support. In the period 2004 to 2008, the total number is approximately 14,400 individual accreditations to include presenters and producers as well as technical staff.[5]

The Main Press Center and the International Broadcasting Center operate in different ways, the latter being one of the most inaccessible

Olympic venues, as it holds the strictly protected "moving image" feed of all sport competitions, currently valued at $1.7 billion and available exclusively to right holders. Nevertheless, they share a series of characteristics as the main official accredited media venues: access to each requires full accreditation under strictly limited quotas (requests are made directly to the IOC), and they can only provide information related to official Olympic events, which essentially comprise the Olympic Torch Relay, the Opening Ceremony, each of the official sporting competitions taking place during the sixteen days of the Games, and the Closing Ceremony. Olympic broadcast right holders have access to all Main Press Center facilities, while the press and photographic media cannot enter the International Broadcast Center. Non rights holding broadcasters may be entitled to apply for accreditation at the Main Press Center to access and distribute text-based information about official events, but, as in the case of the press, they cannot gain access to the International Broadcast Center or any moving images. This stipulation also encompasses the distribution of such images in an online environment (IOC 2006b).

The Olympic Charter specifies the IOC's commitment to protecting the media coverage of the Games as well as the technical regulations imposed on journalists for this purpose (IOC 2004, Rule 51). In particular, it identifies the objective of the IOC as to maximize media coverage and for such coverage to "promote the principles and values of Olympism" (IOC 2004, Bye-Law 1). In so doing, the IOC asserts its authority on the media's governance at each Games. Moreover, the host city is bound by these requirements as an integral part of its contract with the IOC. By extension, the IOC also asserts its exclusive rights by stipulating that

> Only those persons accredited as media may act as journalists, reporters or in any other media capacity. . . . Under no circumstances, throughout the duration of the Olympic Games, may any athlete, coach, official, press attaché or any other accredited participant act as a journalist or in any other media capacity. (IOC 2004, Article 51, Bye-Law 3)

It is worth mentioning other ways of regulating what images are transmitted to those in the host city and the world as well. Host governments, at the behest of the IOC, often institute legislation to govern the protection of the Olympic identity. For example, for the London 2012 Olympic Games, the British Government instituted an "Olympic

Bill" (House of Commons 2005). These stipulations reveal that the IOC considers the Games to be its core property, not that of the host city, which is borrowing the association. This indicates aspects of a division in directing the narrative—between the IOC, which is setting the conditions of the stage, and the host city, which is facilitating its orchestration. The Olympic Charter offers further details. Specifically, Rule 53 notes that

> . . . 2 No form of advertising or other publicity shall be allowed in and above the stadia, venues and other competition areas which are considered as part of the Olympic sites. . . .
>
> 3 No kind of demonstration or political, religious or racial propaganda is permitted in any Olympic sites, venues or other areas. (IOC 2004, 101)

The effects of such guidelines are clearly visible in the stadia, where spectators, athletes, and officials are prohibited from doing or wearing anything that might act contrary to this rule. Furthermore, areas of IOC regulation continue to expand. For instance, during recent Olympics, *all* billboard space within the city center and areas surrounding the Olympic venues was offered to Olympic sponsors or else left empty to avoid ambush marketing. In this sense, the entire city is construed as and becomes an "Olympic site."

To understand the full implications of this situation, it is important to note the nature of delivery structures within the Olympic Games. The city authorities are in charge of establishing an Organizing Committee that will deliver the Games according to IOC regulations, but with funding and support from local, regional, and national government agencies. The IOC delimits what is "owned" by the Olympic Movement—thus granting privileged access to members of the Olympic Family—during the period of the Games. Yet, local authorities have also attempted to protect ownership of other spaces that may use the Games as a platform to promote activities other than the official Olympic program and parts of the Olympic program not set as priority by the IOC. The latter include the Cultural Olympiad[6] and education activities, which tend to focus on the representation of local and national identities. The establishment of Nonaccredited Media Centers could be described as one of the most paradigmatic examples of such attempts at protecting ownership by the local hosts of platforms outside the obligations of the Host City Contract and IOC regulations.

325

Dealing with the New Journalistic Masses: From
Sydney 2000 to Torino 2006

Following the establishment of strict Olympic media regulations in the 1980s, the first organized attempt at coping with the large number of journalists outside the official accredited list is found at the Barcelona 1992 Games. The Barcelona City Council recognized the importance of using the Games as a platform for promoting the city and region. It realized that it was fundamental to nourish and attract the attention of media writers from non–Olympic rights holding organizations that would not have access to the sporting venues. As such, it supported the creation of a center within the Barcelona "Welcome Operation," called the Barcelona Press Service. This center was organized in collaboration with the Autonomous University of Barcelona and focused its services on the specialist press and scholars interested in the history of Barcelona and Catalonia, and in particular the Catalan cultural identity. This experience was highly regarded by local authorities and served as the basis for intervention by subsequent Olympic host cities. However, the Barcelona center lacked visibility and relied on very limited technical and financial resources. By the Sydney 2000 Olympic Games, the commitment to such centers had been upgraded considerably. Local authorities raised the priority in terms of expenditure and care in catering to a far wider band of individuals engaged in journalistic activity. And these individuals were encouraged to promote non–sports related stories as a top priority.

In Sydney, the main facility to welcome the broad range of journalistic actors, accredited and nonaccredited, the Sydney Media Center, was situated in the fashionable city center area of Darling Harbour. This Center was the result of a collaboration between the Commonwealth Department of Foreign Affairs and Trade, the Australian Tourism Commission, Tourism New South Wales, the Department of State and Regional Development, and the Sydney Harbour Foreshore Authority. These organizations aimed to enhance the city and regional economic development via the promotion of its leisure and business tourism offerings. Interestingly, the Sydney Media Center was also formed out of concerns that the Atlanta 1996 Games suffered by *not* providing for nonaccredited journalists. As was discussed in an Australian parliamentary debate on the subject:

> As Atlanta found to its cost, if . . . journalists are not looked after by being given good facilities from which to operate, if they are not pro-

vided with assistance in delivering interesting stories, the result is a del-
uge of media coverage critical of the city itself and critical of the
Olympics preparations. We were absolutely determined that this would
not happen in Sydney. (Legislative Assembly 2000, 9070)

As such, the establishment of the Sydney Media Center was both an attempt to promote local causes and a way to ensure that journalists with
no access to the accredited venues had access to other facilities, and
stories. It was a facility-based way of encouraging a broader sense of
what constituted the Olympics narrative and supplementing the work
of the Main Press Center and the International Broadcasting Center,
which were run for the exclusive benefit of the "accredited journalists."
Located at the border of the harbor, the Center provided shooting locations for broadcasters and a spacious bar-restaurant in addition to the
common provision of working and communication facilities, information stands, press releases, daily keynotes, press briefings, promotional
events, and conferences. Some days prior to the start of the Games in
September 2000, the center had registered more than 3,000 media representatives.[7] By the conclusion of the Games, 5,000 journalists had
been accepted at the Media Center (Legislative Council 2000, 9274).
The venue hosted various high-profile events, including athletes' pan-
els and press conferences with key figures from the Opening Ceremony.

In Salt Lake City, provision for the ever broader and technologically
diverse nonaccredited media was distributed between two different
centers, each of which had different purposes and was overseen by different organizations. The Utah Media Center, the direct successor of
the Barcelona innovation, was located in close proximity to the official
Main Media Center in the heart of the city. It was an initiative of the
Utah Travel Council with the support of the Chamber of Commerce
and Visitors and Conventions Bureau in Salt Lake City. A second hub—
the Park City Media Center—was created at the initiative of the Chamber of Commerce and was located in Park City, home of one of the
most popular ski resorts in the area and a central point to access a wide
range of Olympic competition venues. The Utah Media Center was the
largest of the two, and, as in the case of Sydney, it hosted high profile
events such as the only press conference by Rudolph Giuliani, the
mayor of New York City, who discussed the situation in the United
States in the aftermath of 9/11.

In Athens, the main nonaccredited center was located in the
Zappeion Center, directly next to the city's main square, Syntagma.

The Zappeion Press Center was established in a building that had historic value for both the city and the Olympic Movement, as it was the headquarters of the first Modern Olympic Games in 1896. As evidence of the growing relevance of this effort by host cities to go beyond the IOC-approved journalist corps, this Center was far greater in size and political significance than previous versions. The day after the Opening Ceremony, the Zappeion Press Center hosted the formal signing of the Olympic Truce "wall,"[8] which brought heads of state, royalty, and IOC dignitaries to the same press venue. Notably, this took place outside of the normal, expected security requirements of Olympic venues and among the nonaccredited journalists. The Zappeion Center also hosted a number of other important events, such as a presentation for the Melbourne 2006 Commonwealth Games and the presentation of the Cultural Olympiad, which tends to lack media visibility. Each day, there were press briefings by the Ministries of Public Order, Sports, and Culture, and opportunities for journalists to meet athlete celebrities, including Cathy Freeman, the Australian Aboriginal athlete who lit the Olympic cauldron in the Sydney 2000 Games, and the city mayor.

Winter and Summer Olympic hosts always look toward their respective predecessors, and comparing Torino 2006 with Salt Lake City 2002 shows a further increase of provision for the nonaccredited media. The Torino Piemonte Media Center offered unprecedented facilities for journalists, including a vast and richly endowed press room with large-screen projections of athletic events, wireless computing, and gourmet regional cuisine. By 2006, the advance of technology and the social context of reporting had so altered that it is reasonable to suggest that Torino was the first post-Web 2.0 media center. It had a strong representation from online authors and journalists, often, if loosely, described as bloggers. By this time, a number of bloggers had established enough publishing credibility for the organizers to look beyond traditional print and broadcast journalists in determining what efforts should be made to embrace them in official and quasi-official venues. The range of bloggers included local as well as overseas writers, many from Vancouver, the next Winter Olympic host city and one at the forefront of new media development.

The Emergence of the Nonaccredited Media Center

In the previous section, we traced a phenomenon that has had a formal name since the Sydney 2000 Olympics: that is, the Nonaccredited

Media Center. Over the years, some common features have emerged to distinguish these centers. First, they are physically and structurally separate from the major accredited media venues, the Main Press Center and the International Broadcasting Center. In addition, the arrangements for nonaccredited journalists tend to be established by the local host city council and affiliated authorities, rather than the Olympic Organizing Committee. Because of this, the focus of these centers has generally been on the promotion of the local cultural milieu, with an emphasis on tourism and business opportunities, rather than sports (though frequently, screens displaying competitions are focal points for the journalists within the Nonaccredited Media Centers). Also, due to their greater flexibility in the acceptance of users, the nonaccredited centers attract a much wider range of journalists, many of whom are not associated with mainstream media groups. However, these venues are not specifically designed to serve as what has often been called "alternative" or independent media centers (Lenskyj 2002; Neilson 2002), which, as noted by Lenskyj, may facilitate "the organization of (publicly advertised) Olympic-related protest events" (166) and which are "organized by a diverse collective of media activists" (167). While the Nonaccredited Media Centers may include individuals with an overtly anti-Olympic information bent, they are far from being established for that purpose.

Following the success of Sydney, the term *Nonaccredited Media Center* (NAMC) was adopted in Athens, Torino, and Beijing. Despite having been developed outside the official Olympic regulations, the NAMCs have structures and functions that reveal significant commonalities with the form—and thus suggest the potential for a conflict of roles to emerge between them. These commonalities become clear when examining their respective journalist demographics; the characteristics of location, facilities, and stories; and the evolution of an ever-closer relationship with the host city Olympic Organizing Committee.

Journalist Demographics

In contrast to accredited journalists, most of whom represent mainstream media groups, individuals and companies registered at the NAMCs represent a wide variety of organizations, including small outlets such as specialist culture and trade magazines, and community radio stations and independent activist groups, who may have a specific agenda to uncover the most controversial issues emerging during Games time. Furthermore, those at the Nonaccredited Media Center are neither regularly accredited in their own countries nor always professionally trained. Thus, they bring a variety of agendas, demands, experience, and interests to these centers. Those who use these facilities include

- Official IOC accredited journalists who find the location, facilities, and environment more convenient or find the NAMC program of events to be newsworthy.
- Journalists from IOC-accredited media organizations who do not have their own accreditation to the Main Press Center or International Broadcast Center, due to the limited quotas.
- Journalists from mainstream media organizations who do not have official Olympic accreditations.
- Specialist and freelance writers.
- Nonprofessional journalists who have their own publishing outlet.
- Online publishers whose work in online platforms is inseparable from their personal online profile as creative practitioners.
- Nonprofessional "citizen" journalists interested in exploring and portraying alternative impressions of the Games.

Typically, the first four types can be characterized as professional journalists; in the final three categories, far fewer have the marks of professionalism. The last two categories are growing in numbers quite significantly: in Torino, video bloggers (vloggers) were plentiful for the first time. Notably, an increasing number of journalists from Categories 1 and 2 are using the nonaccredited facilities, working within the same environment as journalists from Categories 3–7, who were originally the targeted users.[9] The wide variety of individual backgrounds, and the unique situation of all of these journalists sharing the same facilities and attending the same conferences over a concentrated period of time, offers unexpected opportunities for personal interaction that can lead to quite unusual proceedings. The agenda of a meeting may be radically transformed simply because the interests of the minor press are different; these interactions also raise the possibility of the minor press's capability to influence and transform the agenda of established, mainstream journalists.

Location, Facilities, and Stories

The NAMC tends to be located in a space that is conducive to the city's interest in promoting locally rooted messages. The venue is typically a city center surrounded by relevant cultural attractions and political institutions. In contrast, the accredited centers are located at the main Olympic park area, which is usually outside the city center in new purpose-built facilities. Further, the NAMC tends to emphasize hospitality as much as media information. It is a facility in which those who underwrite it—local and regional authorities as well as corporations—are cajoling as much as hosting, trying to extend the field of vision rather than simply provide access. As a result, the NAMC retains a strong local character, which contrasts sharply with the standardized framework of the Main Press Center and the International Broadcasting Center, where facilities present almost identical features from one Games edition to the next and where stories typically exclude any social, cultural, and political aspects of the local host.

Relationship with "Official" Olympic Structures

The NAMC has no official link to the accredited centers but is increasingly being used to ensure representation of the host city Organizing Committee in non–sporting related issues such as cultural, educational, and environmental matters. For example, one feature that has been integral to the NAMC since Sydney 2000 is a Cultural Olympiad or Olympic Arts Festival press office. This presence is a reflection of the impression that cultural information is marginalized at the Main Media Centers.

The nonaccredited centers have also become hosts of high profile Olympic-related events, such as the Olympic Truce in Athens, and are sites for information about popular Olympic features such as the Medals Plaza during the Winter Games and the LiveSites!—large screens in the open air broadcasting sport as well as concerts and providing free live entertainment. None of these would feature prominently at the accredited media venues. Furthermore, the NAMC has become a hub for official information about Olympic transportation and environmental guidelines.

The increasing level of partnership between these semiofficial or unofficial centers and entire departments or programs within the local Olympic Organizing Committee reveals a trend toward the increasing centrality of the NAMC as a provider of information and media access to relevant dimensions of the Games that are, however, not yet considered a media priority for the IOC. While part of this division has to do with the differing interests of the media—the assumption that local culture and street celebrations are meaningful primarily to local media, whereas elite sport is of global interest—it is also explained through sponsorship structures, which presently do not fund the majority of cultural (nonsport) activities (García 2001).

New Trends, New Media

As demonstrated by the experience in Torino, there are increasing numbers of online journalists present at the Olympics, which presents new opportunities for the NAMC. Some of the fundamental distinctions of Olympic journalism are disrupted by new media, notably the distinction between broadcasters and print media. The collapsing of boundaries is also indicative of the mixed role of new media publishers: they are producers, users, and audiences. Moreover, the process of editorial control is diminished or, at least, replaced by a user-generated agenda, whereby the successful impact of stories is enabled by the syndication of material by the user community.

The IOC has sought to control who can report on the Olympics, but this is increasingly difficult given the emergence of a new community of citizen journalists. So far, athletes and coaches have been forbidden from blogging—or undertaking any practice that could be construed as journalism—during the Olympic fortnight. Regardless of whether this ban on such activities is an unreasonable infringement on the players' rights of self-expression, it is difficult to foresee how such rules can be enforced effectively given the breadth of online publishing that currently exists. Additionally, on-site spectators with high specification telephone cameras are also likely to share firsthand and timely pictures and videos transmitted immediately to their personal blogs and the like. In many cases, this could present a competitive challenge to the fee-paying broadcasters in the struggle for audiences, or at least offer some alternative insight. The impact of new technologies will have to be a particularly prominent issue for China at the Beijing 2008 Games, as it is a country that is considerably advanced in the area of new media innovation, but also imposes specific restrictions on journalistic freedom that are now being contested within the context of the Olympic Games.

The New Media of and in Beijing 2008

Characterizing the subject of new media in the context of China is a multilayered task. First, one can discuss the rise of digital media technologies, as instances of new media proper, in scholarly terms. This would encompass the development of online publishing platforms by established media companies or the emergence of new organizations that are increasingly occupying a stronghold in the dissemination of information and enabling new spaces of communication. A good example of this is the recent emergence of MySpace China (Barboza 2007). However, this category also encompasses discussions over censorship surrounding the presence of, say, YouTube or Google in China. Second, one could speak about the expectant discourse of greater Western media freedom in China as an indication of its new media population. In this regard, the Beijing Olympic Games can be discussed as a mechanism through which this transformation will take place. Third, one must consider the emergence of new media as the disruption of traditional categories of media professions, as with the rise of citizen journalists and the syndication of information via Web 2.0 software. Among these three categories of new media, there is considerable overlap. Already, one can notice how the emergence of on-site amateur photographers is challenging the role of the photojournalist. Thus, the sourcing of images through photo sharing platforms such as flickr.com, using Creative Commons licenses, is evidence of this challenge, particularly when such nonprofessionals are on-site with unrivaled access to a story. Nevertheless, this separation of new media debates in China will enable some distinct points to be made in the context of China generally and the Beijing Olympics specifically.

Beijing's Nonaccredited Olympic Media

Realizing the role the NAMC will play in promoting the historical, cultural, and social elements of Beijing to the world, Beijing's "Service Guide for Foreign Media Coverage of the Beijing Olympic Games and the Preparatory Period" (BOCOG 2007) takes into account provision for the nonaccredited media. In this document, as well as in personal interviews throughout July 2006, the Beijing Organizing Committee of the Olympic Games expressed its intention to host a Nonaccredited Media Center that would accommodate more than 10,000 journalists, including representatives from the more than 2,000 newspapers that exist in China, along with other international media. While this is an interesting development, its implications are not clearly positive. Increased visibility and integration with official structures could lead the NAMC to implement tighter restrictions on access and narrow the range of participants it hosts. In short, one might suppose that this integration within BOCOG is indicative of an attempt to control and restrain the nonaccredited media. However, it might also enable greater and wider journalistic coverage. In support of the positive interpretation of this development, one might cite an interview with Wang Hui, vice-director of BOCOG's media and communications department. Wang emphasized the diversity of media coverage during the Olympics, "as media are concerned not only about who won a gold medal and set a world record during the Olympics, but also about the Olympics hosting country's landscape, the hosting city's characteristics, local people's lives, how they participate in the Olympics" (China.com.cn 2006).

The Beijing Organizing Committee of the Olympic Games suggested that there was some expectation that the NAMC would host professional journalists who did not happen to have access to the Main Press Center and the International Broadcasting Center. In an interview at the Beijing Olympic Media Center, which currently operates as the main point of contact with the press, one journalist from the *China Post* newspaper indicated that the nonaccredited journalists should be professional journalists and have qualifications that would authenticate an application to the NAMC. Yet, as we have suggested in reference to Torino, and given the rise of online usage in China (China Internet Network Information Center 2007), it is unlikely that many of these nonaccredited journalists will be either "professional" in the widely accepted sense or in possession of a national press card. Consequently, while the expectation of the NAMC in Beijing might seem to contradict our expectation, experience at previous Games suggests that these intentions are common when discussed in *advance* of the Games. In each of the cities we have investigated, there was considerably less rigor applied to applications from journalists during Games time itself, as local authorities were pressing to attract publicity about non-Olympic-related causes.

The Beijing Games illustrates a number of other challenges posed by the development of new media in China. For example, one might have concerns about China's capacity to deliver international, online facilities to accommodate the Olympics' new media needs, such as streaming on accredited broadcasters' Web sites. In March 2007, the IOC launched a tender for the sale of the Internet and mobile platform exhibition rights (new media rights) to the Beijing Games, for China's mainland territory. This is the first time that the IOC has separated the sale of television transmission rights from Internet and mobile broadcasting. However, while China endeavors to honor its commitment to the IOC by abiding by the rules of Olympic media coverage, some of its own domestic media management laws and regulations have not been upgraded to meet these commitments. Effective February 2003, China's State Administration of Radio Film and Television (SARFT) instituted the Administrative Measures regarding the Broadcasting of Audiovisual Programs through the Internet and other Information Networks in China, which stipulate that a broadcaster must first apply for a "License to Broadcast Audiovisual Programs by Network" before they can broadcast audiovisual programs through information networks such as the Internet. However, many Internet content providers, such as Sina.com, Sohu.com—the appointed Internet content provider for BOCOG—China Unicom, and QQ, do not have such a "license," which means they may not be able to broadcast under this regulation. At the time of writing, the IOC had not announced the results of the open tender for the rights to broadcast competitions over the Internet. However, in a transcript from Sohu.com in the first quarter of 2007 it indicates that it has no role in the delivery of such content:

> Sohu is the exclusive Internet content provider sponsor for the Beijing 2008 official website, so we are the operator of Beijing2008.com or .cn, for that matter, and all content on that website is provided by Sohu. . . . The new media rights is a separate matter and that is closely tied into with the TV broadcasting rights, so yes, there was a tender but that is separate and distinct from the official website that we operate. So it is almost like TV broadcasting rights in the eyes of the IOC. The outcome of the tender will be known probably—it [*sic*] not during Q2, it will be early Q3. So it is separate and distinct. (Carol Yu, Sohu co-president, chief financial officer, cited in Seeking Alpha 2007)

For the nonaccredited journalist, the implications of this are unclear. While it indicates the IOC's attempt to respond to the potential challenge of online publishing and a recognition that the national television broadcaster is not always best placed to deliver the largest online audience, domestic laws can inhibit this objective. For China, the SARFT regulations indicate that there will be considerable barriers to a non-China-based company delivering such content. Indeed, it is likely that a number of China-based companies will struggle with the regulations. In any case, China-based bloggers—including those who are approved to work from the NAMC—could face unknown penalties for broadcasting material via the Internet, though this is likely to be of concern only in the context of moving sports images. In sum, while it is still unclear what the Chinese Olympic "citizen journalist" might entail, the active Chinese blogs, podcasts, vlogs and so forth are a clear indication of the relevance of such voices in the construction of alternative narratives about China. Moreover, in response to such participation, many mainstream Chinese media companies, such as China Central Television (CCTV), are already engaging in new media practices by adding blogs and podcasting elements to their Web sites.

Discussion: Neither Alternative, Marginal, nor Minor

Nonaccredited Media Centers constitute a mixed zone at the Olympics. They are regulated, but, crucially, they are not official Olympic venues, as the absence of the Olympic rings and the word *Olympic* within the center's branding indicates. As such, they are not subject to the much stricter level of regulation of the Olympic venues. This distinction is important when considering their role in the creation or definition of additional narratives. Moreover, it informs our understanding of what character media coverage of the Games might exhibit. While independent or alternative media centers are sometimes explicitly anti-Olympic, we have been interested in the mixed zones within the Olympic city. In part, this is because there appear to be opportunities from within the system to challenge the dominant media structures. We are not convinced that this has happened through the NAMCs, but the potential is certainly present. Their more relaxed accreditation process, the governmental involvement and capacity to gain access for media to important political and cultural events, and the demographics of journalists present provides a rich set of circumstances through which the highly regulated media structures at the Games can be circumvented.

Furthermore, the NAMC has become an integral part of a host city's programming, though its establishment is not a formal requirement within the IOC Host City contract. Indeed, its existence poses a potential compromise to a range of stakeholders who finance the Games, though it offers a major platform on which the host city can stage itself. To this extent, its position would appear to favor a degree of invisibility at IOC level. If it were to become too successful at influencing TV coverage or column space, Olympic media rights holders might question its legitimacy and even claim breach of contract. Yet, the local authorities benefit considerably from a high-profile NAMC. Indeed, the host city has no such commitment to the long-term relationship of media rights holders to the IOC. Rather, the host's preferred position is to utilize a NAMC as best it can to ensure an overall, positive long-term legacy for the city.

The information provided by NAMCs is essentially different from what is available in the Main Press Center or International Broadcasting Center, but it is not irrelevant in the context of the Games. The sporting focus of the main Olympic media venues may have limited the ability of journalists to gather a detailed understanding of the host community and its potential legacy. Moreover, followers of sporting events seem increasingly interested in security issues, environmental policies, and the social acceptance and sustainability of the event. This makes a case for the provision of information beyond sporting results, Olympic ritual, and athletes' biographies, which are the only explicit media priority for the IOC.

The NAMC as the Institutionalization of New (Olympic) Media

There are an important number of distinctions that need unraveling in the context of the nonaccredited media. First, we might arrive at a reconceptualization of the Olympic media, which can be broken down into three general categories: accredited (those at the International Broadcast Center or Main Press Center), nonaccredited (those at the NAMC), and unaccredited (those at the Independent or Alternative Media Centers, as well as those acting as citizen journalists).

Second, it is necessary to consider the range of ways in which each of these types of journalists contributes to or detracts from the established Olympic narratives. While we might describe the accredited facilities as those that communicate the official IOC narratives, the nonaccredited media centers offer an additional, city-oriented narrative, which has the potential to supplement or compete with the coverage of the former. As such, while one might expect that the local Organizing Committee and the host city should be working toward, mostly, the same goals as the IOC, in practice, each is competing for different kinds of (positive) narratives (and different kinds of media attention). While for the IOC, the Olympic Games is an opportunity to showcase and reinforce the Olympic brand as a global entity, for the host city, the Games as a global brand is an opportunity to showcase its local characteristics.

Third, one of the crucial clarifications that must be addressed throughout this unraveling is the dual process of institutionalization and destabilization associated with the NAMCs. The NAMCs are agents of institutionalization insofar as they are attempts to manage journalists who are external to the Olympic accreditation process and who might, as a result of being unmanaged, negatively portray the Olympics. However, as a result of this process, the NAMCs also risk their stability, since their greater visibility can become a conflict for the exclusive, rights-holding arrangements set up via the Main Media Centers. Presently, the NAMC exists because of the lack of concern from within the Olympic infrastructure to market the city.

Finally, there are two important points to think about in relation to the emergence of new media in general and the citizen journalist specifically. Since Torino, new questions have arisen from the growth of blogging and video blogging as a means of reporting the Games. Admittedly, one cannot assume that bloggers are politically minded or even journalistic in their style of reporting. Indeed, in the context of the Olympics, it is not obvious that "new media" denotes "countermedia," although it is true that a range of new activists are visible due to this phenomenon. While there may be an increasing number of vloggers or bloggers at the Games, they will not all be concerned with criticizing them. Many will most likely want simply to celebrate them. Second, while we suggest that new media platforms have the potential to subvert established media channels, old media are increasingly recognizing the need to *become* new media. A good indication of this is the purchase of YouTube channels by a number of established broadcasters around the world. As this trend develops, the distinction between old and new media—along with new media's subversive potential—might similarly disappear, though we anticipate that the Internet will continue to give rise to resistant structures.

Regardless, we argue that the various complexities of the NAMC will challenge how media coverage of the Games takes place and thus also what the Games themselves mean to nations and people. To the extent that the Olympic Games aspires to be a publicly shared media event, our proposition has been that the NAMC provides a crucial mechanism through which a valuable democratization of the media is taking place, while maintaining the financial infrastructure upon which the Games rely. In some sense, we can describe journalism at the NAMC as a form of *ambush media*—a phenomenon that involves infiltrating the privileged position of traditional media organizations either within a fixed media event or through new media publishing spaces and, usually, a combination of the two. Ambush media implies three key processes: *piggyjacking*[10] on the intellectual property of traditional media to generate competing publicity, turning the cameras on traditional media in action and then broadcasting the results, and infiltrating spaces that are reserved for traditional media. There are many ways in which this latter phenomenon occurs, including the simple act of allowing accredited journalists to enter a non–IOC regulated media space where they will learn about less visible Olympic activities, such as the Olympic Truce and non-Olympic but relevant local host-related activities. However, the NAMC is also a space where nonprofessional journalists can broadcast and write about the Games, thus providing opportunities for a wider range of questions to be asked during the actual event. In this sense, our title for this chapter, "We Are the Media," draws attention to the growing demand for citizen journalism to be given political recognition from institutions and governments and, importantly, the growing acceptance of this recognition. These changes have consequences for how society is (dis)ordered via the media and, indeed, raise questions about whether the notion of a "media event" (Dayan and Katz 1992) is undermined by these new forms of interrogation.

Conclusion

We began this chapter by asking what stories the nonaccredited media tell and what role they have in the construction of the Olympic media event. We have explored the processes through which new kinds of media have become part of the Olympic infrastructure and highlighted the tensions this provokes. In comparison to the accredited journalists, the nonaccredited media are fed different stories, they have different expectations, and they work for different kinds of media organizations. Even without knowing much about what is actually published or broadcast by this community, it is clear that, for such media, the Olympics is not really a sporting event. Rather, it is a moment of intense formal and informal cultural and political presentations and representations.

When examining the evolution of the NAMC, it is remarkable to see how the initiative has progressed from a very modest service in Barcelona whose major asset was the support of a university and whose focus was the press media, to the large venues of recent Games, which provide a wide variety of broadcast services under the auspices of generous tourism boards and other local bodies. The sheer magnitude of these facilities is also intriguing because of the unique political space that they occupy within the organizational structure of the Olympic Games, which is framed by a powerful media mechanism.

We have made a number of claims in this chapter. Our initial premise was that the NAMC—more than the International Broadcast Center or the Main Press Center—is the best place to influence the local and national legacy of the Olympic Games, since it is the key venue that undertakes domestic political communications during Games time. To this extent, it provides an essential space for the host city to orchestrate its narrative, a space that is not offered through the other media venues. It is also a space where new media communities can access structures of governance directly. Yet, we also suggest that the emergence of online publishing and broadcasting, along with the growing prominence of the NAMC, threatens this position. Indeed, one might suggest that these centers might soon die out, before they have really begun to establish the value of their contribution to the presentation of an Olympic city. For now, the Nonaccredited Media Centers are non–Olympic Games time venues where culture, media, and politics collide in ways that are often left unresolved.

As the Beijing Olympic Games approaches, some clear nuances to this discussion are evident. These concern the particular position of media organizations and professions within China during the Games. We note that the new legislation on greater media freedom is directed only toward *foreign* journalists (*China Daily* 2006). Moreover, Beijing's NAMC is being hosted by the Olympic Organizing Committee. Initial arrangements suggest that the registration process will be strict and only granted to professional journalists, though this might change during Games time. The effect of this might be greater limitations on new media journalists, many of whom could be dissuaded from using the NAMC. Equally, China's burgeoning new media population indicates a willingness to engage such communities and one would expect this to shape the NAMC structures before the Games begin.

For the subsequent Olympic cities of Vancouver and London, there is even greater reason to emphasize the changing technological media culture and consider the prospects. During the Torino Games, new media journalists from Vancouver, looking toward the 2012 Games, considered the continued necessity of providing a centralized facility for citizen journalists, given that the increased accessibility of free, publicly available, wireless Internet access somewhat reduces the need for a physical facility. Our expectation is that its role for citizen journalists will be determined by the degree to which such individuals see themselves as either more *citizen* or more *journalist*. However, the notion of a center—where press conferences, key officials, and press officers are located—will continue to have value, since the simple presentation of information will not be sufficient to facilitate the sharing of and access to relevant stories. To this extent, even the strongest claims about virtual societies should not be seen as a replacement for real space interactions. Indeed, one must look toward traditional practices within all forms of journalism to understand that the journalist's presence at the center of an event is a crucial element of its authenticity, originality, and legacy.

The difficulty, we believe, is that these rich and complex social spaces are unlikely to remain outside of the IOC's scrutiny, though the challenge is to convince the IOC that this set of developments can be valuable. Based on the current model, there is no reason to suppose that further integration with IOC venues is likely, since sponsorship negotiations only ensure access to the sports news and venues, which are not the interest of the NAMC. Indeed, integration could lead to undesirable consequences, as it would overburden already saturated Olympic media structures. Moreover, it would most likely be overly restrictive and, potentially, be a disincentive for prospective Olympic cities to bid for the Games, as they might find themselves without the desired platform to promote themselves. Yet the increasing prominence of the NAMC could be seen as detracting from the value media organizations purchase when requesting exclusivity on access to information. If this becomes the perception—which we emphasize, it should not—then one could envisage the end of the Nonaccredited Media Center, as it is currently known.

NOTES

The title of this chapter is from a sticker on the cover of an Apple PowerBook notebook belonging to a Nonaccredited Media Center journalist at the Torino 2006 Winter Games. It refers to the Web site by the same name. Research for this chapter was made possible by the generous support of the British Academy.

1. We do not claim that journalism is deprofessionalized via new media, as this would neglect the advanced skills, ethics, and integrity of so-called citizen journalists. Instead, our reprofessionalization refers to the expansion of journalistic expertise that is achieved by the democratization of technology and publishing channels.

2. The Montreal 1976 Games bankrupted the city and led to a void in the number of applications to host subsequent Games. To confront this crisis, the IOC was forced to revise its core structures and, under the leadership of its new president, Juan Antonio Samaranch, established a model to protect the economic viability of the Games. In the 1980s, the Olympic Games were established as a commercial enterprise with highly regulated protection of its main brand elements. The commercial model for the Olympics relied on two main factors: commercial sponsorship—the TOP program—and, more importantly, broadcasting media rights. Broadcast right holders and sponsors would thus become the main source of funds for the Games and the Olympic Movement at large, and the protection of their interests one of the main tasks of the IOC under its Olympic marketing program.

3. The Olympic Family is defined as the group of organizations involved in promoting the Olympic Movement, which is governed by the IOC. The main Olympic Family member organizations include: the IOC as top governing body; International Federations (IFs); National Olympic Committees (NOCs); respective Organizing Committees for the Olympic Games (OCOGs); national sport associations and sports clubs; national sport teams (comprising the athletes and officials invited to attend respective Games); the main Olympic sponsors (TOP); and Olympic-accredited media, including the press, photographers, and broadcast right-holding organizations.

4. TV rights revenue for the Beijing Olympic Games is estimated at $1,707 million, of which 51 percent is retained by the IOC and 49 percent is directly allocated to the OCOG for the hosting of the Games (IOC 2007).

5. For more on this, see http://www.fouryearstovancouver.com/pb/wp_7882380d/wp_7882380d.html.

6. The IOC specifies that Olympic host cities must organize a program of cultural activities. Since the Barcelona 1992 Games, these programs have taken the form of Cultural Olympiads, covering the four years linking the end of one Winter or Summer Games edition with the next, to present arts and cultural festivals (see García 2001).

7. Figures about attendance at the NAMCs are presented in various forms, including overall visitors per day and total number of registered journalists. The former number is expectedly a much higher figure, which might account for why a report to the British Government as part of fact-finding for the London 2012 Games indicated that there were 20,000 journalists at the Sydney Media Center. This might represent the total number of visits from journalists during the entire Games period to the SMC. However, the total

number of registered journalists is closer to the 5,000 figure indicated at the Legislative Council.

8. Olympic Truce is the IOC's revival of the Ancient Olympic tradition of *Ekexeiria*, which involved an agreement between different regions of Greece to cease conflicts and allow athletes safe passage to Olympia to compete in the Games. The modern version, revived in 1992, aspires to achieve the cessation of global military actions during the time of the Games. It is perhaps the most fundamental link between the IOC and the United Nations, which, every two years, receives a declaration from the IOC president requesting heads of state to observe the Olympic Truce. The signing of the wall by dignitaries is supposed to indicate support for this Truce, though some would regard it as politically inconsequential.

9. By the end of the first week of the 2004 Games, the organizers of the NAMC in Athens claimed that 300 Main Press Center accredited journalists were regularly using their facilities (Zappeion Center Director, personal interview, Athens 2004).

10. This phrase is borrowed from Elihu Katz, who proposed it in the context of a discussion at the Annenberg School of Communication. The term was meant to imply a combination of piggybacking and hijacking and, while meant as a joke, it seems as good a term as any to describe the process. It satisfactorily characterizes the process of capitalizing on the work of official media (hijacking), without intending an obvious corruption of that official journalism or any specific harm to it, hence piggyjacking.

REFERENCES

Barboza, David. 2007. Murdoch Is Taking MySpace to China. *New York Times*, April 27. Available at http://www.nytimes.com/2007/04/27/business/worldbusiness/27myspace.html?ex=1180929600&en=73ecc1e22a92a041&ei=5070 (accessed May 2, 2007).

BOCOG. 2006. BOCOG Will Provide Quality Service for News Media: Liu Qi. Beijing. Available at http://en.beijing2008.cn/72/26/column212022672.shtml.

BOCOG. 2007. Service Guide for Foreign Media Coverage of the Beijing Olympic Games and the Preparatory Period.

Castells, Manuel. 1996. The Rise of the Information Society. Oxford: Blackwell.

China.com.cn. 2006. http://www.china.com.cn/book/zhuanti/qkjc/txt/2006-12/28/content_ 569843.htm.

China Daily. 2006. Foreign Reporters Free to Report in 2008. January 12.

China Daily. 2007. China Has 20.8 Million Bloggers. January 11. Available at http://www.chinadaily.com.cn/bizchina/2007-01/11/content_781038.htm (accessed May 2, 2007).

China Internet Network Information Center. 2007. Statistical Survey Report on the Internet Development in China.

Dayan, Daniel, and Elihu Katz. 1992. *Media Events: The Live Broadcasting of History.* Cambridge: Harvard University Press.

Debord, Guy. [1967] 1994. *The Society of the Spectacle.* New York: Zone Books.

García, Beatriz. 2001. Enhancing Sports Marketing through Cultural and Arts Programmes: Lessons from the Sydney 2000 Olympic Arts Festivals. *Sports Management Review* 4 (2): 193–220.

García, Beatriz. 2004. Urban Regeneration, Arts Programming, and Major Events: Glasgow 1990, Sydney 2000, and Barcelona 2004. *International Journal of Cultural Policy* 10 (1): 103–18.

García, Beatriz. 2005. De-constructing the City of Culture: The Long Term Cultural Legacies of Glasgow 1990. *Urban Studies* 42 (5–6): 841–68.

House of Commons. 2005. London Olympics Bill.

IOC. 2004. The Olympic Charter. Lausanne: International Olympic Committee.

IOC. 2006a. Beijing 2008—Press Accreditation Announcement. Lausanne: International Olympic Committee.

IOC. 2006b. IOC Internet Guidelines for the Written Press and Other Non-Rights Holding Media: XX Olympic Winter Games, Torino 2006.

IOC. 2007. Marketing Revenue. Broadcast Rights. Available at http://www.olympic.org/uk/organisation/facts/revenue/broadcast_uk.asp (accessed May 31, 2007).

Kellner, Douglas. 2003. *Media Spectacle.* New York: Routledge.

Legislative Assembly of New South Wales. 2000. Sydney 2000 Olympic Games. Australian Government, October 11.

Legislative Council of New South Wales. 2000. Minutes. Australian Government, October 13.

Lenskyj, Helen J. 2002. *The Best Olympics Ever? Social Impacts of Sydney 2000.* New York: State University of New York Press.

Miah, Andy. 2000. Virtually Nothing: Re-evaluating the Significance of Cyberspace. *Leisure Studies* 19 (3): 211–25.

Miah, Andy. 2003. (e)text: Error . . . 404 Not Found!, or the Disappearance of History. *Culture Machine* 5 (The e-issue).

Mitchell, Don. 2000. *Cultural Geography: A Critical Introduction.* Oxford: Blackwell.

Mitchell, William J. 1995. *City of Bits: Space, Place, and the Infobahn.* Cambridge: MIT Press.

Moragas, Miquel de. 1992. Los Juegos de la Comunicación: Las múltiples dimensiones comunicativas de los Juegos Olímpicos. Madrid: FUNDESCO.

Moragas, Miquel de, N. Rivenburgh, and F. Larson. 1995. *Television in the Olympics.* London: John Libbey.

Neilson, Brett. 2002. Bodies of Protest: Performing Citizenship at the 2000 Olympic Games. *Continuum: Journal of Media and Cultural Studies* 16 (1): 13–25.

People's Daily Online. 2007. 480 Million Mobile Phone Users in China. April

25. Available at http://english.people.com.cn/200704/25/eng20070425_369708.html (accessed May 12, 2007).

Seeking Alpha. 2007. Sohu.com Q1 2007 Earnings Call. Transcript, May 2. Available at http://china.seekingalpha.com/article/34174 (accessed July 2007).

Li Weitao. 2007. Internet Users to Log in at World No. 1. *China Daily.* Available at http://www.chinadaily.com.cn/china/2007-01/24/content_790 804.htm (accessed April 30, 2007).

Zhang, Lena L. 2006. Behind the "Great Firewall": Decoding China's Internet Media Policies from the Inside. *Convergence: The International Journal of Research into New Media Technologies* 12 (3): 271–91.

Zhihui, Tian. 2005. The Chinese Blogger. Media and Society in China Today: China Media Centre Founding Conference, Harrow Campus, University of Westminster.

Definition, Equivocation, Accumulation, and Anticipation

American Media's Ideological Reading of China's Olympic Games

Sonja K. Foss and
Barbara J. Walkosz

To construct and display itself to its own members and to an external audience, a culture or nation employs many types of texts—legible events or objects—including museums, historic homes and districts, rituals and ceremonies, architecture, shrines, sports events, and artistic performances. Such texts are purposefully used as symbolic resources by the community, engaging the past to forge an image that is "profoundly constitutive of identity, community, and moral vision" (Phillips 2004, 90).

Nowhere is the symbolic function of cultural display more evident than at the Olympic Games. Host nations use the Games "to emphasize [their] claims to having a leading status, mission, and destiny in the world international order and world history" (Roche 2000, 10). Because the Olympics provides the sponsoring country with the opportunity to highlight its achievements to the world (Beck and Bosshart 2003), the Games act as a "potent cultural resource with real implications for international relations and the domestic interest of nation states" (Polumbaum 2003, 57).

The 2008 Olympic Games in Beijing provide an extraordinary opportunity for China to display its culture, ideology, and values to a global audience. China has defined its objectives for sponsoring the Games as being to create "a New Beijing" and to host "a Green Olympics, a High-Tech Olympics, a People's Olympics" (Kolatch 2006). The official theme

346

of the Olympic Games, "One World, One Dream," suggests that China also seeks to position itself as a member of the global community, where it can create a "bright future with the rest of the world" ("One World" 2007). China "considers the Olympics to be modern China's coming-out party to the rest of the world" (Yardley 2005a, 4), and by "taking on the Olympics, China committed itself to demonstrating that it is a world-class power." Its primary objective now is "to impress the world, by whatever means necessary" (Lubow 2006, 68).

China's capacity to accomplish its objectives in hosting the Olympic Games is not, however, entirely under its control. The construction and presentation of its activities in advance of the Olympics is mitigated by media coverage, the primary means by which cultural display is disseminated, particularly to foreigners. The media invite audiences "to understand the world in certain ways, but not in others" (O'Connor and Downing 1995, 16) by framing information to "*select some aspects of a perceived reality and make them more salient in a communicating text, in such a way as to promote a particular problem definition, causal interpretation, moral evaluation, and/or treatment recommendation* for the item proposed" (Entman 1993, 52). As they reinforce, transform, diminish, or ignore the messages China seeks to communicate about itself to the world, then, the media offer "preferred social, cultural, political, and economic meanings" (Danner and Walsh 1999, 64) that easily can become hegemonic in their "symbolic power to map or classify the world for others" (Hall 1988, 44).

In this chapter, we explore the preferred meaning that is being advanced by elite American media concerning China's preparation for the 2008 Olympic Games. To this end, we employ ideological analysis, which focuses on patterns of beliefs that determine a group's interpretations of some aspect(s) of the world and that reflect a group's "fundamental social, economic, political or cultural interests" (van Dijk 1998, 69). As critics make visible the dominant ideology embedded in a particular discursive construction, they are able to discover its preferred reading, what it asks audiences to believe or understand, the arguments it makes, and the ways of seeing it commends. Equally important, an ideological analysis can reveal what a discursive construction does not want audiences to think about or the ways of seeing it asks audiences to avoid (Foss 2004).

The data for our analysis are the eighty-four articles concerning China's preparation for the 2008 Olympics that appeared in the *New York Times* and the *Wall Street Journal* between January 2003, and May

2007. We selected these newspapers as our data because both are widely distributed national newspapers, which means that the issues deemed newsworthy by these newspapers often set the agenda for other Western media outlets, including television, radio, and other newspapers (Dearing and Rogers 1996). Both are highly respected: the *New York Times* is considered the "principal newspaper of record in the United States" (Merrill 1983, 310), and the *Wall Street Journal* is viewed as a leading source of business and financial news in the United States. Because they "provide a site and forum for elite discourse, and produce policy and intellectual discourse for elite consumption" (Lee 2002, 345), they constitute elite American media that are likely to be highly influential in the construction of a hegemonic ideology concerning China (Lee 2002).

An understanding of the ideology behind the discursive construction of China by elite American media is important because of the potential for far-reaching consequences of such a construction. Informed publics often adopt elite cues in the news and utilize those cues to structure their perceptions about specific issues (Zaller 1992). The particular frame used to construct media coverage will affect, for example, whether China achieves its objectives of impressing the world with the Games and positioning itself as a legitimate member of the global community. In addition, the narrative constructed by the media will affect the perceptions of China by Americans and the larger global community, including the nature of outsiders' interactions with the Chinese, their views of Chinese products, and their definitions of themselves vis-à-vis the Chinese.

What we suggest in this chapter is that the elite American media use China's cultural displays in advance of the Olympic Games to construct four ideological spaces—those of definition, equivocation, accumulation, and anticipation. Each of these spaces allows the media to set up a tension between two options concerning a major exigence, something the media identify as "waiting to be done, a thing which is other than it should be" (Bitzer 1968, 6); according to the media construction, each exigence remains unresolved in the space created. We turn now to an explication of each space, followed by a discussion of the reassurance function that we argue these spaces perform for media consumers.

Space of Definition

A major space that is being created in the discursive construction of China by American media is that of definition, which focuses on what

Beijing and China will be like in the future. The exigence that creates this space is the tension between the familiarity and comfort of the West and the uniqueness of Chinese culture. This exigence, the mediated narrative suggests, requires a balance between the desire for China to be much like Westerners' home spaces—comfortable and nonthreatening—and the desire to experience and appreciate what makes China unique. In the space of definition, the key issue, then, is the nature of the "place consciousness" (Glassberg 1996, 18) that China will create.

China as Western

One of the options in the tension that constitutes the space of definition is for China to become Western. American media's coverage of China's cultural displays in advance of the Olympics suggests support for this option in a number of ways. The one that is receiving the most attention is the "demolition of many of the city's old 'hutong' neighborhoods, the ancient, densely populated enclaves of narrow, winding streets and crumbling courtyard homes." The result has been the dislocation of "untold thousands of people, to make room for the thousands of development projects swallowing the city" (Yardley 2006b).

The demolition is exemplified in stories about the historic neighborhood of Qianmen, "once the domain of Qing Dynasty opera singers and classical scholars." One of the last intact hutongs, Qianmen is "home to teachers, shop owners, migrant workers and other working-class people." Because it has fallen into disrepair, however, "many residents believe that officials do not want the neighborhood to be an eyesore at the center of the city during the Olympics." One story quotes a resident who analyzes the situation in this way: "This neighborhood is the face of Beijing to the world. They don't want foreigners to see this scarred old face." As a result, one reporter observers, Qianmen is now "an eerie picture of destruction. Ancient homes lie in rubble. Scavengers squat in alleyways and wait to ransack vacated buildings" (Yardley 2006b).

The presentation of China as part of the West is also evident in coverage of its demolition of archaeological sites. The construction being done for the Olympics is "uncovering so many antiquities that it might be considered a golden era for archaeology—except that sites and antiquities are often simply demolished by bulldozers or looted." The president of the China Archaeological Society, Xu Pingfang, is quoted in one story with an explanation for what is happening in China:

"There are two enemies of antiquity protection. Construction is one. Thieves are the others. They know what they want, and they destroy the rest." The media note that developers and local officials often side-step rules concerning the treatment of archaeological sites "partly because surveys and excavations can be time-consuming and create costly construction delays" (Yardley 2007a). Because archaeological sites delay the construction of modern cities, the news stories suggest, they are often destroyed without excavation so that China may more quickly achieve its goal of Westernization.

The American media's narrative of China as becoming Western can be seen as well in their discussion of the "eye-popping physical transformation of China" through its "craze for theatrically expressive schemes by famous architects." Acknowledging that Chinese "architects were not yet up to the challenge, the Chinese had imported the best the West could offer" to create Western-style buildings. Several factors are cited as facilitating China's embrace of Western architecture: "Cheap labor, at least as much as an unfettered outlook, permits the flourishing in China of avant-garde architecture, with its penchant for original engineering, unorthodox materials and surprising forms." Not all the results have been successful, the media note: the "National Theater is generally seen as a grotesquely inappropriate building on a supremely sensitive site." One story provides an explanation for the less successful architectural results by quoting Peng Pei Gen, an architecture professor: "They couldn't do this in their own country, so they are taking advantage of the Chinese psychology that European thinking is better" (Lubow 2006, 68).

China is also depicted as achieving a Western look because of the kinds of commercial establishments that are taking the place of historic neighborhoods—businesses such as "[n]ightclubs, bars and art galleries." In the area of Houhai, one story reports, "20 or 30 bars all opened up" in one summer; one of these nightclubs is described in detail as "a lounge with a modern décor and a cool minimalist patio," while another is shown as a place where customers come "to dance to the different D.J.'s and drink cocktails like Chivas Regal with green tea" (Yang 2005, 7).

Other typically American institutions that are being introduced into China to make it a more familiar place to Westerners are featured in the news stories. Articles discuss Super 8 Hotels' opening of "six franchise hotels in China, including three in Beijing" (Conlin 2006, 2) as well as the fact that Ticketmaster "won the exclusive contract to supply tickets" for the Olympic Games (Silver 2006). Westerners also will recognize the regional airline on which they fly within China, media coverage notes, because of Mesa Air Group's launch of a regional airline in China in conjunction with Shenzhen Airlines ("U.S. Carrier" 2006).

The disciplining of Chinese citizens to Westernize the country is also the subject of coverage by the media. Much attention has been paid to China's initiation of a campaign to curb public spitting, "a frequent practice in Beijing and even more common elsewhere in China. Health officials, worried about communicable disease, have long tried to curb public spitting, with limited success, given that many people do not consider it unacceptable behavior." The media report that hundreds of volunteers have joined the group known as the *Green Woodpecker Project,* named for the woodpecker's practice of picking up worms and cleaning up the forest. The group members are quoted as saying they want "to clean up the city the same way," which they do by carrying "tissues, which they offer to people as an alternative to spitting on the ground, and try to convince the offender, usually male, to change his ways" (Yardley 2007b).

Yet another way in which China is presented as trying to imitate the West is by cleaning up its English translations: "English translations on signs are considered fashionable and good advertising, as well as a gracious gesture to foreigners baffled by Chinese characters," but many of the translations are poorly done. News stories provide examples of poor translations such as "Racist Park" as the English name for a theme park about China's ethnic minorities and "Sexually Inexperienced Chicken" on menus to describe pullet, a hen less than a year old. The stories applaud Beijing's announcement of "new standards and official translations that can be used on more than 2,000 different types of signs, as well as on menus" (Yardley 2007b) and tell of teams of linguists that will patrol Beijing's public places to cleanse the city of its "often comical English translations" (Fong 2007).

China as Unique

Although a key focus of American media coverage of China's cultural displays is to portray Beijing as a thoroughly modern city devoid of an Asian heritage, the constructed narrative also features China's heritage and its uniqueness as a culture. Although some archaeological sites are being demolished, the narrative asserts, others are not. Archaeological projects, which suggest a reverence for Chinese history, are reported to be "under way all over China," and excavation of archaeological sites is encouraged in many ways, the articles note. They report that a network of government antiquity bureaus "has been established throughout the provinces and major cities. Chinese law also requires that real estate developers receive approval from the local antiquity bureau before proceeding with work." The Olympic site is presented as "an example of how China's antiquities protection system should work" in that "organizers have been careful to work with preservationists." At the sites for the main Olympic stadiums, one story reports, archaeological remains were discovered "tracing back 2,000 years to the Han Dynasty. In all, archaeologists excavated 700 ancient burial sites and recovered 1,538 artifacts, including porcelain urns and jade jewelry, while collecting more than 6,000 ancient coins" (Yardley 2007a).

China is also depicted as unique in articles that note the construction of many new museums designed to showcase key aspects of Chinese culture. Around the country, reporters explain, 1,000 new museums are planned to feature the history of oil lamps, beer, salt and piped water, aerospace, typhoons, tree roots, and smoking. The 2,300 museums that currently exist in China do not compare, news stories note, with the number of museums in developed nations, "especially with China's long history" (Fong 2006b).

There is yet another way in which the media depict China's embrace of its heritage in the space of definition, and that is in the discussion of the Chinese allusions that abound in the most visible buildings being created for the Olympics. The headquarters of CCTV, the national television company, for example, is reported to have been designed to suggest a "calligraphic swoop," while the "airport terminal bears an unmissable resemblance" to a dragon, "a beast revered in traditional Chinese architecture and folklore"; its use of the "imperial colors red and gold" also is noted in media coverage. The bird's nest analogy for the main stadium is described as referencing Chinese culture: "In China, a bird's nest is very expensive, something you eat on special occasions" (Lubow 2006, 85).

The tension that creates the space of definition in the media culture is between transformation of China, and Beijing, in particular, into a modern, Western space that will be familiar to foreign visitors and the preservation and highlighting of China's unique culture. As they do not resolve and, in fact, reinforce the tension between these two options, the media suggest that Beijing can be modern and familiar at the same time that it is historic and unique.

Space of Equivocation

A second space that is created by the American media's presentation of China is a space of equivocation, marked by deliberate ambiguity or evasiveness. This is the space that China's political leaders are shown to occupy, and the focus in this space is on human rights issues. The exigence created in the narrative that constructs this space is the tension between China's meeting of global human rights standards and the sovereignty of Chinese officials to run China's affairs as they choose, which sometimes means controlling Chinese citizens and foreigners. If the political leaders resist global demands and standards for human rights too vigorously, the media observe, they risk losing their place in the global community; if they acquiesce too much to those demands and standards, they lose their power within China.

China as a Violator of Human Rights

One of the major human rights issues that creates the tension in the space of equivocation concerns China's relationship with Darfur in Sudan. The problem is summarized in one article in this way: "China has been criticized for giving strong financial and diplomatic backing to the government of Sudan, which the Bush administration and critics worldwide say has practiced genocide in its southern Darfur region while waging a war against secessionists there" (Kahn 2007c). Another story explains that at least "200,000 people—some say as many as 400,000—mostly non-Arab men, women and children, have died and 2.5 million have been displaced, as government-backed Arab militias called the janjaweed have attacked the local population" (Cooper 2007).

Only three articles about China's economic relationship with Sudan have appeared in the *New York Times* and the *Wall Street Journal* during the time period of our analysis, and one features actor Mia Farrow and her son, Ronan Farrow. An op-ed they coauthored is printed in the *Wall Street Journal,* and their explanation of the relationship between China and Sudan is the most detailed provided in either newspaper: "China is pouring billions of dollars into Sudan. Beijing purchases an overwhelming majority of Sudan's annual oil exports and state-owned China National Petroleum Corp.—an official partner of the upcoming Olympic Games—owns the largest shares in each of Sudan's two major oil consortia. The Sudanese government uses as much as 80% of proceeds from those sales to fund its brutal Janjaweed proxy militia." They also note that China "has used its veto power on the U.N. Security Council to repeatedly obstruct efforts by the U.S. and the U.K. to introduce peacekeepers to curtail the slaughter" (Farrow and Farrow 2007).

That Darfur and the Olympics could collide in the space of equivocation is depicted primarily through the lens of celebrities' activities. In addition to the Farrows, Ira Newble, a professional basketball player with the Cleveland Cavaliers (Beck 2007), and film director Steven Spielberg (Cooper 2007) are cited to create the narrative that "China must use its influence with Sudan's government to improve the situation in Darfur or face a possible backlash against its serving as host of the Games" (Kahn 2007c). Such celebrity protagonists are positioned in the narrative as threatening to shut down the Olympics by disseminating labels such as "Genocide Olympics" to describe the Games (Cooper 2007). The response of the Chinese foreign minister, Yang Jiechi, appears inconsequential in juxtaposition to the star power of the cited celebrities: "There is a handful of people who are trying to politicize the Olympic Games. This is against the spirit of the Games" (Kahn 2007c).

China's restrictions on media access are well known, and coverage of its continued restrictions contributes to a picture of China as a country that violates human rights. Chinese journalists "face heavy censorship" (Yardley 2006c), according to an article that cites as its source Reporters Without Borders. In its annual report on press freedoms, the group asserted "that conditions for the news media and for journalists had deteriorated in China. 'The press is being forced into self-censorship, the Internet is filtered, and the foreign media very closely watched.'" The story continues to quote Reporters Without Borders concerning the status of media restrictions: "Faced with burgeoning social unrest and journalists who are becoming much less compliant, the authorities, directed by president Hu Jintao, have been bringing the media to heel in the name of a 'harmonious society.'" Stories also cover the five-year prison sentence given to a Hong Kong reporter and the three-year sentence given to a researcher in the Beijing bureau of the *New York Times* as examples of efforts to intimidate journalists. In total, one reporter details, "31 journalists were serving jail terms in China and . . . the authorities had convicted 52 more people for posting political views on the Internet" (Kahn 2007b).

Another example of the media's highlighting of the curtailment of press freedoms is a story on China's efforts "to prevent domestic critics from voicing negative views." One Chinese couple, Hu Jia and Zeng

Jinyan, "who have promoted a variety of delicate social and political causes," receive particular attention in the news coverage. The police prevented the couple "from departing from Beijing on a trip to Hong Kong and several European countries," where the two "had planned to call attention to what they described as a neglect of AIDS patients and to defend other Chinese campaigners for human rights who had been prosecuted in recent months." A story reports that the police told the pair that they "were suspected of 'endangering national security' and would be required to stay in their home under police watch for an indefinite period" (Kahn 2007c).

A similar restriction of information is taking place, the media report, in the exhibitions housed in China's new museums. One professor is cited who "fought Shenzhen city authorities when they wanted to omit mention of a devastating 1995 chemical-plant explosion from the city's history museum he was designing. They eventually took his advice, though they played down the significance of the explosion." Likewise, in an exhibition in the new Beijing Capital Museum "designed to show parallels between Beijing and global history," media coverage notes that no mention is made "of an 1860 pillaging of the imperial Summer Palace by British and French troops . . . . Museum head Guo Xiaolin said the period isn't mentioned because it is only a small part of China's history." The media point out that some subjects still cannot be discussed at all: "the 1989 Tiananmen Square killings are still taboo" (Fong 2006b).

China as an Upholder of Human Rights

At the same time that the media's presentation of China depicts it as a violator of human rights, China is also shown to be conforming somewhat to human rights practices. China's loosening of control of the media is one such arena that is reported with the note that "Beijing promised in its bid for the Games that it would . . . open its doors wider, allowing a freer flow of information into and out of the country" (Kahn 2007a). New regulations concerning foreign journalists receive particular attention in the coverage. The rules, announced by the Foreign Ministry, are reported to temporarily "supersede existing restrictions that require journalists to obtain government approval before traveling or conducting interviews. Under the new rules, a foreign journalist will only need to obtain the permission of the person being interviewed" (Yardley 2006c).

Further evidence of the theme that China is willing to share rather than to hoard or restrict information can be seen in coverage of an agreement of cooperation signed between the United States and China in June of 2006. The agreement stipulates that each "country will send delegations of athletes, coaches and administrators to the other to share information about training and research." China has signed such agreements with other countries as well, one article notes. In response to the agreement with the United States, Peter Ueberroth, chair of the United States Olympic Committee, is quoted as saying, "This agreement will benefit the athletes and coaches of each national Olympic committee, but it will also benefit the Olympic movement and sports" (Zinser 2006).

Yet another way in which China is constructed as conforming to global human rights practices is in its transformation concerning Sudan. China's stance toward Sudan changed in April 2007, the media narrative notes, when a senior Chinese official, Zhai Jun, recommended that Sudan allow a United Nations peacekeeping force to support the African Union's efforts in Sudan: "'We suggest the Sudan side show flexibility and accept the United Nations peacekeepers,' he urged." The press note that he "even went all the way to Darfur and toured three refugee camps" (Cooper 2007).

In the space of equivocation, the tension that must be negotiated, according to the media narrative, is between conformity to global requirements for practices concerning human rights and maintenance of power and sovereignty, even at the expense of violating human rights. The media construction of China traditionally has featured the latter, but coverage in advance of the Olympics suggests a nascent effort to construct a different image of China—one that features some degree of conformity with human rights practices.

Space of Accumulation

A third space created by the American media regarding China is a space of accumulation. A primary focus of American media coverage in the construction of this space is on the economic benefits the Olympics will bring. This theme is exemplified in a story that notes that the Chinese consider the number eight to be lucky because it rhymes with the Chinese character for wealth; because the Olympics means the possibility of wealth for the Chinese, it "is no coincidence that the Summer Olympics in Beijing will open on 8/8/08 at 8 p.m." (Yardley 2006a).

The space of accumulation is depicted by the media as an expanding space available for reaping economic rewards. The stakeholders who are situated in the space of accumulation are manufacturers with products to sell and marketers who create markets for those goods among the Chinese and others. But markets can be limited in many ways in China, and when they are, access to economic wealth through the production and marketing of goods is denied or diminished. The exigence that must be negotiated in this space in the media construction is between access and denial of access to new markets.

China as Abundant Resources

The theme of accumulation and access to resources is narratively constructed in stories that feature massive marketing efforts that accompany the Olympics. "In my 20 years in the Olympics, I have never seen the level of interest that I am seeing here," Michael Payne, marketing director of the International Olympic Committee (IOC), is quoted as saying (Chang 2003). The Games, the media reported in May 2007, already "have 55 official sponsors and suppliers, including Coke, Adidas AG, Visa International Inc. and Lenovo Group Ltd.—compared to 38 at the 2004 games in Athens." More "than $5 billion will be spent on ads in China featuring Olympic themes, estimates MindShare, WPP Group PLC's media-buying agency" (Fowler 2007).

Because of China's immense market, the Beijing Games are reported to be drawing "a larger-than-usual field of corporate competitors" (Fowler and Lee 2006, B1). The Olympics traditionally have one "official brand of credit card, one computer, one wristwatch." The 2008 Games, however, "already boast three official beers: Tsingtao, Yanjing and Budweiser. 'One beer cannot cover all China,' says Liu Jun, deputy director of marketing of the Beijing Organizing Committee, or Bocog." China's large number of beer drinkers and the fragmented market are cited to justify the "sudsy trifecta," with each of the beer companies establishing "a different target audience." A Tsingtao representative is quoted to explain the marketing frenzy: "Our point of view is this is the first time that China will conduct the Olympics. We believe it is a great thing that many Chinese brands and businesses are able to participate" (Fowler and Lee 2006).

357

Another way in which accumulation is featured in the media's discursive construction of China is in the proliferation of stories about China's encouragement of its citizens to participate in sports, thereby creating entirely new (and huge) markets for products. One story, for example, discusses how the organizers of the Games are trying to shift local perceptions of bicycling. To most Chinese citizens, "the bike is transportation—a tool for getting from here to there rather than a source of healthful exercise or fun. Now, that is beginning to change." The Olympics organizers "are trying to raise interest in the sport by adding a bicycle-motocross (BMX) event to the 2008 Olympics," at which riders will race on modified bikes on a dirt track. Tang Mingxi, the sales manager at a bicycle manufacturer in China, is quoted to make the point that, not long ago, "you would never see people on the street using their bicycles for exercise, but beginning last year, you see it everywhere. You'll see—the market for BMX and other specialized bicycles is going to grow. When something is popular here, it catches on quickly" (Chao 2007).

Another effort reported by the American media to encourage the Chinese people to participate in new sports and thus to create new markets for sports equipment is China Central Television's launch of a reality show with the theme "'sports can be for all—even the weedy and untrained.' The show aims to pluck someone from the nation's . . . population to become an Olympic athlete"—a coxswain to steer the men's and women's teams of rowers in the Olympics—a position that requires "just a healthy set of lungs and a good sense of direction." The search to find a male and female winner, an article on the new program suggests, "will draw from parts of 'Survivor,' 'The Apprentice,' and 'American Idol' as organizers seek to make stars of China's rowers, whose sport doesn't have much of a following in that country." The story emphasizes as well other ways in which the show will allow access to greater resources: "Of course, the new TV reality show could also draw millions in ad sponsorship for broadcasters" (Fong 2006a).

China as Limited Resources

Although some aspects of the media's narrative tout China as a burgeoning market that will provide greater access to goods and resources for its citizens, it also contains a theme that suggests that access to available resources can be limited. One example is the media's reporting on the Chinese government's stunting of the growth of sports marketing through a "creaking socialist system of state control over athletic careers." As a result, it is a "headache for advertisers counting on Chinese sports heroes to help them grab market share in China's fast-growing consumer market." For advertisers, the narrative continues, securing access to athletes is often difficult because officials want to focus on training them to win medals. One story tells of China's top sports minister, Liu Peng, who "sent ripples through the marketing industry by suggesting to a Beijing newspaper that in order to keep athletes focused on training for the 2008 games, he would ban them from 'social activities.' That has been widely interpreted in China," the media explain, "to include advertising and public-relations work" (Fowler 2007). The media's cautionary note that investing in marketing in China can be risky also can be seen in the example they cite of diver Tian Liang, who won gold and bronze medals in Athens in 2004. He "was kicked off the Chinese national team after appearing in too many commercials" (Fowler and Lee 2006).

That marketers face other problems also is part of the narrative concerning China. As one story explains, "Murky rules make it difficult for advertisers . . . to work with Chinese athletes. 'Brands don't know where to go or how to do it,' says Phil de Picciotto, the president of the athletes and personalities practice at Octagon, a sports-marketing division of Interpublic Group of Companies Inc." As a result, "brands have had to develop relationships with sports federations," which handle athletes' careers, "to gain access to their stars." There are no clear rules "about when and how athletes have to go through their federations or whether they can use individual agents." In addition, the media note, "even scheduling time with some Chinese athletes can take months of planning." Sponsors who "pay as much as $1.3 million" to be associated with famous athletes may not even be allowed access to them "for ad shoots or appearances at their events." Just to get such athletes "once a year for a commercial shoot," according to one story, "they need to pony up nearly $2 million" (Fowler 2007).

China's poor record with intellectual property rights is another potential limitation to access to markets and consumer goods in the media's narrative. Some brands are "nervous about 'ambush marketing' or fu ji shi ying xian, in which brands either steal the Olympics logo or find ways to work Olympic images into their ads" (Fowler and Lee 2006). News stories explain that China is notorious "as a knockoff haven where poor law enforcement has turned a potentially huge consumer market into a land of 75-cent pirated DVDs and $10 fake Louis

Vuitton handbags." If Olympics merchandise is copied, the market for Olympics goods will be dispersed, and the funds expected to pay for the Games may not materialize. "'We have no fixed assets,' says Liu Yan, deputy director of legal affairs for the Beijing Organizing Committee for the Games of the XXIX Olympiad, which operates under the Beijing city government and various national government agencies. 'So the Olympic logo is the most valuable thing we own'" (Fowler 2005). In response to the threat of Olympic knockoffs, one story reports, Olympics officials are reported to have "already shut down some unauthorized use of its logo and is considering launching educational campaigns on state TV to inform the public about the phenomenon" (Fowler and Lee 2006).

In the space of accumulation, according to the elite American media's narrative, manufacturers and marketers are presented as seeking to develop markets and sell goods to a vast market of Chinese and other consumers. At the same time, efforts to gain access to these markets are presented as being mitigated by the government's efforts to rein in and control such efforts.

Space of Anticipation

A fourth space created by the media about China is a future space—a space in which the decision will be made about whether China will be a legitimate and fully participating member of the global community. This space is developed largely through economic themes and is rooted in the constructed tension between growth and control or between China as a strong economic partner and China as an unreliable economic partner.

China as a Powerful Economic Partner

A major way in which the media create a space of anticipation is through discussion of China's rise as an economic power, which is the catalyst that forces China into the global community: "In the last 30 years, no major economy in the world has grown at the speed of China's, and no other country has been able to do it year after year, for over a decade." In 2006, the media exclaim, "China did it again, saying that its economy grew by a whopping 10.7 percent . . . the fastest pace in more than a decade" (Barboza 2007b). According to one story, favorable economic trends continued in 2007, with the economy growing "11.1 percent in the first quarter" of 2007. China's economic growth is compared favorably to that of developing countries; indeed, according to one story, China soon could "overtake Germany to become the world's third-largest economy, behind those of the United States and Japan" (Barboza 2007d).

That China's stock market is booming also receives attention in media coverage. In 2006, "the country's key index—the Shanghai exchange—rose 130 percent to close at 2,675, a record and the best performance of any major stock exchange in the world," and it is reported to have soared even higher in the opening weeks of 2007. The media report that one "Chinese mutual fund raised $5 billion in a single day . . . before closing its doors to new investors." The run-up in the stock market, a reporter explains, means that "companies in China can once again raise money in the Chinese market rather than relying on the Hong Kong stock market" (Barboza 2007a).

Record trade figures are used in the media narrative to provide additional evidence for China as a powerful force in the world economy. As one story notes, "After posting a record $100 billion trade surplus in 2005, much of it with the United States and Europe," China announced in June 2006 "that its total surplus had already reached nearly $47 billion in the first five months of this year, a period that is traditionally slower for exports than the second half of the year." During that time, its "exports rose 25 percent, to $73 billion, while imports rose 22 percent, to $60 billion" (Barboza 2006).

China as an Unreliable Economic Partner

The media's narrative around China also contains the theme that China may be an unreliable economic partner. China does not have much incentive to slow growth, the media explain, because the Communist Party bases "its legitimacy on delivering economic growth," and local officials "are promoted, foremost, for delivering economic growth." High growth "is needed simply to keep unemployment in check, and top leaders fear that a slowdown could lead to social instability" (Yardley 2005b). The government, then, "is determined to keep the economy expanding but is concerned about growing so quickly that the economy might crash before 2008" (Barboza 2007a). "Right now, the economy is growing at the upper limits of what is acceptable," Li Lianfa, an economist at Peking University, is quoted as saying. "The government is facing a lot of challenges." Among the economic challenges, according to one reporter, "are balancing the supersize growth and heavy investment, and trying to distribute the riches as evenly as possible" (Barboza 2007a).

The discursive construction of China also contains the theme that Beijing is under pressure to allow the Chinese currency, the yuan, to appreciate more quickly against the dollar in the hope of easing the country's trade surplus with the United States. Chinese officials, however, assert "that the pace of currency revaluation must be measured and that they will not be pressed into moving hastily" (Barboza 2007d). Reports on the value of the yuan against the dollar are common. One story notes, for example, that the yuan strengthened somewhat against the dollar in 2006, "climbing to about 7.8 yuan to the dollar, from 8.26 yuan in 2005." News stories about the yuan explain that economists "have warned that if the yuan does not continue to appreciate against the dollar and other major currencies, China could face protectionist action, which could pose an even more serious threat to economic growth" (Barboza 2007b).

China also faces concerns about its "enormous rise in bank loans" (Barboza 2006, C8); "too much money in the financial system," the media assert, "could ignite inflation and perhaps fuel a stock market bubble." In January 2007, China's central bank is reported to have "raised the reserve requirement ratio for banks, the fourth increase in six months, to further tighten the nation's money supply," a move that increased "the reserve ratio by half a percentage point to 9.5 percent." "Raising the amount of cash reserves that Chinese banks keep on hand with the central bank," the media's narrative explains, "effectively restricts the amount of money that banks can lend" and curbs "excessive lending to new factories, real estate projects, and road construction" (Barboza 2007a).

China's potential unreliability as an economic partner is also developed in media accounts through stories about the environmental devastation its economic growth has generated. For the Chinese government, these stories assert, the question is how to address the country's environmental problems without crippling the economy: "China, it seems, has reached a tipping point familiar to many developed countries, including the United States, that have raced headlong after economic development only to look up suddenly and see the environmental carnage. The difference with China, as is so often the case, is that the potential problems are much bigger, have happened much faster and could pose greater concerns for the entire world" (Yardley 2005b).

Some stories use prediction of negative consequences to develop this theme. According to one account, pollution levels in China "could more than quadruple within 15 years if the country does not curb its rapid growth in energy consumption and automobile use." Other environmental problems are noted: "China is already the world's second-biggest producer of greenhouse gas emissions and is expected to surpass the United States as the biggest. Roughly a third of China is exposed to acid rain. A recent study by a Chinese research institute found that 400,000 people die prematurely every year in China from diseases linked to air pollution" (Yardley 2005b). One reporter provides an explanation for why China is facing such problems by citing a local official: " 'In the past, we never thought of the capacity of resources,' said Huang Yan, the deputy director of the planning commission in Beijing. 'We only focused on development' " (Yardley 2005a).

All of the ideological spaces constructed through the media's narration concerning China implicitly are designed to address the issue of whether China will become a legitimate participant on the world stage. The space of anticipation, however, is explicitly designed to function in this way as the media present China's credentials as a steady, significant, reliable economic force and weigh those against potential economic problems and the negative environmental impacts of a growing economy.

Spatial Construction of a Rhetoric of Reassurance

The ideological spaces of definition, equivocation, accumulation, and anticipation constructed by the American media regarding China constitute a preferred reading of China that serves an important function for the media themselves and for media consumers. China is, for these audiences, a country with which they are forced to engage because of its economic reach, its manufacture of vast numbers of products distributed worldwide and its sponsorship of the major sports competition in the world, to name a few reasons. But this entity with which they must engage is still largely a mysterious unknown, a perception reinforced when, for example, Zheng Xiaoyu, the head of China's equivalent of the United States' Food and Drug Administration, was executed for accepting gifts and bribes from pharmaceutical companies (Barboza 2007c). Such incidents that suggest a dramatically different system from the one in which they reside make vivid to the international community their lack of knowledge about China, its government policies and judicial system.

In response to the situation of forced engagement with a largely unknown and powerful entity, the American media have chosen to construct a narrative of reassurance. They seek to reassure those who must deal with China—particularly those who have economic and political interests at stake (the targeted audience for the *New York Times* and the *Wall Street Journal*)—that their investments in China will be secure and their relationships with the Chinese will be successful and productive. The spaces function to provide reassurance by educating audiences about China, avoiding construction of China as an enemy and assigning agency to Americans and other outsiders rather than the Chinese.

One of the primary functions of the four spaces is that they educate media audiences about China. For outside observers, the spaces take the vast and complex information available on China and simplify it into easily told and remembered narratives. The spaces reduce China to four primary arenas, each clearly defined, reassuring foreigners that they can gain an understanding of China and can negotiate the culture successfully. Although the ambiguity that derives from the constructed liminal space between two options for the future is crucial for all of the spaces, for audiences outside of China, the spaces limit that ambiguity and make China an entity that is capable of being known. The spaces thus constitute zones of safety and stability in that they help various audiences know the issues and the boundaries with which they must deal.

The ideological spaces provide reassurance as well in that they refrain from making China into an enemy. The constructed narrative avoids such a depiction by presenting a balanced view of the various issues that characterize its content. Certainly, part of the impetus for a balanced presentation is due to the fact that readers' expectations are that the media will provide objective or balanced coverage. But this kind of balance is unusual in an ideological construction; ideologies typically present positive information about a favored person or group and negative information about an opponent. Here, in contrast, when one side of an issue within a space is presented by the media, the other option is also typically presented. Just as China might begin to be seen as negative in the constructed narrative because of its restrictions on the media, for example, the spaces point to China's opening up of opportunities for foreign journalists. Enemies are threatening and create unknown and unstable situations, so lack of construction of an enemy reassures the media audience that its financial investments are safe and its business dealings likely to be ongoing.

The media also eschew presentation of China as an enemy by suppressing story lines already known to American and other audiences in which China is defined as a clear enemy. The prime example is the complete lack of coverage in either newspaper about China's dealings with Tibet and the inclusion of Tibet in the Olympic games. These events include coverage of the activists who protested the route of the Olympic torch over Mount Everest and through Tibet, the "defection" of the Tibetan antelope as an Olympic mascot, and the plans for Team Tibet to bring the FreeTibet2008 message to Chinese embassies and consulates throughout the world on August 8, 2007 (Students for a Free Tibet).

Such coverage would call to mind for many readers China as imperialist, repressive, and seeking to squash negotiations with the Dalai Lama, the spiritual leader of Tibet and recipient of a Nobel Peace Prize. If nothing related to Tibet is covered, this plotline and the concomitant negative perspective on China are less likely to be recalled by audiences. There is another reason, of course, why the elite American media would not want to cover an enemy-sanctioning issue like Tibet: their readers are not likely to be those most concerned about Tibet—an issue that generates the most excitement among economically impoverished college students, American Buddhists, and political activists.

Although coverage of Sudan in the media coverage of China seems to violate the narrative tenet of suppression of story lines that would make China into a clear enemy, that coverage was done in a particular way—largely in terms of celebrities. Although nonpoliticos who act as spokesperson for causes are becoming increasingly common in the context of infotainment-dominated media (Kellner 2003, 13), a degree of trivialization of an issue may evolve when that issue is embraced and advocated for by, for example, an actor. Certainly, celebrities do "attract press attention to various issues and explain why the public should be concerned" and, "with the aid of willing media reporters, this kind of coverage affects the national political agenda and sometimes even the deliberation of congressional legislators" (West and Orman 2003, 74). Celebrities, however, are not always successful in insuring that their causes take precedence over the very nature of their celebrity. In America's infotainment culture (Kellner 2003; West and Orman 2003), the public's attention tends to stay focused more on the celebrities' lives and activities per se and less on the issue itself, which takes back stage to, for example, what the celebrity is wearing, with whom she is seen, her current marital status, what her children are doing, who their father is, and the nightclubs in which she makes an appearance. The presence of a celebrity helps reassure media audiences by placing on center stage someone known and familiar to them rather than a serious issue or China as a potential enemy. In this case, attention on the celebrity is allowed to displace the possibility of an enemy in the narrative.

When China is not constructed as an enemy because of a balanced presentation of issues and lack of coverage of polarizing plotlines, another benefit accrues to the media and media consumers as well. China's image cannot become fixed and settled; one truth, in other words, cannot emerge about China in this media construction. As a result, neither the media corporations nor their audiences can be caught on the wrong side of any particular issue or argument; they are positioned in a liminal space of noncommitment. They can rest easy, knowing that whichever way an issue unfolds or on whatever side a decision is made, they have not committed themselves to the opposite position. As a result of the four spaces in the media's constructed narrative, the truth about China is always fluid and changing, and the media and media audiences are allowed to change with it, positioning themselves in whatever ways are politically and economically most advantageous.

A third way in which the ideological spaces function to provide reassurance to media corporations and audiences is that they make Americans in particular, and outsiders in general, the active agents in the media narrative. The construction of the spaces provides reassurance for audiences that they are in control of the mysterious entity that is China. They are the ones who have the capacity to act and to make a difference in this world, even though they are the outsiders. They function, in a sense, as omnipotent protagonists, and because they are all seeing and all knowing, they are the ones who can act in the most effective ways.

What is striking in the narratives is the extent to which outsiders are depicted as inhabiting the spaces, roaming across them, and playing key roles in them. In the space of definition, they are seen as driving China's transformation into a different kind of physical space. In the space of equivocation, they are positioned as judges, measuring and passing judgment on China's progress on human rights. In the space of accumulation, they are the marketers and investors who stand to benefit from the resources available in China. And in the space of anticipation, they are the ones with the most to gain from China's participation in the global community. Although some Chinese people move from space to space in the media narrative, the consistent occupants of the spaces of China are not the Chinese. That Americans and other outsiders have this capacity surely is reassuring to American corporations and audiences.

Americans and other foreigners are given agency in the narrative as well as in its trivialization of certain aspects of the Chinese culture. The articles often present information about China in a mildly patronizing tone, with readers expected to chuckle at the eccentricities of the Chinese—their spitting and translation practices, bars that serve cocktails of Chivas Regal and green tea, and museums on subjects such as tree roots and piped water, for example. The position created for outsiders in the narrative is thus one of superiority—they belong, the narrative suggests, to a culture that is more civilized, refined, normal, and sensible because it is lacking in the silly or boorish practices that characterize the Chinese culture. Positioned to pronounce judgment on the Chinese, media audiences no longer feel as intimidated by the mysterious, powerful China, and they are reassured that they will be able to handle their interactions with the Chinese successfully.

The elite American media's narrative concerning China in advance of the 2008 Olympic Games offers four spatial arenas that negotiate tensions between opposite perspectives on China in terms of definition, equivocation, accumulation, and anticipation. Although such a balanced approach is unusual for an ideological construction, the preferred reading presented by the media is one designed to serve the interests of its readers as they seek to engage—often unwillingly or at least warily—with China. Lee labels this type of coverage "established pluralism" and notes that it "consists of a plurality of viewpoints within a narrow range of the established order or official circle, thus producing an orchestra of 'diversity within unity' in support of the hegemonic voice" (Lee 2002, 345). In this case, the spaces function to provide reassurance that engagement with the Chinese will be safe, secure, worthwhile and, most important, under the control of the Americans or other outsiders.

That the *New York Times* and the *Wall Street Journal* would construct

China with a balanced narrative that reassures themselves and their audiences concerning the unknown power that is China is not unexpected, of course. As Hallin points out, a newspaper such as the *Times* is "basically a Fortune 500 company that positions its products to have broad appeal and credibility" (2006, 44–45). As part of "a global media market . . . closely linked to the rise of a significantly more integrated 'neo-liberal' global capitalist economy" (McChesney 1999, 78), such newspapers construct news frames for a number of reasons, including newsgathering routines and values, economic factors, government regulation, the physical structure of the medium, the political and economic interests of the country constructing the news, deference to government officials, and journalists' personal biases (Innis 1951; Gitlin 1980; Chomsky 1989; Keshishian 1997). Perhaps most important, they make decisions to frame news coverage in ways that benefit the interests of the elite—the wealthy and powerful few who have the most to gain and lose from interactions with China (Lee 2002; McChesney 1999). The narrative of reassurance created by the four ideological spaces in the news coverage around China is designed to address this audience and to reassure it specifically that interactions with China will create "America's China Dream" and not "America's China Nightmare" (Wasserstrom 2007; also see Wasserstrom's chapter in this volume).

REFERENCES

Barboza, David. 2006. China Posted Trade Surplus of $13 Billion Last Month. *New York Times,* June 13, C8.

Barboza, David. 2007a. China Moves to Tighten the Money Supply. *New York Times,* January 6, C3.

Barboza, David. 2007b. China Says its Economy Grew by 10.7% in 2006, with Little Inflation. *New York Times,* January 26, C3.

Barboza, David. 2007c. A Chinese Reformer Betrays His Cause, and Pays. *New York Times,* July 13, A1.

Barboza, David. 2007d. Chinese Growth Shows Little Restraint, Rising 11.1% in Quarter. *New York Times,* April 20, C3.

Barboza, David. 2007e. China's Mighty Economy. *New York Times,* April 21, C2.

Beck, Daniel, and Louis Bosshart. 2003. Sports, Media, Politics, and National Identity. *Communication Research Trends* 22 (4): 25–26.

Beck, Howard. 2007. Cavalier Seeks Players' Support for Darfur. *New York Times,* May 16.

Bitzer, Lloyd F. 1968. The Rhetorical Situation. *Philosophy and Rhetoric* 1: 1–14.

Chang, Leslie. 2003. Beijing Prepares to Pick Sponsors for the Olympics. *Wall Street Journal*, August 21, B6.

Chao, Loretta. 2007. Memo to China's Hordes of Cyclists: Lighten Up; Olympics' BMX Events Will Show the Dubious How Bikes Can Be Fun. *Wall Street Journal*, January 18, B1.

Chomsky, Noam. 1989. *Necessary Illusions: Thought Control in Democratic Societies*. Boston: South End Press.

Conlin, Jennifer. 2006. Looking to '08 Games, Super 8 Expands in China. *New York Times*, October 22, sec. 5, 2.

Cooper, Helene. 2007. Darfur Collides with Olympics, and China Yields. *New York Times*, April 13, A1.

Danner, Lauren, and Susan Walsh. 1999. "Radical" Feminists and "Bickering" Women: Backlash in United States Media Coverage of the United Nations Fourth World Conference on Women. *Critical Studies in Mass Communication* 16: 63–84.

Dearing, James W., and Everett M. Rogers. 1996. *Agenda-Setting*. Thousand Oaks, CA: Sage.

Entman, Robert M. 1993. Framing: Toward a Clarification of a Fractured Paradigm. *Journal of Communication* 43 (4): 51–58.

Farrow, Ronan, and Mia Farrow. 2007. The Genocide Olympics. *Wall Street Journal*, March 28, A17.

Fong, Mei. 2006a. China's New Reality Show Goes for the Gold. *Wall Street Journal*, August 29, B1.

Fong, Mei. 2006b. Why China Is Letting a Thousand Museums Take Root and Bloom; The Olympics Are Coming, Towns Hope for Tourists; History in the Right Light. *Wall Street Journal*, November 24, A1.

Fong, Mei. 2007. Tired of Laughter, Beijing Gets Rid of Bad Translations. *Wall Street Journal*, February 5, A1.

Foss, Sonja K. 2004. *Rhetorical Criticism: Exploration and Practice*. 3rd ed. Long Grove, IL: Waveland.

Fowler, Geoffrey A. 2005. China's Logo Crackdown: The Nation Is Awash in Phony Western Brands but Draws the Line at Valuable Olympic Symbol. *Wall Street Journal*, November 4, B1.

Fowler, Geoffrey A. 2007. Beijing Olympics 2008: In China, Sports Stars Face Hurdles in the Race for Ad Riches. *Wall Street Journal*, May 15, B1.

Fowler, Geoffrey, and Wendy Lee. 2006. For Sponsors, China's Olympics Have Already Begun. *Wall Street Journal*, August 8, B1.

Gitlin, Todd. 1980. *The Whole World Is Watching: Mass Media and the Making and Unmaking of the New Left*. Berkeley: University of California Press.

Glassberg, David. 1996. Public History and the Study of Memory. *Public Historian*, 18: 7–23.

Hall, Stuart. 1988. The Toad in the Garden: Thatcherism among the Theorists. In *Marxism and the Interpretation of Culture*, ed. Cary Nelson and Lawrence Grossberg, 35–57. Urbana: University of Illinois Press.

Hallin, Daniel C. 2006. Review of *The Record of the Paper: How the* New York Times *Misreports U.S. Foreign Policy*, by Howard Friel and Richard Falk. *Global Media and Communication*, 2 (2): 231–42.

Innis, Harold A. 1951. *The Bias of Communication*. Toronto: University of Toronto Press.

Kahn, Joseph. 2007a. Rights Group Says Conditions in China Worsen as Olympics Near. *New York Times*, January 13, A2.

Kahn, Joseph. 2007b. Journalist Group Criticizes Press Freedoms under Hu. *New York Times*, Feburary 3, A5.

Kahn, Joseph. 2007c. 2 Activists Are under House Arrest and Barred from Leaving China. *New York Times*, May 19, A3.

Katriel, Tamar. 1993. "Our Future Is Where Our Past Is": Studying Heritage Museums as Ideological and Performative Arenas. *Communication Monographs* 60: 69–75.

Kellner, Douglas. 2003. *Media Spectacle*. New York: Routledge.

Keshishian, F. 1997. Political Bias and Non-political News: A Content Analysis of an Armenian and Iranian Earthquake in the *New York Times* and *Washington Post*. *Critical Studies in Mass Communication* 14: 332–43.

Kolatch, Jonathan. 2006. Beijing Practices for the 2008 Olympics. *Wall Street Journal*, September 20, D12.

Lee, Chin-Chuan. 2002. Established Pluralism: US Elite Media Discourse about Chinese Policy. *Journalism Studies* 3 (30): 343–57.

Lubow, Arthur. 2006. The China Syndrome. *New York Times Magazine*, May 21, 68.

McChesney, Robert W. 1999. *Rich Media, Poor Democracy*. Urbana: University of Illinois Press.

McLuhan, Marshall. 1964. *Understanding Media: The Extension of Man*. New York: McGraw-Hill.

Merrill, John C., ed. 1983. *Global Journalism: A Survey of the World's Mass Media*. New York: Longman.

O'Connor, Alan, and John Downing. 1995. Culture and Communication. In *Questioning the Media: A Critical Introduction*, ed. John Downing, Ali Mohammadi, and Annabelle Sreberny-Mohammadi, 3–22. Newbury Park, CA: Sage.

One World, One Dream. 2007. http://en.beijing2008.cn (accessed May 5, 2007).

Phillips, Kendall R., ed. 2004. *Framing Public Memory*. Tuscaloosa: University of Alabama Press.

Polumbaum, Judy. 2003. Capturing the Flame: Aspirations and Representations of Beijing's 2008 Olympics. In *Chinese Media, Global Contexts*, ed. Chin-Chuan Lee, 57–75. New York: Routledge.

Roche, Maurice. 2000. *Mega-events and Modernity: Olympics and Expos in the Growth of Global Culture*. New York: Routledge.

Silver, Sara. 2006. Ticketmaster Prepares to Vault into China; Contract for Beijing Olympics Will Be Used as Springboard into Market for the Long Term. *Wall Street Journal,* October 27, B5.

Students for a Free Tibet. http://www.studentsforafreetibet.com (accessed June 3, 2007).

U.S. Carrier to Help Start Regional Air Venture. 2006. *New York Times,* December 28, C11.

van Dijk, Teun A. 1998. *Ideology: A Multidisciplinary Approach.* Thousand Oaks, CA: Sage.

Wasserstrom, Jeffrey N. 2007. Olympic Dreams and Nightmares. *International Herald Tribune* (published by the *New York Times*), July 28–29, 6.

West, Darrell M., and John M. Orman. 2003. *Celebrity Politics.* Upper Saddle River, NJ: Prentice Hall.

Yang, Andrew. 2005. The Olympics Haven't Begun, but the Party Has. *New York Times,* June 26, sec. 5, 7.

Yardley, Jim. 2005a. Beijing's Quest for 2008: To Become Simply Livable. *New York Times,* August 28, sec. 1, 4.

Yardley, Jim. 2005b. China's Next Big Boom Could Be the Foul Air. *New York Times,* October 30, sec. 4, 3.

Yardley, Jim. 2006a. First Comes the Car, Then the $10,000 License Plate. *New York Times,* July 5, A4.

Yardley, Jim. 2006b. Olympics Imperil Historic Beijing Neighborhood. *New York Times,* July 12, A1.

Yardley, Jim. 2006c. China Plans Temporary Easing of Curbs on Foreign Journalists. *New York Times,* December 2, A6.

Yardley, Jim. 2007a. Olympic Construction Unearths Ancient Treasure Trove. *New York Times,* February 8, A4.

Yardley, Jim. 2007b. No Spitting on the Road to Olympic Glory, Beijing Says. *New York Times,* April 17, A3.

Zaller, John R. 1992. *The Nature and Origin of Mass Opinion.* New York: Cambridge University Press.

Zinser, Lynn. 2006. Exchange Planned with China. *New York Times,* June 10, D6.

IV

Conclusion

Toward the Future

The New Olympic Internationalism

Christopher J. Finlay

The Beijing Olympics represents a turning point for the International Olympic Committee (IOC). Beijing 2008 embodies traditional aspects of the Olympic Movement, but it also can be seen as ushering in a new internationalist role for the IOC, as an organization responding to the demands of twenty-first century globalization. In this nascent role, the IOC offers the Games as a tool for the transcultural negotiation of the global identities of powerful states and other key global actors. Valuable insights about the Olympic Movement can be derived from the cultural imperialism paradigm, but Beijing 2008 also points to the limitations of this paradigm. Marwan Kraidy points to the "growing consensus [that] has emerged to discard cultural imperialism" as a paradigm for thinking about globalization (2002, 335). At the same time, he warns that research that has attempted to push beyond a cultural imperialist model "oftentimes appears to be at best descriptive, at worst a noncritical celebration of transnational culture as global multiculturalism" (2002, 318). He calls for researchers to continue to develop new approaches to understanding global politics through a critical examination of the sociopolitical and economic factors that influence contemporary transcultural exchange. In this chapter, I attempt to take up Kraidy's call via an analysis of recent developments in the Olympic Movement.

When thinking about Olympic internationalism, there is a temptation to use international relations models that divide the world into familiar binaries such as Developed and Developing, North and South, West and the Rest, or Core and Periphery. Implicit in all of these models is a notion of progress, where the development of global actors is measured via comparison with the standards of the West or the core. These measures are calculated based on contestable metrics, geography to geopolitics, from a state's GDP and its willingness to abide by international trade agreements to the development and enforcement of human rights and environmental standards. In effect, the progress narrative that acts as a foundation for these binaries can be said to be a measure of global assimilation to a single set of standards. Yet, the fluidity, hybridity and interdependence of a newly globalizing world have resulted in states who achieve power and global influence without wholly assimilating the norms of "core" actors.

Traditional Olympic internationalism can be understood as a form of global outreach. One of the functions of the global outreach model of the Olympics was, at least on the surface, to measure a state's "progress," or its assimilation of core values, when considering a host city candidate. Thus, when a non-Western host city is granted the right to host the Olympics, Whannel suggests it "constitutes a *rite de passage* into the modern (western) world" (Whannel 1992, 166). I suggest that while this sense of purpose still animates the Movement, a new Olympic internationalism also positions the Games as a vehicle for negotiating the norms, aspirations, and roles of already powerful global actors as they interact in an increasingly interdependent world. If the Olympic Movement was once understood as a unidirectional force for bringing the culture and media of the West into the developing world of the periphery, I suggest that it is now reforming itself so that it operates as an enabling force for the multidirectional flows that bring mutually influencing actors together to challenge old boundaries and distinctions and negotiate the terms of a new global social order.

In some ways the new Olympic internationalism can be said to mirror the triple imperative of Hardt and Negri's *Empire,* which describes a modern shift from colonial imperialism and an accompanying tendency to incorporate, differentiate, and manage in a political order of globalization (2000, 201). In the moment of incorporation, "universal inclusion [is achieved] by setting aside differences that are inflexible or unmanageable" (2000, 198). In the differential moment, cultural differences are celebrated. As Hardt and Negri suggest, cultural differences are thought to be "contingent rather than biological and essential, [and thus] they are thought not to impinge on the central band of commonality or overlapping consensus that characterizes the Empire's inclusionary mechanism" (2000, 199). Finally, fluid and contingent differences create "complex variables that change continuously and admit a variety of always incomplete but nonetheless effective solutions" (2000, 199). New Olympic internationalism differs from the *Empire* model because it does not take the primacy of the United States and its allies as a given. Indeed, it is the function of the new Olympic internationalism in supporting negotiations between powerful global actors, new and old, that leads to the blurring of the distinction between the West and the Rest, thus furthering a global hegemonic order that benefits multiple powerful actors.

It is important to note that the older global outreach model of Olympic internationalism continues to be influential. For instance, while the Beijing and Sochi Olympics can be read on one level as facilitating transcultural negotiation, they also remain opportunities for influencing and pressuring China and Russia to conform to the shared norms of those primarily Western states who continue to hold sway over the IOC. Ultimately, the new Olympic internationalism outlined in this chapter finds the IOC and those who work with it in a transitional moment in which the organization is reluctant to abandon the global outreach model and in which it is just beginning to explore the potential of its new role as facilitating greater interaction and negotiation between powerful global actors.

Future Olympic host cities play an important role in the ongoing construction of this new Olympic internationalist narrative. To date, the IOC has announced three Olympic host cities subsequent to Beijing. In 2012, the next Olympic Games will be held in London. In addition, two Winter Olympics host cities have been chosen: Vancouver in 2010 and Sochi in 2014. The construction of narratives around these host cities contributes to the IOC's new internationalist project by embodying this notion of transcultural negotiation at both the macro and micro level. At the macro level, Beijing 2008 and Sochi 2014 can be understood as IOC attempts to contribute to and strengthen the negotiations between powerful, yet unassimilated, states and those states which have historically been most influential in the development of the modern Olympics. At the micro level, London 2012 and Vancouver 2010, both of which are using the Games to foster greater cultural pluralism, are also addressing similar issues of transcultural negotiation. Together, these host cities aid in a larger Olympic internationalist project of transcultural negotiation.

Olympic Internationalism in the Twenty-first Century

Internationalist aspirations have been a component of the Olympic Movement since Pierre de Coubertin. As Hoberman observes with concern, the Movement is seen as a force for "redemptive and inspirational internationalism" (1995, 1). Redemption and inspiration speak to an almost Hegelian notion of universal progress that animates traditional Olympic internationalism in which the Movement is seen as an agent of change and a tool for measuring the advances and missteps of global actors as they develop. In order to play this dual role, the Olympic Movement purports to have already identified universal ideals and aspirational principles. This is clearly evident in the Fundamental Principles of Olympics recorded in the Olympic Charter:

> Olympism is a philosophy of life, exalting and combining in a balanced whole the qualities of body, will and mind. Blending sport with culture and education, Olympism seeks to create a way of life based on the joy of effort, the educational value of good example and respect for universal fundamental ethical principles. (IOC, 2004)

In this passage, as elsewhere, Olympism remains vaguely defined. Roche notes that the Olympic Movement has always had an adaptive capacity, which he suggests it is "currently displaying again in the contemporary era of globalization" (2006, 29). I contend that the vague universal aspirations of the Movement contribute to the adaptability of Olympism. The IOC has developed a complex bureaucratic system of working groups, committees and Olympic legislation reform procedures for interpreting and adapting Olympism to the demands of an evolving context. The Olympic Charter, for example, has been subject to significant revision. One of the primary duties of the IOC Juridical Commission, founded in 1974, is to consider draft amendments to the Charter. Examples of working groups and committees include the Women and Sport Working Group, established in 1994 and turned into a commission in 2004, and the Sport and Environment Commission, which was created in 1995 after the IOC stated that it "has acknowledged its particular responsibility in terms of promoting sustainable development, and regards the environment as the third dimension of Olympism, alongside sport and culture" (IOC 2007b).

These and other IOC activities have ensured that Olympism is able to stay relevant to an evolving set of global trends while simultaneously remaining true to the principles of Coubertin's philosophy. Although the internal procedures through which the IOC identifies new spaces for broadening the scope of Olympism remain shrouded in secrecy, it is clear that the changes in the focus of the IOC reflect the interests of powerful global actors. This indicates that the IOC is not an independent author of the specific components of the internationalism that it promotes, but rather that it is responsible to the interests of multiple actors in an ever-changing global context. Thus, the IOC is perhaps best understood as a semiautonomous global actor, promoting an internationalist agenda that speaks to the interests of a collection of powerful global actors.

New Olympic internationalism can be linked to an increased recognition of the interdependence—also to be read as vulnerability—of all global actors. As Roche suggests, the desire to steer globalization processes has taken on a greater urgency after the attacks of September 11, 2001 (2006, 27). The IOC has adapted to the demands of this insecure and interdependent world by positioning itself as a tool for helping to steer this process.

Traditional Western, or core, powers continue to be influential actors in the Movement and continue to use the Games to promote their agendas. And yet, the IOC is evolving and increasingly responding to the imperatives of actors who have not traditionally been key players in the organization. Today, the IOC's internationalist agenda is discursively constructed via the interaction of the IOC with three key categories of global actors: states, transnational corporations, and a loose grouping of actors representing what is increasingly called global civil society. These three categories include actors who have been traditionally involved in the Olympic Movement and newer actors who have not. All of these actors share an interest in the new Olympic internationalism because they can use the Games as a tool for expanding their global reach and for constructing a viable position and purpose for themselves.

Transnational corporations play an increasingly vital role in Olympic internationalism. Corporations, such as McDonald's, NBC, or

Samsung (and new entrants like China's Lenovo), who have signed multi-Games sponsorship deals, have a profound impact in shaping the themes of the ongoing Olympic story as it evolves from city to city every two years. Tomlinson (2005), for example, reviewed Coca-Cola's funding of FIFA football initiatives in Asia and Africa. He argues that the corporation's generous funding of initiatives such as the World Youth Cup is, in a large part, responsible for the increase in the number of skilled players from these regions. As he writes, "the FIFA initiatives clearly offered valuable international experience and competition that were to stand Asian and African footballing nations in good stead on the larger world stages of the World Cup and the Olympic Games" (2005, 45). Thus, by contributing to an international environment where fans from these regions could expect their teams to participate competitively in international sporting events such as the Olympics, a new audience was created for the Games and the products that sponsor the event. As Whannel writes, "this then is the new Olympic internationalism—there we are with our Coke in one hand and our Visa card in the other" (1992, 178).

The substantial role of Olympic sponsors in the IOC may lead to accusations that the new Olympic internationalist project is largely a cultural imperialist project. Indeed, the majority of Olympic TOP sponsors continue to have origins in the West. Yet, as transnational sponsors continue to diversify and expand globally, it is becoming increasingly problematic to continue to identify these actors as Western. While the ultimate mission of transnational corporations is to continue to increase sales of their products and services, this mission does not necessarily translate to cultural imperialism. In fact, as transnational corporations open regional offices and target new markets, they may best be understood as trying to accomplish this mission via attempts to become more responsive to a diverse global consumer base. Thus, "the bottom line" for transnational corporations can be said to all but demand that they research, represent, and respond to a growing global plurality of voices and interests.

The state also participates in the discursive construction of new Olympic internationalism. This is especially true when one of its cities is bidding for the Games. States are heavily involved in the funding, promotion, and crafting of the messages created for city bids. In London's final bid presentation, for instance, British Prime Minister Tony Blair appealed to the IOC by stating, "my entire government and the main opposition parties too, are behind this bid. It has total political support. It is the nation's bid" (Blair, 2005). The Vancouver Organizing Committee for the 2010 Olympic and Paralympic Winter Games (VANOC) describes the vision of 2010 as building "a stronger Canada whose spirit is raised by its passion for sport, culture and sustainability" (VANOC 2007b). The Sochi 2014 bid was aided by "the Russian government [which] has offered its full and unqualified support to the Bid and has implemented a US$12 billion Federal investment programme" in the region (Sochi 2014 Bid Committee 2007c). In each case, the host city is explicitly linked to the host state. Thus, in analyzing how Beijing and future host cities contribute to the new Olympic internationalist narrative, attention must be paid to the goals and global geopolitical context of the states where the host cities are located.

It is important also to consider how those global civil society groups that use the Olympics to further their own goals contribute to the construction of new Olympic internationalism. The roster of actors in this category is always shifting as each host city presents a unique set of issues and causes that attract different groups. In the realm of civil society, Western organizations posses the social networking contacts, technological sophistication and, in many cases, a legitimizing history of activism that allows them to most successfully promote their viewpoints. Close, Askew, and Xu suggest these groups play a role in facilitating Western cultural imperialism (2007, 170). The concentration of Western moralists who have learned how to be heard by the IOC has indeed led to a situation where the conscience of new internationalism is primarily dictated by the West.

Consider the human rights groups who have been most successful in presenting a case for boycotting the Beijing Games for issues ranging from Darfur to Burma. They seem almost exclusively based in the West (though this may be because of the mode of coverage of such actors or because the particular forms of civil society that have been popularized are Western in style and structure). And, the Olympic boycott narratives that they have authored have become occasions for debate within the West about the morality of China and, importantly, the morality of the Olympic Movement itself. These debates have the potential to influence the evolution of Olympic internationalism as the IOC strives to stay relevant to the prerogatives of a spectrum of global actors.

Globalization has created an environment where powerful new actors, from rising states and transnational corporations to global civil society groups, have acquired substantial international influence, and the IOC has taken notice. But the transformation is not complete. Power, here as elsewhere, is a function of voice, and the IOC, in an attempt to stay dynamic and relevant, has adapted to make itself a different strategic tool for these new actors. And yet, as the authors in this volume have found, a project of inclusion is hardly complete.

Host Cities and the New Olympic Internationalist Narrative

When the IOC chooses a host for the Olympics, it considers multiple factors that range from basic questions about the ability of the city to engage in the massive infrastructure projects required by the Games to macropolitical questions about the messages that the selection of the city creates. In the history of the modern Olympic Movement, the selection of host-states who are outside or who have contested relationships with the West has served two important functions: graduation and rehabilitation. Black and Van Der Westhuizen include Mexico City 1968 and Seoul 1988 as examples where the Olympics have been used "to signal their 'graduation'" to advanced nation status (2004, 1206). They also suggest that "a succession of World War II Axis powers (Rome 1960; Tokyo 1964; Munich 1972) sought the Olympic Games in part to signal their rehabilitation within the international community" (2004, 1206).

Allusions to these two functions can be found in the rhetoric surrounding Beijing and Sochi, but the rhetoric of the two cities' bids also softly challenges the assumptions of the global paradigm that has enabled traditional Olympic internationalism. Historically, states that sought rehabilitation, such as Germany or Japan, and states that pursued the Games as a rite of passage, such as Mexico or South Korea, were ultimately asking for permission to join an international community of developed and like-minded states. Without this permission, they remained outside and were unable to enjoy the status and economic benefits of membership in the international community. In effect, Games-related rehabilitation and graduation signaling can be understood as sanctioned power grabs. Via the Games, the international community affirmed its own power by taking on the duty of judging which states had earned the right to ask for more global influence.

For the majority of the second half of the twentieth century, the IOC and the community of nations that worked with the organization were in the enviable position of having a monopoly on political and economic power in the Western half of a bipolar world. Today, in a post–Cold War globalized world, characterized by what Miller et al refer to as a "polycentric notion of global flow" (2001, 14), the Western monopoly on power has been challenged by the increased interdependence of states and the rapid rise of new global powers such as China. The question has shifted from whether the IOC should consider the host bids of global powers like China or Russia to a different kind of salience: whether the IOC can afford to *not* hold an Olympics in these states. And this change has occurred in a short period of time.

Consider Beijing's bids for the 2000 and 2008 Games. Samuel Huntington (1996) suggests that in 1993, Beijing's failure to win the 2000 Games was a message to China from the West that China and its policies remained unacceptable. Supporting evidence for Huntington's assertion can be found in the vocal opposition of states and international human rights groups to the bid. In the United States, for example, the House of Representatives passed a resolution against the Beijing 2000 bid with bipartisan support (CNN.com 2001). Close, Askew, and Xu report that although China's human rights violations were not the only reason for opposition to the 2000 Beijing bid, it was a central issue for a range of international groups (2007, 169). And, as Lenskyj reports, competing 2000 host city candidate Sydney attempted to "discredit the Beijing bid by drawing world attention to China's human rights record" (2000, 181). The "rehabilitation function" of the global outreach model of traditional Olympic internationalism serves to explain, in large part, why Beijing did not host the 2000 Games. But the traditional approach does not adequately explain the award for 2008.

In 2001, during their final bid presentation for the 2008 Olympics, the Chinese delegation rhetorically framed the 2000 loss as an appeal to the "rehabilitation function:" "Eight years have already gone by since our first bid for the 2000 Games. During this period of time, my country has made tremendous strides on the road to modernization and social progress" (Beijing Olympic Games Bid Committee [BOBICO] 2006). It cannot be disputed that the transformations that China went through between 1993 and 2001 were significant. China has emerged as the next global superpower, has embraced the technology of the knowledge economy, and appears to follow international trends such as an increased focus on the environment. Beijing's Green Olympics, for example, speaks to China's purported commitment to the global environmental movement. At the same time, China's human rights record has remained a matter of great contention. The 2008 Games have become a touchstone for groups who wish to bring attention to China's internal and external human rights policies. Internal issues that have gained international notoriety include high profile examples such as child labor, suppression of the Falun Gong, the destruction of Tibet, and the absence of a free press. China has been criticized for pursuing a foreign policy that supports violations of human rights in Sudan and, most recently, Burma. As to some of these issues, particularly in foreign policy, geopolitical opinions may differ. But from the perspective of the "rehabilitation function," the award to China was in the category of aspiration rather than recognition of accomplished change. There are those who hope that the Games will act as a mechanism for pressuring China to address its violations of a Western-constructed human rights regime. For instance, Beijing has had a contractual obligation to the IOC that requires it to develop the 2008 Games according to strict IOC regulations. Further, the Olympics placed an international spotlight on China and it is now contending with a much greater level of scrutiny. China is not immune to this pressure as its response to the "Genocide Olympics" campaign indicates, but the minimal adjustments it has made thus far suggest that China will by and large continue to pursue its existing policies. Ultimately, China has little reason to give in to pressure. It is not South Korea, dependent on increasing foreign investment and support to develop. Thus, the expectations of international human rights groups and other actors who are attempting to use Beijing 2008 to further their goals must be tempered by the recognition of the fact that China is already deeply and irreversibly integrated into the interdependent global political economy.

The dynamics of Sochi 2014 are similar to Beijing 2008. Russia is a powerful global actor with a strong economy. Despite inconsistent commitments to democracy Russia's global influence continues to grow. Sochi's bid committee, which included Russia's deputy prime minister Alexander Zhukov and finance minister Alexei Krudrin (Sochi 2014 Bid Committee 2007b), constructed a bid that appeared to hint and nod to the rehabilitation themes of traditional Olympic internationalism but with language so subtle as to recognize the global shift. This is perhaps best captured in the Sochi bid's Olympic Vision, which states that the Winter Olympics is expected to "drive positive change across multiple areas of social life, including integration of people with disabilities, environmental awareness, corporate transparency and accountability" (Sochi 2014 Bid Committee 2007d). In the bid, Sochi addresses the role of the Olympics as an agent of change, but in a carefully cushioned way: "A celebration of the 'new Russia' during the 2014 Olympic Winter Games will showcase the nation's renewal and highlight the contribution of the Olympic Movement to the transformation of developing countries" (Sochi 2014 Bid Committee 2007a).

Both the Chinese and Russian bids, and Beijing's execution of 2008, reflect an intense nationalism and commitment to visions of a return to national glory. The Sochi bid actively positioned the Games as a "Gateway to the Russian Renaissance," expected to "open a door to a dynamic and exciting future for the people of Russia and leave a precedent-setting for the Olympic Movement" (Sochi 2014 Bid Committee 2007d). The term *Renaissance* differs importantly from the terms *New China* and *New Russia,* both of which are also present in discourse about the Olympics and the two cities, because it connects aspirations for future greatness to glorious, even mythical pasts. *Renaissance* points to the restoration of these once great nations to their rightful place as influential global actors. The terms *New China* and *New Russia* could be said to speak for graduation into world power status via assimilation into a global order. At the same time, a renaissance endows the states with a level of autonomy as they pursue a future that speaks to the glories of their own past.

In winning the Games, China and Russia were able to embrace a rhetoric that spoke to traditional Olympic internationalism, while relying on the realpolitik of today's emerging global order. Close, Askew, and Xu state that globalization processes "are being directed mainly by the West and in the interests of the West, Western hegemony and Westernization" (2007, 178). Transformations in the IOC's focus demonstrate that while Western actors certainly have an extraordinary interest and role in shaping globalization processes, globalization alters Western hegemony. The new Olympic internationalism facilitates exchanges and negotiations between Western actors and these new actors, who by virtue of their quick rise to power, almost demand attention.

This chapter has focused on the 2008 and 2014 bids as evidence of the IOC's new internationalism. But a few words about London 2012 and Vancouver 2010 are in order. Asu Aksoy suggests that there has been "a change in the language of inclusion and exclusion, a focus on the economic barriers rather than what had been customarily couched in terms of a political and cultural jargon" (2006, 102). She continues, "it inscribes the issue of social inclusion on a new terrain of economics" (2006, 102). The London 2012 and Vancouver 2010 bids, both of which shared commitments to social and economic outreach to some of the respective nations' poorest and most violent regions, conform to the pattern that Aksoy identifies. Both bids explained how Olympic Legacies programs would directly initiate positive changes via various Olympic-related outreach programs. In both cases, the bids focused on the interaction of economic problems and social problems. In the two bids, the interaction between the social and the economic, as suspected causes of suffering in Vancouver's Downtown Eastside and East London, have been converted into causes for celebration. In both bids, cultural tensions, understood as perpetuating socioeconomic disparities, are challenged by cultural pluralist policies, which perpetuate a positive rendering of cultural difference in the service of universalizing neoliberal economic solutions. Ultimately, both bids can be said to enunciate a universal goal of socioeconomic reform buoyed by a celebration of managed difference. This is a slightly different expression of the new internationalism.

London 2012, more than Vancouver, has aggressively and successfully presented a transcultural vision of itself that speaks to the new internationalism.[1] In a large part this is because, as Modood argues, "London is not simply an English or a British or even a European city, but a world city" (2005, 193). As a world city, London is a key member of what Saskia Sassen (2006) refers to as a network of global cities that operate within nation-states but that are heavily influenced by an economic elite global class who operate in an "intermediate position between the subnational and the global" (2006, 301). There is a growing trend to think about global cities as somewhat autonomous from the state, putting the demands of global actors ahead of the expectations of the state. London's winning transcultural global city bid can be read as evidence of this trend. It worked within a pro-diversity paradigm already given life by London mayor Ken Livingstone, despite years of multicultural policy waffling and missteps by the national Labour Party. However, national support for the bid and the role of the federal government in the organization and thematic construction of the Games must not be underestimated.

As preparations for the 2012 Games continue, the United Kingdom is both using and contributing to the narrative of London, the World City, to try and strengthen its own position as a key global state. The Games are intended to "celebrate cultures, people and languages—in London, the UK and around the world." The organizers "have taken a deliberately broad and inclusive definition of culture, representing the breadth of London's and the UK's expertise and world standing" (London 2012 2007). Massey argues, "London is not *only* multicultural. It is also—for instance—a heartland of the production, command and propagation of what we have come to call neoliberal globalization" (2006, 65). London 2012 is constructing the city as a microcosm of the globalizing world that the new internationalism seeks to work within. In so doing, it is working to challenge critics who argue that *London-istan* (Phillips 2006) is spiraling into multicultural chaos by presenting a transcultural World City whose global competitiveness is due, in part, to the contributions of a diverse population. Although there are doubts about whether 2012 will be successful, the London Games have the potential to contribute significantly to the IOC's new internationalism. Games organizers are promoting London as a city that implicitly encourages the blurring of old binaries by pointing to its multiple populations who represent and can negotiate with different parts of the world. If it can be said that Russia and China, by virtue of their status as emerging global powers, have virtually demanded the IOC's attention, it can be also be said that the IOC's new internationalism must address London, a city whose diverse population makes it a proxy for addressing China, Russia, and other powerful non-Western global actors.

In 1978 Los Angeles was selected to host the 1984 Games because it was the only city willing to bid (Shoval 2002, 583). In 2005 an impressive list of world-class candidate cities including London, Paris, and New York battled viciously for the 2012 Games. Already, a diverse list of host cities are lining up to bid for the 2016 Games. Confirmed bids include Tokyo, Chicago, Madrid, Rio de Janeiro, Doha, and Prague. How did the Olympics transform from a grim duty that nobody wanted to a highly coveted prize in less than three decades? Part of the answer is that the economic debacle of the 1976 Montreal Games (Hamlyn and Hudson 2005; Whitson and Horne 2006) has been forgotten by potential host cities and that the lucrative 1984 Los Angeles Games has become the de facto Olympic model to which host cities point when trying to convince their businesses, their citizens, and themselves that they ought to host the Games (Burbank, Andranovich, and Heying 2001; Whannel 1992). The evolution of new global internationalism is also part of the answer. The IOC has found a narrative that, whether wholly warranted or not, gives it a geopolitical purpose; one in which it puts a fluid and shifting alliance of states and sponsoring corporations in uneasy conversation with global civil society.

NOTE

1. The Vancouver Organizing Committee for the 2010 Olympic and Paralympic Winter Games (VANOC) has committed to "create a strong foundation for sustainable socio-economic development in Vancouver's inner-city neighbourhoods" (VANOC 2002). In Vancouver's Downtown Eastside, infamous for having one of "the highest HIV infection rates of any community in the Western world" (Adilman and Kliewer 2000, 422), soaring rates of injection-drug use related deaths and fetal alcohol syndrome, Aboriginals are disproportionately the victims. Throughout Vancouver 2010's promotional materials, Aboriginal groups are referenced specifically and separately from other references to cultural diversity. For instance, the 2010 Games are expected to "reflect the great cultural diversity, rich Aboriginal heritage and lively, progressive arts scene, of both Vancouver and Canada" (VANOC 2007a). Difference, not assimilation, is promoted, but the implications of difference are reframed in a positive light where Aboriginals are positioned as contributing to a diverse Canada, not as victims of an intolerant state.

WORKS CITED

Adilman, Steve, and Gordon Kliewer. 2000. Pain and Wasting on Main and Hastings: A Perspective from the Vancouver Native Health Society Medical Clinic. *BC Medical Journal* 42 (9): 422–25.

Aksoy, Asu. 2006. London and the Project of Urban Cosmopolitanism. In *Transcultural Europe: Cultural Policy in a Changing Europe,* ed. Ulrike Meinhof and Anna Triandafyllidou, 85–104. New York: Palgrave Macmillan.

Black, David, and Janis Van Der Westhuizen. 2004. The Allure of Global Games for "Semi-peripheral" Polities and Spaces: A Research Agenda. *Third World Quarterly* 25 (7): 1195–1214.

BOBICO. 2006. *Presentation in Moscow.* Available at http://en.beijing2008.com/00/73/column2117300.shtml.

Blair, Tony. 2005. Prime Minister's Address to the 117th IOC Meeting in Singapore. Available at http://www.webcast.ukcouncil.net/hosted/london 2012/.

Burbank, Matthew J., Gregory D. Andranovich, and Charles H. Heying. 2001. *Olympic Dreams: The Impact of Mega-Events on Local Politics.* Boulder, CO: Lynne Rienner.

Close, Paul, David Askew, and Xin Xu. 2007. *The Beijing Olympiad: The Political Economy of a Sporting Mega-event.* London: Routledge.

CNN.com. 2001. China Slams U.S. Olympics Resolution. Available at: http://edition.cnn.com/2001/WORLD/asiapcf/east/03/30/china.olympics/index.html.

CNN.com. 2005. London Wins 2012 Olympics. Available at http://www.cnn.com/2005/SPORT/07/06/singapore.olympics/index.htm.

Downtown Eastside Residents Association. 2007. *Making the Invisible Visible.* Available at http://www.vcn.bc.ca/dera/.

Gamebids.com. 2007. *2014 Winter Olympic Games Bids.* Available at http://www.gamesbids.com/english/archives/arch2014.shtml.

Hall, C. Michael. 2005. Selling Places: Hallmark Events and the Reimaging of Sydney and Toronto. In *The Political Economy of Sport,* ed. John Nauright and Kimberly S. Schimmel. New York: Palgrave Mcmillan.

Hamlyn, P. J., and Z. L. Hudson. 2005. 2012 Olympics: Who Will Survive? *British Journal of Sports Medicine* 39:882–83.

Hardt, Michael, and Antonio Negri. 2000. *Empire.* Cambridge: Harvard University Press.

Hoberman, John. 1995. Toward a Theory of Olympic Internationalism. *Journal of Sport History* 22 (1): 1–37

Huntington, Samuel. 1996. *The Clash of Civilizations and the Remaking of World Order.* New York: Simon and Schuster.

International Olympic Commission. 2004. *Olympic Charter.* Available at http://multimedia.olympic.org/pdf/en_report_122.pdf.

International Olympic Commission. 2007a. *Members.* Available at http://www.olympic.org/uk/organisation/ioc/members/index_uk.asp?tri=2.

International Olympic Commission. 2007b. *The Sport and Environment Commission.* Available at http://www.olympic.org/uk/organisation/commissions/environment/index_uk.asp.

Kraidy, Marwan. 2002. Hybridity in Cultural Globalization. *Communication Theory* 12 (3): 316–39.

Lenskyj, Helen Jefferson. 2000. *Inside the Olympic Industry: Power, Politics, and Activism.* Albany: State University of New York Press.

London 2012. 2007. *Our Plans: Culture.* Available at http://www.london2012.com/plans/culture/index.php.

Massey, Doreen. 2006. London Inside Out. *Soundings* 32:62–71.

Miller, Toby, et al. 2001. *Globalization and Sport.* London: Sage.

Modood, Tariq. 2005. *Multicultural Politics: Racism, Ethnicity, and Muslims in Britain.* Minneapolis: University of Minnesota Press.

Olympic Delivery Authority. 2007. *Demolish Dig Design.* Available at http://www.london2012.com/documents/oda-publications/demolish-dig-design-leaflet.pdf.

Phillips, Melanie. 2006. *Londonistan.* New York: Encounter Books.

Roche, Maurice. 2006. Mega-Events and Modernity Revisited: Globalization and the Case of the Olympics. In *Sports Mega-events: Social Scientific Analyses of a Global Phenomenon,* ed. John Horne and Wolfram Manzenreiter, 27–40. Oxford: Blackwell Publishing.

Sassen, Saskia. 2006. *Territory, Authority, Rights: From Medieval to Global Assemblages.* Princeton: Princeton University Press.

Shoval, Noam. 2002. A New Phase in the Competition for the Olympic Gold: The London and New York Bids for the 2012 Games. *Journal of Urban Affairs* 24 (5): 583–99.

Sochi 2014 Bid Committee. 2007a. *Bid Highlights*. Available at http://sochi2014.com/37404?

Sochi 2014 Bid Committee. 2007b. *Federal Support*. Available at http://sochi2014.com/sch_federalsupport?

Sochi 2014 Bid Committee. 2007c. *Our Bid*. Available at http://sochi2014.com/sch_ourbid.

Sochi 2014 Bid Committee. 2007d. *Positioning Statement*. Available at http://sochi2014.com/38680.

Tomlinson, Alan. 2005. The Making of the Global Sports Economy: ISL, Adidas, and the Rise of the Corporate Player in World Sport. In *Sport and Corporate Nationalisms,* ed. Michael L. Silk, David L. Andrews, and C. L. Cole, 35–66. Oxford: Berg.

VANOC. 2002. 2010 *Winter Games Inner-City Inclusive Commitment Statement.* Available at http://www.vancouver2010.com/resources/PDFs/CommitmentStatement_EN.pdf.

VANOC. 2007a. *Cultural Events.* Available at http://www.vancouver2010.com/en/CultureEducation/CulturalEvents.

VANOC. 2007b. *Defining Sustainability.* Available at http://www.vancouver2010.com/en/Sustainability.

Wasserstrom, Jeffrey N. 2002. Using History to Think about the Beijing Olympics: The Use and Abuse of the Seoul 1989 Analogy. *Harvard International Journal of Press/Politics* 7 (1): 126–29.

Whannel, Garry. 1992. *Fields in Vision*. London: Routledge.

Whitson, David, and John Horne. 2006. Underestimated Costs and Overestimated Benefits? Comparing the Outcomes of Sports Mega-events in Canada and Japan. In *Sports Mega-events: Social Scientific Analyses of a Global Phenomenon,* ed. John Horne and Wolfram Manzenreiter, 73–89. Oxford: Blackwell.

Beyond Media Events

Disenchantment, Derailment, Disruption

Daniel Dayan

The Olympics exemplify a class of occurrences that are not only pre-planned and heralded long in advance, but also inscribed on calendars. The issue is not whether or not they will take place. We know they will. And since the "what" of the event is already known, the "how" be-comes the important issue. Given the predictable nature of the Olympic formula, the Olympics tend to be no longer envisaged as "events-on-their-own" (as expressive actions, or as gestures). They are not seen as messages but as media. They are used as blank slates, as empty stages available for all sorts of new dramaturgies besides their own. The Olympics thus become palimpsests, scrolls that have been written upon, scraped almost clean, and written upon again.

The Olympics have a discontinuous existence made of long intervals and of episodic reenactments. They are an unusual form of "repertory" events. As in repertory theater, each enactment means to be different. Yet the play or event must be recognizable from repeat to repeat, from episode to episode. This might lead to a "freezing" of the event. Short of freezing the event, the organizers try to control its performance.

In the case of the Olympics, two models of episodic reenactments come to mind. The first model is religious. The Olympic "religion" is dominated by an almost mystical entity: the Olympic "spirit," a doc-trine that, like all dogmas, calls for a hermeneutic approach. A body of specialized literature is devoted to identifying, contextualizing, and updating this "spirit" in reference to the pronouncements of the institution's entrepreneurial prophet, Pierre de Coubertin. Conducted in the name of this doctrinal belief, the orthodoxy of the Games generates a whole bureaucracy of semantic gestures, symbolic displays, and ritual manifestations. Like the Vatican bureaucracy, the IOC bureaucracy seems ferociously attached to detail, and the Olympics are not open to unnegotiated change.

Yet, unlike the church, the IOC cannot rely on threats of excommunication. Attempts by the IOC to impose a given reading of the Olympics involve, therefore, another dimension. This second dimension is legalistic. A given script is handed over and must be implemented. Variability is accepted but only within limits. Implementation is governed by contract. In this regard, the IOC is not very different from the Dutch television company, Endemol, whose reality television shows—including the universally imitated Big Brother—are franchised into formats meant to encourage successful reproduction. Like Endemol, the Olympics offer "probabilistic" dramaturgies: ready-to-implement situational plots. Delivered to very different sets of actors and countries, these dramaturgies are meant to function independently of cultural contexts and specific outcomes. In the case of the Olympics, as in the case of Endemol (and, of course in the case of many other serials as well), the dramaturgies are submitted to managerial rationalization. One could describe them as "Taylorized" or "bureaucratic."

In 1992, Elihu Katz and I wrote *Media Events:The Live Broadcasting of History* about those great occasions—mostly occasions of state—that are televised as they take place and transfix a nation or the world. We called these events—which include epic contests of politics and sports, charismatic missions, and the rites of passage of the great—Contests, Conquests, and Coronations. In so doing, we were seeking to identify a narrative genre that employed the unique potential of the electronic media to command attention universally and simultaneously in order to tell a primordial story about current affairs. These were events, we argued, that in effect placed a halo over the television set, thus transforming the viewing experience. Fifteen years have now passed since *Media Events* was first published. The world has changed. We have learned from experience and from the many who have commented on our writings. This volume on the Beijing Olympics provides an opportunity to revisit several aspects of our joint approach to the phenomena of modern communications. For example, in our book, we focused on three story forms, or "scripts," that constitute the main narrative possibilities within the genre of Contests, Conquests, and Coronations. We argued that these three story forms are dramatic embodiments of Weber's (1946) three types of authority: rationality, charisma, and tradition. The present volume opens the possibility of additional themes that are less tied to celebration and that reflect new tensions in the world, including what Tamar Liebes (1998) calls "disaster marathons" and what James Carey (1998) describes as television rituals of "shame" and "degradation."

When we wrote *Media Events,* we found that the fact that the events were preplanned—announced and advertised in advance—was significant, as advance notice gives time for negotiation, but also for anticipation and preparation on the part of both broadcasters and audiences. These broadcast events were generally presented with reverence and ceremony. In the past, journalists who presided over them suspended their normally critical stance and treated their subject with respect, even awe. Even when these programs addressed conflict—as they often did—they frequently celebrated not conflict but reconciliation. On our reading, media events were generally ceremonial efforts to redress conflict or restore order or, more rarely, institute change. They called for a cessation of hostilities, at least for a moment, very much in keeping with the ancient Greek tradition of an Olympic truce. Here too, there have been great changes. Each of us has been contemplating whether there is a retreat from the genres of media events, as we described them, and an increase in the live broadcasting of disruptive events of disaster, terror, and armed conflict.

In our book we also discussed how media events preview the future of media technology. We suggested that when radio became a medium of segmentation—subdividing audiences by age and education—broadcast television replaced it as the medium of national integration. But that too has changed, as so many have recognized. Beijing is not the first Olympics to take place in this fundamentally altered television environment, but it is clearly a theater for seeing the implications of new distribution methods. As new media technology multiplies the number of channels, television has become a medium of segmentation, and television-as-we-knew-it continues to disappear. It is not clear that any medium has replaced or will replace it; if anything, the newest technologies, like mobile, further increase this segmentation. In 1992 we wrote that "the nation-state itself may be on the way out, its boundaries out of sync with the new media technology. Media events may then create and integrate communities larger than nations. Indeed, the genre of media events may itself be seen as a response to the integrative needs of national and, increasingly, international communities and organizations." Beijing seems to be a laboratory for these and related ideas.

The moments that Elihu Katz and I characterized as "Media Events" offered a powerful contrast to ordinary news. Media Events, as we defined them, invite their audiences to stop being spectators and to become witnesses or participants of a television performance. Rephrasing in a slightly different vocabulary the characteristics explored in the original volume, I would hold that the concept of Media Events includes the following four major features:

- Insistence and emphasis
- An explicitly "performative," gestural dimension
- Loyalty to the event's self definition; and
- Access to a shared viewing experience.

The first feature, *emphasis,* is manifested through the omnipresence of the transmitted events; the length of broadcasts that disrupt organized schedules without being themselves disrupted; the live dimension of these broadcasts; and the repetition of certain shots in seemingly endless loops. *Performativity* means that Media Events have nothing to do with balance, neutrality, or objectivity. They are not accounts but gestures: gestures that actively create realities. *Loyalty* consists in accepting the definition of the event as proposed by the organizers. It means that the proposed dramaturgy is not questioned but substantially endorsed and relayed. And, finally, Media Events provide not only knowledge or information but, also, a shared experience. This participatory function leads to formats that rely on narrative continuity, visual proximity, and shared temporality. Media Events, in our original formulation, were about the construction or reconstruction of "we."

The Beijing Olympics exemplify in many other ways the established sense of media events, as defined in the analytical framework we sought to forward in 1992. Audiences recognize Media Events as an invitation—even a command—to stop their daily routines. If festive viewing is to ordinary viewing what holidays are to the everyday, these events are among the highest holy days of mass communication. In keeping with this insight, our original project attempted to bring the anthropology of ceremony (Durkheim 1915; Handelman 1990; Levi-

Strauss 1963; Turner 1985) to bear on the process of mass communication. In this way, we defined the corpus of events in terms of three categories inspired by linguistics—syntactics, semantics, and pragmatics. We showed that a media event, as a contemporary form of ceremony, deals reverently with sacred matters (semantics), interrupts the flow of daily life (syntactics), and involves the response (pragmatics) of a committed audience.

Because the Beijing Olympics is taking place in a different world from the one in which *Media Events* was first published, it is useful to reprise the three categories as a means of marking the contrast. To better understand the nature and some of the consequences of the changes I will briefly explore the semantics of conflictualization, the syntactics of banalization, and the pragmatics of disenchantment. All are characteristics of today's media events and ways of differentiating today's "media events" from the Media Events in the grand sense we implied in 1992.

In terms of semantics, an ideological sea change has taken place. In 1992, what had particular resonance was the end of conflicts, the waning of feuds, the rise of gestures that seemed to lessen the possibility of war. This mood was later captured in the title of Francis Fukuyama's book *The End of History and the Last Man* (1992). On the eve of the Beijing Olympics, the themes that resonate globally are significantly more somber than those of the late 1980s and 1990s. After a long eclipse, Foucault's "order of supplices" seems to be back, lending its macabre accoutrements to televised ordeals, punishments, and tortures. Numerous events are in keeping with, and indeed extend, James Carey's emphasis on stigmatization and shaming. War rituals multiply. Agon is back, where the dramaturgy of "contest" succeeded in civilizing the brutality of conflict. Media events have stopped being "irenic." Their semantics is no longer dominated by the theme of a reduction of conflict through mediation and resolution of differences. Rather, they could be characterized by Gregory Bateson's notion of "schismogenesis" (1935), that process through which one provokes irremediable hostility, fosters divides, and installs and perpetuates schisms.

In terms of syntactics, there is also a significant change. The format of media events has been dismantled into discrete elements, many of which have migrated toward other genres. As a result of this dissemination, the rhetoric of media events no longer stands out as radically distinct. Take the notion of an event that is automatically guaranteed a monopoly of attention, a characteristic imputed to the royal weddings, coronations, and moon walks of an earlier day. This kind of exclusive focusing on one event at any given time is now becoming almost impossible. Instead, there is a "field" of events in which different candidates compete with each other for privileged status, with the help of entrepreneurial journalists. Social and political polarization and its effect on media mean that it is harder to achieve a broad consensus about the importance of particular events. News and media events are no longer starkly differentiated entities but exist rather on a continuum. This banalization of the format leads to the emergence of an intermediate zone characterized by the proliferation of what I would call "almost" media events.

Finally, the pragmatics of media events have also changed. One of the characteristics of classical Media Events was the way in which such events seemed capable of transforming the home into a public space by inviting spectators to assemble into actual viewing communities. The power of those events resided, first and foremost, in the rare realization of the full potential of electronic media technology. Students of media effects know that at most times and places this potential of radio and television is restricted by society. In principle, radio and television are capable of reaching everybody simultaneously and directly; their message, in other words, can be total, immediate, and unmediated. But this condition hardly ever obtains. Messages are multiple; audiences are selective; social networks intervene; diffusion takes time. In the case of media events, however, these intervening mechanisms are suspended. Interpersonal networks and diffusion processes are active before and after the event, mobilizing attention to the event and fostering intensive hermeneutic attempts to identify its meaning. But during the liminal moments we described in 1992, totality and simultaneity were unbound; organizers and broadcasters resonated together; competing channels merged into one; viewers gathered at the same time and in every place. All eyes were fixed on the ceremonial center, through which each nuclear cell was connected to all the rest. Social integration of the highest order was thus achieved via mass communication (Kornhauser 1959).

Since the 1990s, entertainment genres such as reality TV have called for a similar transformation of the home into a communal, public, space while media events themselves have offered less of a communal experience. One may watch the Olympics in a living room or even in a stadium, but in both cases, the ubiquitous cell phone is a constant invitation to disengage from the surrounding community. Reliance on new media has reintroduced individualized reception, and this in turn has led to what seems to me to be one of the most significant differences in context: it is not merely the notion of a shared social experience that wanes, it is the very notion of "communitas." What characterized great Media Events was a kind of agreed conspiracy among organizer, broadcaster, and audience: a tacit decision to suspend disbelief, repress cynicism, and enter a "subjunctive" mode of culture. It is this machinery of suspension that is now at risk.

The resonance of media events used to be associated with what Victor Turner called the "as if" or subjunctive modes of culture. Even when an event was perceived as "mere spectacle," authors like John MacAloon (*Rite, Drama, Festival, Spectacle* 1984) believed in a process through which it would ultimately transcend this status and become truly festive and participatory. But a noticeable change of mood has taken place at the level of reception. Media events produce cynical behaviors. They foster rather than suspend disbelief. Spectators and publics act like Clausewitzian strategists. While they do so, they are themselves being negotiated, acquired, or stolen. Media events still mobilize huge audiences, but they have lost a large part of their enchantment. Bureaucratically managed, they are an exploited resource within a political economy of collective attention. Their magic is dissipating. They have become strategic venues.

These changes in the character of media events have at least two implications. The first implication is theoretical. By virtue of their explicitly "performative" nature, media events are an excellent starting point for understanding the status of news images. Yet the visual "performatives" at play in media events are not to be opposed to some "normal"—that is, devoid of performatives—status of television news images. Quite the contrary. While media events display a spectacular performative dimension, a performative dimension characterizes news as well. Indeed, excluding those systems of unmanned video surveillance (whose function involves neither watching nor showing anything, but retroactively retrieving the recorded traces of past occurrences), television never offers images that are merely informative, images that are enunciatively neutral.

Yet this does not mean that the two performances—news and media events—are or should be identical. They call for a distinct set of rules and for different grammars. And the nature of these grammars brings us to the second implication, a political one. It concerns the quest for proximity that characterizes media events, and almost specializes them in the construction of what I have suggested is a collective "we." In the case of Media Events, the process of "we" construction is perfectly explicit. This process is what the event is about: it is heralded, discussed, negotiated, in advance. The construction of a "we" becomes much less explicit for events in which the sharing of an experience is imposed by a merely journalistic decision. In this case, the construction of a "we" (insufficiently heralded, negotiated, or discussed) intervenes before and/or without any sort of debate. News quietly turns into rituals. When this transformation takes place on a daily basis, when we attend a constant banalization of the format, the very multiplication of "almost" media events leads to the emergence of a "gray" zone, inhabited by images that are neither Media Events nor news.

Any event can be turned into a media event through an addition of specific features. The same event can be given more or less space, more or less attention. The same incident can be summed up in a few shots, or treated as a continuous narrative. It can be told retrospectively or transmitted live. It can be shown once or repeated in a continuous loop. Events, and their producers, contend with each other for being awarded the largest amount of features. In today's "gray zone," where there is a blurring of the limits between media events and news, each event can be treated as a news item *and* as a media event at once. Each situation can be simultaneously addressed through different formats, lending itself to a whole array of discursive statements. Such statements enter in dialogue or debate with each other. Rather than being spoken by a single, monolithic voice—the voice of the nation—any event becomes part of a conversation involving competing versions of the same event, some of them local, some of them foreign. This conversation enacts a new model of public affairs in which the centrality of events seems to have dethroned that of newscasts (Csigo 2007). Instead of dominant media organizing and conferring a hierarchy on the multiplicity of events, dominant events now serve as the contested ground for a multiplicity of media voices.

Following Daniel Hallin (*The Uncensored War: The Media and Vietnam* 1986), Michael Schudson (2006) proposes a strong distinction between two exclusive modes of functioning of the public sphere. One corresponds to the normal regime of a democratic society. It is the "sphere of legitimate controversy." The other corresponds to exceptional moments, such as wars, crises, and periods of redefinition of identity. It is a sphere dominated by consensus and complemented by a mirroring

sphere, the sphere of deviance. One sphere is meant to allow deliberation and debate. The other sphere is meant to stifle it in the name of
some higher general interest.

I would suggest that one sphere is characterized by the normal, critical, informative functioning of news while the other is characterized
by a situation where all news items tend to be treated as if they were
media events. Schudson points to the danger of allowing the sphere of
consensus/deviance to persist beyond moments of acute crisis, of allowing it to take over functions that are normally performed in the
sphere of debate. This—I believe—is the danger involved in the undue
generalization of a media event model to all news forms, in the rampant progression of the gray zone.

Disenchantment and the Loss of the "We"

These issues are obviously relevant to the Beijing Olympics and the
contested territory of media events. Events compete with each other
for the conquest of public attention. All aspire to the privilege of being
on all media at once. In this competition, there will be not only efforts
by the organizers of an event to persuade but efforts by many to shape
the pattern of that persuasion. Any media event happens because it is
willed by some entity, but every media event is also offered as a "public" event. This dual status entails a series of tensions. Such tensions are
first of all a matter of production versus reception. From the point of
view of spectators, it is clear that the producers of an event have no
right to claim ownership over its meaning. The event's meaning depends on their own responses and interpretations. But there are other
tensions as well: between the ratified performers of a given event and
other would-be performers; between the "bona fide" definition of the
event and alternative definitions of the same event; between the core
of the event and the crowd of parasitic manifestations that proliferates
around it, as so many doppelgangers or satellites, as discussed in Price's
chapter in this volume.

In the contest for ownership, media events lend themselves to a rich
grammar of appropriations. They fall prey to entities that are neither
their organizers nor their publics. They may be subverted (denounced),
diverted (derailed), or perverted (hijacked). They can be used as Trojan
horses or placed under the threat of a sword of Damocles. These multiple tensions and the calculated moves of various public actors inter-

ested in the exploitation of the event's charisma ask the question of "legitimate ownership" and undue appropriation. Can anyone own a public event?

This legalistic question is in a way typical of today's media events. It is one of the main questions raised by the Beijing Olympics and by the general transformation undergone by the Games. The Olympics, meant to propose a normative enactment, have become a provider of collective attention on a grand scale. For the IOC, international power consists in brokering such attention. For political publics, the Olympics provide an opportunity of harnessing that attention to the benefit of neglected agendas. For national organizers, the Games offer the prospect of a *rite de passage* into a certain "elite" of nations. For advertisers, this attention is available in serendipitous quantities. For spectators they are a spectacle or entertainment. What about those who embody that attention? What about the public and the spectators? Is it cynicism or communitas, skepticism or suspension of disbelief?

In each case what seems at risk is a certain form of "enchantment." Of course disenchantment is not a particularly new development. John MacAloon's classical analysis of the Olympic experience (*Rite, Drama, Festival, Spectacle* 1984) is centrally concerned with this disenchantment, a disenchantment it does acknowledge but transforms into a mere prelude to the real experience of the Games. Thus a complex initiation process takes the spectators of the Olympics through a succession of steps, or frames. The Olympic experience is framed as spectacle, festival, ritual, and finally as access to truth. MacAloon's process starts with skepticism (spectacle) and ends with belief (truth). Is this progression still conceivable today? Is there any room for an Olympic experience framed as an access to some truth? Or should we rewrite MacAloon's sequence in a style inspired by Baudrillard: "spectacle, festival, ritual, and finally: . . . simulacrum?"

REFERENCES

Bateson, Gregory. 1935. Culture Contact and Schismogenesis. *MAN* 35, article 199. Republished in *Steps to an Ecology of Mind*. New York: Ballantine Books, 1972.

Carey, James. 1998. Political Ritual on Television: Episodes in the History of Shame, Degradation and Excommunication. In *Media, Ritual, and Identity*, ed. Tamar Liebes and James Curran. London: Routledge.

Csigo, Peter. 2007. Ritualizing and Mediating "Ordinary" Reality in the Era of

"Event Television." Paper presented at International Conference, Media Events, Globalization, and Cultural Change, Bremen, July 5–7.

Dayan, Daniel. 2006. "Terrorisme, Performance, Representation." In *La Terreur Spectacle*, ed. Daniel Dayan. Paris: INA-De Boeck.

Dayan, Daniel, and Elihu Katz. 1992. *Media Events: The Live Broadcasting of History*. Cambridge: Harvard University Press.

Durkheim, Emile. 1915. *The Elementary Forms of the Religious Life: A Study in Religious Sociology*. Trans. J. W. Swain. London: Allen and Unwin.

Fukuyama, Francis. 1992. *The End of History and the Last Man*. New York: Free Press.

Hallin, Daniel. 1986. *The Uncensored War: The Media and Vietnam*. New York: Oxford University Press.

Handelman, D. 1990. *Models and Mirrors: Towards an Anthropology of Public Events*. New York: Cambridge University Press.

Katz, Elihu, and Tamar Liebes. 2007. No More Peace: How Disaster, Terror, and War Have Upstaged Media Events. *International Journal of Communication* 1 (1): 157–66.

Kornhauser, W. 1959. *The Politics of Mass Society*. New York: Free Press of Glencoe.

Levi-Strauss, Claude. 1963. The Effectiveness of Symbols. In *Structural Anthropology*, trans. Claire Jacobson and Brooke Grundfest Schoepf, 186–205. New York: Basic Books.

Liebes, Tamar. 1998. Television's Disaster Marathons: A Danger to Democratic Processes? In *Media, Ritual, and Identity*, ed. Tamar Liebes and James Curran. London: Routledge.

MacAloon, John, ed. 1984. *Rite, Drama, Festival, Spectacle*. Philadelphia: Institute for the Study of Human Issues.

Schudson, Michael. 1989. How Culture Works: Perspective from Media Studies on the Efficacy of Symbols. *Theory and Society* 18:153–80.

Schudson, Michael. 2006. L' Extraordinaire Retour du Journalisme Politique Ordinaire. In *La Terreur Spectacle*, ed. Daniel Dayan, 153–65. Paris: INA-De Boeck.

Turner, Victor. 1985. Liminality, Kabbala, and the Media. *Religion* 15:205–17.

Weber, Max. 1946. *From Max Weber: Essays in Sociology*. New York: Oxford University Press.

Author Biographies

Sandra Collins is Lecturer in Japanese History and Culture in the history department at San Francisco State University. She was recently a Visiting Scholar at the Center for Japanese Studies, University of California, Berkeley, as she completed her manuscript for *The 1940 Tokyo Games: The Missing Olympics: Japan, the Asian Olympics and the Olympic Movement* (Routledge, forthcoming). She has published several works on the role of Japan in the Olympic Movement and served as a guest editor for the special issue of the IOC and the *International Journal of the History of Sport* (2006). She received her PhD in modern Japanese history from the University of Chicago, where she began her research on the canceled 1940 Tokyo Games. She was also an inaugural Post-Graduate Research Scholar for the International Olympic Committee and a Fulbright-Hays Scholar at the University of Tokyo Institute for Socio-Cultural Information Studies.

Nicholas J. Cull holds a joint appointment with the University of Southern California's Annenberg School and School of International Relations, where he serves as Professor of Public Diplomacy and Director of the Master's in Public Diplomacy Program. His research and teaching interests are broad and interdisciplinary, centering on the role of culture, information, news, and propaganda in foreign policy. He has written widely on media and history, including the forthcoming *The Cold War and the United States Information Agency: American Propaganda and Public Diplomacy, 1945–1989* (Cambridge University Press, 2008). He is the president of the International Association for Media and History.

Daniel Dayan is Directeur de Recherche at the Centre National de la Recherche Scientifique, Paris; a member of the Marcel Mauss Institute (École des Hautes Études en Sciences Sociales); and Professor of Media Sociology at the University of Geneva. He holds degrees in anthropology, comparative literature, semiotics and film studies from Stanford University; the Sorbonne; and the École des Hautes Études en Sciences Sociales, where he received a PhD in aesthetics.

Dayan started his academic career as Roland Barthes's assistant. He has been a lecturer, professor, or visiting professor at numerous universities. His most recent books are *La Terreur Spectacle: Terrorisme et télévision* (INA.-De Boeck, 2006) and *Televisão: Das Audiências aos Públicos* (with J. C. Abrantes) (Livros Horizonte, 2006). Written during a long collaboration with Elihu Katz, *Media Events: The Live Broadcasting of History* (Harvard University Press, 1992) has been translated into eight languages.

Jacques deLisle is the Stephen Cozen Professor of Law at the University of Pennsylvania, a member of the faculty of the university's Center for East Asian Studies, and Director of the Asia Program at the Foreign Policy Research Institute. His writings address Chinese law and politics (including the roles of law in economic and political reform in contemporary China), Taiwan's international legal and political status, and U.S. laws and policies to promote reform or advance human rights in China and the postcommunist world. He received a JD degree from Harvard, graduate education in political science at Harvard, and an AB from Princeton. He clerked for Stephen Breyer (then Chief Judge of the First Circuit Court of Appeals) and served as attorney-adviser in the Office of Legal Counsel, U.S. Department of Justice, where his work focused on separation of powers and foreign affairs law.

Christopher J. Finlay is a PhD candidate at the University of Pennsylvania's Annenberg School for Communication. He holds an MA in political science from Carleton University (Ottawa, Ontario) and a BA in political science and history from Simon Fraser University (Vancouver, British Columbia). His research interests include cultural studies, international communication, and political communication. He is particularly interested in exploring the complex relationships between individual and group identities and notions of national, regional, and global citizenship. His dissertation will examine how the Olympics, as a global media event, frames notions of citizenship and nationalism while simultaneously promoting cultural diversity at both the global and local levels.

Sonja K. Foss is Professor in the Department of Communication at the University of Colorado at Denver. Her research and teaching interests are in contemporary rhetorical theory and criticism, visual rhetoric, feminist perspectives on communication, the incorporation of marginalized voices into rhetorical theory and practice, and the reconceptualization of communication in the change process. She is the author or coauthor of the books *Rhetorical Criticism: Exploration and Practice, Contemporary Perspectives on Rhetoric, Feminist Rhetorical Theories, Destination Dissertation: A Traveler's Guide to a Done Dissertation, Inviting Transformation: Presentational Speaking for a Changing World,* and *Women Speak: The Eloquence of Women's Lives.* Her essays in communication journals have dealt with topics such as feminine spectatorship in Garrison Keillor's monologues, agency in the film *Run Lola Run,* invitational rhetoric, feminist rhetorical theory, visual argumentation, and body art. Dr. Foss earned her PhD in communication studies from Northwestern University and previously taught at Ohio State University, the University of Oregon, the University of Denver, Virginia Tech, and Norfolk State University.

Beatriz García is the Director of Impacts 08—European Capital of Culture Research Programme and Lecturer in Sociology at the University of Liverpool. She is an active researcher in urban sociology focused on the study of cultural policy and event-led city regeneration. She has developed a model for the longitudinal assessment of the cultural impact and legacy of regeneration initiatives and has directed projects assessing the legacy of cultural programming within major events such as the Olympic Games (from Barcelona 1992 onward), the Commonwealth Games (Manchester 2002), and the European Capital of Culture (Glasgow 1990 and Liverpool 2008). She has received funding from the IOC–Olympic Museum, the International Olympic Academy, and the British Academy to assess the cultural policy dimension of the Olympic Movement and the experience of Olympic Arts Festival and Cultural Olympiad programming in Sydney, Salt Lake City, Athens, Torino, and Beijing. She is also funded by the Liverpool City Council, the Arts and Humanities Research Council, and the Economic and Social Research Council in the United Kingdom to study the EU-led European Capital of Culture program. She has acted as academic adviser to the London 2012 Culture and Education team since the bid stage and is coeditor of *Culture @ the Olympics* magazine.

Heidi Østbø Haugen holds an MPhil degree in human geography from the University of Oslo, and has read Chinese at Beijing Normal University and Princeton University. She did fieldwork in Beijing around the time when the city was awarded the Olympic Games. She has also carried out research among Chinese entrepreneurs in Africa and is currently working as a food security analyst for the United Nations World Food Programme in West Africa.

Lee Humphreys is Associate Lecturer in Communication Arts at the University of Wisconsin. She completed her PhD at the Annenberg School for Communication at the University of Pennsylvania in 2007. Her dissertation, *Mobile Sociality and Spatial Practice: A Qualitative Field Study,* explored how mobile telephony can facilitate and encourage the development, maintenance, and strengthening of social connections in urban public spaces. Past research projects have explored the social norms of cell phone use in public spaces, the use of digital photos on online dating sites, and the role of technology in singles bars. Her work has appeared in journals such as *New Media and Society, Journal of Technical Writing and Communication,* and *Social Epistemology.* With Paul Messaris, she is coeditor of *Digital Media: Transformations in Human Communication* (Peter Lang, 2006).

Christopher Kennett is Head of Research at the Olympic Studies Centre, Universitat Autònoma de Barcelona (UAB); Associate Lecturer at UAB's Department of Sociology, and the head of the Sports Management specialization at the La Salle Universities International Programme (Barcelona Campus). He holds a PhD in sport studies and management from Loughborough University and has worked on a series of international research projects since joining the Olympic Studies Centre in 2002. He has published in the areas of sports management, communication and the Olympic Movement, the legacy of the Olympic Games, and the role of sport in issues of social inclusion.

Carolyn Marvin is the Frances Yates Professor of Communication at the Annenberg School for Communication at the University of Pennsylvania. Her research interests include public space, freedom of expression, social construction of taboo, symbols and rituals of nationalism, and the history of communication technologies. She is the author of *Blood Sacrifice and the Nation: Totem Rituals and the American Flag* with David W. Ingle (Cambridge University Press, 1999) and *When Old Technologies Were New: Thinking about Electric Communication in the Late Nineteenth Century* (Oxford University Press, 1988).

Andy Miah is Reader in New Media and Bioethics at the University of the West of Scotland and Fellow in Visions of Utopia and Dystopia, Institute for Ethics and Emerging Technologies. His research is informed by an interest in applied philosophy, technology, and culture, and he writes broadly about emerging technological cultures. His publications include *Sport Technology* (Elsevier, 2002), *Genetically Modified Athletes* (Routledge, 2004), and the coauthored volume *The Medicalisation of Cyberspace* (Routledge, 2007). In 2003, he was Visiting Professor at the International Olympic Academy. He has conducted British Academy–funded research and given lectures at the last four Olympic Games cities (Sydney, Salt Lake, Athens, and Torino) under invitation by various organizations. He has been researching the cultural, political, and media structures of the Olympic Movement since 2000, most recently examining the role of the Olympic Truce in international peace processes and the emergence of new media.

Miquel de Moragas is Professor in Communication at the Universitat Autònoma de Barcelona (UAB). He has served as Director of the UAB's Olympic Studies Centre since its creation in 1989 and as Director of the Institut de la Comunicació–UAB since its creation in 1998. He has widely published on communication and the Olympic Games, in particular on the interpretation and dissemination of the cultural and social values of Olympism and sport, the development of Olympic Studies, and the impacts of the Barcelona 1992 Olympic Games. He was a member of the Research Council of the IOC Olympic Studies Centre (1998–2002), Dean of the Faculty of Communication at the UAB (1978–80 and 1982–84), and Vice-Rector of Research at the UAB (1985–89).

Monroe E. Price is Director of the Center for Global Communication Studies at the Annenberg School for Communication at the University of Pennsylvania and Professor of Law at the Benjamin N. Cardozo School of Law at Yeshiva University. He also serves as Director of the Stanhope Centre for Communications Policy Research in London and Chair of the Center for Media and Communication Studies at Central European University in Budapest. He served as Dean of Cardozo School of Law from 1982 to 1991. Among his many books are a treatise on cable television, *Cable Television and Other Nonbroadcast Video: Law and Policy; Media and Sovereignty;* and *Television, the Public Sphere, and National Identity.*

Hai Ren is Professor and Director of the Centre for Olympic Studies in Beijing Sport University and a Chief Expert for the China Sport Science Institute. His academic interests are primarily focused on cross-cultural sport studies and Olympic issues, and he is currently working on projects on Olympic reform and its impacts and the historical process of interaction between the IOC and China. He edited *The Olympic Movement,* the first Chinese textbook used for university students majoring in sport science in China, as well as several recent books related to the Beijing Olympics, including the Olympic readers for primary and secondary school students in China. He received his doctoral degree from the University of Alberta Canada.

Briar Smith is a current PhD student at Annenberg School for Communication who recently returned from teaching at the Center for Global Communication Studies' first Penn-in-Beijing undergraduate summer program for undergraduate students. She has a B.A. in psychology as well as in Chinese language and literature from Swarthmore College and spent a semester abroad in Beijing in 2001. Her research interests are in cultural studies, with a current focus on Asia, including the Olympics and Muslim populations in China. In the summer of 2006, she assisted in the organization of and gave a lecture at a three-week summer school at Beijing University in which Annenberg faculty gave lectures to Chinese communication master's students. She also helped organize a jointly hosted Olympics conference in Beijing with Communications University of China during the same summer.

Alan Tomlinson is Professor of Leisure Studies at the University of Brighton, where he is Head of Research at the Chelsea School. He teaches courses on the social history of sport, sociology, and cultural studies and supervises research students on media/sport cultures and comparative sports cultures and politics.

His publications include *Sport and Leisure Cultures* (University of Minnesota Press, 2005), *National Identity and Global Sports Events: Culture, Politics, and Spectacle in the Olympics and the Football World Cup* (edited with C. Young) (State University of New York Press, 2006), *The Game's Up: Essays in the Cultural Analysis of Sport, Leisure, and Popular Culture* (Ashgate, 1999), and *FIFA and the Contest for World Football: Who Rules the People's Game?* (with John Sugden) (Polity, 1998). He was editor of the International Review for the Sociology of Sport for the issues from 2000 to early 2004.

Barbara J. Walkosz is a faculty member in the Department of Communication at the University of Colorado at Denver. Her scholarship and teaching focus on the role of mass media in society, civil discourse, political communication, health communication, social marketing, and community development. In the area of health communication, she has been engaged in research programs on tobacco and skin cancer prevention and media literacy education. Her publications have examined such topics as the effects of health communication programs, media representation of the Ladies Professional Golf Association, and political decision making. She received her PhD from the University of Arizona and was previously a faculty member at Montana State University-Billings.

Jeffrey N. Wasserstrom is Professor of History at the University of California, Irvine. He specializes in the study of modern and contemporary China and is the author of *Student Protests in Twentieth-Century China: The View from Shanghai* (Stanford University Press, 1991; paperback edition 1997) and *China's Brave New World: and Other Tales for Global Times* (Indiana University Press, 2007). He is also the editor, coeditor, or coauthor of five other books, including *Human Rights and Revolutions* (Rowman and Littlefield, 2000 and 2007 editions) and *Chinese Femininities/Chinese Masculinities: A Reader* (University of California Press, 2002).

He has served as a consultant to the Long Bow Group, makers of award-winning documentaries, including *The Gate of Heavenly Peace* (1995), a film about the 1989 Tiananmen protests. His current research interests include Shanghai's two great periods of internationalization (the subject of a book in progress), the Boxer Rebellion, and American images of China.

Tian (Tina) Zhihui is Associate Professor of Communication and a PhD candidate in communication at the Communication University of China. From 2004 to 2005, she was a Visiting Scholar at the University of Westminster, where she studied with Colin Sparks. Her research interests include new media, online journalism, and user-created content.

Index

Text design by Mary H. Sexton
Typesetting by Delmastype, Ann Arbor, Michigan
Text font: Stone Serif
In 1987, Sumner Stone completed his designs for the
Stone type family, which consists of three subfamilies, Serif, Sans,
and Informal. In 1992, John Renner finished designing phonetic
companion faces for ITC Stone Sans and ITC Stone Serif.
The result is a font palette that can be combined successfully
over a broad spectrum of typographic applications.
—courtesy www.adobe.com